Survival Reading Skills for Secondary Students

Wilma H. Miller, Ed.D.

Published by Jossey-Bass
A Wiley Imprint
989 Market Street, San Francisco, CA 94103-1741
www.josseybass.com

Jossey-Bass books and products are available through most bookstores. To contact Jossey-Bass directly, call our Customer Care Department within the U.S. at (800) 956-7739, outside the U.S. at (317) 572-3993 or fax (317) 572-4002.

Jossey-Bass also publishes its books in a variety of electronic formats. Some content that appears in print may not be available in electronic books.

Library of Congress Cataloging-in-Publication Data

Miller, Wilma H.
Survival reading skills for secondary students / Wilma H. Miller.
p. cm.
Includes bibliographical references.
ISBN 0-7879-6597-9 (alk. paper)
1. Reading (Secondary) 2. Education, Secondary—Activity programs.
I. Title.
LB1632.M534 2003
428.4'071'2—dc21
2003010398

Printed in the United States of America
FIRST EDITION
PB Printing 10 9 8 7 6 5 4 3 2 1

In loving memory of my beloved parents,
William and Ruth Miller

Acknowledgments

I would like to thank Steve Thompson, Elisa Rassen, and Pamela Berkman at Jossey-Bass, as well as copyeditor Sandra Beriss and proofreader Diane Turso, for their hard work on this project.

The Practical Help This Resource Provides

Most students learn the basic word-identification techniques and comprehension skills in the primary grades. However, by the time they reach the intermediate grades, a number of them have difficulty reading content material. This is especially the case with social studies, science, and mathematics materials. Students who earlier were good or adequate readers may have great difficulty responding at the interpretive and critical levels of comprehension and may dislike all reading activities. This may happen because they have not learned the specialized reading skills that are necessary to interpret the vocabulary and organizational patterns found in these content area books. Unless students are given specific instruction and reinforcement in these unique reading skills, they may have difficulty reading content area material.

However, this does not need to be the case for most students in contemporary schools. Most, including those with special needs such as learning disabilities, or those who belong to minority groups, should be able to experience academic success in all their subjects, including subjects requiring specialized vocabulary skills and unique patterns of organization, and be able to read content textbooks and other content materials such as informational trade books, material found on the World Wide Web, print and on-line encyclopedias, and magazines and newspapers.

Providing practical, time-saving help for classroom teachers, reading specialists, special education teachers, content teachers, reading tutors, reading curriculum coordinators, administrators, and family members is the primary focus of *Survival Reading Skills for Secondary Students.* All of the strategies, activities, and ready-to-duplicate activity sheets are geared toward students in grades 5 to 12, which have been given limited emphasis in professional textbooks in the past. Many reading textbooks focus on the primary grades, with limited emphasis on grades 5 to 8 and virtually none on grades 9 to 12. This teacher's resource is unique because it provides guidance in teaching reading in grades 5 to 12—a much wider scope than most others.

This resource contains numerous classroom-tested strategies and reproducible activity sheets that are referenced to specific reading problems of students. The reproducibles are valuable because they are designed to improve competence in all the important reading skills, especially those that are required for academic success in grades 5 to 12. The strategies and reproducibles included in *Survival Reading Skills for Secondary Students* are highly motivating and challenging, and they are designed to present content information in the areas of literature, social studies, science, and mathematics. Therefore, they are informative and interesting as well as being constructed to present specific reading study skills that are necessary for academic success in grades 5 to 12. Students who have used such worksheets have found them very interesting and have been able to transfer the skills that were taught to their academic subjects.

The following paragraphs explain the kind of help that is offered in each chapter of this practical resource.

Chapter One, "Informal Reading Assessment Tools for Older Students," contains a number of classroom-tested, easy-to-use, and effective informal assessment devices. It includes the graded reading passages for Forms A and B of the *Content Reading Inventory,* an informal assessment device that reading and content teachers can use to determine their students' approximate reading levels and reading strengths and weaknesses. It also includes the *San Diego Quick Assessment List,* a very useful, quick way to determine a student's approximate instructional reading level. In addition, this chapter includes lists of sample words from the content areas of English (literature and grammar), social studies, science, and mathematics. The chapter also contains an informal assessment of basic survival words, and inventories in phonic analysis, word structure, and context clues.

Chapter Two, "Strategies and Activities for Improving Content Sight Word Identification," contains reproducible copies of daily living words for students in grades 5 to 12 and words needed for computer literacy. Then the chapter describes numerous classroom-tested strategies for improving ability in recognizing and identifying important content and daily living words. All the strategies are both motivational and functional. This chapter closes with six reproducible activity sheets, including an activity sheet on words borrowed from other languages, a reversed crossword puzzle using computer literacy terms, and a magic square from science.

Chapter Three, "Strategies and Activities for Improving Basic Phonic Skills," describes the basic phonic elements in which older students should be competent. The chapter also contains seven helpful phonic generalizations. Then the chapter provides a sampling of useful strategies for general phonics instruction, such as cross-checking word identification strategies, word detectives, Hinks Pinks, discovering a code, and making words using age-appropriate rimes. The chapter ends with six ready-to-duplicate activity sheets, including completing a torn grocery shopping list, discovering a secret code, and finding food words with double letters.

Chapter Four, "Strategies and Activities for Improving Basic Word Structure Skills in Content Reading," explains the usefulness of word roots, prefixes, and suffixes in determining the meaning of the specialized vocabulary terms that are found in the various content areas. It includes comprehensive lists of the most useful elements of word structure that can help students read and study content materials effectively. The chapter also contains a sampling of classroom-tested strategies that should help students improve ability in word structure. Some of these are as follows: studying words "borrowed" from various cultures, "adding the points," "Can of Words," a generalization strategy for teaching syllabication, and the Compound Word Game. The chapter also contains seven reproducible activity sheets, including determining word etymologies, selecting and writing in the suffix that gives the correct meaning to words, the Compound Word Game, and determining the correct accent.

Chapter Five, "Strategies and Activities for Improving Use of Context Clues to Identify New Words," first explains context clues and stresses their importance to effective reading in grades 5 to 12. It also presents a useful classification scheme for context clues. The chapter then presents a number of classroom-tested strategies for using context clues while reading content material in grades 5 to 12. Several of these are self-monitoring and self-correcting while reading silently and orally: Dahl and Samuel's strategy for using context clues, Edwards and Dermott's method of teaching context clues, cryptology and mutilated messages, "Help the Dragon Get Home," and musical cloze. The section ends with seven reproducible activity sheets for improving ability in context clue usage, including choosing the correct word in sentence context, writing an answer in place of the make-believe word, and working with the random cloze procedures from social studies and science.

Chapter Six, "Strategies and Activities for Improving Comprehension Skills While Reading Content Material," opens by briefly describing reading comprehension and levels of comprehension—textually explicit, textually implicit, and critical or evaluative. It then describes a myriad of classroom-tested strategies for improving comprehension, including predictive QARs, guided reading, the anticipation-reaction guide, semantic webs and weaves, generating reciprocal inferences procedure (GRIP), cybernetic sessions, the investigative questioning procedure (InQuest), the *click or clunk* strategy, fix-up strategies, and Brown and Day's rule for summarizing. The chapter closes with seven reproducible activity sheets for improving comprehension skills while reading content material, including an anticipation-reaction guide, using partial headlines from social studies, determining which is the better invention, completing a job application form, and determining what an author was trying to do—inform, entertain, or persuade.

Chapter Seven, "Strategies and Activities for Improving Study Skills in the Content Areas," opens by describing the basic study skills, which are classified in the following manner: selecting and evaluating, organizing, following directions, locating information, using graphic aids, reading rate and flexibility, and test-taking strategies. The chapter also describes the specialized study skills that students need while reading specific content material. Chapter Seven then illustrates a multitude of classroom-tested strategies for improving study skills, which are referenced to the categories of study skills that were mentioned earlier. It closes with seven classroom-tested reproducible activity sheets for improving elements of the general and specialized study skills, including organizing material, using the Dewey Decimal System, interpreting a bar graph, skimming for specific purposes, and using the newspaper effectively.

Readers will find the following unique features in *Survival Reading Skills for Secondary Students*:

- It is published in a lay flat format that makes reproducing the material very easy.
- It contains reproducible copies of classroom-tested, easy-to-use, and effective assessment devices: Forms A and B of the Content Reading Inventory; the San Diego Quick Assessment List; sample words from the content areas of English (literature and grammar), social studies, science, and mathematics; the basic survival words; and inventories in phonic analysis, word structure, and context clues.
- All classroom-tested reading strategies and reproducibles are referenced to specific common problems in the reading skill areas of content sight word identification, basic phonic skills, word structure, context clues, comprehension skills while reading relevant material, and study skills in the content areas. This makes locating appropriate materials for all students, including those with learning disabilities and other special needs, very easy.
- All of the classroom-tested strategies and reproducibles will save any classroom, reading, special education, or content teacher much time and effort in teaching reading skills to all types of readers in grades 5 to 12—above average, average, below average, and those with special needs.

- It contains numerous reading strategies and reproducible activity sheets that will help reading and literature teachers plan and present reading and literature (including grammar) skills to students in grades 5 to 12.
- It includes many strategies and reproducibles that social studies, science, and mathematics teachers can use to present and reinforce the specialized reading skills that are needed in their content areas.
- It provides family members of students in grades 5 to 12 with countless practical, easy-to-use strategies and reproducibles that they can use to reinforce the various important general and content reading skills.
- The reproducibles included are designed to teach important, motivating content in literature, social studies, science, or mathematics as well as relevant reading skills. The relevant content is presented and reinforced along with the reading skills that are emphasized.
- It contains strategies and reproducibles for use with students in grades 5 to 12. In contrast, many other teacher resource books and professional books in reading emphasize teaching reading in the primary grades but deemphasize it in the intermediate grades, middle school, and secondary school.
- It provides reproducible lists of basic survival words and words needed for computer literacy. The lists of survival words are especially applicable for students with special needs, while the list of words needed for computer literacy is equally applicable with all types of students.
- It provides valuable lists of word roots and their meanings, prefixes and their meanings, and suffixes and their meanings, and scope and sequence charts suggesting when these elements of word structure should be taught. These reproducibles should be motivating to most students in grades 5 to 12 whether or not they have learning or reading disabilities.
- It provides readers with a good description of reading comprehension along with numerous strategies and reproducibles designed to improve ability in literal, interpretive, and critical comprehension. Using these materials with students of varying reading abilities should help them improve specific areas of reading comprehension in which they are weak.
- The reproducibles included in this volume are highly motivating, challenging, and functional. Because effective comprehension, including critical reading, is of primary importance in reading instruction, this volume should be of invaluable help to classroom, reading, special education, and content teachers as well as to reading tutors.
- It provides a comprehensive description of the *basic study skills* as well as a complete description of the *specialized study skills* that students need while reading specific content material in English (literature and grammar), social studies, science, and mathematics and includes a multitude of classroom-tested strategies and reproducibles for improving basic and specialized study skills in grades 5 to 12. The mastery of these study skills is a prerequisite for academic success in these grades and for success in later life.
- The *Survival Reading Skills for Secondary Students* is very *reader-friendly* and should save teachers and tutors much time and effort in locating appropriate reading materials for students in grades 5 to 12 no matter their reading ability.

After teaching and writing about reading for more than forty years, I firmly believe that teachers and tutors can help almost all students to read both narrative and content material effectively. Often teachers and tutors are unable to locate effective relevant motivating materials quickly and easily. The strategies and reproducible activity sheets in this volume are extremely helpful. It is obvious that no single book can solve all reading problems. However, the information and materials contained in this book should enable classroom, reading, special education, and content teachers, as well as tutors, to make a good beginning. It is my hope that this resource can provide them with much time-saving and effective help and also provide students with many motivating, challenging, and concrete ways to improve both their reading and study skills.

Wilma H. Miller

About the Author

A former classroom teacher, Wilma H. Miller, Ed.D., taught at the university level for thirty-three years. She is continuing her writing career in retirement, having authored six teacher resource books since leaving her position as professor of education at Illinois State University in Normal. She completed her doctorate in reading at the University of Arizona under the direction of the late Dr. Ruth Strang, a nationally known reading authority.

Dr. Miller has contributed more than two hundred articles to professional journals and is the author of more than thirty other works in the field of reading education. Among the latter works are *Identifying and Correcting Reading Difficulties in Children* (1972), *Diagnosis and Correction of Reading Difficulties in Secondary School Students* (1973), *Reading Diagnosis Kit* (1975, 1978, 1986), *Corrective Reading Skills Activity File* (1977), *Reading Teacher's Complete Diagnosis & Correction Manual* (1988), and *Reading Comprehension Activities Kit* (1990), all published by The Center for Applied Research in Education. In addition, she has authored *Complete Reading Disabilities Handbook* (1993), *Alternative Assessment Techniques for Reading & Writing* (1995), *Ready-to-Use Activities and Materials for Improving Content Reading Skills* (1999), *The Reading Teacher's Survival Kit* (2001), *Phonics First! Ready-to-Use Phonics Worksheets for the Primary Grades* (2001), *Phonics First! Ready-to-Use Phonics Worksheets for the Intermediate Grades* (2001), and *Reading Skills Problem Solver* (2002), all published by Jossey-Bass.

Dr. Miller also is the author of an in-service aid for teachers entitled *Reading Activities Handbook* (1980) and several textbooks for developmental reading, including *The First R: Elementary Reading Today* (1977) and *Teaching Elementary Reading Today* (1983), all published by Holt, Rinehart and Winston. She has also published *Teaching Reading in the Secondary School* (1974) with Charles C. Thomas and *Strategies for Developing Emergent Literacy* (2000) with McGraw-Hill.

Dr. Miller's doctoral dissertation received a citation of merit from the International Reading Association in 1968. Dr. Miller also received the 1998 Outstanding Contribution to Education Award from Northern Illinois University, DeKalb.

Contents

Informal Reading Assessment Tools for Older Students

Jamie is an eighth-grade student of average intelligence but superior mechanical ability. He is already able to take apart and repair his father's excavating and logging equipment. In addition, with his own money he has purchased and reconditioned a used snowmobile and boat motor. Jamie loves to hunt and fish and does both very well, but he struggles with reading and does not like to read for pleasure or for information either at school or at home. The only reading materials he likes are magazines and pamphlets that are related to his interests: machinery, hunting, fishing, and boating.

Nevertheless, Jamie should be able to read up to grade level with proper instruction. It is important that his precise reading strengths and weaknesses be correctly diagnosed and appropriate reading instruction then be provided for him. If this is done, Jamie should be able to make a significant reading improvement, especially if he has a good relationship with his reading teacher or tutor.

This chapter is designed to help reading teachers and tutors, classroom teachers, and content teachers quickly and accurately diagnose a student's specific reading strengths and weaknesses and reading levels. It contains numerous classroom-tested, easy-to-implement, and useful informal assessment devices. In general, informal assessment devices are fairly easy to administer and evaluate and are very helpful in determining a student's reading skills. They often are more user-friendly than many standardized tests. After reading this chapter, teachers and tutors should better understand informal assessment devices and how to use them effectively in a reading program.

The first section of the chapter explains how informal assessment can help instruction and describes a system of miscue analysis. The second section provides reproducible graded reading passages of the Content Reading Inventory. The last section of the chapter provides reproducible assessment inventories of several different reading skills.

Assessment and Instruction

Assessment can be defined as gathering information to meet the specific reading needs of a student. It involves determining what a student can and cannot achieve. Although assessment usually is informal, it often can be very helpful. *Evaluation* is judging the information that has been gathered by assessment. It is evaluating the responses that a student made, and it is usually more formal than assessment. Determining a student's understanding of the meaning of prefixes by using a checklist is an example of assessment, whereas determining that understanding by using an individual or group reading test is an example of evaluation.

The main purpose of assessment is to provide teachers and tutors with information that will help them improve a student's specific reading skills. Assessment should always point the way to subsequent instruction. In addition, students should not be taught reading skills that they already have. Reading teachers and tutors should never assess a student's reading skills without knowing why it is being done and without concern for his or her improved instruction. Integrating assessment with instruction makes it likely that the information gained from assessment will be used, not just filed in a student's cumulative folder. Informal assessment always should occur continuously to be effective.

Informal assessment can take many different forms: surveys, checklists, miscue analyses, various kind of informal inventories, QARs (question-answer relationships; see Chapter Six), conferences and interviews, retellings, and dialogue and response journals, among many others.

Advantages of Informal Tests

Here are the main advantages of using *informal assessment devices* in any reading improvement program in grades 5 to 12:

- They usually reflect the information that is being taught in a reading improvement program.
- They often are more *authentic* in evaluating a reading program.
- They emphasize the *process aspects* of reading rather than the *product aspects*, as traditionally is done by standardized tests.
- They usually more accurately reflect the accomplishments and attitudes of learning disabled, reading disabled, slow learning, and minority students than do standardized tests. Such students often are discriminated against in standardized tests, and their lower scores may not accurately reflect their true reading skills.
- They usually reflect the different styles of teaching and learning more effectively than do standardized tests.
- They are able to assess the affective (emotional, interest, or attitudinal) aspects of reading quite effectively.
- They do not have the prescribed, rigid directions and time limits that usually are found on standardized tests. Thus, "at-risk" students may not experience as much test anxiety. In addition, standardized tests often penalize the slow, but accurate, reader.
- Finally, they may be more motivating for at-risk students than are standardized tests.

MISCUE ANALYSIS

Miscue analysis can be very helpful in diagnosing the specific strengths and weaknesses of students in grades 5 to 12. Miscue analysis is based on the study of *psycholinguistics.* It is a method of analyzing how a student approaches the reading process and determining how he or she views it. According to this theory, deviations from the printed material are not really *errors* but instead are *miscues* that may or may not interfere with comprehension.

Miscues usually are classified into some variation of the following:

- *Graphophonic (graphonic or graphic) miscues*—are deviations in which there is a *graphic change* (the substitution of *thorough* for *through).*
- *Semantic miscues* are those deviations in which there is a *meaning change* (the substitution of *copper* for *cooper).*
- *Syntactic miscues* are those deviations in which there is a *substitution in the grammatical structure* of the sentence (for example, turning a statement into a question).

Advantages of Miscue Analysis

The following are the main advantages of using miscue analysis in an informal assessment program in grades 5 to 12. These are the reasons that every reading teacher and tutor should learn at least one miscue analysis system.

- The reading teacher or tutor can learn a great deal about how a student understands or views the purpose and content of the reading process.
- The reading teacher or tutor can learn whether or not a student's miscues usually interfere significantly with comprehension. As stated earlier, those miscues that do interfere are considered more important than those that do not.
- The reading teacher or tutor can learn if a student has difficulty with graphophonic (phonic) analysis, and specifically with word beginnings, middles, or endings. In addition, the teacher can learn if a student has difficulty with word structure, specifically with prefixes, suffixes, syllabication ("chunking"), or accent.
- The reading teacher or tutor can learn if a student self-corrects while reading.
- The reading teacher or tutor can learn if a student's deviation from the printed text results in graphic change, meaning change, or grammatical change.
- Miscue analysis is a good way to observe a student's reading informally. This can help a teacher to teach reading much more effectively.
- Miscue analysis is a fairly accurate way to assess reading strengths and weaknesses if it is done by an experienced, well-trained reading teacher or tutor. However, it does require some practice to become proficient in marking the miscues and evaluating them. Furthermore, miscue analysis should be considered an *approximation* of a student's reading strengths and weaknesses and reading levels.

Using the Miscue Analysis Described in This Book

Later, this chapter contains two forms of a reproducible Content Reading Inventory (Forms A and B) that can be duplicated and used with students from the fifth- through the twelfth-grade reading levels.

Here's how you can use them: in *oral reading,* you mark the miscues; in *silent reading,* you evaluate comprehension based on the student's responses to the questions that follow the passage. You can also use a combination of oral-silent-oral reading; silent-oral-silent reading; and pre- and post-testing.

Because it takes considerable practice to become adept at marking oral reading miscues, it's a good idea to tape-record the oral reading. Then you can mark the miscues while playing back the tape recording.

The student's oral reading can be marked with a variety of systems. Here is the one recommended in this book:

- Omission—Circle the entire word or letter sound.

- Addition—Insert with a caret.

  famous

- Substitutions/Mispronunciations—Draw a line through the word and write in the substituted word.

  ~~criminal~~ crime

- Reversals—Use the transposition symbol.

  exploration scientific

- Repetitions—Use a wavy line to indicate a repetition of more than two words.

  their unsuccessful attempt

- Words Aided—If a student says nothing after about five seconds, provide the word and cross it out.

  ~~cheetah~~

The following are guidelines to keep in mind when using this system of miscue analysis:

1. Count as a *major oral reading miscue* and deduct *one point* for any error that interferes with comprehension. Some examples are *frozen* for *fracture, rough* for *enough, angle* for *angel,* and *satisfactory* for *satellite.*

2. Count as a *minor oral reading miscue* and deduct *one-half point* for any deviation from the printed text that does *not* seem to interfere significantly with comprehension. Some examples are *terrible* for *disastrous, interesting* for *fascinating, heavy* for *torrential,* or *friendly* for *docile.*

3. Count an *addition* as *half an oral reading miscue* if it does not significantly alter the meaning of the material. Usually an addition or insertion is a minor oral reading miscue because it does not significantly change the meaning of the material.

4. Do *not* count a *self-correction* as a miscue if it occurs within a short period of time, such as five seconds. A self-correction usually indicates that the student is *monitoring* his or her reading and attempting to read for meaning.

5. Count a *repetition* as *half an oral reading miscue* if it occurs on *two or more words.* A repetition of a single word may indicate that the student is trying to monitor his or her own reading or correcting the miscue.

6. Do not count more than *one oral reading miscue* on the same word in any one passage. For example, if the student mispronounces the same word more than once while reading a passage, count it as a miscue only once.

7. Do not count an oral reading miscue on any *proper noun* found in a passage.

8. Deduct *one point* for any word that a student cannot pronounce after about five seconds *if that word interferes with comprehension.* Deduct *one-half point* for any word that a student cannot pronounce after about five seconds *if that word does not seem to interfere with comprehension.*

9. Do not count oral reading miscues that seem to exemplify a student's *cultural or regional dialect.* To consider this point, you should be quite familiar with the basic characteristics of the student's speech patterns, such as in the African American dialect or the Latino dialect.

When you have marked all of the oral reading miscues from the material that the student has read, you can use the information to determine the student's approximate *independent, instructional,* and *frustration reading levels.*

The characteristics of the three main reading levels usually are as follows:

- *Independent (easy) reading level:* The point at which a student is about *99%* accurate in word identification and has about *95%* or better comprehension.
- *Instructional (learning) reading level:* The point at which a student is about *90%* accurate in word identification and has about *75%* or better comprehension.
- *Frustration (hard) reading level:* The point at which a student is less than about *90%* accurate in word identification and has less than *50%* accuracy in comprehension.

After using this system of miscue analysis with thousands of students over a period of many years, I have found that adding several other reading levels to the three basic levels is helpful in placing students in reading materials that they can read independently or with teacher help. Therefore, you can also use the following three sublevels:

- Low independent reading level
- High instructional reading level
- Low instructional reading level

The paragraphs included in the Content Reading Inventory near the end of this chapter use the three subcategories of reading levels in addition to the three basic ones. Because any content IRI (individual reading inventory) is an *informal assessment device,* teachers and tutors should use their own judgment in arriving at these reading levels, and should take a student's word identification miscues and comprehension score into account together. *The student's performance on comprehension should be weighted more highly than the performance on word identification because comprehension always is more important.*

Using the three additional approximate reading levels is justified because the graded oral reading passages always are *informal assessment devices.* They never should be considered completely accurate indicators of a student's reading level.

As already mentioned, a student's responses to the comprehension questions can also be evaluated. Here's how to do it. On the first line by each question after a passage under the word *Score,* write the number *1* for a correct answer and the number *0* for an incorrect answer. On the second line by each answer under the word *Appropriateness,* write a + for a complete or insightful answer or a ✓ for a completely irrelevant answer. You do not have to put down either of these marks if they are not pertinent. If more than one-third of a student's answers have been marked with a ✓ then the student probably does not have a true idea of the purpose of the passage and does not comprehend well. If the student has a number of +'s, then he or she probably understands the material very well.

Then determine the student's comprehension score on each of the passages. If there are six comprehension questions accompanying a passage, the following scores are needed *either in oral or silent reading* to attain the various reading levels.

- Independent (easy) reading level: 6 correct
- Instructional (learning) reading level: 4–5 correct
- Frustration (hard) reading level: 3 or fewer correct

If there are eight comprehension questions accompanying a passage, the following scores are needed *in either oral or silent reading* to attain the different reading levels.

- Independent (easy) reading level: 8 correct
- Instructional (learning) reading level: 5–7 correct
- Frustration (hard) reading level: 4 or fewer correct

In addition, you can assess the student's *self-monitoring* of his or her comprehension informally by noticing his or her responses to the questions that follow the comprehension questions for each passage. As you will notice when you review the passages in Forms A and B, the following is how self-monitoring of comprehension is assessed in this book:

How well do you think you answered these questions?

very well _________

all right _________

not very well _________

You can then make an informal comparison between each student's responses on these questions and his or her actual score on the comprehension questions. The following probably are the most comparable responses:

Student's Response	Comprehension Score on the Passage	
	6 total questions	8 total questions
very well	6	8
all right	4–5	5–7
not very well	3 or fewer	4 or fewer

A significant deviation from this pattern of responses *may indicate* that the student does not monitor his or her comprehension as effectively as possible.

Interpreting a Student's Performance

A reading teacher or tutor can use the information about determining *oral reading miscues* to analyze a student's pattern of errors. Obviously, this analysis is not applicable when the student reads a passage silently. In that case, *comprehension* of the material is all that can be evaluated.

As noted earlier, a student's oral reading miscues can be analyzed in terms of the following: *omissions*, *additions*, *substitutions/mispronunciations*, *reversals*, *repetitions*, and *words aided* or *words supplied.*

Briefly, here's how to analyze the oral reading miscues: divide the total number of words in the passage into the total number of words that the student pronounced correctly to obtain the *percentage* of correct words. For example, *325* total words in a passage divided by *296* total words correct in the passage equals *.90* or *90%* accuracy in word identification, which is the instructional (learning) reading level.

You can use the percentages that are supplied in the Content Reading Inventory included in this chapter. However, if you want detailed information about analyzing a student's oral reading miscues, consult *Alternative Assessment Techniques for Reading & Writing* (Miller, 1995, pp. 127–129).

Record Sheet of Miscue Analysis

The following is a *sample blank record sheet for miscue analysis.* I encourage you to duplicate it and use it if you want to have a *graphic record* of the type of oral reading miscues a student makes. You may want to place it in his or her cumulative folder, or share it with family members during a conference.

Name ______________________ Grade ___ Teacher ___________ Date _________

Record Sheet for Miscue Analysis *#+

Text	Miscue	Omission	Addition	Substitution/ Mispronunciation	Repetition	Word Aided/ Supplied

Name ______________________ **Grade** ___ **Teacher** ___________ **Date** _________

Record Sheet for Miscue Analysis, continued

Text	Miscue	Omission	Addition	Substitution/ Mispronunciation	Repetition	Word Aided/ Supplied
________	__________	___	___	____	___	___
________	__________	___	___	____	___	___
________	__________	___	___	____	___	___
________	__________	___	___	____	___	___
________	__________	___	___	____	___	___
________	__________	___	___	____	___	___
________	__________	___	___	____	___	___
________	__________	___	___	____	___	___
________	__________	___	___	____	___	___
________	__________	___	___	____	___	___
________	__________	___	___	____	___	___
________	__________	___	___	____	___	___
________	__________	___	___	____	___	___
________	__________	___	___	____	___	___
________	__________	___	___	____	___	___
		Total	Total	Total	Total	Total

Total number of words in the passage _____

Total number of major miscues _____

Total number of minor miscues _____

Total number of major and minor miscues ___________

Percentage of words correctly supplied ___________

Approximate reading level ___________

Independent (easy) reading level approx. *99%*

Instructional (learning) reading level approx. *90%*

Frustration (hard) reading level less than *90%*

---

* Major miscue: Deduct one point.

\# Minor miscue: Deduct one-half point.

\+ Repetition of two or more words: Deduct one-half point.

REPRODUCIBLE CONTENT READING INVENTORY

This section of the chapter provides the graded reading passages that make up Forms A and B of the Content Reading Inventory. They are designed for use at the fifth- through the twelfth-grade reading levels. Duplicate one set of the graded reading passages at the appropriate levels, omitting the questions to assess prior knowledge and interest in the passage, the comprehension questions, and the self-monitoring questions. This is the set from which students will read aloud or silently. Make a second set containing the questions and the formula for scoring; this is the set you will evaluate. The student set can be laminated for durability.

The following code has been placed on each of the graded reading passages so that you, but not the students, can determine the levels of the passages they are reading.

Fifth Reader Level

Sixth Reader Level

Seventh Reader Level

Eighth Reader Level

Ninth Reader Level

Tenth Reader Level–Twelfth Reader Level

Additional sets of graded reading passages can be found in several sources: *Alternative Assessment Techniques for Reading & Writing* (Miller, 1995, pp. 174–185, 204–215); *Reading Diagnosis Kit* (Miller, 1986, pp. 213–228, 244–259); and *The Reading Teacher's Survival Kit* (Miller, 2001, pp. 92–116). These additional graded reading passages can be used for pre- and post-testing or with different types of administration, such as oral-silent-oral, silent-oral, oral-silent, or silent-oral-silent.

Because it is very difficult to discriminate between the tenth-grade reading level and the twelfth-grade reading level, Forms A and B each contain one passage that is designed for use in the tenth through the twelfth grades. However, the reading levels from these two passages always should be considered *tentative.*

Form A Passages

Name ______________________ Grade ___ Teacher ___________ Date _________

Oral Reading Passage: Venus Williams, Tennis Champ* ___

Venus Williams, an African American tennis star, probably owes much of her success to her father Richard Williams, her tennis coach and mentor. Venus was born in the Watts section of Los Angeles, California, on June 17, 1980, the fourth of five daughters born to Richard and his wife.

Richard decided to help his two youngest daughters, Venus and Serena, to become tennis stars. Venus began playing tennis when she was only four and practiced on the free public courts in the middle of gang territory in Compton, California. Venus and her sister Serena were shot at by gang members while practicing and learned to hit the ground quickly.

Venus was a very talented tennis player who loved the game and was well known throughout the country before she was twelve. Although Venus practiced every day, her parents also encouraged her to do well in school, and she was an excellent student.

In 1991 her family moved to Florida so Venus and her sister could get better training. Venus turned professional at the age of fourteen and from that time on has been a familiar figure in tennis tournaments—a tall, athletic African American wearing cornrow braids with beads.

By 1995 Venus had signed a multimillion-dollar endorsement deal with Reebok, and the family moved to a ten-acre estate in Palm Beach Gardens, Florida, where Venus and Serena could practice on their own tennis courts.

From that time on Venus has steadily improved until she is recognized as probably the best woman tennis player in the world. In 2000, after being sidelined for six months with tendonitis in both wrists and thinking about retirement, she won the singles championship at Wimbledon in England. She was the first black women's champion there since Althea (Ăl thēə) Gibson in 1957 and 1958. In 2001 she entered twelve tennis tournaments and won six of them, including Wimbledon and the U.S. Open.

In 2000 the magazine *Sports Illustrated Women* named Venus "Sportswoman of the Year." In 2000 Venus and Serena built an expensive home next to their parents with part of their 45 million dollars of earnings.

Both Venus and Serena are close to their family and are religious. They love to shop and have fun "horsing around." However, both are talented and are positive role models for thousands of young women.

---

* The readability level of this passage was computed by the Dale-Chall Readability Formula.

Before Reading "Venus Williams, Tennis Champ"
Assessing Prior Knowledge and Interest

1. What do you know about Venus Williams, the tennis champion?
2. Do you think that you will like reading this passage? Why? Why not?

After Reading

Number of words in this selection *389*

Number of word identification miscues ________

Word Identification Miscues

Independent reading level approx. *0–5*

Low independent reading level approx. *6–14*

High instructional reading level approx. *15–24*

Instructional reading level approx. *25–35*

Low instructional reading level approx. *36–39*

Frustration reading level *40+*

Assessing Comprehension

Score *1* for a correct response and *0* for an incorrect response in the appropriate column. Score ✓ for any answers that are clearly illogical or + for any answers that are very good, detailed, or insightful.

Reading the Lines	**Score**	**Appropriateness**
1. How many children are in Venus's family? **(five)**	_____	_____
2. What kind of student was Venus? **(excellent, very good, good)**	_____	_____
3. In 2000 what honor was given to Venus by the magazine *Sports Illustrated Women*? **(Sportswoman of the Year)**	_____	_____
Reading Between the Lines		
1. Why do you think Venus is an outstanding tennis player? **(she has natural talent; she practices a lot; she loves to play tennis)**	_____	_____
2. Why do you think Venus wears her hair in cornrow braids? **(it is easy to take care of; it shows her African American heritage; she likes the way it looks)**	_____	_____
3. Why do you think Venus developed tendonitis (soreness) in her wrists? **(she used her wrists a lot while playing tennis; she has played tennis a long time)**	_____	_____

Reading Beyond the Lines	**Score**	**Appropriateness**
1. Would you like to grow up to be a famous tennis player like Venus Williams? Why? Why not? **(any logical answer—some examples: YES I would like to earn all that money; it would be fun to have a job playing tennis; I would like to travel all over the world; NO it would be hard not to have any privacy; I would not enjoy practicing tennis every day for hours; I would not like to get injured)**	_____	_____
2. Would you like to be a role model for thousands of young women? Why? Why not? **(any logical answer—some examples: YES it would be great to be admired by thousands of young women; it would make me feel proud; NO I would be afraid that I would do something wrong and disappoint them; it would be a burden to always have to do everything right)**	_____	_____

Number of comprehension questions correct _____

Comprehension Score

Independent reading level *8*

Instructional reading level *5–7*

Frustration reading level *4 or fewer*

Self-Monitoring of Comprehension

How well do you think you answered these questions?

very well _____

all right _____

not so well _____

Name ______________________ Grade ___ Teacher ___________ Date _________

Oral Reading Passage: Gold—The Metal of Kings*

Gold has always been valued very highly because it is both beautiful and rare. Only five-billionths of the earth's crust is made of gold.

Because gold reacts with few other chemicals, it usually is found in its pure form and is extracted in tiny crystals barely a few millimeters in size. However, sometimes prospectors locate larger lumps of gold called *nuggets.* When gold is discovered in loose chunks in sand or gravel, the chunks are called *placer deposits.*

The leading areas for gold mining are found in South Africa, what was formerly called Russia, the United States, Canada, Australia, Brazil, and China. The Transvaal province of South Africa now produces one-quarter of the world's annual gold production. Although the oceans that cover about three-quarters of the earth's surface contain a higher proportion of gold than the land, it would not be cost effective to extract gold from sea water.

Ancient peoples such as those in Egypt and Persia panned for gold using river water. They washed sand or gravel through a sieve, leaving lumps of gold behind in the sieve to collect. Ancient Egyptians who associated glistening gold with their sun god used it as a decoration in life and in death. The tombs of the pharaohs in Egypt contained fantastic artifacts of gold. Perhaps the gold mask of the young Egyptian pharaoh king Tutankhamen (Tŭt) that was discovered in 1922 best displays the brilliance and durability of gold.

Pure gold, which is 24 karats, is too soft to use for jewelry making. Most jewelry is made from gold that is 14 or 18 karats—meaning 14 or 18 parts of gold out of a possible 24 parts. The remaining parts usually are silver, copper, nickel, palladium, or zinc. This is the reason that most jewelry is made of yellow gold but also can be made from white or rose gold.

Because gold is extremely easy to work with, it can be *cast*—melted, poured into a mold, and then left to cool. However, it also can be beaten into *gold leaf* to cover large areas extremely thinly. It also can be pressed or plated on silver, which creates vermeil (ver mēl), a slightly less expensive material that looks and feels like solid gold.

Most interestingly, gold is useful in medical science and is safe to use within the body because it reacts with very few chemicals. For example, pellets of gold can destroy cancerous cells in such parts of the body as the prostate gland and the ovaries. Compounds containing gold can stop the growth of some bacteria.

* The readability level of this passage was computed by the Dale-Chall Readability Formula.

Before Reading "Gold—The Metal of Kings"
Assessing Prior Knowledge and Interest

1. What do you currently know about gold?
2. Do you think that you will like reading this passage? Why? Why not?

After Reading

Number of words in this selection ___*434*___

Number of word identification miscues _____

Word Identification Miscues

Independent reading level approx. ___*0–7*___

Low independent reading level approx. ___*8–16*___

High instructional reading level approx. ___*17–26*___

Instructional reading level approx. ___*27–37*___

Low instructional reading level approx. ___*38–47*___

Frustration reading level ___*48+*___

Assessing Comprehension

Score *1* for a correct response and *0* for an incorrect response in the appropriate column. Score ✓ for any answers that are clearly illogical or + for any answers that are very good, detailed, or insightful.

Reading the Lines	**Score**	**Appropriateness**
1. What is a gold nugget? **(a fairly large lump of gold)**	_____	_____
2. What country produces the greatest amount of gold? **(South Africa)**	_____	_____
3. What is vermeil? **(gold that is plated on silver)**	_____	_____
Reading Between the Lines		
1. Why did the Ancient Egyptians associate gold with their sun god? **(both the sun and gold are yellow and shine brightly)**	_____	_____
2. Why is 24-karat gold not practical to use for jewelry? **(it is so soft that it would not hold its shape; the jewelry made of it would "squish")**	_____	_____
3. Why is gold leaf popular? **(it looks beautiful but is not as expensive as thicker gold; it makes the gold go a long way)**	_____	_____

Reading Beyond the Lines	**Score**	**Appropriateness**
1. It is still possible to pan for gold in parts of the American West. Are you interested in doing that? Why? Why not? **(any logical answer—some examples: YES it would be fun; I could find gold and sell it for the money; I would like to see what the prospectors did; NO it would take too long to find gold; it would be boring)**	_____	_____
2. Would you like to visit a working gold mine? Why? Why not? **(any logical answer—some examples: YES it would be interesting to see how gold is mined; I am interested in learning more about gold; NO I do not want to go that deep into the earth; I am not interested in gold)**	_____	_____

Number of comprehension questions correct _____

Comprehension Score

Independent reading level ___*8*___

Instructional reading level ___*5–7*___

Frustration reading level ___*4 or fewer*___

Self-Monitoring of Comprehension

How well do you think you answered these questions?

very well _____

all right _____

not so well _____

Name ______________________ Grade ___ Teacher ____________ Date _________

Oral Reading Passage: Solar Power—Renewable Source of Energy* 

Sunlight, or solar power, is an energy source that is renewable, clean, and environmentally friendly in comparison to coal, oil, and natural gas.

Although the sun appears to be a glowing ball of burning gas, it is actually a giant nuclear reactor. It is so huge that more than a million earths would fit inside it. At its center, hydrogen atoms collide with each other with such tremendous force that they combine to form *helium.* This type of reaction, called *nuclear fusion,* releases enormous amounts of energy. Most of this energy is given off as heat and light, which stream out into space in all directions. After a journey of 93 million miles through space, a small fraction of this solar energy reaches the earth.

People have treated the sun as miraculous for thousands of years because it brought life-sustaining light and heat. Many ancient civilizations believed that the sun was a god or that it was moved across the sky by a god each day. The Ancient Egyptians believed that the sun was a god who sailed across the sky in a heavenly ship while the Ancient Greeks worshipped the sun god Helios (Hē lē ōs). The Aztecs, an ancient Mexican civilization, made human and animal sacrifices in high temples and on mountain tops to worship their sun god.

Solar energy as an alternative energy source has been researched since the nineteenth century in such experiments as a solar-powered printing press, furnace, and water heater. At the present time flat-plate solar collectors are sold to supply homes with hot water for heating and washing. An efficient flat-plate collector can heat water to a temperature of 194° F. In northern countries, the solar collectors are tilted toward the south, while in countries south of the equator, they are tilted northward. At the equator, they face straight up at the sky.

Solar One, the world's biggest solar power plant, was built in 1982 in the Mojave Desert in California. It supplies 10,000 homes with electricity by using almost 2,000 mirrors laid out in semicircles. These mirrors reflect sunlight onto a boiler at the top of a high control tower. When solar energy reflects from the mirrors and falls onto the boiler, it glows white hot, and oil flowing through it is rapidly heated. Then the hot oil is piped away and used to heat water in a boiler. It is then converted to steam, which drives a generator to make electricity.

There currently are solar cars that race in Australia every three years in the World Solar Challenge. These cars average 56 miles an hour, are silent, and are very small, seating only two people. They also are very expensive, costing up to a million dollars to build.

* The readability level of this passage was computed by the Dale-Chall Readability Formula.

Before Reading "Solar Power—Renewable Source of Energy"
Assessing Prior Knowledge and Interest

1. What do you know about solar energy?
2. Do you think that you will like reading this passage? Why? Why not?

After Reading

Number of words in this selection ___*455*___

Number of word identification miscues _____

Word Identification Miscues

Independent reading level approx. ___*0–7*___

Low independent reading level approx. ___*8–16*___

High instructional reading level approx. ___*17–26*___

Instructional reading level approx. ___*27–37*___

Low instructional reading level approx. ___*38–47*___

Frustration reading level ___*48+*___

Assessing Comprehension

Score *1* for a correct response and *0* for an incorrect response in the appropriate column. Score ✓ for any answers that are clearly illogical or + for any answers that are very good, detailed, or insightful.

Reading the Lines	**Score**	**Appropriateness**
1. What are some of the advantages of using solar power as an energy source? **(it's renewable, clean, environmentally friendly)**	_____	_____
2. Why did some ancient peoples worship the sun? **(it brought them light and heat)**	_____	_____
3. Where was the solar plant Solar One built? **(in the Mojave Desert; in California)**	_____	_____
Reading Between the Lines		
1. Why do you think solar power is considered an energy source? **(the sun should continue to give light and heat forever; the world cannot use up solar energy)**	_____	_____
2. Why do you think flat-plate solar collectors face south in the Northern Hemisphere? **(they face in the direction of the sun to get the most light and heat possible)**	_____	_____
3. Why do you think a solar power plant is not practical in crowded urban (city) areas? **(the mirrors that they use require a lot of land)**	_____	_____

Reading Beyond the Lines	**Score**	**Appropriateness**
1. Would you like to own a completely solar-powered home in the future? Why? Why not? **(any logical answer—some examples: YES it would be clean and friendly to the environment; it would be attractive with its glass solar collectors; NO it would be very expensive to use solar power; it might not provide enough heat and light)**	_____	_____
2. Sometime in the future would you like to drive a solar car? Why? Why not? **(any logical answer—some examples: YES it would be environmentally friendly; it would be exciting and different; it seems natural to use solar power for energy; NO it would be too small; it would be much too expensive; it would not be practical)**	_____	_____

Number of comprehension questions correct _____

Comprehension Score

Independent reading level *8*

Instructional reading level *5–7*

Frustration reading level *4 or fewer*

Self-Monitoring of Comprehension

How well do you think you answered these questions?

very well _____

all right _____

not so well _____

Name ______________________ Grade ___ Teacher ____________ Date _________

Oral Reading Passage: The Chipewyans of the North* 

The Chipewyans (Chip ∂ wâns) of northern Canada live in the forest-tundra ecosystem, a narrow zone of thinning forest between the tundra bordering the Arctic Ocean to the north and the forests to the south.

The Chipewyans have created a way of life that for centuries relied on the extreme cold of this region instead of defying it. Freezing winds caused caribou to seek winter homes in the shelter of valleys where they were stalked by Chipewyan hunters. The deep snow also yielded animal tracks, such as those of rabbits and other small animals, so the Chipewyan women could position snares to capture them.

The caribou was of primary importance to the Chipewyan native peoples. The customs, spiritual culture, and economic and social structure all depended on the pursuit of the caribou. Caribou provided meat and fat for food, skins for shelter and clothing, and horn and bones for primitive but functional tools. Chipewyan hunters wore breechcloths, shirts, and moccasins made of caribou hide, which was warm, light, and easy to fashion. The name "Chipewyan" probably came from a Cree word meaning "pointed skins," referring to the traditional caribou-skin shirts that come to a point in the back.

The Chipewyans are an excellent example of hunter-gatherers, those people whose sustenance depends upon their ability to hunt prey and gather food of various types. Because the Chipewyans had to follow the caribou in their migrations in order to survive, a hunter and his family had to be ready to move at a moment's notice. Therefore, the Chipewyans built no permanent cities with buildings. However, their adaptation to the harsh conditions of their way of life indicates that they were not truly primitive peoples.

The child-rearing duties of the Chipewyan women were complicated because they had to be ready to move their camp at a moment's notice, and because they were responsible for transporting equipment from camp to camp. Since the Chipewyan men needed to be able to pursue game or defend the group from enemy attack, the Chipewyan women carried camp equipment and pulled heavy sledges packed with tents and other items. Chipewyan women carried their babies under their clothing, and the baby was held in place by a belt. Moss was used instead of diapers to keep the baby dry.

Chipewyan children enjoyed games such as stickball with caribou-skin balls stuffed with dried moss, peashooters made from a hollow swan bone, and a "bull-roarer," a toy made of a slab of notched wood attached to a long strip of partially tanned caribou hide. When this toy was whirled in the air, it made a low noise like the roaring of a bull.

* The readability of this passage was computed by the Dale-Chall Readability Formula.

Before Reading "The Chipewyans of the North"
Assessing Prior Knowledge and Interest

1. What do you know about the Chipewyans, the native peoples of northern Canada?
2. Do you think that you will like reading this passage? Why? Why not?

After Reading

Number of words in this selection ___*441*___

Number of word identification miscues _____

Word Identification Miscues

Independent reading level approx. ___*0–7*___

Low independent reading level approx. ___*8–16*___

High instructional reading level approx. ___*17–26*___

Instructional reading level approx. ___*27–37*___

Low instructional reading level approx. ___*38–47*___

Frustration reading level ___*48+*___

Assessing Comprehension

Score *1* for a correct response and *0* for an incorrect response in the appropriate column. Score ✓ for any answers that are clearly illogical or + for any answers that are very good, detailed, or insightful.

Reading the Lines	**Score**	**Appropriateness**
1. How did the Chipewyan women hunt for rabbits and other small animals? **(using snares)**	_____	_____
2. What animal was most important to the Chipewyan? **(the caribou)**	_____	_____
3. What are "hunter-gatherers?" **(people whose life depends upon their ability to hunt and gather food)**	_____	_____
Reading Between the Lines		
1. Why do you think the Chipewyan wanted to hunt for caribou in the valleys? **(they were easier to hunt because they couldn't run as far or as fast as they could on open ground)**	_____	_____
2. Why do you think it was difficult for the Chipewyan women to transport equipment from camp to camp? **(it probably was heavy to carry; they also had to care for the children; they were not as strong as the men)**	_____	_____
3. Why do you think moss was used in place of diapers? **(it was soft; it absorbs liquids well; it was easily available)**	_____	_____

Reading Beyond the Lines	**Score**	**Appropriateness**
1. The Chipewyan still live in parts of northern Canada, and anthropologists can still learn about them. Would you like to study them someday? Why? Why not? **(any logical answer—some examples: YES I enjoy learning about native peoples; I enjoy the wilderness and people who live there; NO the area is too isolated for me to enjoy visiting it and living there awhile; I don't like wilderness areas)**	_____	_____
2. Compare your life to the life of a traditional Chipewyan child your age. **(any logical answer—some examples: we live in one place and don't move from place to place; it is not as cold here as northern Canada; this is not a wilderness area; we have more modern conveniences such as a TV and computer; we don't eat the caribou that we hunt; our lifestyle is more "civilized"—different, but not necessarily better)**	_____	_____

Number of comprehension questions correct _____

Comprehension Score

Independent reading level *8*

Instructional reading level *5–7*

Frustration reading level *4 or fewer*

Self-Monitoring of Comprehension

How well do you think you answered these questions?

very well _____

all right _____

not so well _____

Name ______________________ Grade ___ Teacher ___________ Date _________

Oral Reading Passage: Learning about Stress* ☆

Stress is anything that upsets the body's natural means of self-regulation. Moment by moment the body adjusts its blood pressure, temperature, heart rate, hormonal levels, and a myriad of other variables. These are all controlled by a pea-sized organ deep inside the brain called the *hypothalamus.*

The hypothalamus also is the location where emotions and memories are processed and basic feelings and urges such as hunger, thirst, desire, panic, anger, and pain are controlled.

Any event that provides intense feelings, whether painful or pleasurable, can trigger a stress reaction. The common denominator of stress is *change,* whether for the better or the worse.

Stress is often manifested in the "fight or flight" response. The instant the brain senses a crisis, it sends danger signals in the form of chemical messengers that alert the body to prepare for action. The hypothalamus sets the stress response in motion with a direct command to the *adrenal glands* to "release adrenaline." This powerful hormone increases blood pressure and heart rate and also releases *cortisol,* a hormone that helps move *glucose* (the sugar the body uses for fat) out of storage and into circulation.

There are many other changes in body chemistry during the "fight or flight" response. The bone marrow increases production of blood cells to fight infection. The thyroid gland secretes hormones to speed metabolism, providing an energy boost; however, prolonged stimulation can lead to increased appetite and insomnia. The lungs expand to deliver more oxygen to the heart and muscles. The heart beats harder, potentially resulting in a heart attack or stroke from the additional strain. The pancreas secretes extra *insulin* for a burst of energy. Blood sugar soars and may stay high for awhile, setting the stage for *diabetes.* The liver pumps out extra *cholesterol* to provide slow-burning fuel where blood sugar leaves off. If stress is chronic, hardening of the *arteries* may result. Activity in the stomach and intestines shuts down to conserve energy, and stomach acid rises, which may cause nausea and vomiting. Sweat glands work harder to cool heated muscles, and tiny blood vessels near the surface contract and hairs stand on end—a reaction that made our ancestors seem larger to their enemies.

Because of all these potentially damaging changes in the body, it is vital for a person to learn how to control stress effectively.

* The readability level of this passage was computed by the Dale-Chall Readability Formula.

Before Reading "Learning about Stress"
Assessing Prior Knowledge and Interest

1. What do you know about the body's reaction to stress?
2. Do you think that you will like reading this passage? Why? Why not?

After Reading

Number of words in this selection ___*390*___

Number of word identification miscues _____

Word Identification Miscues

Independent reading level approx. ___*0–5*___

Low independent reading level approx. ___*6–14*___

High instructional reading level approx. ___*15–24*___

Instructional reading level approx. ___*25–35*___

Low instructional reading level approx. ___*36–39*___

Frustration reading level ___*40+*___

Assessing Comprehension

Score *1* for a correct response and *0* for an incorrect response in the appropriate column. Score ✓ for any answers that are clearly illogical or + for any answers that are very good, detailed, or insightful.

Reading the Lines	**Score**	**Appropriateness**
1. What is stress? **(something that upsets the body's means of self-regulation)**	_____	_____
2. What response often is the result of stress? **(fight-or-flight response)**	_____	_____
3. What does the heart do during stressful times? **(it beats harder)**	_____	_____
Reading Between the Lines		
1. Why do you think the hypothalamus is placed deep in a person's brain? **(since it is important to body functions, it is very well protected by the skull)**	_____	_____
2. Why do you think our ancestors found the fight-or-flight response useful? **(for survival; they often were required to fight their enemies or escape from them)**	_____	_____
3. Why do you think the thyroid gland secretes hormones to provide an energy boost during the fight-or-flight response? **(additional energy may be needed either to stay and fight enemies or to escape from them)**	_____	_____

Reading Beyond the Lines	**Score**	**Appropriateness**
1. When you are "stressed out" about a difficult upcoming exam, what examples of the "fight or flight" response have you noticed? **(any logical answer—some examples: either I am very hungry or I can't eat at all; I don't sleep well, my heart beats harder, I feel hot and sweaty; I have "butterflies" in my stomach)**	_____	_____
2. What are some ways you deal with stress? **(any logical answer—some examples: exercise, walk or run; have a pet; pursue a hobby; talk to a friend or friends; read a good book; smile at someone; laugh at a good joke; read the comics; pray; take a warm bath)**	_____	_____

Number of comprehension questions correct _____

Comprehension Score

Independent reading level *8*

Instructional reading level *5–7*

Frustration reading level *4 or fewer*

Self-Monitoring of Comprehension

How well do you think you answered these questions?

very well _____

all right _____

not so well _____

Name ______________________ Grade ___ Teacher ___________ Date _________

Oral Reading Passage: Abu Simbel, Monument to Ramses the Great*

Abu Simbel (Abū Sĭm bəl), located in southern Egypt, is the most imaginative and extravagant construction of the renowned and whimsical pharaoh of Egypt, Ramses II, also called Ramses the Great.

Constructing these temple represented a daunting challenge to the pharaoh's architects because it was carved out of a solitary piece of rock 65 meters long and 35 meters wide.

The façade consists of four colossal statues of Ramses II seated on a throne, each 20 meters tall and 4 meters wide from ear to ear. The statues not only are monuments to the accomplishments of this pharaoh-king but also are indispensable, because they support the façade, which is 31 meters high.

The temple wall decorations celebrate the military grandeur and resourcefulness of Ramses II. The poet Pentaur, who served at the court of this mighty pharaoh, composed a lengthy epic poem about the expedition of Ramses II into Syria. This poem is engraved in hieroglyphics at Abu Simbel and graphically illustrates his military valor. According to the poet Pentaur, Ramses the Great was ambushed and suddenly surrounded by enemy troops. Extending his body to full height and his chariot pulled by two horses, Ramses II flung himself into battle to confront the enemy completely alone. Although surrounded by 2,500 chariots, each bearing three enemy soldiers, he addressed a fervent prayer to the supreme god of the pharaohs and was granted an overwhelming victory with the support of his generals and horsemen, who sprang forward.

Adjacent to the temple of Ramses II is a much less officious temple, barely ten meters long, dedicated to his most honored wife, Nefertari. Never before in Egypt had the wife of a pharaoh been accorded such a phenomenal honor. However, even at this temple, statues of Ramses the Great are found adjacent to those of Nefertari.

For untold centuries the temples at Abu Simbel stood as unyielding memorials to the divinity and greatness of Ramses II, lapped by the eternal waters of the Nile. The probability that the temples would be submerged due to the waters of the artificial Lake Nasaar that had been created, had worldwide repercussions. UNESCO immediately formed two commissions to study the dilemma of salvaging the temples from destruction. The final suggestion was made by Sweden, recommending cutting up the temples and reconstructing them on a plateau 90 meters above their original level. Seventeen thousand holes were made in the stone, through which resin was injected to consolidate the structures. The monuments were sawed into 1,036 segments whose average weight was thirty tons, to which were added 1,110 pieces from the surrounding rock.

The removal of the temples from their original site was barely completed in time. By the end of summer 1965, the waters of the Nile started submerging the cavern where the temples had once stood.

---

* The readability level of this passage was computed by the Dale-Chall Readability Formula.

Before Reading "Abu Simbel, Monument to Ramses the Great"
Assessing Prior Knowledge and Interest

1. What do you know about Abu Simbel in southern Egypt?
2. Do you think that you will like reading this passage? Why? Why not?

After Reading

Number of words in this selection ___*470*___

Number of word identification miscues _____

Word Identification Miscues

Independent reading level approx. ___*0–8*___

Low independent reading level approx. ___*9–17*___

High instructional reading level approx. ___*18–27*___

Instructional reading level approx. ___*28–38*___

Low instructional reading level approx. ___*39–48*___

Frustration reading level ___*49+*___

Assessing Comprehension

Score *1* for a correct response and *0* for an incorrect response in the appropriate column. Score ✓ for any answers that are clearly illogical or + for any answers that are very good, detailed, or insightful.

Reading the Lines	**Score**	**Appropriateness**
1. In what pharaoh's honor was the temple at Abu Simbel built? **(Ramses II; Ramses the Great)**	_____	_____
2. What is the name of the poet who wrote the epic poem about Ramses II's military victory that is displayed on the temple walls at Abu Simbel? **(Pentaur)**	_____	_____
3. What country suggested the final solution to the problem of how to move the temples at Abu Simbel? **(Sweden)**	_____	_____
Reading Between the Lines		
1. Why do you think Ramses II constructed such an elaborate temple in his honor at Abu Simbel? **(he was proud of his accomplishments and wanted his subjects to be aware of them; he was an egotistical man; he enjoyed seeing statues of himself)**	_____	_____
2. Why do you think Pentaur's epic poem about Ramses II may have exaggerated his military feats? **(he was the pharaoh and was said to have divine powers; it would be virtually impossible for one pharaoh and some generals and men to defeat twenty-five hundred chariots, each containing three men; he undoubtedly would not begin to fight an army by himself)**	_____	_____

	Score	Appropriateness
3. Why do you think moving the temples at Abu Simbel was such a monumental task? **(the site was very huge and heavy; it had to be constructed exactly as it had been in its original position; there was a very limited time period in which to do the reconstructing)**	_____	_____

Reading Beyond the Lines

1. Would you like to visit Abu Simbel sometime in the future? Why? Why not? **(any logical answer—some examples: YES it must be magnificent to see; I enjoy traveling to unique places; I would like to see it since it is an engineering marvel; I am interested in Egypt and Egyptian history; NO I am not interested in traveling overseas; I am not interested in Ancient Egypt; I am not interested in archaeological sites)**	_____	_____
2. Would you like to have been involved in the relocation of Abu Simbel? Why? Why not? **(any logical answer—some examples: YES I would like to have contributed to the saving of a site that is so beautiful and historical; I am interested in engineering and construction; I would like to have traveled to Egypt; NO I am not interested in engineering and construction; it would have been much too difficult a job; I would have not been competent to do the job)**	_____	_____

Number of comprehension questions correct _____

Comprehension Score

Independent reading level *8*

Instructional reading level *5–7*

Frustration reading level *4 or fewer*

Self-Monitoring of Comprehension

How well do you think you answered these questions?

very well _____

all right _____

not so well _____

Form B Passages

Name ______________________ **Grade** ___ **Teacher** ____________ **Date** _________

Oral Reading Passage: Arthur Ashe, Tennis Great and Man of Courage*

Arthur Ashe was born in Virginia on July 10, 1943. When Arthur was four, his father got a job as a special police officer in charge of the largest playground in the city of Richmond—Brook Field. It had four tennis courts and a backboard as well as a large swimming pool, basketball court, and baseball diamonds.

Arthur started playing tennis when he was six years old and was good at it because his reflexes were very quick. He was known as "the little boy who could play tennis." However, he also was an excellent student who earned A's and was elected class president in sixth grade.

Arthur's mother died when he was seven, and he was raised by his father, his stepmother, and an elderly widow his father hired. Arthur was a sickly, thin boy and did not appear to be very athletic.

However, Ronald Charity, an African American tennis instructor at Brook Field, spent hours teaching Arthur tennis. When his teacher was not there, Arthur spent countless hours hitting a ball against the backboard to perfect his swing.

When Arthur was ten, he began studying tennis with Robert Walter Johnson, an African American doctor, tennis fan, and teacher. Arthur stayed with Dr. Johnson at his home in Lynchburg (Lĭnch berg), Virginia. Dr. Johnson also stressed being a gentleman while playing tennis, and Arthur always remembered that lesson. He spent every summer there until he was eighteen.

Arthur went to college at UCLA in California on a tennis scholarship and also was enrolled in Officer's Training. In 1964 he was named the third best male tennis player in the country, but that was just the beginning.

His later tennis career included the national singles and doubles titles, the U.S. Open men's singles titles, the Wimbledon singles title in England, and being ranked the top male tennis player in the world in 1975.

Arthur also spent his life fighting for the rights of blacks, both in this country and in Africa, especially South Africa, where the racial discrimination was very bad at that time.

Arthur suffered major health problems in his life. He had a heart attack and open-heart surgery in 1979. From the blood that he was given during surgery, he developed AIDS. He died in 1993 of AIDS-related pneumonia.

Because of his tennis ability and all he did to fight racial discrimination, the National Tennis Center in New York named its stadium the Arthur Ashe Stadium. This is a fitting honor to the great African American tennis star.

---

* The readability level of this passage was computed by the Dale-Chall Readability Formula.

Before Reading "Arthur Ashe, Tennis Great and Man of Courage"

Assessing Prior Knowledge and Interest

1. What do you know about the great tennis star Arthur Ashe?
2. Do you think that you will like reading this passage? Why? Why not?

After Reading

Number of words in this selection __*420*__

Number of word identification miscues _____

Word Identification Miscues

Independent reading level approx. __*0–6*__

Low independent reading level approx. __*7–15*__

High instructional reading level approx. __*16–25*__

Instructional reading level approx. __*26–36*__

Low instructional reading level approx. __*37–40*__

Frustration reading level __*41+*__

Assessing Comprehension

Score *1* for a correct response and *0* for an incorrect response in the appropriate column. Score ✓ for any answers that are clearly illogical or + for any answers that are very good, detailed, or insightful.

Reading the Lines	**Score**	**Appropriateness**
1. What was the main reason why Arthur Ashe was a good tennis player? **(his reflexes were quick)**	_____	_____
2. What was the name of the place where Arthur learned to play tennis? **(Brook Field)**	_____	_____
3. For whose rights did Arthur spend much of his life fighting? **(African Americans, blacks)**	_____	_____
Reading Between the Lines		
1. Why do you think Arthur became a top-ranked tennis player? **(he had quick reflexes; he practiced a lot; he had very good teachers)**	_____	_____
2. Why do you think Arthur was well-suited to fight for the rights of African Americans? **(he had experienced discrimination; he was very well-known; people admired and respected him)**	_____	_____
3. Why do you think Arthur developed AIDS from a blood transfusion? **(because AIDS was not known then, blood was not screened for it at that time)**	_____	_____

Reading the Lines	**Score**	**Appropriateness**
1. In what sports are you most talented and interested in? Are you interested in becoming as famous in that sport as Arthur was? Why? Why not? **(any logical answer—some examples: YES I would like to earn all that money; I would like to be famous; I could buy a fancy house and car; NO I would not like to travel that much; there would be too much pressure; I would not want to get injured)**	_____	_____
2. Would you like to watch the famous tennis matches at Wimbledon? Why? Why not? **(any logical answer—some examples: YES I like to watch tennis very much; I would like to travel to England; it would be very exciting; NO I don't understand the scoring in tennis; I think tennis is boring; I don't like crowds)**	_____	_____

Number of comprehension questions correct _____

Comprehension Score

Independent reading level ___*8*___

Instructional reading level ___*5–7*___

Frustration reading level ___*4 or fewer*___

Self-Monitoring of Comprehension

How well do you think you answered these questions?

very well _____

all right _____

not so well _____

Name ______________________ Grade ___ Teacher ____________ Date _________

Oral Reading Passage: Copper—Versatile Metal*

Copper is a soft orange-brown metal that has been used by humans for about 10,000 years. It has proven to be an extremely useful metal.

Copper and its compounds are used in many ways in contemporary society. Its attractive color has made it popular for use in decorative items such as wall ornaments and kettles. Because copper is an excellent conductor of electricity and heat, it is used in electrical wiring and heating systems. It is also necessary to ensure the health of most animals and plants.

Similar to other metals, copper is made up of tiny crystals too small to be seen by the eye. Copper crystals are not brittle like salt crystals, so the sheets of atoms that form them can slide past one another without coming apart. That is the reason that copper can be beaten into shape and drawn into a wire.

Copper is commonly found on earth in compounds called *carbonates*, *chlorides*, and *sulfides*, and as a free metal. Copper is not very reactive and is often found as the pure metal.

Copper has been used in metalworking for thousands of years in western Asia. Somewhat later, people in that region began to use heat to *smelt* (separate) copper from its ores so that they could make tools and weapons. About 3500 B.C., *bronze*, which is an *alloy* (mix) of copper and tin, was developed, and the Bronze Age of Europe and Asia began. A new weapon—the sword—was made from bronze. Metalworking techniques are recorded in great detail in the tomb paintings of Ancient Egypt. Later *brass*, an alloy of copper and zinc, was introduced.

Pure copper has many uses in today's society. For example, about four million tons of copper are used every year to make electrical wiring, and copper also is commonly used to make water and gas pipes in homes and commercial buildings because it bends easily. In addition, copper is poisonous to bacteria and ensures a safe water supply. In construction, copper is often used to protect the roofs of public buildings. Copper gradually corrodes if it is left outdoors, and as well as protecting the copper from further corrosion, the layer of copper carbonate that develops on its surface is green and is valued as decoration.

Copper is vital to the body chemistry of most animals and plants, and the body chemistry of many organisms would not work without it. Copper is required to make the hemoglobin that is found in red blood cells. Copper is also found in many proteins called *enzymes*, which are used to *catalyze* (speed up) biological reactions.

---

* The readability level of this passage was computed by the Dale-Chall Readability Formula.

Before Reading "Copper—Versatile Metal"
Assessing Prior Knowledge and Interest

1. What do you know about the metal copper?
2. Do you think that you will like reading this passage? Why? Why not?

After Reading

Number of words in this selection *389*

Number of word identification miscues ____

Word Identification Miscues

Independent reading level approx. *0–7*

Low independent reading level approx. *8–16*

High instructional reading level approx. *17–26*

Instructional reading level approx. *27–37*

Low instructional reading level approx. *38–47*

Frustration reading level *48+*

Assessing Comprehension

Score *1* for a correct response and *0* for an incorrect response in the appropriate column. Score ✓ for any answers that are clearly illogical or + for any answers that are very good, detailed, or insightful.

Reading the Lines	**Score**	**Appropriateness**
1. What color is copper? **(orange-brown)**	____	____
2. What is the alloy bronze composed of? **(copper and tin)**	____	____
3. To what is copper poisonous when it is used in water pipes? **(bacteria)**	____	____
Reading Between the Lines		
1. Why do you think copper is often used on the bottom of cooking pots? **(it is an excellent conductor of heat)**	____	____
2. What would be the main disadvantage of using a sword made of pure copper? **(it would bend easily since copper is soft; it would not hold its shape)**	____	____
3. How do archaeologists know that Ancient Egyptians knew how to work with copper? **(drawings of metalworking were found on the walls of tombs that have been excavated)**	____	____

Reading the Lines	**Score**	**Appropriateness**
1. If you have seen the green-colored corrosion (patina) on the copper roofs of public buildings or copper statues, do you think it is attractive? Why? Why not? **(any logical answer—some examples: YES the green color is a unique, pretty color; it seems appropriate for an old building or statue; NO the copper is no longer shiny; it looks kind of dirty)**	_____	_____
2. Since copper decorations tarnish fairly easily, would you enjoy polishing them with copper cleaner? Why? Why not? **(any logical answer—some examples: YES I would enjoy making them shiny and clean again; I would enjoy polishing them since I would enjoy looking at them; NO it would be a lot of work; it would be a very dirty job)**	_____	_____

Number of comprehension questions correct _____

Comprehension Score

Independent reading level *8*

Instructional reading level *5–7*

Frustration reading level *4 or fewer*

Self-Monitoring of Comprehension

How well do you think you answered these questions?

very well _____

all right _____

not so well _____

Name ______________________ Grade ___ Teacher ___________ Date _________

Oral Reading Passage: Using the Wind for Energy*

As the world's population increases and people use more machines to do work, more energy will be needed to power them. Although it seems difficult to comprehend, the world's demand for energy has increased tenfold since the beginning of the twentieth century.

Much of this energy has been produced by the burning of *fossil fuels*—oil, natural gas, and coal. Unfortunately, there is a very limited amount of fossil fuel remaining in the world, and fossil fuels that required millions of years to formulate are being consumed at the rate of over half a million tons an hour. At this rate of usage, virtually all of the world's oil and gas will be depleted by the year 2040.

In addition, fossil fuels cause serious damage to the earth's environment because as they burn they produce poisonous gases that turn into *acid rain*, which pollutes vast areas of the world, killing wildlife, fish, and trees. Some of these gases also contribute to the *greenhouse effect*, a gradual warming of the earth's atmosphere.

Because of the problems associated with the burning of fossil fuels, scientists are searching for alternative sources of energy. One of the most promising of these is *wind energy*, valued because it is inexpensive, safe, clean, and renewable.

The moving air in any wind contains great amounts of *kinetic energy* that can be used to do work. In the past, wind energy was employed to drive mighty sailing ships called *clippers* and to grind grain and pump water by using *windmills*. Holland was famous for its windmills, having about 12,000 of them in 1800; however, only 1,000 operating windmills remained by 1960.

Currently people all over the world are interested in wind energy, especially to generate electricity, which provides heat, light, and power. Wind machines that produce electricity are called *wind turbines*—*horizontal-axis turbines* and *vertical-axis turbines*. Wind turbines usually have two or three blades with curved surfaces like those on an airplane. As the wind pushes against the blades, it turns the turbine that is connected to a generator. As the turbine turns the generator, it produces electricity. The blades of a turbine must be light enough to turn easily but strong enough to withstand fierce gale-force winds. The blades may be made of fiberglass, carbon fiber, or steel.

Modern turbines are much more powerful than traditional windmills, and the amount of electricity a turbine can produce depends on the strength of the wind and the size of the blades.

Wind farms are part of a power network, and wind farm owners are paid for the electricity that they produce. The optimum locations for wind farms are seacoasts, high plains, and mountain passes where the wind blows much of the time.

* The readability level of this passage was computed by the Dale-Chall Readability Formula.

Before Reading "Using the Wind for Energy"

Assessing Prior Knowledge and Interest

1. What do you know about wind energy?
2. Do you think that you will like reading this passage? Why? Why not?

After Reading

Number of words in this selection *455*

Number of word identification miscues _____

Word Identification Miscues

Independent reading level approx. *0–7*

Low independent reading level approx. *8–16*

High instructional reading level approx. *17–26*

Instructional reading level approx. *27–37*

Low instructional reading level approx. *38–47*

Frustration reading level *48+*

Assessing Comprehension

Score *1* for a correct response and *0* for an incorrect response in the appropriate column. Score ✓ for any answers that are clearly illogical or + for any answers that are very good, detailed, or insightful.

Reading the Lines	**Score**	**Appropriateness**
1. What are the three fossil fuels? **(oil, natural gas, coal)**	_____	_____
2. What kind of energy is found in the wind? **(kinetic energy)**	_____	_____
3. What do you call the wind machines that produce electricity? **(wind turbines)**	_____	_____
Reading Between the Lines		
1. Why it is imperative to find an alternative energy source to fossil fuels as soon as possible? **(when they run out, there will be no energy to generate electricity; when they run out, there will be no heating fuel; when they run out, there will be no fuel to power automobiles, trucks, buses, or airplanes)**	_____	_____
2. Why do you think that the number of windmills greatly decreased in the past two hundred years? **(fossil fuels have been used more commonly than wind energy; wind energy probably was considered "old-fashioned" and obsolete)**	_____	_____

	Score	Appropriateness
3. Why do you think that wind farms are not more popular than they currently are? **(they require a large investment of money before they can be used effectively; wind has been considered a nontraditional source of energy)**	_____	_____

Reading Beyond the Lines

1. Would you like to own a home powered solely by wind energy? Why? Why not? **(any logical answer—some examples: YES it might be more economical and safer and cleaner; it would be environmentally friendly; NO it does not seem as reliable as fossil fuels)**	_____	_____
2. Would you like to work on a wind farm sometime in the future? Why? Why not? **(any logical answer—some examples: YES it would be worthy and valuable work; it would contribute in a positive way to the betterment of people; it would lower the need for fossil fuels; NO I would not like to work outside that much; I am not interested in working with any type of fuel—whether wind or fossil)**	_____	_____

Number of comprehension questions correct _____

Comprehension Score

Independent reading level *8*

Instructional reading level *5–7*

Frustration reading level *4 or fewer*

Self-Monitoring of Comprehension

How well do you think you answered these questions?

very well _____

all right _____

not so well _____

Name ________________________ Grade ___ Teacher ____________ Date __________

Oral Reading Passage: The Kwakiutl People*

The Kwakiutl (Kwâ gēē ōōlth) are the native Americans who have lived for generations along the northern and eastern shores of Vancouver Island and the nearby mainland of British Columbia, Canada.

The Kwakiutl's traditional stories is an enlightening way to learn about how they viewed the world. These legends usually showed the links between the Kwakiutl, their ancestors, and animals. Most of the families traced their origin to a spirit, most common of which was the Raven. They believed that such a spirit could grant a family the right to fish or pick berries in a special place or even grant them magical powers. Each family had its own dances and songs that told the story of how the spirit helped them.

Anthropologists have studied the Kwakiutl extensively by examining the tools and other objects that they made long ago. Through this extensive study they have learned much about these fascinating and ingenious native people.

Since they lived in the mild temperatures and heavy rainfall of the Pacific Northwest, with its forests of towering trees, the heavy underbrush made walking virtually impossible. The life of the Kwakiutl therefore focused on the Pacific Ocean, which offered unlimited fishing grounds. The most important fish to the Kwakiutl were the *salmon*, which live in the ocean but swim up rivers each year to lay their eggs. The Kwakiutl caught and ate fresh salmon during the summer but also preserved salmon to eat during the winter. Other fish the Kwakiutl caught were herring, smelt, cod, and eulachon (ōō lă kĕn), a fish that contains so much fat that if a wick were placed in its mouth and lit, the entire fish would burn like a candle. The Kwakiutl also hunted seals, porpoises, sea otters, and seabirds.

The Kwakiutl often erected a cedar pole called a *totem pole* outside their house to show the status of the people who lived there. Totem poles were carved and sometimes painted with *crest symbols*—images of humans, animals, and supernatural beings or spirits to whom the family was spiritually connected.

Perhaps the most important wooden object that the Kwakiutl made was the canoe, because they could not have lived on the seacoast without a way to travel on water. A canoe maker created a canoe from a single cedar log—a lengthy and arduous task that required much tedious work.

The most unique element of the Kwakiutls' life was their belief that the spirits gave them mystical powers. Their performances were filled with magic tricks and theatrical effects, including statues that seemed to move, objects that appeared to fly through the air, people walking on water or holding fire in their hands, and people who appeared to be dead only to return to life.

* The readability level of this passage was computed by the Dale-Chall Readability Formula.

Before Reading "The Kwakiutl People"
Assessing Prior Knowledge and Interest

1. What do you know about the Kwakiutl Native American people?
2. Do you think that you will like reading this passage? Why? Why not?

After Reading

Number of words in this selection *452*

Number of word identification miscues _____

Word Identification Miscues

Independent reading level approx. *0–7*

Low independent reading level approx. *8–16*

High instructional reading level approx. *17–26*

Instructional reading level approx. *27–37*

Low instructional reading level approx. *38–47*

Frustration reading level *48+*

Assessing Comprehension

Score *1* for a correct response and *0* for an incorrect response in the appropriate column. Score ✓ for any answers that are clearly illogical or + for any answers that are very good, detailed, or insightful.

Reading the Lines	**Score**	**Appropriateness**
1. Where did the Kwakiutl live? **(along the northern and eastern shores of Vancouver Island near British Columbia)**	_____	_____
2. What group of people have studied the Kwakiutl? **(anthropologists)**	_____	_____
3. What kind of fish was the most important to the Kwakiutl? **(salmon)**	_____	_____
Reading Between the Lines		
1. Why do you think that the Kwakiutl believed in legends? **(it gave them a way to understand their life)**	_____	_____
2. Why do you think totem poles were made of cedar wood? **(cedar logs are long since cedar trees are tall; cedar trees were common; cedar logs were easy to carve)**	_____	_____
3. Why do you think canoes were so important to the lives of the Kwakiutl? **(they were needed for fishing; they were needed for travel on the ocean; their lives depended on transportation on the water)**	_____	_____

Reading Beyond the Lines	**Score**	**Appropriateness**
1. Would you like to have lived as the Kwakiutl did? Why? Why not? **(any logical answer—some examples: YES I would like to have viewed the magic performances; I like to eat seafood; their life sounds interesting; NO it would have been a very difficult life; I don't like to eat fish; they had no modern conveniences)**	_____	_____
2. Would you have liked to view a performance that emphasized mystical powers? Why? Why not? **(any logical answer—some examples: YES it would be fascinating; I like to watch magic shows; NO I am not interested in magic; I am not interested in the occult)**	_____	_____

Number of comprehension questions correct _____

Comprehension Score

Independent reading level ___*8*___

Instructional reading level ___*5–7*___

Frustration reading level ___*4 or fewer*___

Self-Monitoring of Comprehension

How well do you think you answered these questions?

very well _____

all right _____

not so well _____

Name ________________________ Grade ___ Teacher ____________ Date _________

Oral Reading Passage: The Immune System* ☆

Although it may sound unbelievable, your immune system saves your life every day. A vast network of white blood cells, chemicals, and organs working together, the *immune system* recognizes millions of potentially harmful invaders. It then destroys them before they injure healthy cells, deplete the body's nutrients, or damage vital organs.

The first line of defense against illness and disease is the body's *skin*, which serves as its primary armor against bacteria and viruses. It is formulated of a protein called *keratin*, which is difficult to break down. However, even before germs land on the skin, they may be stopped by hairs that aid in keeping out microorganisms and dirt. If some microorganisms get past the hair, cells in the *epidermis* of the skin wait to ingest unwelcome microbes.

Vulnerable areas of the body such as the eyes are protected by mucous membranes, skin-like surfaces coated with secretions that fight germs. These membranes are found in the natural openings of the body, places unprotected by the skin, such as the eyes, nose, mouth, and reproductive tract. The thick, sticky film produced by mucous membranes traps yeasts, viruses, bacteria, dirt particles, pollen grains, and almost anything else that attempts to enter the body through the openings.

However, sometimes invaders bypass the first lines of defense—the skin and mucous membranes—and travel into the bloodstream and organs. When they do, the *innate immune system*, a complex group of specialized molecules and white blood cells, is there to meet them.

The first and most important function of the immune system is to determine what is foreign and what is not. *Antigens* provide the clues. These molecules cover the surface of every cell and act as the cell's calling card. If the cell belongs to the body, the calling card is engraved with the message "self" and the immune system cells do not attack. However, if the cell belongs to an invader, the calling card reads "foreign," which sounds the signal for the immune system to attack.

After an antigen is detected, the many millions of white blood cells called *leukocytes* mobilize to fight the invader microorganisms. Alongside them are *lymphocytes*, or *B-cells*, an elite group of white blood cells whose job it is to custom-make proteins called *antibodies*, which recognize and bind to a particular invader. A given antibody matches an antigen much as a key matches a lock.

* The readability level of this passage was computed by the Dale-Chall Readability Formula.

Before Reading "The Immune System"
Assessing Prior Knowledge and Interest

1. What do you know about the body's immune system?
2. Do you think that you will like reading this passage? Why? Why not?

After Reading

Number of words in this selection ___*398*___

Number of word identification miscues _____

Word Identification Miscues

Independent reading level approx. ___*0–5*___

Low independent reading level approx. ___*6–14*___

High instructional reading level approx. ___*15–24*___

Instructional reading level approx. ___*25–35*___

Low instructional reading level approx. ___*36–39*___

Frustration reading level ___*40+*___

Assessing Comprehension

Score *1* for a correct response and *0* for an incorrect response in the appropriate column. Score ✓ for any answers that are clearly illogical or + for any answers that are very good, detailed, or insightful.

Reading the Lines	**Score**	**Appropriateness**
1. What is the body's first line of defense against illness? **(the skin)**	_____	_____
2. What protects the natural openings in the body against germs? **(mucous membranes)**	_____	_____
3. What is a leukocyte? **(white blood cell)**	_____	_____
Reading Between the Lines		
1. Why do you think infection is one of the greatest dangers of a severe burn? **(the skin can no longer protect the body against foreign invaders if it is burned)**	_____	_____
2. Why do you think it is important to have a way to fight invading microorganisms at the body's openings? **(it is easy for invading microorganisms to get into the body there)**	_____	_____
3. What do you think happens when the body makes too few white blood cells? **(the person has a hard time fighting off infections)**	_____	_____

Reading Beyond the Lines	**Score**	**Appropriateness**
1. Would you like to be a microbiologist someday? Why? Why not? **(any logical answer—some examples: YES I enjoy studying science; it would be fascinating; it would be great to find a cure for an illness like AIDS; NO I don't like science and am not good at it; I am not interested in learning how various parts of the body work; I would not enjoy working in a lab)**	_____	_____
2. What are some things that you can do **to keep your immune system healthy? (any logical answer—some examples: avoid tobacco smoke and air pollution; get plenty of rest; eat wisely; take antibiotics only when they are really needed; exercise; avoid stress)**	_____	_____

Number of comprehension questions correct _____

Comprehension Score

Independent reading level *8*

Instructional reading level *5–7*

Frustration reading level *4 or fewer*

Self-Monitoring of Comprehension

How well do you think you answered these questions?

very well _____

all right _____

not so well _____

Name ______________________ Grade ___ Teacher ____________ Date _________

Oral Reading Passage: Death and Mummification in Ancient Egypt*

Because the immortality of the soul was fundamental to the religious beliefs of the ancient Egyptians, pyramids, mastabas, and tombs all were constructed to house the souls of the deceased. Numerous frescoes representing the immortality of the soul and other religious scenes have been found in the dwellings that housed the pharaohs.

Because the religious beliefs of ancient Egypt stipulated that a deceased person must retain his or her body to enter the afterlife, *mummification* was practiced to preserve the physical body. The term *mummy* is derived from the Arabic *mumiya* or *mumyai*, which refers to *bitumen*, or a mixture of *pitch* and *myrrh*, a material that was utilized extensively in the embalming of corpses. Some of the mummies, however, were created solely by the extremely arid Egyptian climate, with its sand and total absence of bacteria in the air causing a kind of natural embalming.

Embalming of the dead was conducted by specialists, and the initiating operation consisted of extracting the brain by means of a hooked instrument. The brain cavity was then filled with material consisting primarily of liquid bitumen, which hardened on cooling. The eyes were then extracted and replaced with porcelain substitutes. By means of a sharpened stone, an incision was made in the left side of the corpse, and the intestines and internal organs were removed. They were then treated with boiling bitumen and wrapped, as were the brain and liver. The viscera were preserved in four canopic (căn ō pĭc) jars made of clay, limestone, or alabaster. The jars were then situated in a coffer near the mummy and contained lids, each of which was graced with a unique head: man, jackal, sparrow-hawk, and dogfaced baboon.

The cavities in the intestines were carefully washed with palm wine, dried with a powdered mixture of aromatic plants, and subsequently filled with myrrh or perfumed sawdust. Finally the corpse was placed in a solution of *natron* (sodium carbonate) and left there for seventy days.

Bandages impregnated with resin were wound around each finger, then around each hand, and finally around each arm. The same procedure was carried out on the remainder of the corpse.

Much is known about how funerals were conducted in ancient Egypt from the presence of paintings and bas-reliefs found in tombs. Opening the funeral procession was an assemblage of slaves carrying offerings and objects belonging to the deceased. Next came a group of professional mourners uttering piercing sounds, tearing their hair, and singing dirges. Behind the master of ceremonies and the priest was the *catafalque*, in the shape of a solar barge, mounted on a sledge pulled by a team of oxen. Last, relatives and friends followed dressed in mourning clothes and uttering lamentations. At the conclusion of the procession was an assemblage of persons singing the praises of the deceased.

* The readability level of this passage was computed by the Dale-Chall Readability Formula.

Before Reading "Death and Mummification in Ancient Egypt"
Assessing Prior Knowledge and Interest

1. What do you know about death and mummification in ancient Egypt?
2. Do you think that you will like reading this passage? Why? Why not?

After Reading

Number of words in this selection ___*468*___

Number of word identification miscues _____

Word Identification Miscues

Independent reading level approx. ___*0–8*___

Low independent reading level approx. ___*9–17*___

High instructional reading level approx. ___*18–27*___

Instructional reading level approx. ___*28–38*___

Low instructional reading level approx. ___*39–48*___

Frustration reading level ___*49+*___

Assessing Comprehension

Score *1* for a correct response and *0* for an incorrect response in the appropriate column. Score ✓ for any answers that are clearly illogical or + for any answers that are very good, detailed, or insightful.

Reading the Lines	**Score**	**Appropriateness**
1. Why was mummification practiced in ancient Egypt? **(it was believed that a dead person needed a body to enter the afterlife)**	_____	_____
2. What was the first procedure in mummification in ancient Egypt? **(removing the brain)**	_____	_____
3. Into what solution was the corpse placed near the end of mummification? **(natron [sodium carbonate])**	_____	_____
Reading Between the Lines		
1. Why do you think that it required specialists to embalm corpses in ancient Egypt? **(it was a complex process; it required special training to learn; it required practice)**	_____	_____
2. Why do you think porcelain substitutes were used in place of the eyes? **(they looked liked actual eyes; the eyes disintegrate after death)**	_____	_____
3. Why do you think that the funeral processions were so elaborate in ancient Egypt? **(they were trying to honor the deceased; death was made into a "production" there)**	_____	_____

Reading Beyond the Lines	**Score**	**Appropriateness**
1. Would you like to be involved in preserving a corpse by mummification? Why? Why not? **(any logical answer—some examples: YES it would be fascinating; I enjoy working with scientific projects; NO I could never work with a dead body; it would be a very "gross" procedure)**	_____	_____
2. Would you like to view the ancient mummies found in the Egyptian Museum in Cairo? Why? Why not? **(any logical answer—some examples: YES it would be very interesting; I would like to visit Egypt; I am very interested in history and ancient Egypt; NO I would not enjoy seeing any kind of dead body; I think mummies are ugly; I would not enjoy traveling overseas as far as Egypt)**	_____	_____

Number of comprehension questions correct _____

Comprehension Score

Independent reading level ___*8*___

Instructional reading level ___*5–7*___

Frustration reading level ___*4 or fewer*

Self-Monitoring of Comprehension

How well do you think you answered these questions?

very well _____

all right _____

not so well _____

San Diego Quick Assessment List

The *San Diego Quick Assessment List* is a helpful, quick way to determine a student's *approximate instructional reading level.* It is *not* a substitute for the graded reading passages of the Content Reading Inventory. However, if you want a *very easy, quick estimate of a student's approximate instructional reading level,* it is very useful for that purpose.

Administration

1. Type each list of words on an index card.
2. Begin with a card that is at least two years below the student's grade-level assignment.
3. Ask the student to read the words aloud to you. If he or she misreads any words on the list, drop to easier lists until he or she makes no errors. This indicates the *base level.*
4. Write down all incorrect responses, or use diacritical marks on your copy of the list. For example, *capacious* might be read and recorded as *capricious. Zany* might be read and recorded as *zăny.*
5. Encourage the student to read words that he or she does not know so that you can identify the techniques he or she uses for word identification.
6. Have the student read from increasingly difficult lists until he or she misses at least *three words.*

Analysis

1. The list in which the student misses no more than *one of ten words* is the level at which he or she can read *independently.* Two errors indicate the *instructional reading level.* Three or more errors on a list may indicate material that *probably is too difficult (frustration reading level).*
2. An analysis of the student's errors is useful. Among those errors that occur with the greatest frequency are the following:

Error	**Example**
reversal	*baldpie* for *piebald*
consonant	*moment* for *comment*
consonant blend	*fright* for *blight*
short vowel	*grime* for *grim*
long vowel	*mŏlĕcūle* for *mŏlĕcūle*
prefix	*protext* for *pretext*
suffix	*amazing* for *amazed*
miscellaneous	accent in the incorrect place, and so on

3. As with all informal assessment devices, teacher observation of student behavior is very important. Such characteristics as posture, facial expression, and voice quality may signal nervousness, lack of confidence, or frustration while reading.

San Diego Quick Assessment List*

Grade 3	**Grade 4**	**Grade 5**
city	decided	scanty
middle	served	business
moment	develop	amazed
frightened	silent	considered
exclaimed	wrecked	discussed
several	improve	behave
lonely	certainly	splendid
drew	entered	acquainted
since	realized	escaped
straight	interrupted	grim
Grade 6	**Grade 7**	**Grade 8**
bridge	amber	capacious
commercial	dominion	limitation
abolish	sundry	pretext
trucker	capillary	intrigue
apparatus	impetuous	delusion
elementary	blight	immaculate
comment	wrest	ascent
necessity	enumerate	acrid
gallery	daunted	binocular
relativity	condescend	embankment
Grade 9	**Grade 10**	**Grade 11**
conscientious	zany	galore
isolation	jerkin	rotunda
molecule	nausea	capitalism
ritual	gratuitous	prevaricate
momentous	linear	risible
vulnerable	inept	exonerate
kinship	legality	superannuate
conservatism	aspen	luxuriate
jaunty	amnesty	piebald
inventive	barometer	crunch

*Word list and excerpt from LaPray, M., and Ross, R. "The Graded Word List: Quick Gauge of Reading Ability." *Journal of Reading*, 1969, *22*, 305–307.

INFORMAL ASSESSMENT OF CONTENT WORDS

The chapter now includes lists of sample words from the content areas of English (literature and grammar), social studies, science, and mathematics. Each list is designed to assess a student's competency in content words in either grades 5 to 8 or grades 9 to 12. If a student is able to identify about *99%* or more of the words of the words on a list, he or she is considered to be on the *independent reading level.* If the student is able to identify about *90 to 98%* of the words on a list, he or she is considered to be on the *instructional reading level.* Finally, if he or she identifies fewer than *90%* of the words correctly on a list, he or she is considered to be on the *frustration reading level.* The number of words that a student must be able to identify for a particular reading level is located at the bottom of the lists.

To score each list of words, mark each word the student correctly identifies with a +, and mark each word that the student cannot identify with a – or *0.* Then count the total number of words that the student has identified correctly and consult the numbers under the list to determine the reading level.

As an additional assessment, have the student try to provide a short definition for each word or use it in a sentence; this will let you see if he or she can determine its meaning. Thus, each list can be used both for content word identification and word meaning.

Content Word List: LITERATURE

Grades 5 to 8	Grades 9 to 12
autobiography	alliteration
ballad	hyperbole
cliché	onomatopoeia
dialogue	oxymoron
epic	ode
simile	genre
metaphor	antithesis
idiom	assonance
characters	chiasmus
fantasy	anadiplosis
folk tale	allegory
imagery	chronological order
irony	stanza
narrator	kenning

Independent—15 correct on a word list

Instructional—13 to 14 correct on a word list

Frustration—12 or fewer correct on a word list

Content Word List: GRAMMAR

Grades 5 to 8	Grades 9 to 12
preposition	gerund
passive	interjection
conjunction	auxiliary verb
subordinate	phrasal verb
article	participle
adjective	transitive
adverb	intransitive
adverbial	conditional
clause	lexical morpheme
grammatical morpheme	nominative
predicate	dative
neuter	accusative
masculine	reflexive pronoun
feminine	modal

Independent—15 correct on a word list

Instructional—13 to 14 correct on a word list

Frustration—12 or fewer correct on a word list

Content Word List: SOCIAL STUDIES

Grades 5 to 8	Grades 9 to 12
agribusiness	apartheid
amendment	armistice
assassinate	czar
bureaucracy	demarcation
caucus	fascism
emancipation	habeas corpus
inaugurate	laissez-faire
monarchy	megalopolis
monopoly	mercantilism
neutral	monotheism
nuclear weapon	muckraker
preamble	pacifist
prohibition	protectorate
recession	reapportionment
referendum	transcontinental
representative	alluvial
resolution	archipelago
contour	cartographer
continental divide	coniferous
deciduous	polytheism
diversity	hydroelectric
environment	meridian
evaporation	seismograph
geologist	topography
hemisphere	Mercator map

Independent—24 to 25 correct on a word list

Instructional—22 to 23 correct on a word list

Frustration—21 or fewer correct on a word list

Content Word List: SCIENCE

Grades 5 to 8	Grades 9 to 12
adrenal	carcinogen
antibiotic	chloroplast
astronomy	cytoplasm
benign	dendrite
cardiac	diatom
duodenum	electrolyte
electrode	exothermic
enzyme	fluorescent
fertilization	galvanometer
genetics	genotype
glucose	geothermal energy
herbivore	hallucinogen
igneous	homeostasis
kinetic	hypothalamus
neutron	incandescent
photosynthesis	interferon
precipitation	meniscus
psychological	nucleolus
respiration	ossification
sedimentary	pheromone
stratosphere	pseudopod
symbiosis	rarefaction
synapse	reverberation
trachea	rhizoid
velocity	thermocouple

Independent—24 to 25 correct on a word list

Instructional—22 to 23 correct on a word list

Frustration—21 or fewer correct on a word list

Content Word List: MATHEMATICS

Grades 5 to 8	Grades 9 to 12
Celsius	abscissa
Fahrenheit	cosine
commutative property	exponential notation
minuend	histogram
parenthesis	micron
subtrahend	permutation
congruent	reflexive property
exponent	topology
rhombus	trigonometry
symmetrical	concave polygon
vertex	equiangular triangle
inverse	hypotenuse
linear	isosceles triangle
multiplicand	Pythagorean theorem
quadrant	scalene triangle
bisect	tessellation
Venn diagram	milliliter
obtuse triangle	centiliter
tangent	foci
trapezoid	theorem
perpendicular	truncate
concentric	circumscribe
quartile	tangent ratio
hexagon	permutation
linear	perpendicular bisector

Independent—24 to 25 correct on a word list

Instructional—22 to 23 correct on a word list

Frustration—21 or fewer correct on a word list

Informal Assessment of Survival Words

Survival words are those sight words that older students and adults should immediately recognize for their health, safety, and daily living needs. These words often are especially useful to students with learning and reading disabilities at the middle school level and beyond. This section contains a list of *sample survival words* that can be used for assessing a student's probable competency in such words.

If a student can identify about *99%* or more of these words accurately, the words on the list probably are on the student's *independent reading level.* If a student can identify approximately *90 to 98%* of the words correctly, he or she may be at the *instructional reading level*, and if a student is able to identify fewer than *90%* of the words accurately, he or she probably is at the *frustration reading level.* You can use the numbers under the list to determine a student's approximate reading levels.

List of Sample Survival Words

elevator

flammable

pedestrian

caution

merging traffic

immigration

signature

combustible

oxygen

keep refrigerated

perishable

fragile

equal opportunity employer

dependent

construction zone

concourse

low clearance

aspirin

itemized deductions

directory assistance

confidential

explosive

Social Security number

résumé

restaurant

classified directory

cafeteria

physician

ambulance

rest rooms

Independent—24 to 25 correct on a word list

Instructional—22 to 23 correct on a word list

Frustration—21 or fewer correct on a word list

Oral Inventory of Basic Phonic Skills for Older Students

The chapter now includes an oral inventory of *basic phonic skills* for older students. It is designed for students in grades 5 to 12. You can duplicate and use this inventory in its present form or modify it in any way you wish.

Answer Key

1. The student should underline the first letter in each of these twenty-five words.

2. transitive   propaganda   stratosphere   platelet   gravity
statistics   freight   clamor   swamp   smuggle
blockade   graduate   breathe   cleaver   drought
flammable   glacier   frequency   stimulus   plasma
species   transfusion   stanza   twentieth   praline

3. grōss   cĕll   phāse   crĕst   lāser
fūse   vălve   nōde   gēne   swĭtch
optĭcal   lĕns   dēgree   expănd   gĭlls
hătch   pōlar   dāta   dĕlta   grĭd
fŏssil   scāle   glōbe   vēto   gŭlf

4. shampo͞o   kangaro͞o   carto͞on   sho͝ok   bo͞oth
bro͞od   bambo͞o   wo͝od   dro͞op   ho͞oves
sho͝ok   sto͝od   bro͝ok   lo͞op   ho͝of

5. system   microscope   xylophone   bacon   minus
pupil   button   rural   central   tyrant
civil   legal   delta   climate   neutral

6. canin~~e~~   biom~~e~~   dendrit~~e~~   ~~w~~rist   ~~g~~nom~~e~~
incubat~~e~~   tim~~e~~lin~~e~~   resi~~g~~n   impe~~a~~ch   fle~~e~~t
h~~e~~ight   revolv~~e~~   molecul~~e~~   eclips~~e~~   ~~w~~rest

7. aggressor   liberal   geyser   horizon   cartilage
centimeter   hibernate   molar   fracture   circuit
worthwhile   mortify   barefoot   curse   assertive

8. pagan   changeable   admiration
silica   lance   commendation
rifle   crocus   annex
labor   civilize   window
canteen   pupil   plunge

Name __________________________ **Grade** ___ **Teacher** _____________ **Date** __________

Oral Inventory of Basic Phonic Skills for Older Students

1. Pronounce each of these words and then *underline the initial consonant in each word.*

dominant	pioneer	longitude	bacteria	vitamin
geometry	nuclear	circulation	manufacture	hurricane
recoil	parenthesis	maximum	numerator	lynch
significant	temperate	constellation	fertilization	diffusion
kinetic	judicial	sediment	wilderness	zoology

2. Pronounce each of these words and then *underline the two-letter or three-letter consonant blend in that word.*

transitive	propaganda	stratosphere	platelet	gravity
statistics	freight	clamor	swamp	smuggle
blockade	graduate	breathe	cleaver	drought
flammable	glacier	frequency	stimulus	plasma
species	transfusion	stanza	twentieth	praline

3. Pronounce each of these words and *mark each vowel in the middle either long (–) or short (˘).*

gross	cell	phase	crest	laser
fuse	valve	node	gene	switch
optical	lens	degree	expand	gills
hatch	polar	data	delta	grid
fossil	scale	globe	veto	gulf

Name ______________________ Grade ___ Teacher ____________ Date _________

Oral Inventory of Basic Phonic Skills for Older Students, continued

4. Pronounce each of these words and *mark the double oo's either long (–) or short (˘).*

shampoo	kangaroo	cartoon	shook	booth
brood	bamboo	wood	droop	hooves
shook	stood	brook	loop	hoof

5. Pronounce each of these words and *underline the vowel that represents the schwa (ə) sound.*

system	microscope	xylophone	bacon	minus
pupil	button	rural	central	tyrant
civil	legal	delta	climate	neutral

6. Pronounce each of these words and *mark the silent letter or letters with a forward slash mark (/).*

canine	biome	dendrite	wrist	gnome
incubate	timeline	resign	impeach	fleet
height	revolve	molecule	eclipse	wrest

7. Pronounce each of these words and then underline the *r-controlled vowel.*

aggressor	liberal	geyser	horizon	cartilage
centimeter	hibernate	molar	fracture	circuit
worthwhile	mortify	barefoot	curse	assertive

8. Pronounce each of these *words that have been spelled phonetically.*

pā' gən	chānj 'ə bəl	ăd mə 'rā shən
sĭl ĭk ə	lăns	kŏm mĕn dā' shən
rī fəl	krō kəs	ă nĕks'
lā' bər	sĭv' ĭl īz	wĭn' dō
kăn tēn'	pū' pəl	plŭnj

GROUP-ADMINISTERED STRUCTURAL ANALYSIS INVENTORY FOR OLDER STUDENTS

This section of the chapter contains a group-administered structural analysis inventory for older students. It is applicable *with appropriate modifications* for students in grades 5 to 12. It probably will need to be simplified for students in grades 5 and 6 as well as for some older students. You can duplicate it and use it in its present form or modify it in any way you wish.

Answer Key

1.

humanitarian	tonsillectomy	postscript	illegitimate	monorail
contraband	comatose	midsummer	retroactive	immature
ultraconservative	hyperactive	gigabyte	capitalism	pasteurize
forgery	internship	blockade	affirmative	dietetic
humanoid	clockwise	fruity	poetic	superscript

2. Japan is usually considered to be a progressive and homogenous society that thrives on competition.

3.

subordinate	circumnavigate	hypothermia	neophyte	polysyllabic
antebellum	intramural	retroactive	transatlantic	omnipotent
cooperate	dysfunction	neonatal	aftertaste	prototype
ambidextrous	telepathy	equidistant	nonfiction	underground
irresponsible	malfunction	centimeter	precaution	paralegal

4. Emily seems to be a hypersensitive and irresponsible young woman who undoubtedly had a dysfunctional and unhappy childhood.

5.

repentance	claustrophobia	standardization	assistant	bronchitis
capitalism	computerize	alphabetic	docile	aviatrix
different	loquacious	contemptuous	westernmost	loyalty
yearling	martyrdom	formulae	autocrat	strengthen
showmanship	scholarly	earthen	warmth	honorary

6. The new superintendent of schools in our community is a former teacher with an excellent reputation.

7.

rect/an/gle	cog/ni/zant	doc/u/ment	ca/dav/er	in/sur/gent
pseu/do/nym	prov/i/dence	bel/li/cose	vol/un/teer	hos/pice
fig/ment	ten/don	pro/nounce	pop/u/la/tion	tur/bu/lent

8.

ma' ni a	div' i dend	re gress'	doc' u ment	bank' rupt
ad' vent	stag' nant	con vince'	cit' a del	fil' a ment
im pe' ri al	ma' trix	in' su lin	hal' o gen	in cred' i ble

Name ________________________ Grade ___ Teacher ____________ Date _________

Group-Administered Structural Analysis Inventory for Older Students

1. Underline the *base or root word* in each word.

humanitarian	tonsillectomy	postscript	illegitimate	monorail
contraband	comatose	midsummer	retroactive	immature
ultraconservative	hyperactive	gigabyte	capitalism	pasteurize
forgery	internship	blockade	affirmative	dietetic
humanoid	clockwise	fruity	poetic	superscript

2. Underline each word in this sentence that contains a *base or root word.*

   Japan is usually considered to be a progressive and homogenous society that thrives on competition.

3. Underline the *prefix* in each word.

subordinate	circumnavigate	hypothermia	neophyte	polysyllabic
antebellum	intramural	retroactive	transatlantic	omnipotent
cooperate	dysfunction	neonatal	aftertaste	prototype
ambidextrous	telepathy	equidistant	nonfiction	underground
irresponsible	malfunction	centimeter	precaution	paralegal

4. Underline each word in this sentence that contains a *prefix.*

   Emily seems to be a hypersensitive and irresponsible young woman who undoubtedly had a dysfunctional and unhappy childhood.

Name ______________________ Grade ___ Teacher ____________ Date _________

Group-Administered Structural Analysis Inventory for Older Students, continued

5. Underline the *suffix* in each word.

repentance	claustrophobia	standardization	assistant	bronchitis
capitalism	computerize	alphabetic	docile	aviatrix
different	loquacious	contemptuous	westernmost	loyalty
yearling	martyrdom	formulae	autocrat	strengthen
showmanship	scholarly	earthen	warmth	honorary

6. Underline each word in this sentence that contains a *suffix*.

   The new superintendent of schools in our community is a former teacher with an excellent reputation.

7. Divide each of these words into syllables by placing a forward slash mark (/) between each syllable.

rectangle	cognizant	document	cadaver	insurgent
pseudonym	providence	bellicose	volunteer	hospice
figment	tendon	pronounce	population	turbulent

8. *Mark the accented syllable* in each word in this way: **main tain'**.

ma ni a	div i dend	re gress	doc u ment
bank rupt	ad vent	stag nant	con vince
cit a del	fil a ment	im pe ri al	ma trix
in su lin	hal o gen	in cred i ble	

Group-Administered Inventories in Context Clues for Older Students

The chapter now includes four group-administered inventories in context clues that can be used with older students. The inventories assess use of context clues in the following four content areas: *literature*, *social studies*, *science*, and *mathematics*.

Although the inventories may be useful with students in grades 5 to 12, they may need to be simplified, especially for students in grades 5 and 6. You can duplicate and use these inventories in their present form or modify them in any way you wish.

Answer Key for Literature

1. cliché; 2. Alliteration; 3. ode; 4. oxymoron; 5. simile; 6. dialogue; 7. onomatopoeia; 8. Allegory; 9. Genre; 10. ballad

Answer Key for Social Studies

1. sovereignty; 2. amnesty; 3. filibuster; 4. navigable; 5. apartheid; 6. monotheism; 7. typhoon; 8. hydroelectric; 9. steppe; 10. Fascism

Answer Key for Science

1. cholesterol; 2. fluorescent; 3. cataract; 4. Kinetic; 5. cerebellum; 6. platelet; 7. carnivore; 8. calorie; 9. estrogen; 10. antibiotic

Answer Key for Mathematics

1. polyhedron; 2. Pi; 3. minuend; 4. geometry; 5. equation; 6. Symmetry; 7. theorem; 8. graph; 9. median; 10. exponent

Name ________________________ **Grade** ___ **Teacher** ____________ **Date** _________

Group-Administered Context Clue Inventory for Older Students: Literature

Choose the one word that belongs in each sentence.

1. A __________________ is a phrase in literature that is overused and therefore may become somewhat meaningless—such as "pretty as a picture," "happy as a lark," "mad as a hatter."

   ballad cliché conclusion

2. __________________ occurs when two or more words have the same beginning sound.

   Alliteration Chiasmus Hyperbole

3. An ________________ is a poem written in praise of someone or something.

   inference opinion ode

4. An ________________ is the use of words with contradictory ideas next to one another.

   oxymoron epic irony

5. A comparison of two things using the word "like" or "as" is called a ______________.

   simile rhyme personification

6. A conversation between characters in a story or play is called a _________________.

   conflict dialogue moral

7. ________________ is when the sounds of words suggest their meaning.

   Metaphor Onomatopoeia Idiom

8. ________________ links the objects, characters, and events of a story with meanings beyond the literal meanings of the story.

   Antithesis Allegory Comparison

9. ________________ is a category or type of writing, such as fiction, nonfiction, biography, mystery, or science fiction.

   Genre Imagery Inference

10. A ________________ is a long poem, usually with rhythm and rhyme, that tells a story.

    fantasy ballad narrative

Name ______________________ Grade ___ Teacher ___________ Date _________

Group-Administered Context Clue Inventory for Older Students: Social Studies

Choose the one word that belongs in each sentence.

1. It is foolhardy to challenge the absolute ________________ of the United States Supreme Court in determining the legality of a decision of a lower court.

   prohibition sovereignty recession

2. After the man was sentenced to prison for treason, he was granted ________________ by the president of the United States.

   amnesty emigration recall

3. It is the absolute right of a United States senator to ______________ legislation with which he or she does not agree.

   fascism filibuster secede

4. The Nile River in Egypt is one of the world's longest ____________ rivers, and it also is one of the most fascinating.

   neutral navigable nationalism

5. Although racial ______________ was practiced in South Africa for many years, it has since been abolished.

   apartheid diplomacy monarchy

6. Since the Lutheran faith is state-supported in Sweden, this country's religion is an example of ________________.

   mercantilism monotheism laissez-faire

7. A ______________ is a violent tropical storm.

   typhoon geyser plateau

8. A ______________ plant uses water power to generate electricity.

   navigation hydroelectric petroleum

9. A _____________ is a vast, generally treeless and uncultivated plain, as is found in southeastern Europe and Asia.

   seismograph archipelago steppe

10. ______________ is a system of government characterized by dictatorship, belligerent nationalism, racism, and militarism.

    Fascism Filibuster Commonwealth

Name ______________________ Grade ___ Teacher ____________ Date __________

Group-Administered Context Clue Inventory for Older Students: Science

Choose the one word that belongs in each sentence.

1. To be considered within the normal range, an adult's ______________ level should have a reading of two hundred or below.

   cholesterol diffusion chromosome

2. A ________________ lamp is a glass tube coated on the inside with a substance that gives off light when mercury vapor in the tube is acted on by a stream of electrons.

   cilium conductor fluorescent

3. An opaque condition of the lens of the eye causing blindness or partial blindness is called a __________________.

   retina cataract convex

4. ________________ energy is derived from movement.

   Homeostasis Ossification Kinetic

5. The _________________ is a section of the brain behind and below the cerebrum whose function is to coordinate voluntary movements.

   cerebellum cytoplasm epidermis

6. A ________________ is one of a series of substances alike in percentage composition but differing in molecular weight.

   proton platelet polymer

7. A dog is an example of a mammal called a ________________ that likes to eat meat.

   herbivore carnivore polymer

8. A _______________ is the amount of heat needed to raise the temperature of a gram of water from 15° to 16° Celsius.

   calorie cartilage coefficient

9. The hormone that stimulates the development of feminine characteristics is called __________________.

   exothermic ecology estrogen

10. The prescription drug Keflex is an example of a(n) ______________.

    antibiotic diatom alloy

Name ______________________ Grade ___ Teacher ____________ Date _________

Group-Administered Context Clue Inventory for Older Students: Mathematics

Choose the one word that belongs in each sentence.

1. A ________________ is a solid figure with more than six faces.

   percentage polyhedron correlation

2. ________________ is a symbol for the ratio of the circumference of a circle to the diameter, approximately 3.14.

   Pi Quartile Sine

3. The ________________ is the number from which another is to be subtracted.

   vertex multiplicand minuend

4. The branch of mathematics dealing with the properties, measurements, and relationships of points, lines, planes, and solids is called ________________.

   geometry calculus percentiles

5. A(n) ________________ is a formal statement of equivalence often used in algebra and denoted by the = sign.

   exponent graph equation

6. ________________ is the state in which one part exactly corresponds to the other in size, shape, and position.

   Symmetry Segment Subscript

7. A ________________ is a proposition that can be proved from accepted principles.

   cosine theorem power

8. A ________________ is a diagram representing the successive changes in the value of a variable quantity or quantities.

   deviation graph mean

9. The ________________ is the middle number in a series of numbers.

   median concentric tangent

10. An ________________ is a number written above and to the right of a mathematical expression to indicate the operation of rising to a power.

    inference equivalent exponent

For Additional Reading

Barbe, W., and Allen, H. *Reading Skills Competency Tests: Fifth Level.* Paramus, N.J.: Center for Applied Research in Education, 1999.

Barbe, W., and Allen, H. *Reading Skills Competency Tests: Sixth Level.* Paramus, N.J.: Center for Applied Research in Education, 1999.

Barbe, W., Allen, H., and Sparkman, B. *Reading Skills Competency Tests: Advanced Level.* Paramus, N.J.: Center for Applied Research in Education, 1999.

Fry, E., Kress, J., and Fountoukidis, D. *The Reading Teacher's Book of Lists* (4th ed.). San Francisco: Jossey-Bass, 2000.

Heilman, A., Blair, T., and Rupley, W. *Principles and Practices of Teaching Reading* (pp. 452–496). Upper Saddle River, N.J.: Prentice Hall/Merrill, 1998.

Miller, W. *Alternative Assessment Techniques for Reading & Writing.* Paramus, N.J.: Center for Applied Research in Education, 1995.

Pavlak, S. *Informal Tests for Diagnosing Specific Reading Problems.* Paramus, N.J.: Parker Publishing, 1985.

Reutzel, D., and Cooter, R., Jr. *Teaching Children to Read* (pp. 346–396). Upper Saddle River, N.J.: Prentice-Hall/Merrill, 2000.

Shanker, J., and Ekwall, E. *Locating and Correcting Reading Difficulties* (pp. 241–358). Upper Saddle River, N.J.: Prentice Hall/Merrill, 1998.

Stieglitz, E. *The Stieglitz Informal Reading Inventory.* Needham Heights, Mass.: Allyn and Bacon/Longman, 2002.

Works Cited in Chapter One

LaPray, M., and Ross, R. "The Graded Word List: Quick Gauge of Reading Ability." *Journal of Reading*, 1969, *22*, 305–307.

Miller, W. *Alternative Assessment Techniques for Reading & Writing.* San Francisco: Jossey-Bass, 1995.

Miller, W. *Reading Diagnosis Kit.* Paramus, N.J.: Center for Applied Research in Education, 1986.

Miller, W. *The Reading Teacher's Survival Kit.* San Francisco: Jossey-Bass, 2001.

2

Strategies and Activities for Improving Content Sight Word Identification

Emily is a sixth-grade student at Mountain View Elementary School in Arizona. In the primary grades Emily had good word identification and comprehension skills and enjoyed reading for pleasure, but she began to experience some difficulty reading content materials in fourth grade. In sixth grade, she is having great difficulty reading social studies and science materials and no longer enjoys reading for pleasure. What do you believe may have happened to change her reading skills and attitudes?

The likely reason is that she has difficulty instantly recognizing the specialized vocabulary terms found in her content textbooks. A number of social studies and other content textbooks in middle school and high school are written far above the actual reading level of the students. This is primarily because the content areas of social studies and science, and to a somewhat lesser degree literature and mathematics, contain a number of difficult vocabulary that students must be able to identify immediately in order to comprehend the material.

Chapter Two is designed to help any reading teacher, reading tutor, classroom teacher, or content teacher learn how to present and review the specialized terms that students need to know to comprehend content and daily living materials. The chapter first provides reproducible copies of daily living words and words needed for computer literacy. Then it describes classroom-tested strategies for improving ability to recognize and identify important content and daily living words; most of these strategies are motivational as well as functional. The chapter ends with six reproducible activity sheets that provide students with motivating ways to improve their ability to identify important content words.

After reading this chapter, any teacher or tutor should be well-equipped to provide students with appropriate instruction and practice in this important reading skill.

Content Sight Words and Why It Is Important to Be Able to Identify Them

Sight word recognition and *sight word identification* are both components of *sight word knowledge.* Sight word recognition is *recognizing,* or being able to select, a word immediately when it is located with other words that appear similar. In contrast, sight word identification is the ability to *pronounce* a word immediately when it is encountered while reading. Although sight word identification is the more difficult skill, it is the one that readers need to have.

Readers distinguish sight words from one another through a variety of techniques. One of these is *configuration,* in which the student mentally "frames" the word to note its unique shape, if any. Configuration can be a helpful strategy if the target word has a unique shape. Here are several examples of content words that a student may be able to identify using configuration: *megalopolis, typhoon, cholesterol, zoology,* and *onomatopoeia.* In contrast, here are some content words whose identification probably is not aided by using configuration: *concave, caucus, oasis, aurora,* and *ozone.*

Another technique is to focus on the *top half of the word.* This portion of the word is usually more helpful in word identification than the bottom half. This can be illustrated by the following word:

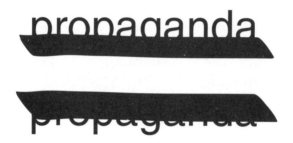

The *beginning and final elements* of words often are the most useful in identification. For example, the *beginning* of the following words probably greatly aids in their identification: *royalist, seismograph, flammable, alliteration,* and *symmetry.* However, the *ending* of these words may be useful in their identification: *monotheism, medulla, photosynthesis, cliché,* and *cosine.*

The *context* in which a word is placed is of added importance to its *appearance* and enhances the student's ability to identify it. The following sentences illustrate the effectiveness of context clues in identifying content words:

> A *fascist* government usually is a dictatorship that encourages racism and militarism.
>
> Zoologists are very concerned about protected animals that are currently endangered. They fear that they may become *extinct.*
>
> The statement "The billowy clouds in the summer sky look like fluffy cotton balls" is an example of *imagery.*
>
> In an arithmetic problem the *subtrahend* is the number that is to be subtracted from the minuend.

Because content reading materials, especially in social studies and science, contain numerous difficult vocabulary terms, it is essential that students be able to identify them *immediately* in order to comprehend the materials. Although structural and phonic analysis may at first be helpful in analyzing difficult vocabulary terms (see Chapters Three and Four), students soon need to be able to identify them *automatically* so that they do not fail to understand a sentence or paragraph while pausing to analyze them. They need to be able to identify content words immediately and accurately so that they have reading fluency in both content and narrative material.

The strategies and materials contained in this chapter are useful when beginning to help students to identify important specialized content and daily living terms rapidly. You are encouraged to modify these materials based on the needs and interests of your own students.

Reproducible Lists of Daily Living Words

This section of the chapter provides reproducible lists of daily living words. They are organized into the following categories: *basic survival words*, *travel words*, *application words*, and *work words*.

Although all students should be able to recognize these words instantly, teachers usually need to emphasize them particularly with students who have special needs, such as learning or reading disabilities.

Basic Survival Words

Survival words are those sight words that older students and adults should be able to identify immediately for their health and safety. These words may be especially useful to students with learning and reading disabilities at the middle-school level and beyond. This section includes a brief list of the most important survival words. For a more comprehensive list of such words see *The Reading Teacher's Book of Lists* (4th ed.) by Fry, Kress, and Fountoukidis (2000, pp. 376–377).

Travel Words

Travel words are words that older students and adults need to be able to identify for successful travel. Although they are generally not as important as the survival words, they still should be mastered if possible.

Application Words

Here is a sampling of words that older students and adults may need to identify in order to *complete applications* of various types. Being able to identify these words should help students and adults to function more effectively in both their professional and personal lives.

Work Words

Here is a sampling of *work words and phrases* that older students and adults should be able to identify immediately. (For a comprehensive list of such words, consult Fry, Kress, and Fountoukidis, 2000, pp. 380–385.)

Daily Living Words: Basic Survival Words

acid
ambulance
apartment
area code
ATM
bank
bus stop
cab
cafeteria
caution
check
close door
combustible
confidential
coupon
customer service
danger
dentist
dial tone
doctor
do not drink
don't walk
down
drinking water
drugstore
elevator
emergency
emergency exit
entrance
exit
fire
fire alarm
fire escape
fire exit
first aid
flammable
food
fragile
fuel
gas
gentlemen
handle with care
harmful if swallowed
help wanted
hospital
keep out
keep refrigerated
ladies
laundry
license number
local call
long distance
M.D.
medicine
men working
men working above
newspaper
no admittance
no smoking
no trespassing
nurse
one way
open door out
out of order
oxygen
parking
pedestrians
perishable
physician
poison
police
post office
private
public parking
railroad station
receipt
refund
repair service
rest rooms
sales tax
schedule
school zone
smoking prohibited
stairs
STOP
swim at your own risk
taxi
telephone
this way
timetable
toll booth
use other door
warning
watch your step
women
X-ray

Daily Living Words: Travel Words

bike route
bridge may be slippery
caution
children crossing
construction ahead
dangerous intersection
dead end
deer crossing
detour
divided highway
do not enter
emergency parking only
entrance
exit
expressway
four-way stop
freeway
fuel
hidden driveway
highway ends
hospital zone
intersection
keep right (keep left)
left lane must turn
low clearance
mechanic on duty
merging traffic
narrow bridge
no left (right) turn
no stopping
no U turn
one way
pass with care
pedestrian crossing
railroad crossing
ramp speed
school crossing
school zone
signal ahead
slippery when wet
slow traffic keep right
soft shoulder
speed limit 55 mph
through traffic keep right
tow-away zone
truck crossing
winding road
wrong way
yield

Daily Living Words: Application Words

application
apply in person
available immediately
bonus
certificate
claim form
compensation
dependents
dues
earn
eligible
employment
equal opportunity
employer
exemptions
experience
fringe benefits

graduated
health plan
human resources
identification
incentives
income
insurance
intern
landlord
lease
license
maiden name
married
overtime
part-time
pension plan
permanent
personnel

reference
résumé
salary
seniority
shift
signature
Social Security number
status
temporary
trainees
union
vacation
volunteer
widow
widower
withholding
work history

Daily Living Words: Work Words

Danger Words

- break glass
- danger—slow
- do not close switch
- do not open valve
- do not stand up
- do not wear loose clothing or gloves around machines
- equipment must not be taken within 10 feet of electric lines
- fire exit only
- keep hands and arms inside car
- proceed with caution
- report dangerous conditions at once
- watch out for persons below
- your eyes are priceless—wear proper protection

Want Ads

- assembler
- attendant
- automotive mechanic
- counterman
- janitor
- maintenance
- production workers
- rotating shift
- stock man
- warehouseman

Income Tax

- balance due
- deductions allowed
- dependent
- dividends
- enter total wages
- exemptions
- if filing joint return
- interest
- itemized deductions
- joint return
- married filing jointly
- married filing separately
- middle initial
- refund
- spouse's
- total federal income tax withheld
- total income tax from tax table
- withholding allowances

Daily Living Words: Work Words, continued

Credit Terms

bank balance
checking account
contract expires
creditors
excluding overtime
extension
finance company
insurance coverage
landlord
list your debts
loan value
mortgage payments
purchase price
registration number
rent

Trucking

C.O.D. (collect on delivery)
commodities rate
consignor
delivery number
destination
explosives
gross load
gross weight
prepaid
pro number
protective signature service
received in good condition
second-class rates
storage
vehicle number

Construction

caution—keep walking, paths clear

cement

employees only allowed past this point

heater room

kerosene

men working above

mortar cement

pile all materials properly

replace guards and barriers immediately

riding on this forbidden

solvent

stop machines before cleaning or adjusting

this hoist for materials only—do not ride

warning—stop machines before clearing jams or repairing

wear your hard hat

Reproducible List of Computer Literacy Words

In the contemporary information age, older students and adults must be able to identify and understand words that are related to the use of *computers*. Because many of the terms on this list are fairly difficult, they may be most applicable for students in upper middle school and above.

Although the list is not exhaustive, it is fairly comprehensive. To make it more useful for reading teachers, tutors, and students, I have included definitions for each term on the list.

Words Needed for Computer Literacy

A

abort To stop a program or function before it is completed naturally.

alias An alternative name for an object such as a variable, file, or device.

application A specific use of the computer, such as for inventory or billing.

archive To copy computer files onto a long-term storage device for safekeeping.

arrow keys Most computer keyboards contain four arrow keys for moving the cursor or insertion point right, left, up, or down.

B

backbone The main cable that connects devices on a computer network.

bit Another name for binary digit—that is, the smallest unit of information used by computers.

bookmark To mark a Web address or document for easy later retrieval.

boot To start a computer by loading the operating system.

browser Computer software used to search the Web and display information.

bug An error in the computer software or hardware that causes a malfunction.

byte Groups of eight bits that can be used to represent numbers and letters of the alphabet.

C

cache A special high-speed storage mechanism.

CD-ROM (Compact Disk-Read Only Memory) A type of compact disk designed to have information read from it but not to have information stored on it.

chip An extremely small piece of silicon on which thousands of electronic elements are implanted.

click To tap the mouse button. "Click on" means to select an item on the screen by pointing the cursor to it and tapping the mouse button.

clip art Electronic graphics that are often part of a software package, and usually royalty-free, that can be inserted into a document.

close box To finish work on a data file and save it.

compact disk (CD) A disk (disc) with one or more metal layers used to store digital information that is read by a laser.

cookie Information that is given to the Web browser by a server to identify a user when that user accesses the server in the future.

crash A major failure in the computer that results from a failure in either the hardware or the software.

cursor A symbol, usually blinking, that indicates where the next character will appear on the screen.

Words Needed for Computer Literacy, continued

D

database	A computer file or collection of data.
default	A value or setting that is preset by the manufacturer or program and remains that way until changed.
desktop	The primary display screen with icons representing programs, files, and so on.
dial-up access	Connection to the computer by telephone and modem.
disk	A plate on which data can be encoded; two types are hard disk and floppy disk.
disk drive	A device that reads and writes data to a disk.
document	A file created with a word processor. Documents can include text, graphics, and charts.
download	To copy a file, program, and so on from a main source such as the Internet or a mainframe computer to a local computer or printer.
drag	To move an icon or other image on a display screen.

E

electronic mail (e-mail)	A message sent over a communication network.
ESC	The escape key on the keyboard; it is used to exit a program quickly.
execute	To run a program or perform a command or function.

F

file	A collection of data or information that has a name (the filename).
finder	The desktop management system for Apple Macintosh computers.
floppy disk	Disks that are designed to be removed from computers and thus are portable. These disks used to be sold in sealed envelopes and "flopped" when shaken. Now they are usually encased in a rigid shell.
folder	In graphical user interfaces, such as Windows, and in the Macintosh environment, a folder is an object that contains multiple documents.
font	A design for a set of characters. A font is a combination of typeface and other qualities, such as size, pitch, and spacing.
freeware	Software given away by its author that is available over the Internet.

Words Needed for Computer Literacy, continued

G

graphical interface Allows the user to give the computer commands by pointing to and activating icons on the computer screen.

H

hard disk A rigid magnetic disk sealed inside the computer on which data can be stored.

hardware The actual computer and other objects, such as monitor, keyboard, printer, and so on, that connect to it.

highlight To make an object on a display screen stand out by displaying it in a different mode from other objects.

homepage The main page of a Web site—often the first page accessed by visitors to that site.

HTML (HyperText Markup Language) The language used to create documents on the World Wide Web.

I

icon A small picture appearing on the computer screen that represents something larger, such as a program, folder, or object.

initialize In programming to assign a starting value to a variable.

insertion point In graphics-based programs the point where the next character typed from the keyboard will appear on the display screen. It is usually represented by a blinking vertical line.

Internet A large number of computer networks that are interconnected and make it possible for millions of computers around the world to communicate with each other.

J

java A programming language that allows small applications to be downloaded to a computer for playback.

K

kilobyte (KB) 1,024 bytes, or approximately a thousand bytes.

L

laptop A small, portable computer.

laser printer A high-speed, high-resolution printer that uses a laser beam for printing.

log on To access a computer system by providing a password or other identification.

Words Needed for Computer Literacy, continued

M

mainframe	The largest computers to which terminals or personal computers may be linked.
megabyte (MB)	1,048,576 bytes, or approximately a million bytes.
memory	Storage area in the computer.
modem (fax/data modem)	A device that makes it possible for a computer to send and receive data over telephone lines.
monitor	A screen for displaying computer information.
mouse	A small device connected to a computer that controls the movement of the cursor.
multimedia	The use of computers to present voice, video, and data in an integrated way.

N

network	Two or more computers linked together.
notebook	A lightweight and portable computer; another term for laptop.

O

online	Turned on and connected to the Internet.
operating system	The most important program that runs on a computer.

P

password	A series of characters that is kept secret and allows the user to gain access to files, e-mail, computers, and so on.
personal computer (PC)	A microcomputer that has its central processing unit etched onto a single chip; the most common type of computer in use today.
print queue	The operating system of the computer lines up the documents to be printed by placing them in a special area. The printer pulls the documents off the queue one at a time.
printer driver	A program that controls the printer. When a document is printed, the printer driver feeds the data to the printer with the correct control commands.
program	Any set of rules that tells a computer what to do.
purge	To remove or delete unneeded files.

R

RAM (Random Access Memory)	The most common type of memory found in computers.
read-only	Capable of being displayed but not modified or deleted.
ROM (Read-Only Memory)	The most common type of memory found in computers.

Words Needed for Computer Literacy, continued

S

save	To copy data from a temporary to a more permanent storage area in a computer so that it can be accessed at a later time.
search engine	A program that searches for information on the World Wide Web.
server	A computer or other device that manages resources on a network.
shareware	Software that is readily available over the Internet; users are allowed to try it out with the understanding that if they decide to keep it, they will pay for it.
shortcut key	A special combination of keys that causes a specific command to be executed.
software	Computer programs and accompanying documentation.
spreadsheet	Software for working with data (both words and numbers) in rows and columns.
system	A combination of components working together. A computer system includes hardware and software.

T

title bar	The bar at the top of the window that contains the name of the file application.

V

virtual reality	An artificial environment created with computer hardware and software and presented to the user so that it appears to be real.
virus	Computer code that is introduced to the computer from an outside source, without the user's knowledge, and causes problems.

W

Webmaster	An individual who manages a Web site.
Web page	A document on the World Wide Web.
Web site	A collection of interrelated Web pages.
window	An enclosed rectangular area on a display screen.
word processor	Computer software used to produce and edit text.
World Wide Web (WWW, www)	A hypermedia system on the Internet that makes it possible to browse through information.

STRATEGIES FOR CORRECTING DIFFICULTIES IN SIGHT WORD IDENTIFICATION

This section of the chapter offers a sampling of classroom-tested strategies for improving ability to recognize general and content sight words. Although all of these strategies are helpful in grades 5 to 12, you should modify any of them based on the abilities and interests of your own students. This section has two parts: strategies for correcting difficulties in general sight word recognition and identification, and strategies for correcting difficulties in content sight word recognition and identification in literature, social studies, science, and mathematics.

Contextual Reading of Easy, Motivating Material

Wide reading of easy, motivating material undoubtedly is the most effective way to learn sight words that already have been presented. Many reading teachers and tutors have stated that a student may need as many as 120 to 140 meaningful exposures to a word before that word becomes part of his or her sight word bank (the words that he or she can immediately recognize). Some students with special needs, such as those with learning or reading disabilities, may need even more exposures before a word can be immediately identified.

Some students with special needs, however, do not enjoy reading any type of material either for information or pleasure. Therefore, it is important for the reading teacher or tutor to provide such students with a wide variety of easy, highly motivating reading material. As much as possible, the material should be on the student's independent (easy) or high instructional reading level and reflect his or her unique interests.

However, it often is necessary for students with special needs to read content textbooks in which they are not particularly interested. Although there is not one single method to motivate them, locating easy material on the selected topic may be helpful—for example, interesting, easy-to-read mass-market books, magazines, newspapers, and material on the World Wide Web, among many others.

In any case, contextual reading is one of the most effective ways to learn both general sight words and content vocabulary and should be encouraged whenever possible.

Three-Step Strategy for Teaching Difficult Sight Words

Here is a useful *three-step strategy* for teaching sight words to older students, especially those with learning or reading disabilities:

1. *See:* Write the target word on the chalkboard and pronounce it. Call attention to features of the word—such as the initial consonant, consonant blend, or word ending—that are similar to words the student already knows. Use each word in a sentence similar to the way in which it will be used in the student's narrative or content reading.

2. *Discuss and define:* If the meaning of the new word is not familiar to the student, discuss the word in detail. If possible, students should use their prior knowledge to figure out the meaning; they can also look it up in the dictionary.

3. *Use and write:* If possible, have the student use the new word in speaking and writing. Ask the student to make up a sentence containing the word and write the sentence on the chalkboard, chart paper, or an overhead transparency. The student can include the word in his or her word bank if desired. New words become completely learned through repeated exposure when they occur in the sentences and material that students read and when they are often used in their writing.

Gipe's Clueing Strategy

Research conducted by Gipe (1980, 1987) indicated that new word identification and meanings are most effectively taught when they appear in an appropriate and familiar context. Gipe's clueing technique teaches words that should eventually become immediately recognized by first presenting a series of sentences that rely on *clueing.* All of the sentences used in the clueing technique are filled with familiar words and situations.

Here's how this procedure works. Students are given a passage in which the first sentence uses the new word appropriately, thus providing valuable semantic and syntactic information. The second sentence of the passage describes some of the characteristics or attributes of the unknown word. The third sentence of the passage defines the unknown word again, being certain to use familiar concepts (Gipe, 1987, p. 152). The last sentence has students relate the new word to their own lives. At this point the students write an answer to a question or complete an open-ended statement requiring application of the word meaning.

Here is an example of how this strategy can be used with an unknown science word.

> Ryan is an eighth-grader who has always been fascinated by *astronomy.* At night he enjoys looking at planets, stars, and the moon with his telescope. Astronomy is the study of the stars and other heavenly bodies that make up the universe. Are you interested in visiting a planetarium so you can become more knowledgeable about the science of astronomy? Why or why not?

After students complete this reading and writing procedure, their responses can be shared in a group discussion. The reading teacher or tutor can write the answers to the final question or open-ended statement on the chalkboard or on chart paper. If a student is keeping an individual word bank, he or she can add the new word, making it available for later study and use.

RIVET

RIVET is a strategy formulated by Cunningham (2000) that is designed to help students activate their prior knowledge about a topic and make predictions about what they are about to read with the purpose of recognizing and identifying important content words.

To plan a RIVET lesson, read the content selection that you want to use and select six to eight words that you want students to learn to identify. Cunningham suggests that they be polysyllabic words or important concept words. Start the RIVET procedure by writing numbers and drawing lines on chart paper, a chalkboard, or a dry-erase board to indicate how many letters are found in each word. Have students copy this information on a sheet of paper, or give them a duplicated version if you want to save time. The chalkboard and their papers might look like this:

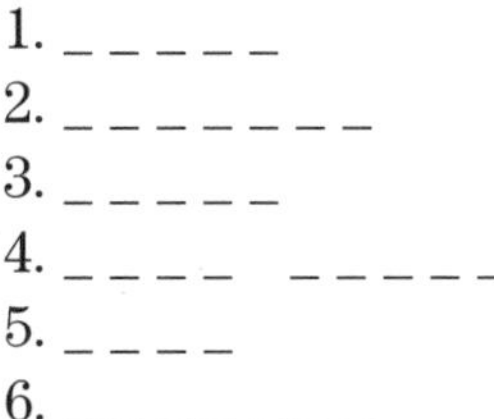

1. _ _ _ _ _
2. _ _ _ _ _ _ _
3. _ _ _ _ _
4. _ _ _ _ _ _ _ _ _
5. _ _ _ _
6. _ _ _ _ _ _ _

Begin the whole-group or whole-class lesson by filling in the letters of the first word slowly, one letter at a time. Have the students copy the letters as you write them and ask them to guess what the word might be as soon as they can.

The first word might first appear like this when you begin the lesson:

1. *E g* _ _ _

It then looks like this after someone guesses and helps you finish the spelling:

1. *E g y p t*

Continue in the same way until the students have completed the list, as in the example shown.

1. *E g y p t*
2. *p y r a m i d*
3. *m u m m y*
4. *N i l e R i v e r*
5. *t o m b*
6. *p h a r a o h*

Once all the words have been filled in, ask the students to use them to predict what the passage they are about to read will be about; also write down some questions that they may have on the topic.

The RIVET strategy helps students learn to recognize and identify important content words and improves their prediction and comprehension skills. It also is a motivating, challenging, and enjoyable activity.

The Omnibus Strategy

Manzo and Manzo (1993) suggested the *omnibus strategy* for improving immediate sight word identification. This strategy uses voice variations and questions about the target word to provide necessary repetitions and attention to its distinguishing features and to build eidetic imagery. Because it incorporates several other strategies, Manzo and Manzo named it the omnibus strategy.

This strategy can be carried out with one or more students. It probably should be used only with learning or reading disabled students and only with those content words that are crucial for comprehending an assignment. Hold up a flash card or write the word on the chalkboard.

TEACHER: See this word? The word is *patriot.* Everyone look at this word and say it together.
STUDENTS: Patriot.
TEACHER: That's correct. Now say it five times while looking at it.
STUDENTS: Patriot, patriot, patriot, patriot, patriot.
TEACHER: Good. Now say it louder.
STUDENTS: *Patriot!*
TEACHER: I know you can say it louder than that!
STUDENTS: *PATRIOT!*
TEACHER: I have three other cards here (*pacifist, persecute, politics).* When I show a card that is not *patriot,* say No! in a loud voice. But when you see the word *patriot,* say it in a whisper.
STUDENTS: No!
STUDENTS: No!
STUDENTS: *(in a whisper) Patriot.*
TEACHER: That's great. Look at the word carefully and when I take it away, close your eyes and try to picture the word in your mind. Do you see it? Good. Now say it in a whisper again.
STUDENTS: *Patriot.*
TEACHER: Very good. Now spell the word.
STUDENTS: P-A-T-R-I-O-T.
TEACHER: Now pretend to write it in the air in front of you with your finger while saying each letter.
STUDENTS: P-A-T-R-I-O-T.
TEACHER: Now describe the word in the same way you would describe a new student to a friend who hasn't seen that student yet.
STUDENT 1: It has seven letters.
STUDENT 2: It begins with the letter "p" and ends with the letter "t."
STUDENT 3: It looks like the word "patriotism."
TEACHER: What is the name of the word again?
STUDENTS: *Patriot.*
TEACHER: Can anyone use it in a sentence?
STUDENTS: The chaplain of the New York firefighters who died on September 11, 2001, is an example of an American *patriot.*
TEACHER: When you read your social studies assignment later today, search for the word *patriot* and see if you can count the number of times it appears in your assignment. I'll ask you tomorrow how many times it appeared.

The next day the teacher or tutor asks the students to point out each place in their assignment where the word *patriot* appeared.

The omnibus strategy should not be used often because it is time-consuming and can become boring.

Configuration Clues

As noted earlier, *configuration clues* are when a student observes the *total shape* of a word as an aid to its identification. Although configuration clues were used for many years—especially in the primary grades—as an aid in sight word recognition and identification, the strategy fell out of favor because a number of words have the same configuration or shape. However, it is currently regaining popularity, and it may be useful as one strategy among others for identifying general or content terms. Reading teachers and tutors may recommend that students use it *as one strategy for identifying unknown words found in their reading.*

To use configuration as a word identification strategy with older students, print a target word such as the following on the chalkboard or a sheet of chart paper:

zygote

Then draw a frame around the word and have the students try to visualize the configuration or unique shape of the word.

Here is one activity that can be used to improve ability in word configuration. Construct an activity sheet containing sentences with one omitted content word. In place of each omitted word draw a configuration frame with a line between each letter. Then have the students read the sentences silently and print what they believe to be the omitted word in the correct spaces in the word configuration frame. Here are two examples:

Since Dr. Bertsche is a devout Mennonite who does not believe in war, he can be called a pacifist.

The Sonoran Desert in southern Arizona is very arid and receives very little precipitation.

The Drastic Strategy

If a student with learning or reading disabilities has extreme difficulty in learning a critical general or content sight word, it may be necessary to use the *drastic strategy.* This strategy was developed by Cunningham (1980). Very briefly, it consists of the following steps:

1. Write the target word on a card and give it to the student.
2. Read a paragraph or passage aloud in which the word is used several times. Have the student hold up the card every time he or she hears the word.
3. Have the student compose a paragraph—either orally or in writing—that uses the target word.

4. Have the student cut the written target word into separate letters. Then have him or her reassemble the letters to form the word.
5. Write the word on the chalkboard. Have the student memorize the word and spell it from memory three times.
6. Have the student read another paragraph or passage containing the word. Have him or her point out the word whenever he or she encounters it.

Important: Do not use this technique often because it is intensive. Students can easily become bored and frustrated.

Borrowed Words from Other Languages

Many words that have come into common usage in English were borrowed from other languages. Because the spellings of such words are often unusual, they may be best taught as *sight words*. Fry, Fountoukidis, and Kress compiled a comprehensive list of foreign words in their book *The Reading Teacher's Book of Lists* (2000, pp. 114–116).

Here is a brief list of words that have been borrowed from other languages. Students can add to the list by exploring the language and origins of their own cultural heritage.

African	**Arabic**	**Dutch**	**East Indian**
marimba	alcohol	monsoon	catamaran
mumbo jumbo	carafe	skipper	cheetah
safari	kebab	sloop	dinghy
samba	tariff	wagon	khaki
zombie	zero	yacht	teak

French	**German**	**Italian**	**Japanese**
ambiance	angst	cavalry	bonsai
boulevard	delicatessen	confetti	jujitsu
caprice	gestalt	fiasco	origami
fiancée	sauerkraut	incognito	sayonara
impromptu	schema	virtuoso	tycoon

Portuguese	**Russian**	**Spanish**	**Yiddish**
commando	commissar	albino	bagel
pagoda	intelligentsia	armada	kibbutz
peon	parka	cafeteria	klutz
	politburo	flotilla	pastrami
	sputnik	junta	schmaltz

Connected Flash Cards

May (1998) recommended using *connected flash cards* to review general or content sight words. He believed that when flash cards are presented in the order of a sentence, they are much more motivating than when they are presented in isolation. May described the following advantages of using connected flash cards:

- It is more like the actual reading act to review general or content sight words *in context* rather than in unrelated fashion.
- Once the students have learned the particular words in context, the teacher can challenge them by mixing up the cards and presenting them in an unrelated order if possible.
- This procedure can be adapted to any sight words that the teacher wishes to have students learn.

The following is an example of connected flash cards of words from the content area of science.

Peyer's
patches,
oval
lumps
of
tissue
similar
to
the
tonsils
and
adenoids,
are
found
on
mucous
membranes
lining
the
small
intestine.

Semantic Maps or Webs

Students often learn sight words more easily if they are *grouped into meaningful contexts.* Among the most effective strategies are *semantic maps or webs,* which are also called *advance organizers, graphic organizers,* or *think-links.* They can improve ability in identifying content words, and they also can be used in grades 5 to 12 to improve reading comprehension and to motivate writing. To improve ability to identify content words, use them either before or after reading.

Although there are slight variations between these strategies, they are all very similar. They use *graphic representations* of the relationships between the important content terms in the material and are designed to organize vocabulary so that it can be retained more effectively. There are as many variations of semantic maps or webs as there are reading teachers and tutors, so you should experiment until you find your own version of the strategy.

To formulate a semantic map or web, it is first useful to display a completed map on the chalkboard or a transparency using the important terms from a content assignment or narrative (mass-market) book that your students will read shortly. Then place a partially completed map on the chalkboard or a transparency either before or after they read a portion of the material. They can then complete it with your help, if necessary.

Only after students have had considerable experience with completing semantic maps or webs should they be asked to construct one independently or with a partner or partners. When they are ready to do so, it often is preferable to have them construct it with one or more partners. However, if you do not present semantic mapping carefully, students may become extremely frustrated and not want to use this strategy again. It also is important to use semantic mapping fairly often if it is eventually to be used independently.

Here is a sample semantic map constructed from material on the network of organs that make up the immune system.

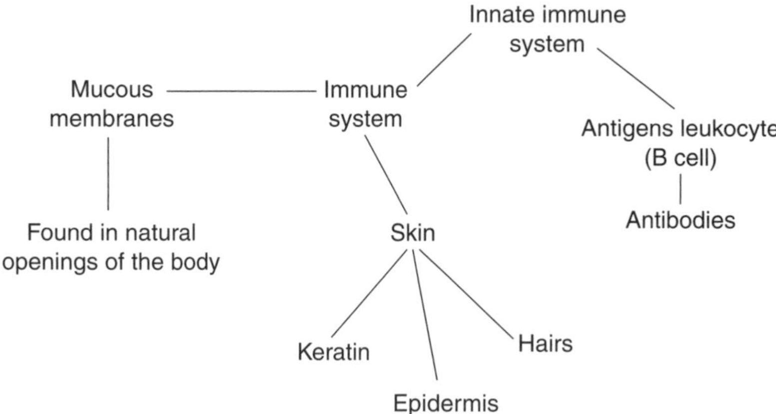

Study Buddies

Use *study buddies* in the classroom or tutoring setting. Here's how. Match learners with fellow students who are able to identify and define content words that are unknown to the first group. Make sure you teach the "tutors" the basic strategies to use in reinforcing unknown content words. A reward of some kind should be given to both tutors and tutees once the latter have attained their goal.

PUZZLE-LIKE STRATEGIES FOR REVIEWING GENERAL AND CONTENT SIGHT WORDS

There are a number of highly motivating puzzle-like strategies that reading teachers and tutors can use to review general and content sight words. Most of them can be completed by an individual student or with a partner or partners. The next paragraphs provide examples of several of these very interesting strategies. I have used all of them successfully in tutoring sessions with both students who have special needs and students who are average or able readers.

Sight Word Search

A *sight word search* can be used with students in grades 5 to 12. To construct a sight word search, select important vocabulary terms from a topic in the content areas of literature, social studies, science, or mathematics. Then, depending on the ability of the student who is to complete the search, either list the terms underneath the sight word search or include only the *definitions* of the terms. You can use computer software to formulate a sight word search if you wish. One such source is *Wordsheets v 5.1* published by Qualint (www.qualint.com/purchase.html; send e-mail to info@qualint.com).

Have the student circle the targeted content words. The words can be written horizontally either forward or backward, vertically either forward or backward, or diagonally either forward or backward. If you want, later have the student pronounce each of the located words.

Crossword Puzzle

A *traditional crossword puzzle* can be a very effective tool for reviewing the specialized terms in a content assignment that have already been presented. A reading teacher or tutor can easily construct a traditional crossword puzzle with a computer software program by entering the target content terms on the keyboard in either the *across* or *down* column. The computer then prints a completed crossword puzzle using the target terms. This saves a great deal of time, although teachers or tutors can construct their own puzzle if they want to. I have easily done so many times. *Wordsheets v 5.l* (see previous section for access information) offers one such software program. *Eclipse* publishes another such software program; information is available on its Web site (EclipseCrossword.com).

Most students enjoy completing crossword puzzles although some, especially those with special needs, may want to work with a partner to avoid frustration. Although the *target terms* can be included in a crossword puzzle along with the definitions, you may not want to include them, depending on your students' abilities.

Reversed Crossword Puzzle

In a *reversed crossword puzzle*, the target words are placed in the crossword puzzle. Usually the terms have previously been taught. The student or students then must provide a definition for each of the words found in the *across* and *down* columns.

To do this, students usually will have to research the definitions of the target words by using content textbooks, the World Wide Web, or a dictionary, among other sources. In some ways a reversed crossword puzzle may be somewhat easier than a traditional crossword puzzle because the terms are already written down.

Word Puzzle or Acrostic

A variation of a *word puzzle* or *acrostic* can be highly motivating for *reviewing* specialized vocabulary terms that have been presented in a content unit or chapter. A student can complete such a word puzzle independently or with a partner.

Here are several examples of word puzzles or acrostics.

Write the three-syllable word that is the name of a normally colorless, odorless, highly flammable gas that is the simplest and lightest of the elements.
h _ /_ _ _ /_ _ _ (hydrogen)

Write the three-syllable word that is the name of an element that is found free as a colorless, tasteless, odorless gas in the atmosphere, of which it forms about 21%.
o _ / _ /_ _ _ (oxygen)

Write the three-syllable word that is the name of a silver-white, light, malleable, ductile metallic element that commonly occurs in nature.
m _ _ /_ _ /_ _ _ _ (magnesium)

Magic Square

A *magic square* is a challenging and creative technique to improve knowledge of content vocabulary terms and can be used effectively in grades 5 to 12. Magic squares are special arrangements of numbers that *when added across, down, and diagonally always equal the same sum.*

Reading teachers and tutors can construct content term exercises by having students match a lettered column of words to a numbered column of definitions. Letters on each square of the grid match the lettered words. Students then try to find the magic number by matching the correct word and definition and entering the number in the appropriate square on the grid. A magic square is fairly easy to construct, and some students in middle and secondary school will enjoy constructing their own magic squares either independently or with one or more partners.

Scrambled Words

Scrambled words can be used to help students *review* the specialized vocabulary terms found in a content unit or assignment. Scrambled word activity sheets can be completed by a student independently or working with a partner or partners.

Categorization Exercise

A *categorization exercise* can help students practice reviewing important content words that they have learned. To construct a categorization exercise, select a topic from a content unit or book chapter and write the major categories (the headings) of this topic along the top of an activity sheet. Then write the significant content terms related to these categories in random order. Have students then put each term under the proper category or heading.

The following illustration of a scrambled list that the students will need to sort out should clarify this technique:

The Digestive System	**The Circulatory System**	**The Respiratory System**
____________	____________	____________
____________	____________	____________
____________	____________	____________
____________	____________	____________
____________	____________	____________
____________	____________	____________
____________	____________	____________
heart	lungs	large intestine
bronchi	arteries	veins
insulin	blood vessels	esophagus
stomach	mouth	liver
capillaries	pancreas	colon
small intestine	blood cells	nose
pleura	larynx	heart

Reproducible Activity Sheets for Improving Content Sight Word Identification

This last section of the chapter provides six reproducible activity sheets for improving specific difficulties in content sight word identification. They can be duplicated in their present form or modified in any way you wish based on the needs and interests of your own students. In addition, they should serve as models for you in constructing similar activity sheets to reinforce both general and content sight word knowledge.

The six activity sheets included here are as follows: Crossword Puzzle Using Survival Words—Seventh- to Twelfth-Grade Level; Words Borrowed from Other Languages—Seventh- to Twelfth-Grade Level; Using the RIVET Technique in Social Studies—Sixth-Grade Level; Reversed Crossword Puzzle Using Computer Literacy Terms—Seventh- to Twelfth-Grade Level; Magic Square from Science—Sixth-Grade Level; Scrambled Words from Mathematics—Seventh- to Eighth-Grade Level.

Answer Key for Crossword Puzzle of Survival Words

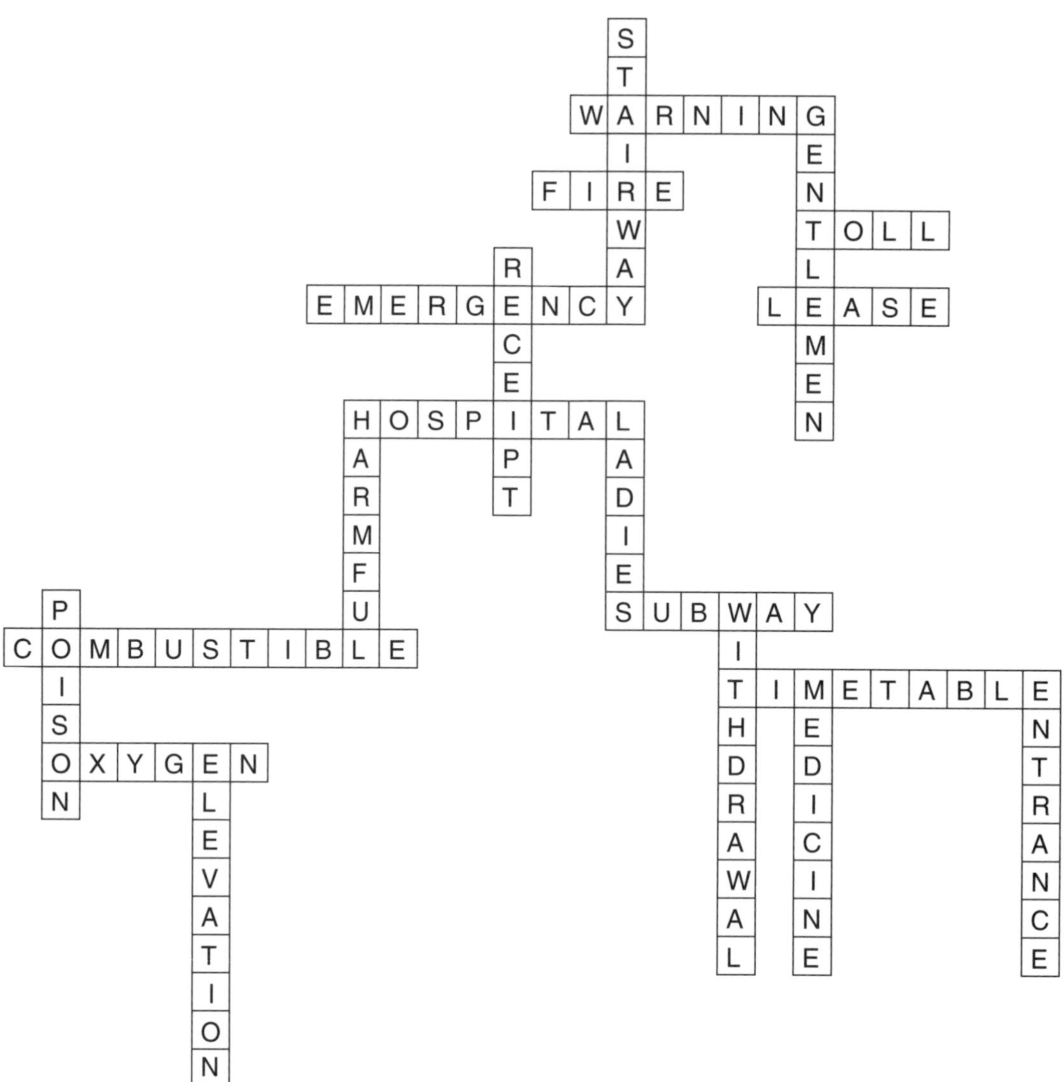

Answer Key for Words Borrowed from Other Languages

Note: These answers are shown in random order. There is no correct order within each classification. *French:* parfait, bureau, rotisserie, ambiance, ballet, bouquet, gourmet, morgue, protégé, résumé, suite, morale, boulevard; *Spanish:* mesquite, palomino, pueblo, enchilada, serape, avocado, burro, coyote, chocolate, junta, mosquito, plaza, potato, tobacco, taco, hombre, albino, lariat; *German:* bratwurst, zwieback, delicatessen, hamburger, pumpernickel, strudel, diesel, kaput; *Italian:* spaghetti, opera, piano, alfresco, casino, gondola, macaroni, stucco, volcano; *Native American:* pemmican, kayak, sequoia, cayuse, catawba; *Chinese:* shantung, tea, tofu, soy, kowtow, typhoon, mahjong.

Answer Key for RIVET Technique in Social Studies

1. terra cotta; 2. warriors; 3. archaeologists; 4. site; 5. burial tomb; 6. clay; 7. excavated; 8. spears; 9. chariots; 10. Chinese

Answer Key for Reversed Crossword Puzzle

Note: The students' wording may be somewhat different; just make sure the definitions are correct. *Across:* 1. software that is easily available, often on the World Wide Web, that allows a person to try it out with the understanding that if he or she decides to keep it, he or she must pay for it; 2. anything that comes out from the computer; 3. computer software used to search the World Wide Web and display information; 4. to find and remove errors from a program; 5. turned on and connected; 6. to tap a mouse button; "click on" means to select an item on the screen by pointing the cursor at it and tapping the menu button; 7. groups of eight bits that can be used to represent numbers and letters of the alphabet; 8. to copy a file, program, and so on, from a main source, such as the Internet or a mainframe computer, to a local computer; 9. a little picture appearing on the computer screen that represents something larger, such as a program, object, or choice of action; 10. a plate on which data can be encoded. *Down:* 1. a lightweight and portable computer; 2. a system of writing and displaying text in which there are links that allow the reader to browse and find connections with related documents; 3. to mark a World Wide Web address or document for later retrieval; 4. to stop a program or function before it finishes; 5. two or more computers linked together; 6. an extremely small piece of silicon on which thousands of electronic elements are implanted; 7. information that is given to a Web browser by a server to identify a user when the server is accessed; 8. the primary display screen with icons representing programs, files, and so on; 9. etiquette for posting messages on computer networks, mainly the Internet; 10. 1,024 bytes, or approximately a thousand bytes.

Answer Key for Magic Square from Science

The magic number is *15*.

A 4	B 9	C 2
D 3	E 5	F 7
G 8	H 1	I 6

Answer Key for Scrambled Words from Mathematics

1. theorem; 2. percentile; 3. hexagon; 4. bisect; 5. exponent; 6. axis; 7. graph; 8. micron; 9. cosine; 10. cubic; 11. median; 12. tangent; 13. kilometer; 14. radius; 15. cone; 16. rhombus; 17. polygon; 18. sphere; 19. ray; 20. numeral

Name ______________________ Grade ___ Teacher ____________ Date _________

Crossword Puzzle of Survival Words

This activity sheet contains a crossword puzzle using *survival words.* The longest word, "combustible," has been written for you. Try to write the rest of the words contained on this sheet on the puzzle. Keep trying until you can find a way to write in all of them. You may work with a partner or partners on this crossword puzzle if you wish.

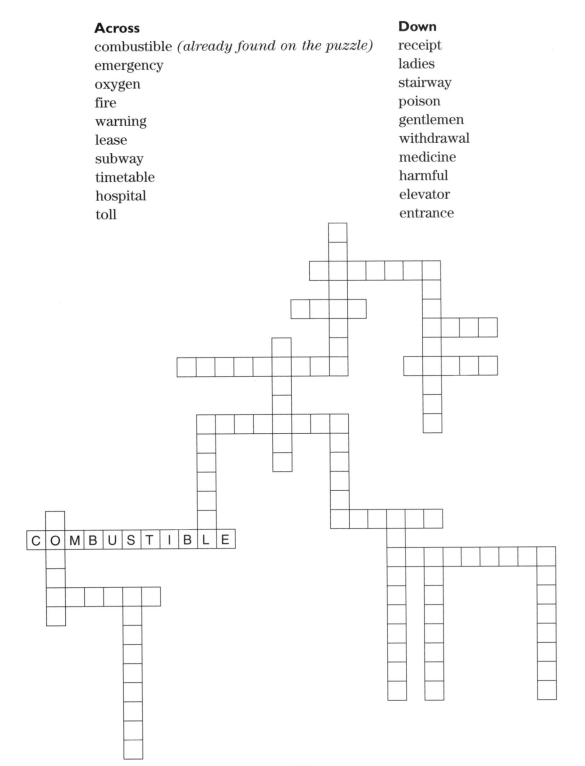

Across	**Down**
combustible *(already found on the puzzle)*	receipt
emergency	ladies
oxygen	stairway
fire	poison
warning	gentlemen
lease	withdrawal
subway	medicine
timetable	harmful
hospital	elevator
toll	entrance

C O M B U S T I B L E

Name ______________________ Grade ___ Teacher ____________ Date __________

Words Borrowed from Other Languages

Here is a list of words borrowed from other languages. *Classify each of them* into the language from which it was borrowed by writing it under the correct heading. You can work with a partner or partners if you wish. You may want to consult the World Wide Web or a dictionary.

mesquite	cayuse	tobacco	morale	catawba	typhoon
delicatessen	diesel	plaza	alfresco	ballet	coyote
junta	burro	tofu	gondola	spaghetti	opera
kayak	protégé	avocado	zwieback	sequoia	mahjong
rotisserie	potato	pueblo	enchilada	piano	pemmican
lariat	boulevard	morgue	soy	ambiance	gourmet
résumé	pumpernickel	strudel	chocolate	palomino	casino
macaroni	bureau	shantung	stucco	volcano	kowtow
albino	hombre	bratwurst	suite	mosquito	parfait
tea	hamburger	serape	bouquet	kaput	taco

French **Spanish** **German**

Italian **Native American** **Chinese**

Name ____________________________ **Grade** ___ **Teacher** ______________ **Date** __________

RIVET Technique in Social Studies

Later you will read a passage about a very well-known attraction that can be seen in *China*. Before you read that passage, complete the word puzzles below. Each puzzle contains an important term that you will find in the passage. You can work with a partner or partners in completing the word puzzles if you want.

1. *t e* ___ ___ ___ *c o t* ___ ___
2. *w a* ___ ___ ___ ___ ___ *s*
3. *a r c h a e* ___ ___ ___ ___ ___ ___ ___ *s*
4. *s* ___ ___ ___
5. *b u* ___ ___ ___ ___ *t* ___ ___ ___
6. *c l* ___ ___
7. *e x c* ___ ___ ___ ___ *e d*
8. *s p* ___ ___ ___ *s*
9. *c h a r* ___ ___ ___ *s*
10. *C h i* ___ ___ ___ ___

Now predict what you think this passage will be about. Then read the passage and *underline the target words* from the puzzles to find out if your predictions were correct. You can work with a partner or partners in formulating your predictions if you want.

Terra-cotta warriors were accidentally discovered by Chinese peasants while digging a well. Their discovery prompted archaeologists to travel to Xian ('Shē än), China, to investigate. No one knows why this amazing site became buried and lost for thousands of years.

What the archaeologists found was the ancient burial site of the first Chinese emperor, Qin. This site contained three underground, timber-lined vaults. The terra-cotta warriors were placed around the emperor's burial tomb, a massive clay army to protect him in the afterlife since there had been three attempts to assassinate him during his life.

Name ____________________ Grade ___ Teacher ____________ Date _________

RIVET Technique in Social Studies, continued

The first site was excavated in 1974. It contained six thousand pottery figures. The bodies of the soldiers had been formed out of terra-cotta clay and then baked in a kiln. They were then positioned in an oblong shape that shows an actual battle formation of the troops.

The warriors are dressed and ready for battle and carry spears and other combat weapons. Each is wearing an army uniform that distinguishes the soldier's rank. The uniforms are painted either red or green, and they also wear either brown or black armor. The different types of warriors include bowmen and infantrymen. Horses and chariots are also found at this site. Although all the warriors are life-size, the commanders are the tallest.

The second excavation occurred in 1976. This pit contained fourteen hundred warriors with horses and sixty-four chariots. There are infantrymen, cavalrymen, and commanders. The facial expressions of these warriors seem less clearly defined than those in the first pit.

The third pit, discovered in 1980, is the smallest of the three. It contains about seventy figures.

All of the warriors at this site demonstrate the quality of Chinese art thousands of years ago. The Qin Terra-Cotta Museum, a hangar-like building constructed over Pit 1, opened in 1979, and Pit 2 opened to the public in 1994. The museum is a wonderful display that every visitor to China should see.

Name ____________________ Grade ___ Teacher ___________ Date _________

Reversed Crossword Puzzle of Computer Literacy Terms

This activity sheet contains a *reversed crossword puzzle.* Although the crossword puzzle has the answers filled in, it does not contain the definitions or clues to the answers. Write the correct definition or clue beside the correct numbers both across and down. You may work with a partner or partners in completing the definitions or clues if you want to. You also may consult the World Wide Web, an encyclopedia, or a dictionary.

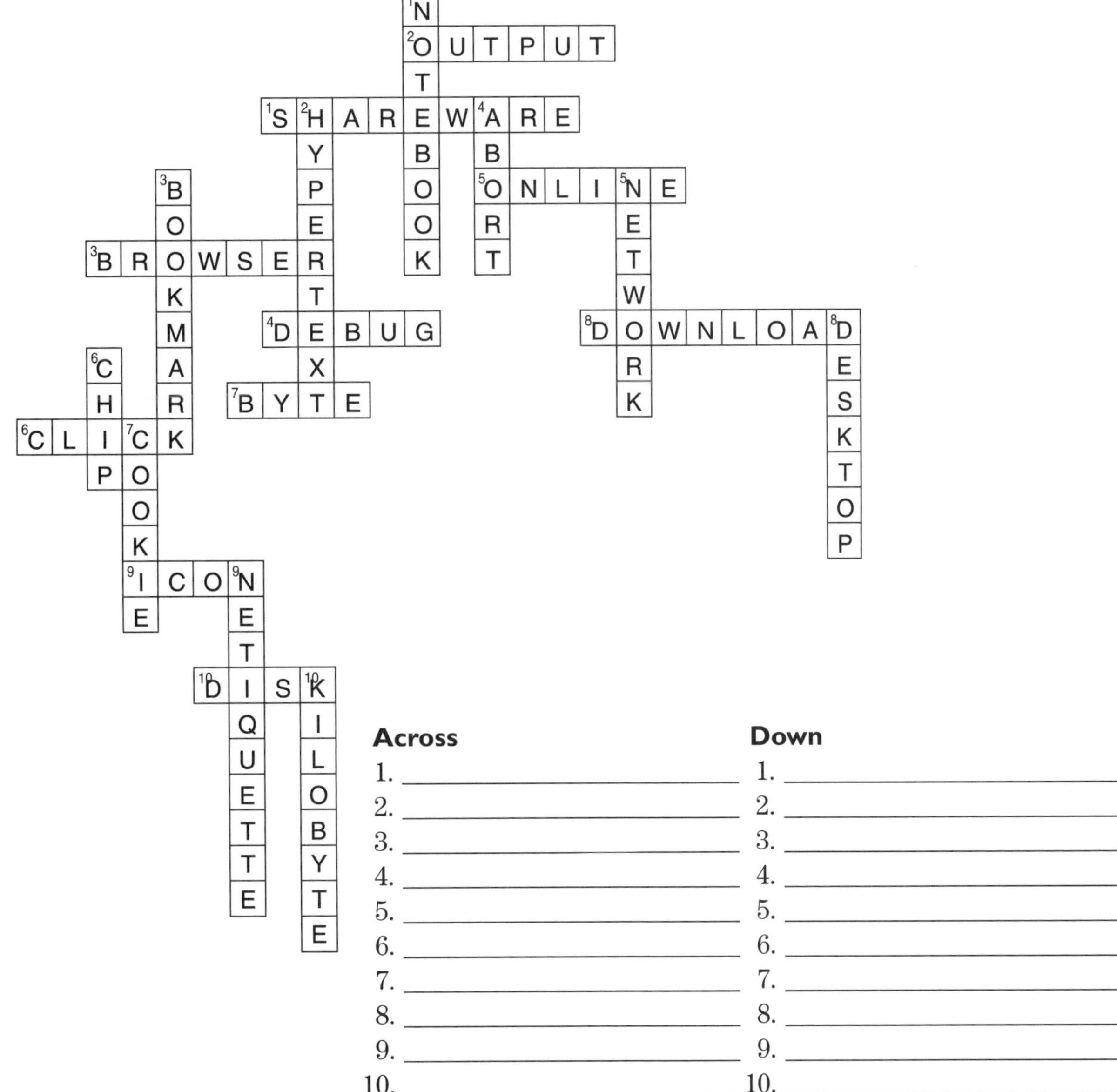

Across

1. ____________________
2. ____________________
3. ____________________
4. ____________________
5. ____________________
6. ____________________
7. ____________________
8. ____________________
9. ____________________
10. ____________________

Down

1. ____________________
2. ____________________
3. ____________________
4. ____________________
5. ____________________
6. ____________________
7. ____________________
8. ____________________
9. ____________________
10. ____________________

Name ______________________ Grade ___ Teacher ___________ Date _________

Magic Square from Science

Select from the numbered statements the best match for each vocabulary term. Put the number in the proper space. The total of the numbers will be the same across each row and down each column. Try to find the *Magic Number!*

Plants Are Able to Make Food

A. photosynthesis	1. a gas or chemical element that combines with hydrogen to form a type of food for plants
B. xylem	2. small openings found in the layers of protective cells on the surfaces of leaves
C. stomates	3. the green structure in plants where food is made
D. chloroplast	4. the process by which plants make food
E. oxygen	5. a gaseous element without taste, color, or smell that is given off and moves out of plant leaves
F. chlorophyll	6. the energy source that changes the raw material into food
G. sugar	7. a green pigment or coloring material
H. carbon dioxide	8. a type of food
I. sunlight	9. a type of tissue made of tubes

A	B	C
D	E	F
G	H	I

Name ______________________ Grade ___ Teacher ___________ Date _________

Scrambled Words from Mathematics

Read the definition following each word. Then unscramble the letters to form the word that corresponds to the definition and write it in the blank. You may work with a partner or partners if you wish.

1. emhtroe ________________________________

   A proposition that can be proved from accepted principles.

2. tlpeercnie ________________________________

   A percentage rank based on a scale of 100.

3. gohxean ________________________________

   A figure with six sides and six angles.

4. sbiect ________________________________

   To divide into two equal parts.

5. eetnponx ________________________________

   A number written above and to the right of a mathematical expression to indicate the operation of raising to a power.

6. xisa ________________________________

   A central line about which the parts of a figure are symmetrically arranged.

7. pharg ________________________________

   A diagram representing the successive changes in the value of a variable quality.

8. rominc ________________________________

   A unit of length—10 meters.

9. siocen ________________________________

   One of the six functions of an angle, the ratio of the base to the hypotenuse.

10. bicuc ________________________________

    Of the third power or degree.

Name ______________________ Grade ___ Teacher ___________ Date _________

Scrambled Words from Mathematics, continued

11. diemna ______________________________________

The middle number in a series of numbers that is ranked from highest to lowest.

12. ntegant ______________________________________

A line that touches a curve.

13. loikreemt ______________________________________

A unit of length equal to 1,000 meters or 32,808.8 feet.

14. uisdar ______________________________________

A straight line from the center of a circle to the circumference of the circle to a point on the surface of a sphere.

15. ecno ______________________________________

A solid figure with a circular or elliptical base tapering to a point.

16. mbrhosu ______________________________________

A parallelogram whose adjacent sides are unequal and whose angles are not right angles.

17. gonylop ______________________________________

A plane figure bounded by straight lines.

18. spreeh ______________________________________

A solid body bounded by a surface of which all points are equidistant from a center.

19. yar ______________________________________

Any of several lines radiating from a center.

20. relamun ______________________________________

A symbol or a group of symbols used to express a number.

For Additional Reading

Allen, H., Barbe, W., and Levesque, T. *Ready-to-Use Vocabulary, Word Attack, and Comprehension Activities* (pp. 24–31). Paramus, N.J.: Center for Applied Research in Education, 1998.

Fry, E., Kress, J., and Fountoukidis, D. *The Reading Teacher's Book of Lists* (4th ed.). San Francisco: Jossey-Bass, 2000.

Heilman, A., Blair, T., and Rupley, W. *Principles and Practices of Teaching Reading* (pp. 150–161). Upper Saddle River, N.J.: Prentice Hall/Merrill, 1998.

Lapp, D., and Flood, J. *Teaching Reading to Every Child* (pp. 223–231). New York: Macmillan, 1992.

McCormick, S. *Remedial and Clinical Reading Instruction* (pp. 230–249). Upper Saddle River, N.J.: Prentice Hall/Merrill, 1987.

Reutzel, R., and Cooter, K., Jr. *Teaching Children to Read* (pp. 228–235). Upper Saddle River, N.J.: Prentice Hall/Merrill, 2000.

Works Cited in Chapter Two

Cunningham, P. "Teaching Was, With, What, and Other 'Four-Letter' Words." *Reading Teacher*, 1980, *34*, 160–163.

Cunningham, P. *Phonics They Use: Words for Reading and Writing* (pp. 147–150). White Plains, N.Y.: Longman, 2000.

Fry, E., Kress, J., and Fountoukidis, D. *The Reading Teacher's Book of Lists* (4th ed.; pp. 114–116). San Francisco: Jossey-Bass, 2000.

Gipe, J. "Use of a Relevant Context Helps Kids Learn New Word Meanings." *Reading Teacher*, 1980, *33*, 398–402.

Gipe, J. *Corrective Techniques for the Classroom Teacher*. Upper Saddle River, N.J.: Gorsuch Scarisbrick, 1987.

Manzo, A., and Manzo, U. *Literacy Disorders: Holistic Diagnosis and Remediation* (pp. 236–237). Orlando: Harcourt Brace Jovanovich, 1993.

May, F. *Reading as Communication* (pp. 162–163). Upper Saddle River, N.J.: Prentice Hall/Merrill, 1998.

3

Strategies and Activities for Improving Basic Phonic Skills

"Phonics is only for kids in the primary grades. It's a waste of time to teach phonics to students in the middle school and above." I have heard both teachers and parents make statements like this, and you probably have too. Do you believe that older students have no need to master the basic phonic skills? This certainly is not the case. All students, including those in grades 5 to 12, should have a mastery of the basic phonic skills so that they can effectively decode the multisyllabic words that they meet in their content reading. For example, I have tutored a number of junior high school students who did not know the short vowel sounds. However, phonic instruction in grades 5 to 12 always should be age-appropriate and should use the students' own content reading materials if possible.

This chapter opens by briefly describing the basic phonic elements in which older students should be competent using age-appropriate words. The following sounds are described: long vowel sounds, short vowel sounds, consonant sounds, consonant blends, r-controlled vowels, the schwa ə sound, and analogies. Next the chapter discusses seven useful phonic generalizations.

The chapter then describes a sampling of useful strategies for general phonics instruction, including cross-checking word identification strategies, word "rubber banding," word sorts of various kinds, word detectives, "the Wheel," making words, Hinks Pinks, discovering a code, interpreting phonetic spellings, and making words using age-appropriate rimes.

The chapter closes with six reproducible activity sheets for improving general phonics skills in grades 5 to 12 and one reproducible activity sheet that can be used to improve ability in short vowel sounds. After reading this chapter, classroom teachers, special reading teachers, and content teachers should all understand the importance of teaching basic phonic elements in grades 5 to 12 and how to teach these elements most effectively.

Basic Phonic Elements in Which Older Students Should Be Competent

Here is a brief description of the most basic phonic elements in which students in grades 5 to 12 should be competent. Each element is illustrated with age-appropriate content words.

Vowels

Vowels result when the organs of speech modify the resonance chamber without stopping the flow of the outgoing breath. All vowels are voiced, and there are no nasal vowels in the English language. One vowel is distinguished from another by the *quality* of its sound.

Here are examples of the *long vowels,* which always have the same name as the actual *letter name.*

long /*a*/—*a*gency　　long /*e*/—*e*quation　　long /i/—*i*deology
long /*o*/—*o*pine　　long /*u*/—*u*ranium
long /*y*/ (long /*i*/ sound)—g*y*roscope
long /*y*/ (long /*e*/ sound)—quantit*y*

Here are examples of the *short vowel sounds.* They may be difficult for some students in grades 5 to 12 to discriminate because of their similarity in sound, especially the sounds of short /*e*/ and short /*i*/.

short /*a*/—*a*pprehend　　short /*e*/—*e*pilogue　　short /*i*/—*i*nsulin
short /*o*/—*o*ptic　　short /*u*/—*u*lceration　　short /*y*/—mang*y*

Note that the pronunciation of the short /*y*/ is unique to some English dialects.

Consonants

A *consonant* is caused when the outgoing breath stream is blocked by an organ of speech. The organs of speech are the hard palate, the soft palate, the larynx, the tongue, the teeth, the lips, and the vocal chords. Here are examples of the *consonant sounds* using age-appropriate words:

/*b*/—*b*onanza
/*c*/ (soft sound)—*c*ircuit
/*f*/—*f*ertile
/*g*/ (soft sound)—*g*enerate
/*j*/—*j*udicial
/*l*/—*l*ubricate
/*n*/—*n*eutron
/*q*/—*q*uartz
/*s*/—*s*imulator
/*v*/—*v*ibrate
/*y*/—*y*ogurt
/*c*/ (hard sound)—*c*ompromise
/*d*/—*d*ermis
/*g*/ (hard sound)—*g*overnment
/*h*/—*h*emisphere
/*k*/—*k*ilometer
/*m*/—*m*eteor
/*p*/—*p*ancreas
/*r*/—*r*evolution
/*t*/—*t*itanium
/*x*/—*x*enophobia
/*z*/—*z*irconium

Consonant Blends

A *consonant blend* consists of two or three consonant letters that appear together. Each consonant retains some element of its own sound while blending with that of the others. Although most consonant blends occur at the beginning of words, they also are found at the end. According to Heilman, Blair, and Rupley (1998), there are 24 two- and three-letter consonant blends that may be divided into three major groups on the basis of a common letter contained in them.

- Those consonant blends that begin with *s: sc, sk, sm, sn, sp, st, sw*
- Those consonant blends that end with *l: bl, cl, fl, gl, pl, sl, spl*
- Those consonant blends that end with *r: br, cr, dr, fr, gr, pr, scr, spr, str, tr*

Here are examples of age-appropriate words containing consonant blends:

bl—*bl*ockade	*br*—*br*omide	*cl*—*cl*imate
cr—*cr*anium	*dr*—*dr*edge	*fl*—*fl*uctuate
fr—*fr*ustrate	*gl*—*gl*ucose	*gr*—*gr*anular
pl—*pl*asma	*pr*—*pr*emier	*sc*—*sc*affold
sc—*sc*enic	*sk*—*sk*eleton	*sl*—*sl*oop
sn—*sn*orkel	*sp*—*sp*erm	*spl*—*spl*endor
spr—*spr*inkle	*st*—*st*ingy	*str*—*str*uctural
sw—*sw*itchback	*tr*—*tr*adition	

R-Controlled Vowels

R-controlled vowels are vowels whose sound is altered by the *r* that follows them. Such vowels are neither long nor short but rather have a unique sound. Here are some examples of age-appropriate words that contain r-controlled vowels.

ar—p*ar*liament	*ar*—c*ar*otene	
er—op*er*ate	*er*—electione*er*	*er*—p*er*ishable
ir—wh*ir*l	*ir*—h*ir*eling	
or—l*or*ry	*or*—w*or*ldwide	
ur—d*ur*ess	*ur*—sec*ur*ity	*yr*—M*yr*tle

The Schwa Sound

The *schwa sound* (ə) is the unstressed vowel sound in a word of more than one syllable. Any one of the five vowel letters can be a schwa sound when it is located in an unaccented syllable. The schwa has a sound that is similar to that of the short /*u*/. Here are some age-appropriate words that contain a schwa sound: mocc*a*sin, ten*ement,* el*i*gible, retr*o*grade, thromb*u*s.

Analogy: Onsets and Rimes

Analogy involves using *onsets* (beginning consonants, consonant blends, or consonant digraphs) and *rimes* (word families or phonograms). Onsets and rimes are easier to analyze than single phonemes (sounds) because of the relative high stability of vowel sounds in most of the rimes.

For a complete list of all the rimes contained in content words, see *The Reading Teacher's Book of Lists* (Fry, Kress, and Fountoukidis, 2000, pp. 31–40).

Useful Phonic Generalizations

According to May and Elliot (1978), only a few phonic generalizations have a fairly high level of consistency and therefore should be taught to students. Students in grades 5 to 12 should use these generalizations along with appropriate structural generalizations to identify unknown words in their content material.

The C Rule

The letter *c* is an irregular consonant that has no phoneme of its own. Instead, it takes the sound of two other phonemes found in different words, /*k*/ and /*s*/. Usually when the letter *c* is followed by *a, o,* or *u,* it takes the sound of the letter *k,* also known as the hard /*c*/ sound. Some age-appropriate words containing this sound are *c*ondensation, *c*orruption, and *c*ompatible.

When the letter *c* represents the sound associated with the letter *s,* it is referred to as the soft /*c*/ sound. This sound is usually heard when the letter *c* is followed by *e, i,* or *y.* Examples of the soft /*c*/ sound are found in the words *c*irculation, *c*erebellum, and *c*ensus.

The G Rule

The letter *g* also has a hard sound and a soft sound. When the letter *g* is followed by *a, o,* or *u,* it usually represents the hard or regular sound, as in the words *g*arnet, *g*overnor, and *g*uarantee. However, when the letter *g* is followed by *e, i,* or, *y,* it represents the soft /*g*/or /*j*/ sound, as in the words *g*eriatric, *g*errymander, and *g*ymnastics.

The CVC Pattern

When a vowel comes between two consonants, it usually has the short vowel sound. Examples of words following the *CVC pattern* are *hack, pelt, mince, rock,* and *musk.*

Vowel Digraphs

When two vowels come together in a word, the first vowel is usually long and the second is silent. This is especially true with the *oa, ee,* and *ay* combinations. Some age-appropriate examples are *float, fleet,* and *bray.*

The VCE (Final E) Generalization

When two vowels appear in a word and one is an /*e*/ at the end of the word, the first vowel is usually long and the final *e* is silent. Examples are *rave, scene, chime, cloze,* and *dupe.*

The CV Pattern

When a consonant is followed by a vowel, the vowel usually produces a long sound. This pattern is especially well-illustrated in two- or three-letter words such as *we* and *go.*

R-Controlled Vowels

As already noted, vowels that appear before the letter *r* usually are neither long nor short but have a sound that is altered by the *r* that follows it. Some age-appropriate examples are *intern, pastor, pirogue,* and *urchin.*

Types of Phonic Analysis

There are two main types of phonic analysis—*analytic* and *synthetic phonic analysis.* In analytic phonic analysis the entire word is analyzed by first dividing it into syllables, then analyzing each syllable using the appropriate phonic elements, and finally placing the entire word together. This is an example of going from a whole to parts and is the most appropriate way to use phonics with content words in grades 5 to 12. In contrast, synthetic phonic analysis begins with individual phonic elements and attempts to construct the entire word from these individual elements. It normally is not effective.

STRATEGIES AND ACTIVITIES FOR IMPROVING BASIC PHONIC SKILLS

The chapter now offers a sampling of classroom-tested strategies and activities for improving basic phonic skills. Although all of them are helpful in grades 5 to 12, you should modify any of them in light of the needs and interests of your own students.

Many of the strategies included in this section of the chapter are applicable with any phonic element, but a few are better suited for one of the following phonic analysis subskills: strategies for general phonics instruction, strategies for long vowel sounds, strategies for short vowel sounds, strategies for the schwa ə sound, and strategies for using rimes and analogies. Use your judgment in making this determination.

Cross-Checking Word Identification Strategies

It is crucial that students in grades 5 to 12 learn the value of *cross-checking word identification* strategies by using more than one *cueing system.* Although structural analysis usually is a more important cueing system for older students than phonic analysis, it is a good idea for students to analyze phonetically the words that they have already divided into syllables. Students can identify a number of words by thinking about what word would make sense in a sentence and then noticing whether the initial consonant or consonant blend in that word matches the word they are thinking about.

Often ability to use the initial consonants in a word along with the context is the most important decoding strategy. A student should do two things simultaneously—think about the syllables and the letters and sounds in the word, and think about what word would make sense in context. Many students, especially those with reading or learning disabilities, use one or the other but not both strategies. Thus, some students may guess an unknown word, supplying a word that makes some sense in context, whereas others guess a word that begins with the correct consonant but makes no sense in the sentence.

Sound-Sense Strategy

The *sound-sense strategy* (1981) is a useful strategy that should be taught to all students in grades 5 to 12 if they do not already use it. Teach the student to pause briefly at an unknown word and then follow these steps:

- Skip the unknown word and read to the end of the sentence.
- Return to the unknown word and associate appropriate sounds for its initial and final letters.
- Return to the beginning of the sentence and reread, attempting to identify the unknown word.

Word Rubber Banding

Word rubber banding is a simple technique that can be used to help students pronounce unknown printed words. The teacher may demonstrate rubber banding by saying: "Stretch the word like a rubber band . . . and listen to the sounds. . . . What sounds do you hear?" (Calkins, 1986, p. 174). Students always should begin by using context as the first word identification strategy in determining what word makes sense in the material they are reading. By stretching the word out phoneme by phoneme—or more preferably in grades 5 to 12, by onsets and rimes or by syllables—sound clues are provided that help students determine unknown words.

Topic Word Boards

Teachers can reserve one of the bulletin boards in their rooms for use as a *topic word board.* Here's how to do it. Display some pictures that are related to a thematic unit in social studies or science and tell students that you want them to find large content-related words that are needed to learn about this topic. Leave a supply of colored index cards next to the board, and as you and your students explore the unit, ask them for suggestions of topic-related words to add to the collection. When students suggest words, have them explain why that word is particularly important to the topic. Write the words that the class decides belong in the collection with a black, permanent marker.

As you and the students explore the topic, call attention periodically to a target word when it is used in discussion, reading, or writing. Help students focus on the spelling of the target words by having them chant the spelling of the words in cheerleader style with you. Then have them close their eyes and chant the spelling again. Have students use as many of the target words as possible in a sentence that makes reasonable sense. Help students develop positive attitudes toward learning large content-related words by telling them that every content area has a number of critical words that are required for effective comprehension in that field.

RIVET

Although RIVET (Cunningham, 2000) was described in detail in Chapter Two, it is briefly reviewed here since this technique is as useful in phonic analysis as it is in sight word identification.

Very briefly, the RIVET strategy involves selecting six to eight important words from a content reading assignment. Here's how to do it. Write numbers and draw underlines on the chalkboard to indicate how many letters each word has. Have the students then fill in the letters to the first word one at a time, encouraging them to guess what the entire word is as soon as they can. Continue, having them complete all the blanks in each target word in the content assignment. Finally, have the students use the target words to predict some of the events in the story. Encourage divergent predictions; ask the students questions that lead them to consider various possibilities. (For more detail on this strategy, see Chapter Two.)

Word Detectives

Cunningham (2000) has suggested another interesting strategy called *word detectives* that can be used with students in grades 5 to 12. She stressed that teachers should emphasize these questions with their students:

"Do you know any other words that look and sound like this word?"

"Are any of these look-alike/sound-alike words related to each other?"

According to Cunningham, the answer to the first question should help students pronounce and spell a word, while the answer to the second question should help students discover what, if any, meaning relationships exist between the unknown word and words they already know.

For example, students in a science class may encounter the following unknown word: *pollution.*

The teacher and some students provide examples of pollution, which helps to build meaning for the concept. Then the teacher asks the students to pronounce *pollution* and try to think of other words that look like it and sound like it. The students may mention the following words: *multiplication, nation, pollute, equation, vacation.*

The teacher then lists the words, underlining the parts that look the same. The students pronounce the words, emphasizing the part that is pronounced in the same way. The teacher then points out to the students that thinking of a word that looks and sounds the same as the new word helps them to remember how to pronounce the new word and also helps them spell it. Next, the teacher explains that not all words that look and sound alike are related.

Throughout the school day, students encounter many new words. Because English is a morphologically related language, most new words can be connected to other words by their spelling and pronunciation, and many new words have meaning-related words already known to the students. Some students who are word-sensitive become word detectives on their own—they notice patterns and use them to learn and retrieve words. Other students, however, try to pronounce, spell, and associate meaning with each of these words as separate entities. Asking the two critical questions that were mentioned earlier takes only a few minutes in the introduction of key content vocabulary and can help many students become word detectives.

The Wheel

The popular television game show *Wheel of Fortune* is based on the idea that meaning and a few letters can allow a person to guess many words. In this game, meaning is provided by the category the words belong to. A variation of this game can be used to introduce polysyllabic words and teach students to use meaning and all the letters that they know to determine a word. Very briefly, here is how students play *The Wheel.*

Tell students that they can figure out words when they are unable to see all of its parts if they think about what word might make sense and whether it has parts that they know in the proper places. Ask students if they know how to play the television game *Wheel of Fortune,* and then tell them that this is how the *teacher's version* is played:

1. Students guess all the letters without considering if they are consonants or vowels.

2. Students must have *all* the letters filled in before they can say the word. (This encourages them to learn to spell.)

3. Students win some type of tokens instead of expensive prizes.

To begin, write the category for the game on the chalkboard and draw blanks for each letter.

Have a student begin by asking: "Is there a . . . ?"

If the student guesses a correct letter, fill that letter in. Give the student one token for each time that letter occurs in the puzzle. Let the student continue to guess letters until he or she gets a "no" response. When a student asks for a letter that is not there, write the letter above the puzzle and then go on to the next student.

Be sure that all the letters are filled in before anyone is allowed to guess the word. Give the student who correctly guesses the word five bonus tokens. If a student says the answer out of turn, award the bonus tokens to the student whose turn he or she has taken. The student who has the most tokens at the end of the game is the winner.

Here is an example of how to play *The Wheel.* The teacher draws eleven blanks on the chalkboard and says: "The category is science, and the first word has eleven letters. Allison, please guess a letter."

_ _ _ _ _ _ _ _ _ _ _

Allison asks for an *n*. There is no *n*, so the teacher calls on Mike who asks for an *f*. There is no *f*, either. Next Latasha asks for and gets an *s*.

s _ _ _ _ _ _ _ _ _ _

Latasha has another turn and ask for a *d*.

s _ d _ _ _ _ _ _ _ _

Next, she asks for a *y*.

s _ d _ _ _ _ _ _ _ y

Then Latasha asks for a *p*. There is no *p*, so Lucy has a turn and asks for an *m*. Then Lucy asks for an *e*.

s e d _ m e _ _ _ _ y

Finally Lucy asks for an *i, n, t, a,* and *r.* Lucy wins the game by correctly spelling and pronouncing the word *sedimentary*. If you wish, bonus points can be given a student who uses the target word correctly in a sentence.

Making Words

Choose eight to twelve content words and prepare sets of letter cards for the *making words activity* (Gunning, 1995). Then have students use the letter cards to practice spelling words and review spelling patterns and rules. Students arrange and rearrange the cards to spell one-letter words, two-letter words, three-letter words, and so forth until they use all the letters to spell the *original word.*

With students in grades 5 to 12, teachers should select words from thematic units for this activity. For example, during a unit on the Civil War, one fifth-grade teacher selected the word *confederate,* and the students spelled these words:

One-letter words: *a*
Two-letter words: *on, to, at, an, no, do*
Three-letter words: *ate, ton, can, fan, Dan, tan, rat, cat, fat*
Four-letter words: *done, rate, fate, tear, neat, race, date, cane, coat, fade, feat, fond*
Five-letter words: *canoe, cadet, frond, trade, fetor*
Six-letter words: *nectar, recent, redact, trance, finder, contra, cornea, fedora*
Seven-letter words: *refence*
Eight-letter words: *federate, conferee*
Entire target word: *confederate*

Have students manipulate the letter cards to spell the words. Then list them on the chart, beginning with the one-letter words, and making increasingly longer words until the students have used all of the letters to spell *confederate.* As students work, they can consult dictionaries to check the spelling of possible words and to present their case for including a certain word on the chart. In this activity students manipulate many different spelling patterns and review various phonic elements, rhyming words, and homophones as well as prefixes and suffixes. (These elements of structural analysis are discussed in Chapter Four.)

Word Sorts

Students can use *word sorts* to explore, compare, and contrast word features as they sort a pack of word cards. Teachers can prepare word cards so that students can sort them into categories depending on their spelling patterns or other criteria (Bear, Invernizzi, Templeton, and Johnson, 1996). When teachers tell students what categories they should use, it is called a *closed word sort.* When students must determine the categories for themselves, it is an *open word sort.* In general, an open word sort is more difficult because students must discover the categories for themselves.

Students can sort the word cards and then return them to an envelope to be used later. Word cards can be sorted in a variety of ways, such as by spelling patterns (CVC, CVCe, CVVC, CVV); words having the schwa sound; words containing an r-controlled vowel; and words containing onsets and rimes.

Proofreading

Proofreading is a very valuable strategy to help older students notice certain phonic elements and spelling. Proofreading is a special kind of reading that students use to locate misspelled words and other mechanical errors in rough drafts of writing, whether they wrote the material themselves or someone else did.

In-depth instruction about how to proofread to locate spelling errors and then correct these errors leads to both improved spelling and an awareness of phonic elements. Teachers can provide mini-lessons in which students learn to proofread sample student papers and mark the misspelled words. Then, working with a partner or partners, students can correct the misspelled words, noticing phonic elements as they do so.

Making and Writing Words Using Letter Patterns

Readers use *letter patterns* to help them decode words they do not know (Adams, 1990). The basic patterns that students use are the parts of syllables called *onsets* (initial consonants, consonant blends, or consonant digraphs) and *rimes* (the vowel and the succeeding consonants in a syllable). The other common patterns in English that are useful in decoding and understanding words are prefixes, suffixes, inflected endings, and derivations (all discussed in Chapter Four).

Making and writing words with letter patterns (Rasinski and Padik, 2001) is a very useful activity for students in grades 5 to 12. Instead of individual letters, older students should use onsets, rimes, and patterns. This activity helps them develop a greater awareness of onsets, rimes, and other patterns in the unknown words that they encounter in their content reading. Because onsets and rimes are more complex than individual letters, using them helps older students deal with the longer, more complex words that they encounter in their content reading.

The form that follows can be used to simplify the MWW-LP process. Before going ahead with this activity, the teacher should identify the onsets, rimes, and other patterns to be stressed. One of the most effective ways to do this is to begin with a long word that contains several onsets and rimes. List them in the appropriate boxes. Then add other onsets, rimes, and patterns to create many words of one, two, three, or more syllables. You will find a comprehensive list of rimes in Fry, Kress, and Fountoukidis (2000, pp. 31–41). See the "Works Cited" section at the end of this chapter for complete publishing information.

When the patterns and words to be used are found and planned in the correct order, students should be given a copy of the form, and this activity can begin. In the example shown here, the multisyllabic word *cataract;* the onsets *c, r,* and *t;* the rimes *-at, -act, -age, -ave, -est, -oad, -oop, -ug;* and the prefix *re-* are used.

Then students can make the words shown in the figure. If you want, you can list the words with semantic clues, although in many cases students should make the words after simply hearing them. Students write the words in the appropriate boxes on the blank form as they are pronounced. After students finish writing about and discussing their words, the teacher proceeds to the transfer section of the MWW-LP form. At this point, the teacher asks students to use their recently learned knowledge of word parts to make and write new words. The new words contain some of the word parts and patterns, but not all of them.

Onsets	Rimes	Prefix
c, r, t	-at, -act, -age, -ave, -est, -oad, -oop, -ug	re-

1 cat	2 rat	3 tat	4 react	5 rest
6 test	7 cave	8 toad	9 rave	10 cage
11 coop	12 tug	13 rug	14 crave	15 troop
16 crane	17 crest	18 tact	19 road	

In the final part of the MWW-LP process, the teacher encourages students to cut out each of the words from the blank MWW-LP form. The word cards are then placed in an envelope and for the next several days students practice the words with a partner, play games with the word cards, and participate in word sort activities. The word sort categories can include rime (word family), number of syllables, words that have one meaning and words that do not, words that have positive connotations and words that have negative connotations, and words that describe things.

In summary, MWW-LP is a good activity for older students who must decode longer and more complex words than students in the lower grades. It allows them to examine the structure of specialized terms, providing them with strategies for decoding these more difficult words.

Hinks Pinks

Hinks Pinks is a highly motivating strategy to use in teaching or reviewing onsets and rimes. These are rhyming pairs that students like to make up, illustrate, and then use to solve riddles. Teachers also like them because they stress the spelling pattern-rhyme relationships (onsets—rimes) and provide students with a real purpose for searching for and manipulating onsets and rimes. Hinks Pinks is probably most appropriate in the fifth and sixth grades, and especially with students who have learning or reading disabilities.

Here are examples of Hinks Pinks that you can use in your classroom. However, students are motivated to construct many of their own Hinks Pinks after they understand their purpose and have started doing so.

loose moose	fake snake	slim Kim	light night
goat coat	spring swing	plump lump	round mound
cute flute	bold gold	pink mink	wide bride
sell bell	green queen	lean Jean	tan bran
tall mall	brain drain	quaint paint	pale whale

Secret Messages

Have students create *secret messages* by substituting onsets in familiar words and then putting the newly constructed words together to make a secret message (QuanSing, 1995). In addition to being motivating, secret messages help students focus on the onsets and rimes in words and improves their comprehension. Once students become familiar with this procedure, they can construct their own secret messages either individually or with a partner or partners. This activity probably is most appropriate in grades 5 and 6, especially with students who have learning and reading disabilities. Here is a sample secret message:

1. Take *r* from *rake* and substitute *J.*
2. Take *th* from *thought* and substitute *b.*
3. Take *h* from *hive* and substitute *f.*
4. Take *g* from *gong* and substitute *str.*
5. Take *sh* from *shine* and substitute *sw.*

Answer: Jake bought five strong swine.

Discovering the Code

Students in middle school may enjoy an activity that emphasizes *discovering a code.* In this activity each consonant or vowel in a sentence, paragraph, or passage is replaced by a number, and the student has to interpret the material by substituting the correct letter in the material.

Here is the code that is used in the following example: a = 1, e = 2, i = 3, o = 4, u = 5, y (used as a vowel) = 6, w (used as a vowel) = 7.

> J41n w45ld l3k2 t4 b2 1n 1str4n15t wh2n sh2 gr1d51t2s fr4m c4ll2g2. (Joan would like to be an astronaut when she graduates from college.)

Variability Strategy

It is important that students learn to be *flexible* in their decoding. They should be taught the following *variability strategy.*

- First try the main pronunciation of the letter—the one that the letter usually stands for.
- If the common pronunciation gives a word that is not a real word or does not make sense in the sentence, then try the other pronunciation.
- If you still get a word that is not a real word or does not make sense in the sentence, ask for help.

Interpreting Phonetic Spellings

Students in grades 5 to 12 are required to interpret the phonetic spellings that are found in dictionaries and the glossaries of their content textbooks. Some of the phonetic spellings are difficult for both average and above-average readers at this level, so obviously they will be even more difficult for students with learning or reading disabilities. Students must have considerable practice before they become adept at interpreting phonetic symbols. Nevertheless, they must master the skill in order to be able to use dictionaries and glossaries effectively.

Unfortunately, it is often very difficult to motivate students to search a dictionary or textbook glossary for the pronunciation or spelling of unknown words that they meet while reading. Usually it is most effective to coordinate mini-lessons in interpreting phonetic spellings with a student's actual reading assignments in a content area such as social studies or science.

The following words, selected from intermediate-grade science, clearly illustrate the difficulty in interpreting phonetic spellings and the necessity for providing students with meaningful instruction and review of this element of phonic analysis.

biome	'bī - ōm
dendrite	'den - drīt
osmosis	äz - 'mō - səs
malignant	ma - 'lig - nənt
igneous	'ig - nē - əs

Reproducible Activity Sheets for Improving Phonic Analysis

Chapter Three now contains six reproducible activity sheets for improving specific skills in phonic analysis. You can duplicate and use them in their present form or modify them in any way you wish based on the needs and interests of your students. In addition, they may also serve as models for you in constructing similar activity sheets to reinforce phonic elements.

The activity sheets included here are Providing a Word That Says It Better—Eighth-Grade Level; Completing a Torn Grocery Shopping List—Sixth-Grade Level; Discovering a Secret Code—Fifth-Grade Level; Changing One Letter at a Time to Make a Different Word—Fifth-Grade Level; Finding Food Words with Double Letters— Sixth-Grade Level; and Short Story with All Vowels Deleted—Seventh-Grade Level.

Answer Key for Providing a Word That Says It Better

Note: The following are examples of possible answers. Use your own judgment in determining if an answer is correct. 1. exclaimed, muttered, explained, opined, requested, suggested, murmured, pleaded, stated, reminded; 2. attractive, pretty, lovely, beautiful, appealing, charming, engaging, winsome, pleasing, wistful; 3. wonderful, magnificent, fabulous, monumental, keen, marvelous, stupendous, special, fantastic, unique; 4. tiny, minute, minuscule, trivial, petite, miniature; 5. virtuous, kind, respectable, pleasing, pleasant, agreeable, well-bred, correct, cooperative, likeable; 6. cantankerous, ignoble, small-minded, sordid, contemptible, cranky, crabby, unpleasant, disagreeable; 7. gigantic, humongous, imposing, preeminent, pretentious, magnanimous, imposing, generous; 8. marvelous, astonishing, admirable, awesome, wondrous, astounding, amazing, incredible, miraculous, phenomenal; 9. rotund, portly, heavy, obese, plump, copious, overweight, well-endowed; 10. amusement, enjoyment, pleasure, gratifying, satisfying, rewarding

Answer Key for Completing a Torn Grocery Shopping List

1. bananas; 2. milk; 3. popcorn; 4. potato(es); 5. apple(s); 6. steak; 7. butter; 8. oatmeal; 9. raisins; 10. oranges; 11. bread; 12. beans; 13. lettuce; 14. cauliflower; 15. mustard; 16. soda; 17. catsup; 18. sugar; 19. soup; 20. carrots; 21. broccoli; 22. liver; 23. pickles; 24. yogurt; 25. coffee

Answer Key for Discovering a Secret Code

1 = a; 2 = e; 3 = i; 4 = o; 5 = u; 6 = y (used as a vowel)

Answer Key for Changing One Letter at a Time to Make a Different Word

1. mint: *mine nine nice rice;* 2. welt: *wilt wild weld held;* 3. pant: *pane pine mine mane;* 4. mass: *mast fast fist fish;* 5. send: *sent seat seal meal;* 6. time: *tame lame lamp lump;* 7. slid: *slip slap flap flat;* 8. chop: *chap slap clam cram;* 9. mall: *pall pail sail said;* 10. swim: *slim slam slap slip*

Answer Key for Finding Food Words with Double Letters

Note: The following are possible answers; students may come up with additional foods containing double letters. The answers are presented here in random order: beets, apples, lettuce, cabbage, broccoli, eggs, butter, mushrooms, pepper, walleye (pike), cottage cheese, pudding, pizza, cookies, rolls, dressing, cranberries, blueberries, strawberries, boysenberries, gooseberries, jelly roll, jelly, marshmallows, applesauce, pineapple, chicken noodle soup, cherries.

Answer Key for Short Story with All Vowels Deleted

The bald eagle is the national emblem of the United States. An adult eagle has a blackish-brown back and breast; a white head, neck, and tail; and yellow feet and beak. It is easily recognizable since there are no other large black birds in North America with a white head and tail.

Bald eagles weigh from 10 to 14 pounds and have a wingspan from 72 to 90 inches. Even though wild bald eagles may live as long as thirty years, the average life expectancy is about fifteen to twenty years.

A bald eagle has a high tolerance to cold since its skin is protected by feathers lined with down. Its feet also are cold resistant since they are mostly tendon. The outside of the beak is mainly nonliving material with little blood supply. Although a bald eagle's beak is a strong weapon, it also is delicate enough to feed a small portion of food to a newly hatched chick.

Although eagles mate for life, if its mate dies, the surviving eagle often accepts a new mate. The shrill, high pitched call may be a way of reinforcing the bond between a male and female eagle and to warn other eagles and predators that an area is defended.

North American Native Americans believe a single eagle feather conveys great power and have used eagle feathers in their ceremonies and legends.

Name ________________________ **Grade** ___ **Teacher** ____________ **Date** _________

Providing a Word That Says It Better

Students often use words in their writing that are *overworked* or *uninteresting*. Your writing will be much more interesting if you use longer, more descriptive terms. This activity sheet contains 10 *overworked words*. Write as many words that mean almost the same thing as you can to replace each of the overworked words. Consult a dictionary or thesaurus for help, and use the *phonetic spellings* if necessary to help you pronounce the new words. You can work with a partner or partners if you want.

1. said

____

____

2. cute

____

____

3. great

____

____

4. little

____

____

5. nice

____

____

6. mean

____

____

7. big

____

____

8. wonderful

____

____

9. fat

____

____

10. fun

____

____

Name ______________________ Grade ___ Teacher ____________ Date _________

Completing a Torn Grocery Shopping List

Many shoppers make a list before they go grocery shopping. Pretend that your parent's grocery list was torn in several places right after you arrived at the supermarket. Only a few letters from each item to be purchased are left on the list. Write the name of each item on the list in the blank space beside it. *Note:* No brand names are contained on the list. You can work with a partner or partners if you want to.

1. anas ____________________
2. lk ____________________
3. popc ____________________
4. tato ____________________
5. app ____________________
6. ste ____________________
7. tter ____________________
8. atmea ____________________
9. rai ____________________
10. anges ____________________
11. ead ____________________
12. bea ____________________
13. ttuc ____________________
14. aulifl ____________________
15. must ____________________
16. sod ____________________
17. atsu ____________________
18. gar ____________________
19. up ____________________
20. arro ____________________
21. broc ____________________
22. liv ____________________
23. ickl ____________________
24. yog ____________________
25. ffe ____________________

Name ____________________ Grade ___ Teacher ____________ Date _________

Discovering a Secret Code

The following passage is written *in code.* All of the *vowels,* except those found in proper nouns, have been replaced by *numbers.* Read the *entire passage* silently and try to determine which numbers correspond to each of the vowels: *a, e, i, o, u,* and *y (used as a vowel).* Write the correct vowel next to the numbers listed underneath the coded passage. You can work with a partner or partners if you want to.

The Golden Retriever

Th2 g4ld2n r2tr32v2r 3s 1 r2l1t3v2l6 y45ng br22d 1nd 4n16 d1t2s 1s f1r b1ck 1s th2 m3d-19th c2nt5r6. D2v214p2d b6 Lord Tweedmouth n21r th2 English-Scottish b4rd2r, th2 g4ld2n c4mb3n2s th2 bl44d 4f 1 r2tr32v2r, Tweed w1t2r sp1n32l, s2tt2r, 1nd s1nd6-c4l4r2d bl44dh45nd.

Th2 g4ld2n r2tr32v2r 3s 1 p4p5l1r br22d d52 t4 3ts v2ry fr32ndl6, w2ll-m1nn2r2d n1t5r2. 3t d42s w2ll 3n 4b2d32nc2 tr13n3n 1nd 3s 1r2l31bl2 h5nt3ng d4g. Th2 g4ld2n 3s 1ls4 h1pp6 3n 23th2r 5rban 4r r5r1l 1r21s 3f 3t g2ts 3n45gh 45td44rs 2x2rc3s2. 3t 3s 1 w4nd2rf5l d4g 1r45nd ch3ldr2n 1nd r21ll6 2nj46s pl163ng w3th th2m.

Th2 g4ld2n h1s 1 w1tt2r-r2p2ll2nt c41t w3th 1 m4d2r1t2 5nd2rc41t. Th2 t2xt5r2 4f th2 c41t 3s n23th2r s3lk6 n4r c41rs2 1nd c1n b2 w1vy b5tl32s fl1t. 1 g4ld2n sh45ld b2 br5sh2d 4n 1 r2g5l1r b1s3s. 1lth45gh th2 g4ld2n r2t32v2r 3s c4ns3d2r2d 1 sp4rt3ng d4g b6 th2 American Kennel Club, 3t m1k2s 1n 3d21l c4mp1n34n f4r n21rl6 2v2r64n2 3ncl5d3ng p24pl2 wh4 h1v2 1 d3s1b3l3t6.

Now write the vowel letter that corresponded to each number in the passage "The Golden Retriever."

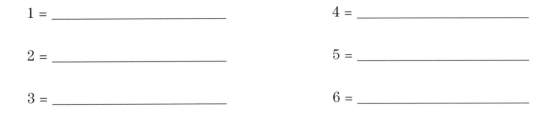

1 = ____________________ 4 = ____________________

2 = ____________________ 5 = ____________________

3 = ____________________ 6 = ____________________

Name ______________ Grade ___ Teacher ____________ Date _________

Changing One Letter at a Time to Make a Different Word

Changing only one letter at a time, the word *hold* becomes *file.* Starting with *hold* the word changes to *hole,* then to *pole,* then to *pile,* and finally to *file.* Here are ten words and the words that they will become four steps later. Write the changes, in order, in the four blank spaces that follow each target word. You may work with a partner or partners if you wish.

1. Change *mint* to *rice.*

   ________ ________ ________ ________

2. Change *welt* to *held.*

   ________ ________ ________ ________

3. Change *pant* to *mane.*

   ________ ________ ________ ________

4. Change *mass* to *fish.*

   ________ ________ ________ ________

5. Change *send* to *meal.*

   ________ ________ ________ ________

6. Change *time* to *lump.*

   ________ ________ ________ ________

7. Change *slid* to *flat.*

   ________ ________ ________ ________

8. Change *chop* to *cram.*

   ________ ________ ________ ________

9. Change *mall* to *said.*

   ________ ________ ________ ________

10. Change *swim* to *slip.*

   ________ ________ ________ ________

Name ________________________ Grade ___ Teacher ____________ Date __________

Finding Food Words with Double Letters

The names of some foods we eat contain double letters: *carrots,* for example. Write the names of as many foods containing double letters as you can. If you are able to write down *thirty,* you are a genius! If you can find *twenty-five,* that is excellent, and *twenty* is very good. If you get stumped, work with a partner or partners.

1. ______________________
2. ______________________
3. ______________________
4. ______________________
5. ______________________
6. ______________________
7. ______________________
8. ______________________
9. ______________________
10. ______________________
11. ______________________
12. ______________________
13. ______________________
14. ______________________
15. ______________________
16. ______________________
17. ______________________
18. ______________________
19. ______________________
20. ______________________
21. ______________________
22. ______________________
23. ______________________
24. ______________________
25. ______________________
26. ______________________
27. ______________________
28. ______________________
29. ______________________
30. ______________________

Name ______________________ Grade ___ Teacher ____________ Date _________

Short Story with All Vowels Deleted

This activity sheet contains a passage about the American bald eagle. Read the passage silently and *print each omitted vowel in it.* Vowels are not omitted in proper nouns in this passage. You can consult a dictionary if you wish. You also may work with a partner or partners if you like. Reread the entire passage when you are finished to make sure that it is completely correct.

The American Bald Eagle

Th_ b_ld _ _gl_ _s th_ n_t_ _n_l _mbl_m _f th_ United States. _n _d_lt _ _gl_ h_s _ bl_ck_sh-br_ _n b_ck _nd br_ _st; _ wh_t_ h_ _d, n_ck, _nd t_ _l; _nd y_ll_ _ f_ _t _nd b_ _k. _t _s _ _s_l_ r_c_gn_z_bl_ s_nc_ th_r_ _r_ n_ _th_r l_rg_ bl_ck b_rds _n North America w_th _ wh_t_ h_ _d _nd t_ _l.

B_ld _ _gl_s w_ _gh fr_m 10 t_ 14 p_ _nds _nd h_v_ _ w_ngsp_n fr_m 72 t_ 90 _nch_s. _v_n th_ _gh w_ld b_ld _ _gl_s m_y l_v_ _s l_ng _s th_rt_ y_ _rs, th_ _v_r_g_ l_fe _xp_ct_anc_ _s _b_ _t f_ft_ _n t_ tw_nt_ _ _ _rs.

_ b_ld _ _gl_ h_s _ h_gh t_l_r_nc_ t_ c_ld s_nc_ _ts sk_n _s pr_t_ct_d b_ f_ _th_rs l_n_d w_th d_ _n. _ts f_ _t _ls_ _r_ c_ld r_s_st_nt s_nc_ th_ _ _r_ m_stl_ t_nd_n. Th_ _ _ts_d_ _f th_ b_ _k _s m_ _nl_ n_nl_v_ng m_t_r_ _l w_th l_ttl_ bl_ _d s_ppl_. _lth_ _gh _ b_ld _ _gl_'s b_ _k _s _ str_ng w_ _p_n, _t _ls_ _s d_l_c_t_ _n_ _gh t_ f_ _d _ sm_ll p_rt_ _n _f f_ _d t_ _ n_ _l_ h_tch_d ch_ck.

lth _gh _ _gl_s m_t_ f_r l_f_, _f _ts m_t_ d_ _s, th_ s_rv_v_ng _ _gl_ _ft_n _cc_pts _ n_ _ m_t_. Th_ shr_ll, h_gh p_tch_d c_ll m_y b_ _ w_ _ _f r_ _nf_rc_ng th_ b_nd b_tw_ _n _ m_l_ _nd f_m_le _ _gl_ _ _d t_ w_rn _th_r _ _gl_s _nd pr_d_t_rs th_t _n _r_ _ _s d_f_nd_d.

North American Native Americans b_l_ _v_ _ s_ngl_ _ _gl_ f_ _th_r c_nv_ _s gr_ _t p_w_r _nd h_v_ _s_d _ _gl_ f_ _th_rs _n th_ _r c_r_m_n_ _s _nd l_g_nds.

For Additional Reading

Allen, H., Barbe, W., and Levesque, M. *Ready-to-Use Vocabulary, Word Attack, and Comprehension Activities: Sixth-Grade Reading Level* (pp. 88–107). Paramus, N.J.: Center for Applied Research in Education, 1998.

Cunningham, P. *Phonics They Use: Words for Reading and Writing.* White Plains, N.Y.: Longman, 2000.

Fry, E., Kress, J., and Foutoukidis, D. *The Reading Teacher's Book of Lists* (4th ed.). San Francisco: Jossey-Bass, 2000.

Gaskins, I., Cress, C., O'Hara, C., and Donnelly, K. *Benchmark Word Identification/Vocabulary Development Program.* Media, Penn.: Benchmark School, 1986.

Gunning, T. *Building Words: A Resource Manual for Teaching Word Analysis and Spelling Strategies.* Needham Heights, Mass.: Allyn and Bacon, 2001.

Heilman, A. *Phonics in Proper Perspective.* Upper Saddle River, N.J.: Prentice Hall/Merrill, 1998.

Heilman, A., Blair, T., and Rupley, W. *Principles and Practices of Teaching Reading* (pp. 163–181). Upper Saddle River, N.J.: Prentice Hall/Merrill, 1998.

Hull, M., and Fox, B. *Phonics for the Teacher of Reading.* Upper Saddle River, N.J.: Prentice Hall/Merrill, 1998. (This is an excellent self-instruction manual for teachers and tutors who want to learn common phonic elements and rules.)

May, F. *Reading as Communication* (pp. 173–203). Upper Saddle River, N.J.: Prentice Hall/Merrill, 1998.

Miller, W. *Phonics First! Ready-to-Use Phonics Worksheets for the Intermediate Grades.* San Francisco: Jossey-Bass, 2001.

Rasinski, T., and Padak, N. *From Phonics to Fluency.* White Plains, N.Y.: Longman, 2001.

Rinsky, L. *Teaching Word Recognition Skills.* Upper Saddle River, N.J.: Gorsuch Scarisbrick, 1997.

Tompkins, G. *Literacy for the 21st Century* (pp. 172–181). Upper Saddle River, N.J.: Prentice Hall/Merrill, 2001.

Vacca, J., Vacca, R., and Gove, M. *Reading and Learning to Read* (pp. 277–290). New York: HarperCollins, 1995.

Wilson, R., and Hall, M. *Programmed Word Attack for Teachers.* Upper Saddle River, N.J.: Prentice Hall/Merrill, 1997.

Works Cited in Chapter Three

Adams, M. *Beginning to Read: Thinking and Learning About Print.* Cambridge, Mass.: MIT Press, 1990.

Bear, D., Invernizzi, M., Templeton, S., and Johnson, R. *Words Their Way: Word Study for Phonics, Vocabulary, and Spelling Instruction.* Upper Saddle River, N.J.: Prentice Hall/Merrill, 1996.

Calkins, L. *The Art of Teaching Writing.* Portsmouth, N.H.: Heinemann, 1986.

Cunningham, P. *Phonics They Use: Words for Reading and Writing* (pp. 147–150). White Plains, N.Y.: Longman, 2000.

Fry, E., Kress, J., and Foutoukidis, D. *The Reading Teacher's Book of Lists* (4th ed.). San Francisco: Jossey-Bass, 2000.

Gunning, T. "Word Building: A Strategic Approach to the Teaching of Phonics." *Reading Teacher,* 1995, *48,* 484–488.

Heilman, A., Blair, T., and Rupley, W. *Principles and Practices of Teaching* Reading (p. 175). Upper Saddle River, N.J.: Prentice Hall/Merrill, 1998.

May, F., and Elliot, S. *To Help Children Read: Mastery Performance Models for Teachers in Training.* Upper Saddle River, N.J.: Prentice Hall/Merrill, 1978.

QuanSing, J. "Developmental Teaching and Learning Using Developmental Continua as Maps of Language and Literacy Development Which Links Assessment to Teaching." Paper presented at the annual meeting of the International Reading Association. Anaheim, Calif., May 1995.

Rasinski, T., and Padak, N. *From Phonics to Fluency* (pp. 90–94). White Plains, N.Y.: Longman, 2001.

Sound-Sense Strategy. Boston: Houghton Mifflin, 1981.

Strategies and Activities for Improving Basic Word Structure Skills in Content Reading

Can you identify this fairly uncommon word—*megalomania*? If you know that the prefix "mega" means "large," then you probably can infer that *megalomania* is a person's desire to perform in a great or grandiose manner. If you are able to do this, you are using word structure to help identify the word. In contrast, if you see this word in the following sentence, you may be able to determine its meaning from its context: *Since Richard passionately believes that he is far superior to anyone else in everything he does, he may be a person who has a degree of megalomania.* A reader may not be able to pronounce this word correctly, but often the pronunciation is not as important as determining the word's approximate meaning. Structural analysis is often most effective when it is combined with phonic analysis and context.

Chapter Four is designed to help reading teachers, reading tutors, and special education teachers understand the elements of structural analysis and how to present and reinforce it most effectively in grades 5 to 12. Word structure is especially effective at these levels. It often helps students both to determine the meaning of words and to analyze them successfully. The chapter first briefly describes how to use word structure in content reading. It then provides lists of common Greek and Latin word roots and their meanings, common prefixes and their meanings, and common suffixes and their meanings. A list of common syllable and accent generalizations and a list of compound words that may be used in grades 5 to 12 follow.

The chapter then provides a sampling of classroom-tested strategies to improve structural analysis skills in grades 5 to 12, including using word root webs, using word roots to create new words, studying "borrowed" words from around the world, playing "add the points," and others. The chapter closes with seven classroom-tested reproducible activity sheets to help improve students' basic word structure skills. The chapter will equip teachers to teach these skills effectively.

Structural Analysis Skills in Content Reading

Structural analysis or *word structure analysis* consists of using *word parts* to determine the pronunciation and meaning of an unknown word. It enables a reader to decode an unknown word and determine its meaning by considering word roots, prefixes, suffixes, syllabication, homophones, compound words, and accent. It also includes consideration of free and bound morphemes. This word identification technique is especially effective if it is used together with phonic analysis and context clues. It is particularly helpful for readers in grades 5 to 12 and adults.

Many words that students encounter in grades 5 to 12 are multisyllabic and must be attacked in some way—either by syllabication or "chunking." Usually, it is helpful to remove the prefix and suffix to identify a word. Often the most effective technique in word identification is first to consider context, then analyze the word structure, and finally analyze the phonics.

Structural analysis (analysis of word structure) includes a number of subskills. One is knowledge of *word roots*. In the intermediate grades and higher, students encounter a number of words with Greek or Latin roots. Especially in the area of science, knowing Greek and Latin word roots can significantly help students to read effectively. In addition, knowing word roots can add many words to a student's meaning vocabulary. The roots that are taught to students should be the most common and useful ones. Students who are average or above-average readers often are fascinated by the history of the English language because it provides interesting information about word meanings and spellings (Tompkins and Yaden, 1986; Venezky, 1999).

The English language began in 447 A.D. when the Angles, Saxons, and other Germanic tribes invaded the land we now call England. Anglo-Saxon English was first written down by Latin missionaries around 750 A.D. The language of the period from 450 to 1100 is known as Old English. During this time, it was a very phonetic language and followed many Germanic syntactic patterns. However, the Vikings, who plundered villages along the English coast, also contributed many new words, such as *egg*, *they*, *sky*, *husband*, and *window*.

Middle English (1100–1500) began with the Norman Conquest in 1066, when William, Duke of Normandy, invaded England and became king. William, his lords, and the royals who followed him all spoke French, and that was the language spoken for nearly two hundred years. French became the official language of England. Therefore, many French words came into English, and French spellings took the place of English spellings. In Old English, *niht* was the spelling for *night* and *cwen* was the spelling for *queen*. During this period words also were borrowed from Dutch, Latin, and other languages.

The invention of the printing press marked the transition from the Middle English period to the Modern English period (1500 to the present). William Caxton brought the first printing press to England in 1476, and soon books and pamphlets were being mass-produced. Spelling became standardized as Samuel Johnson and other lexicographers compiled dictionaries. But borrowed words are still being introduced into contemporary English. Chapter Two contains lists of words borrowed from around the world, and you can consult them. New words are added to English continuously from various sources, with some recent examples being *e-mail*, *gigabtye*, *Internet*, *cosmonaut*, *modem*, and *print queue*.

Even though words have entered contemporary English from a variety of sources, the three most common are Old English, Latin, and Greek. Words derived from Old English are usually one- or two-syllable commonly used words, whereas many Latinate words are similar to words in French, Spanish, or Italian. Greek words are the most unusual because many are long, and their spellings seem unfamiliar.

Word Roots

Word roots that should be taught are those that appear often, transfer to other words, and are on the appropriate level of difficulty. A knowledge of word roots can add countless words to a student's general meaning vocabulary, and they usually should be taught inductively. For example, if students do not know the meaning of *fratricide*, the teacher can discuss such known words as *fraternity*, *fraternize*, and *fraternal*. Students should be helped to determine that all these words are related in some way to *brother*.

Gunning (1996) has proposed a useful scope-and-sequence chart for the common word roots.

Grade	Word Root	Meaning	Example
3	graph	write	autograph
	tele	distance	telegram
4	port	carry	import
	saur	lizard	brontosaurus
	phon	sound	phonics
	vid, vis	see	visible
5	ast	star	astronaut
	cred	believe	credible
	duc	lead	educate
	tri	three	trifecta
6	aud	hear	auditorium
	auto	self	autograph
	bi	two	bicycle
	ology	study of	geology
	scrib, script	write	prescription
	therm	heat	thermometer
7	mid	middle	midlevel
	ped	foot	pedestal
	chrono	time	synchronize
	dic	speak	contradict
	hemi	half	hemisphere
	man	hand	manuscript
8	bio	life	biopsy
	geo	earth	geophysics
	mono	one	monologue
	some	group	twosome

The following is a sample list of common word roots and their meanings. For a comprehensive list, consult *The Reading Teacher's Book of Lists* (Fry, Kress, and Fountoukidis, 2000, pp. 106–113).

Word Root	**Meaning**	**Example**
agr	field	agriculture
aqua	water	aquarium
biblio	book	bibliography
chron	time	chronological
cycle	circle, ring	recycle
dic	speak	diction
graph	write	graphite
mar	sea	marine
mater, matr	mother	maternal
miss, mit	send	missile
ped	foot	pedal
phon	sound	telephone
photo	light	photosynthesis
port	carry	porter
psych	mind, soul	psychopath
sci	know	omniscient
scribe, script	write	transcribe
scope	see	periscope
terr	land	terrararium

Prefixes and Suffixes (Affixes) and Morphemes

Another subskill of word structure is attaching a *prefix* or a *suffix (an affix)* to a base or root word to form a derivative. A student can determine the meaning of a number of words simply by knowing the meaning of the *prefix* in those words. Some examples are *benevolent*, *dysfunctional*, *omnipotent*, and *prototype*.

Derivational *suffixes* change the part of speech of a word or its function in some way. Common derivational suffixes may form nouns, as in the words *despotism*, *equestrienne*, *appendicitis*, and *auditorium*. In contrast, some derivational suffixes may form adjectives, as illustrated in the words *loquacious*, *statuesque*, *comatose*, and *tempestuous*. Others change the function of a verb so that it indicates a *person*, as in the words *shipper*, *murderer*, and *farmer*. There are a few derivational *adverbial suffixes*, such as *largely*, *sideways*, and *lengthwise*.

Other suffixes are called *inflectional suffixes*. These indicate grammatical terms and include the plural *-s*, as in *alligators*, the third-person singular *-s* in *strolls*, the present participle *-ing* in *stealing*, the past tense *-ed* in *transported*, the past participle *-en* in *gladden*, the comparisons *-er* and *-est*, as in *shorter* and *shortest*, and *-ly*, as in *rapidly*.

Knowing the *morpheme* also is a subskill in structural analysis. A morpheme is the smallest unit of meaning in language, and it can be either *free* or *bound*. A free morpheme is made up of a group of letters that form a meaningful word, such as *constitution*, *dinosaur*, *republican*, or *computer*. A bound morpheme is made up of a group of letters that cannot stand alone as actual words. Some examples of bound morphemes are the prefix *semi-* as in *semiannual*, the prefix *macro-* as in *macrocosm*, the suffix *-en* as in *frighten*, and the suffix *-mony* as in *matrimony*.

Prefixes

Gunning (1996, p. 140) provides the following scope-and-sequence chart illustrating the most common prefixes taught in grades 5 to 8:

Grade	Prefix	Meaning	Example
5	im-	not	immature
	in-	not	indecisive
	pre-	before	preamble
	sub-	under	subordinate
6	ex-	out, out of	export
	ex-	former	ex-student
	inter-	among, between	intermission
	mis-	not	misunderstand
	mis-	bad	misfortune
7	en-	forms verb	enlarge
	ir-	not	irresponsible
	trans-	across	transatlantic
8	anti-	against	antilock
	pro-	in favor of	pro-American
	super-	above	supernatural

The English language includes a small number of prefixes that are especially worth teaching because of their frequent occurrence. The following list, based on the work of White, Sowell, and Yanagihara (1989), illustrates the most frequently occurring prefixes and the number of words in school writing that contain each one. These prefixes are used in more than twenty-five hundred words, and the four most common—which White and his colleagues call *the big four* (*un-*, *re-*, *in-* [*im-*, *ir-*, *il-*], and *dis-*)—account for about 65% of these words.

Prefix	Number of Words Containing
un-	782
re-	401
in-, im-, ir-, il-	313
dis-	216
en-, em-	132
non-	126
in-, im-	105
over-	98
mis-	83
sub-	80
pre-	79
inter-	77
fore-	76
trans-	47
TOTAL	2,686

Some 88% of prefixed words take the prefixes *sub-*, *pre-*, *inter-*, and *fore-*. White, Sowell, and Yanagihara (1989) found that thirteen prefixes—*un-*, *re-*, *in-*, *im-*, *ir-* (meaning not), *dis-*, *en-*, *em-*, *non-*, *in-*, *im-* (meaning in or into), *over-* (meaning too much), and *mis-*—account for 76% of the prefixed words in the *Word Frequency Book* (Carroll, Davies, and Richman, 1971). An analysis of their word count also would add the prefixes *sub-*, *pre-*, *inter-*, and *fore-* to the recommended list because they occur as frequently as *over-* and *mis-*, thus totaling 88% of words with prefixes.

The following list shows the common prefixes, their meanings, and a word that contains that prefix. Once again, for a comprehensive list, consult *The Reading Teacher's Book of Lists* (Fry, Kress, and Fountoukidis, 2000, pp. 85–92).

Prefix	**Meaning**	**Example**
anti-	against	antifreeze
auto-	self	autoimmune
bene-	good	benefactor
contra-	against	contraband
dis-	not, opposite	dissimilar
dys-	bad	dysentery
hemi-	half	hemisphere
hyper-	excessive	hyperactive
im-, in-	not	impassable
inter-	among, between	inter state
milli-	thousand	milligram
mon-, mono-	one	monocular
multi-	many, much	multimillionaire
non-	not	nonresistant
poly	many	polysyllabic
post-	after	postdate
pre-	before	prelude
pro-	favor	pro-union
pseudo-	false	pseudoclassical
re-	again	reclaim
semi-	half	semiannual
sub-	under, below	submarine
trans-	across	translate
ultra-	beyond	ultraconservative
un-	not	unbeaten
uni-	one	unicorn

Suffixes

Gunning (1996, pp. 142–143) also has provided the following scope-and-sequence chart for common derivational suffixes and the grade level at which they should be presented.

Grade	Suffix	Meaning	Example
5	-ian	one who is in a certain field	optician
	-ic	of; having	historic
	-ish	having the quality of	brownish
	-ive	being	negative
6	-ian	one who	physician
	-ist	a person who	geologist
	-ity	state of	passivity
	-ize	make	terrorize
7	-ar	forms adjective	muscular
	-age	forms noun	pillage
	-ess	female	countess
8	-ary	forms adjective	honorary
	-ette	small	marionette
	-some	forms adjective	irksome

The following is a sample list of suffixes, their meanings, and examples. For a more comprehensive list, again consult Fry, Kress, and Fountoukidis (2000, pp. 93–99).

Suffix	Meaning	Example
-able, -ible	is, can be	perishable
-ar, -er, -or	one who	editor
-acious	inclined to	fallacious
-ance	state or quality of	annoyance
-arian	one who	librarian
-ation, -ition	state or quality of	desperation
-ble	repeated action	mumble
-dom	state or quality of	boredom
-ectomy	surgical removal of	hysterectomy
-ery	state or quality of	slavery
-est	most	quickest
-etic	relating to	poetic
-hood	state or quality of	statehood
-ial, -ian	relating to	remedial
-ide, -ine	chemical compound	peroxide
-ious	state or quality of	ambitious
-ism	doctrine of	communism
-ity, -ty	state or quality of	necessity
-ive	inclined to	positive
-ize	to make	computerize
-ous	full of	wondrous
-phobia	fear of	acrophobia
-some	inclined to	tiresome
-th, -eth	numbers	twentieth
-ular	relating to	singular
-ulent	full of	fraudulent
-uous	state or quality of	sensuous
-ward	direction	backward
-wise	manner, direction	counterclockwise

Syllabication and Accent

Another subskill in word structure analysis is *syllabication.* A syllable is a group of letters that forms a pronunciation unit, and each syllable contains a vowel sound. A vowel sound may form a syllable by itself, as in the word *a/bound.* Only in a syllable that contains a diphthong (*oi, oy, ou, ow, ew*) is there more than one vowel letter. There are two types of syllables: *open* and *closed.* An open syllable ends with a vowel, whereas a closed syllable ends with a consonant. Two examples of open syllables are ***'ce****/ment,* ***'na****/tion;* two examples of closed syllables are ***en'****/code,* ***'mam****/moth.*

Syllables also can be classified as *accented*—where they are given greater stress—or *unaccented*—where they are given lesser stress. Syllabication can be helpful in analyzing an unknown word. However, the accent has a great deal to do with the vowel sound that is heard in a syllable. Multisyllabic words may have primary (strongest), secondary (second strongest), and tertiary (third strongest) accents. The vowel sound in an open accented syllable usually is long (*'flu/id, 'so/da)*; the second syllable in each of these examples is unaccented; and the vowel sound is represented in the schwa (ə) sound that usually is found in unaccented syllables. A single vowel in a closed accented syllable usually has a short sound unless it is influenced by another sound in that syllable: *'cres/cent, 'fris/son.*

Some reading specialists, notably Patrick Groff (1981), recommend dividing unknown words into "chunks of meaning" instead of into traditional syllables because these may be easier to analyze. For example, the word *cotton* traditionally is divided this way: *'cot/ton.* However, a more useful way of dividing it may be *'cott/on.* A number of reading specialists similarly believe that traditional syllabication may not be particularly useful today because computer word-processing systems do not require it for writing.

I believe that the following procedure should be used when a student encounters an unknown word while reading: (1) use context clues; (2) divide the word into "chunks of meaning" or syllables if required; (3) analyze it phonetically if necessary; (4) determine how accent affects the vowel sounds; (5) blend the syllables together to form a word; and (6) place the word back into context to be sure that it makes sense in the sentence. Syllabication is very important in grades 5 to 12 because by far most of the words students meet in reading at those levels are *polysyllabic.*

Here are some generalizations about *syllabication* and *accent* that you may find useful.

- Words contain as many syllables as they have vowel sounds (counting diphthongs as one unit). Here are some examples: *cy/ber'/net/ics, 'el/e/ment,* and *fowl* (the diphthong is treated as a unit).
- In a word with more than one sounded vowel, when the first vowel is followed by two consonants, the division usually is between the two consonants. Two examples are *'dic/tate, il'/lit/er/ate.*
- Consonant blends and consonant digraphs are considered as one unit and are not divided. Here are two examples: *li'/thog/ra/phy, de'/spise.*
- In a word that contains more than one sounded vowel, when the first vowel is followed by only one consonant or consonant digraph, the division is usually after the vowel. Here are some examples: *'fre/quent, 'le/gal, 'vo/cal.* There are, however, a number of exceptions to this rule. For example, *'lem/on* and *'mon/u/ment* have short initial vowel sounds.

- When a word ends in *-le* preceded by a consonant, the preceding consonant plus *-le* constitute the final syllable of the word. This syllable is never accented, and the vowel sound heard in it is the schwa. Here are two examples: *'ob/sta/cle, 'sin/gle.*
- Prefixes and suffixes usually form separate syllables. Here are examples: *pre'/judge, sub'/merge, se'/lec/tion, spe'/cial/ize.*
- A compound word is divided between the two words that make up the compound word as well as between syllables within the component words. Here are examples: *'land/scape, 'main/frame.*
- Prefixes and suffixes usually are not accented. Here are examples: *sub'/scrip/tion, sub'/ur/ban/ite.*
- Words that may be used as both nouns and verbs are accented on the first syllable when used as nouns and on the second syllable when used as verbs. Here are examples: *'con/tract* (noun), *con/'tract* (verb).
- In two-syllable root words, the first syllable usually is accented, unless the second syllable has two vowel letters. Here are examples: *'slum/ber, com/'mode.*
- Words containing three or more syllables are likely to have secondary (and perhaps tertiary) accents in addition to primary accents. Here are examples: *'he/mo/'glo/bin, 'pig/men/'ta/tion.*

Compound Words

Understanding *compound words* is another element of structural analysis, with complex compound words being learned in fifth grade and above. Students should learn that the meaning of compound words often can be derived from the meaning of the two individual words in the compound. Compound words can be *solid (anchorperson), hyphenated (e-mail),* or *open (pinch hitter).* Because English is continuously evolving, it is being enriched by the creation of new compound words. Indeed, about 60% of the new words being added to English today are compound words, such as *freeware, megabyte, Webmaster, space station,* and *outer space.*

Here is a sample list of solid-spelled compound words that students may encounter in reading in grades 5 to 12. For a comprehensive list of compound words, refer again to Fry, Kress, and Fountoukidis (2000, pp. 330–332).

anchorperson	airborne	backbreaking
bookmark	brainstorm	burnout
checkup	cockpit	copyright
cyberspace	database	download
drawbridge	folklore	freeware
handcuff	handlebar	hardware
huckleberry	keyboard	landscape
lightheaded	loudspeaker	mainframe
motorcycle	network	newscast
overpass	paperback	quicksand
screwdriver	shareware	shipwreck
skyscraper	software	spacecraft
spotlight	spreadsheet	starboard

sunstroke	sweatshirt	teammate
thunderstorm	timetable	touchdown
turnpike	undertake	videotape
vineyard	watermelon	wheelchair
whirlpool	windshield	weatherman
windsurf	wiretap	wristwatch

Strategies for Improving Ability in Word Structure Analysis

The chapter now offers a sampling of classroom-tested strategies for improving ability in the various elements of word structure analysis. Although all are useful in grades 5 to 12, you can modify any of them based on the abilities and interests of your own students. You can easily determine the elements of word structure analysis for which each strategy is most useful.

The strategies presented here are as follows: using word roots to identify content words and their meanings, using prefixes to identify content words and their meanings, using suffixes to identify content words and their meanings, using syllabication or "chunking" to determine word meanings, and using accent to determine word meanings.

Word Root Webs

Construct a *word root web* on the chalkboard or a transparency. Afterward, you can give students—especially those who are average or above-average readers—word roots and have them try to construct their own word root webs independently or with a partner or partners. This activity is most appropriate for students in the intermediate grades and beyond. It usually is too difficult for students with reading or learning disabilities. Here is an example of a web that was constructed from the root word *phon*, which means "sound."

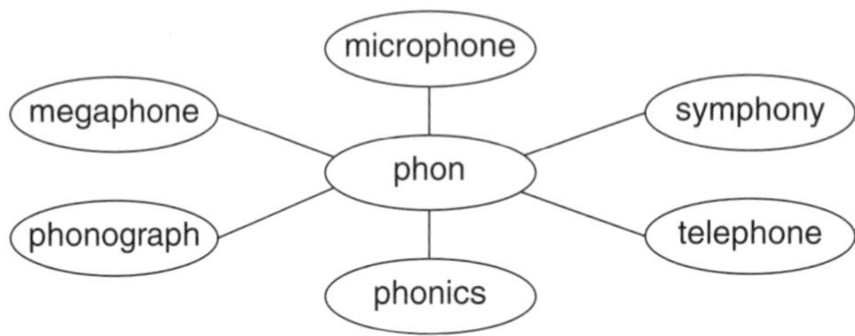

Here are some other root words and words that are derived from them that can be included in such a web. For additional ones, again consult Fry, Kress, and Fountoukidis (2000, pp. 106–113).

aero (air)—aerodynamics, aeronautics, aerate, aerobics
agr (field)—agriculture, agribusiness, agronomy, agrarian
aqua (water)—aquatic, aquarium, aquamarine, aqua (the color), aqueous, aqueduct
biblio (book)—bibliophile, bibliography, Bible, bibliotherapy
card, cord (heart)—cardiology, cardiac, cardiology, cardiologist, cardiogram, cordial, accord, concord, discord

cred (believe)—credible, incredible, credit, discredit, credential, credulous
fac, fic (make, do)—manufacture, factory, benefactor, efficient, facsimile, proficient, beneficial, sufficient
gen (birth, race)—genocide, generate, progeny, genealogy, generation
gram (letter, written)—diagram, telegram, grammar, epigram, autograph, monograph, monogram, phonograph, photograph
jud, jur, jus (law)—judge, judicial, jurisdiction, jury, justice, justify, prejudge
mater, matr (mother)—maternal, maternity, matricide, matrimony, matron
miss, mit (send)—missile, missive, mission, remiss, dismiss, transmit, admit, submit, remit
mort (death)—mortician, mortuary, mortal, immortal, mortify, postmortem
ped (foot)—pedestrian, pedal, pedestal, biped, moped
phil (love)—Anglophile, philharmonic, philanthropist, philosophy, philology
port (carry)—import, transport, portable, porter, export
rad (ray, spoke)—radium, radio, radiator, radiology, radius, radiation
sci (know)—conscience, science, conscious, subconscious, omniscient, unconscious
scribe, script (write)—transcribe, inscribe, prescribe, prescription, scripture, describe, script
spec (see)—spectator, inspect, suspect, respect, spectacle, spectacles (eyeglasses)
terr (land)—terrarium, terrestrial, terrace, territory, terrain
urb (city)—urban, suburban, suburb, urbane, suburbanite, urbanite
vid, vis (see)—video, videotape, visible, invisible, evidence, provide, providence
volv (turn)—involve, revolve, evolve, evolution, revolution, revolver

Word Roots, Prefixes, and Suffixes and "New" Words

Average and above-average readers in the intermediate grades and beyond often enjoy using *word roots*, *prefixes*, and *suffixes* to create new words that are not in the dictionary. This activity is too difficult for many students with learning or reading disabilities.

First, present this concept to them. They can then practice this activity either independently or with a partner or partners. If you like, create an activity sheet for this exercise that will challenge good readers. Here are several examples that can be included in this activity.

beneterr—good land
subaqua—under water
premort—before death
cardectomy—removal of the heart
hyperphil—excessive love
milliann—thousand years
malsaur—bad lizard
graphacious—inclined to write
telefrater—distant brother
genphobia—fear of birth

"Borrowed" Words from Around the World

Average and above-average students in the intermediate grades and beyond often enjoy learning "borrowed" words from around the world. This activity may be very motivating for them and encourage them to use elements of word structure such as word roots, prefixes, and suffixes to identify these words. Students can try to determine the country of origin for each word by using various resources, such as the Internet, the dictionary, a thesaurus, or a resource book of some type.

Chapter Two of this volume contains a fairly good list of foreign words that English has borrowed. In addition, a comprehensive list of such words can be found in Fry, Kress, and Fountoukidis (2000, pp. 114–116).

Here is a sample of words that have been borrowed from other cultures.

Africa (many different languages)—*aardvark, banjo, cola, gumbo, jumbo, mumbo, safari, trek, zombie*
Arabic—*alcohol, assassin, magazine, zero*
Aboriginal or New Zealand—*boomerang, kangaroo, kiwi*
Chinese—*chop suey, tea, typhoon, wok*
Dutch—*caboose, frolic, pickle, waffle, yacht*
Eskimo—*igloo, kayak, mukluk, parka*
Finnish—*sauna*
French—*à la carte, ballet, beige, chauffeur, chic, hors d'oeuvres, restaurant, sabotage*
German—*kindergarten, noodle, poodle, pretzel, sauerkraut, waltz*
Greek—*biology, chaos, epidemic, helicopter, hero, pentagon, siren, thermometer*
Hawaiian—*aloha, hula, lei, luau, ukulele*
Hebrew—*cherub, hallelujah, jubilee, kosher, rabbi*
Hindi—*bangle, dungaree, juggernaut, jingle, shampoo*
Hungarian—*goulash, paprika*
Icelandic—*geyser*
Irish—*leprechaun, shamrock*
Italian—*extravaganza, motto, piano, pizza, spaghetti, umbrella, violin*
Japanese—*hibachi, honcho, judo, origami*
Mexican Spanish—*adobe, bonanza, chocolate, coyote, tacos, tamales, burritos, tomato*
Native American (many languages)—*barbecue, canoe, moccasin, papoose, raccoon, tepee, tomahawk*
Persian—*bazaar, khaki, orange, peach, sherbet, turban*
Polynesian—*taboo, tattoo*
Portuguese—*albino, cobra, coconut, piranha*
Russian—*czar, sputnik, tundra, vodka*
Scandinavian—*fjord, husband, knife, skate, ski, sky, window*
Scottish—*clan, golf, slogan*
South American Spanish–Portuguese—*jaguar, llama*
Spanish—*guitar, hurricane, lasso, mosquito, potato, vanilla*
Turkish—*caviar, khan, kiosk, yogurt*
Yiddish—*bagel, chutzpah, klutz, pastrami*

Add the Points

Add the Points is a spelling game similar to Scrabble. This activity can help improve spelling, vocabulary, and word structure analysis. It also is an enjoyable activity for students in grades 5 to 12, and it can be done independently or with a partner or partners.

Students can use the following point values for each letter and spell words of any length as they try to construct the word with the highest point total: a = 1; f = 5; k = 5; p = 3; u = 2; z = 12; b = 3; g = 4; l = 2; q = 12; v = 6; c = 3; h = 4; m = 2; r = 1; w = 3; d = 2; i = 2; n = 2; s = 1; x = 10; e = 1; j = 8; o = 1; t = 1; y = 4. Using this scoring system, the word *xenophobia* would get 28 points, for example.

Inductive Learning

Inductive learning is also called "discovery" learning. It is based on the principle that if people do something enough times, they finally realize that they have learned a skill. Inductive learning is designed to accommodate different learning styles, and it encourages students to experiment and to learn by doing. This is in contrast to more traditional methods in which students are told exactly how to proceed in a step-by-step manner. Instead, inductive learning allows students to determine their own steps and draw their own conclusions as they learn a specific skill.

To use inductive learning effectively, the teacher should provide experiences that shape and structure what students are doing so the skill will be discovered naturally as part of the process. The principle can be applied effectively to the learning of both prefixes and suffixes. The following illustration should clarify how to use inductive learning with prefixes. As you read this fifth-grade classroom dialogue, you should be able to see how the teacher structures the experience to facilitate the students' discovery of the meanings associated with target prefixes.

MS. GOLDMAN: Today we're going to play a game about prefixes. I'll make three columns. Each column contains a different prefix. I'll give each of you a different root word, and you should place the root word into a prefix column to create a new word. However, it has to be a real word, not a make-believe word. The first prefix is *sub-*. *(Ms. Goldman puts the card on an easel so all the students can see it.)* The second prefix is *im-*. (She puts the second card next to the first.) The third prefix is *pre-*. *(She puts the third card next to the second. She then gives a different root word card to each student.)*

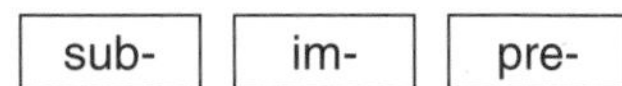

MS. GOLDMAN: I'll take the first one. My root word is *merge.* I can make a new word here. *(She puts* merge *under* sub-.*)* Now part of this game is that I must explain what the root word means. The root word means to "plunge or engulf in something." The prefix *sub-* means *under,* so to submerge means to put under water or put under something else. Who would like to go next? Michael, which column will you put your root word in?

MICHAEL: *Im-*.

MS. GOLDMAN: What is the new word that you have made?

MICHAEL: *Immature. (Michael puts his card in the* im- *column.)*

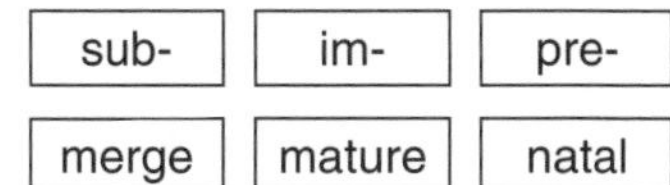

MS. GOLDMAN: What does *mature* mean?
MICHAEL: To be grown up, or like an adult.
MS. GOLDMAN: What happens to the word when you put *im-* in front of it?
MICHAEL: It changes the meaning to "not mature or grown up."
MS. GOLDMAN: Great. Elia, what's your word?
ELIA: *Prenatal. (She puts the card in the* pre- *column.)*

After helping the students place and define their words, Ms. Goldman concludes the lesson by helping them discover the common meanings of the three prefixes.

MS. GOLDMAN: Does the prefix in the first column have the same meaning for every word that you made? *(She points to the prefix* sub-.*)*

SANDI: Yes, it means that something is *under* something else.

MS. GOLDMAN: How about the words in the second column. Does the prefix *im-* mean about the same thing in every word?

TAMIKA: Yes, it always means *not.*

MS. GOLDMAN: How about the words in the third column? Does the prefix *pre-* mean about the same thing every time in the words in that column?

JUAN: Yes, that prefix means *before.*

MS. GOLDMAN: That's right. You have discovered that each of these prefixes keeps its meaning, and that each one affects the meaning of the root word. Now you can use these new prefixes and their meanings to help you identify the meanings of some new words that you meet while you are reading.

As the example shows, a teacher can structure an experience to facilitate the students' *discovery* of the meaning of prefixes. Inductive learning usually is very effective because the students have insights themselves; this usually means that they remember better what they have learned.

Gunning's Strategy for Learning Prefixes

Gunning (1996) also has a strategy that is designed to help *students learn prefixes.* According to Dale and O'Rourke (1964; cited in O'Rourke, 1974), it is easier for students to learn prefixes than suffixes. In addition, according to Graves and Hammond (1980), there are relatively few prefixes and they usually have constant, concrete meanings—unlike suffixes—and fairly consistent spellings. Very briefly, here is Gunning's strategy for learning prefixes.

Step 1: Construct the Meaning of the Prefix

Write the following words on the chalkboard:

antisocial, antiwar, antislavery, antifreeze, antiracism, anticruelty, anticlimax

Discuss the meaning of these words and places where students may have seen them. Have students notice how the prefix *anti-* changes the meaning of the word it precedes and help them formulate a definition for *anti-*. Encourage students to understand that *anti-* is a prefix. In addition, discuss the purpose of prefixes and how they help readers determine the meaning of unknown words. Illustrate how words that contain prefixes are syllabicated, and how the knowledge of prefixes can be used in decoding words and determining their meanings.

Step 2: Guided Practice

Have students complete practice exercises similar to the following example:

Complete the blanks with these words containing prefixes: *antisocial, antiwar, antislavery, antifreeze, antiracism, anticruelty, anticlimax*

> Since it is going to be very cold tonight, my father is taking the car to the service station to have the ___________________ checked.
> The conclusion of the play that we saw last evening certainly was an
> _______________________.
> During the Vietnam era, there were many __________________ protests.
> Karl seems like an __________________ person.
> Everyone should be ___________________ in our democratic, divergent society.
> Since I love animals, I support the _________________ society in my city.
> During the Civil War most people in the North were _________________.

Step 3: Application

Have students read sentences that contain the prefix *anti-* and have them notice its use in real-life materials.

Step 4: Extension

Present the prefix *pro-* and contrast it with *anti-*. Since *pro-* is the opposite of *anti-*, this should help to clarify the meaning of *pro-*.

Irvin's Strategy for Teaching Word Parts

Irvin's *strategy for teaching word parts* (1998) can be very effective in teaching prefixes to students. Briefly, here is the procedure:

1. Write on the chalkboard two familiar words containing the target prefix and have the students define the prefix.

2. Underline the prefix and have students notice its spelling. Then explain the meaning of the prefix or have the students provide it.

3. Write an unfamiliar word that contains the prefix in a sentence on the chalkboard and model the process that should be used in determining its meaning. For example, you can write the word *super-* in a sentence such as this: "The United States of America is considered to be a superpower." Then think aloud as you analyze the prefix and the word to determine its meaning: "In analyzing this word, I notice that the word begins with the prefix *super-*, and I know that the prefix *super-* means *above* or *beyond.* Therefore, *superpower* must mean one of the world's most important countries. Next, I'll try using the meaning in a sentence: "The United States is considered to be a very important country."

4. After you have modeled the procedure several times, provide students with an opportunity to try it themselves. Let them work with a few other words that take the prefix *super-*, following the same procedures that you followed with *superpower.* The words *supernatural, supersonic, superman, superscript, supercharge, superstructure,* and *superfine* could be used. Help students as

necessary, joining in when appropriate. Do not provide too much support, however, because students should become competent in this procedure independently.

5. Provide an example of a word students know in which the letter group that was just taught does not represent the meaning of that prefix. Tell them that letter groups that look like prefixes sometimes are merely "groups of letters." For example, the letter group *super* in the word *superb* has no meaning separate from the meaning of the entire word.

As a culminating activity, have students look for examples of the prefix *super-* over the next few days and bring the examples to class along with the sentences in which they occur. Ask students to explain how they used the meaning of the prefix and root word to arrive at the word's meaning and how they checked the word's meaning in the context in which the word occurred.

Can of Words

The game *Can of Words* probably can be used in grades 5 and 6 to give students practice in adding both prefixes and suffixes to root words. To construct this game, obtain three coffee cans and label them *Prefixes*, *Root Words*, and *Suffixes*. Then construct several three- by five-inch cardboard-backed cards. On each card write a prefix, suffix, or root word.

Have the students draw a card from each can and try to make a word using all three pieces. Here are several examples: *un comfort able, pre caution ary, dys function al.*

If a prefix or suffix does not apply in a particular word, the students need use only one (rather than both). Each student tries to make as many words as possible.

Prefixes in Content Assignments or Articles

Have students read a content assignment or a periodical article, and if possible, circle all the words in that material that contain a prefix. If it is not possible to circle the prefixes in the actual material, then have them write each prefixed word in the content assignment or article on a separate sheet of paper. They can share their prefixed words with the other members of the class or a group, if you wish.

Analogy or Pronounceable Word Parts Strategy

Using the *analogy strategy* with *rimes* (word families) greatly helps students in grades 5 to 12 to pronounce words of more than one syllable. Students with reading or learning disabilities often are unable to decode long, complex words. They usually either do not try to identify them or else guess wildly at them while paying no attention to their use in context.

Using the analogy strategy with rimes helps students combine vowel patterns (phonics) and syllabication (word structure). As an example, examine the two following words and the two different ways that each word theoretically can be pronounced.

CV Pattern	VC Pattern
de/fense	def/ense
ba/lance	bal/ance

A student should learn to read aloud or silently a content word such as these *in context*, and then select the correct pronunciation (that is, the pronunciation that makes sense in the sentence context). The analogy approach using rimes should be a tool that is used in a *flexible way*—it should not be an exercise in merely drawing lines between syllables with no regard for whether the pronounced word makes sense in context.

Decoding Long Words

Students who have difficulties in word structure analysis cannot decode or attack long, polysyllabic words that contain prefixes or suffixes. They may use the six-step strategy for identifying difficult words presented shortly to help them identify such words.

Word Octopus or Word Tree

A *word octopus* or a *word tree* can be used to illustrate the relationships between a *word root* and its derivatives. They are especially useful in demonstrating the relationships between a word root and a suffix.

Draw either an octopus or a tree on the chalkboard. After students have carefully examined it, have them construct their own octopus or tree on a sheet of paper. Here are some *root words* that can be used in this activity:

kind—*kinds, kinder, kindest, kindly, kindness*
soft—*softer, softest, softly, soften, softness*
quick—*quicker, quickest, quicken, quickly, quickness*
child—*childlike, childhood, childless, childish*
rain—*rains, rained, raining, rainy, rainless*

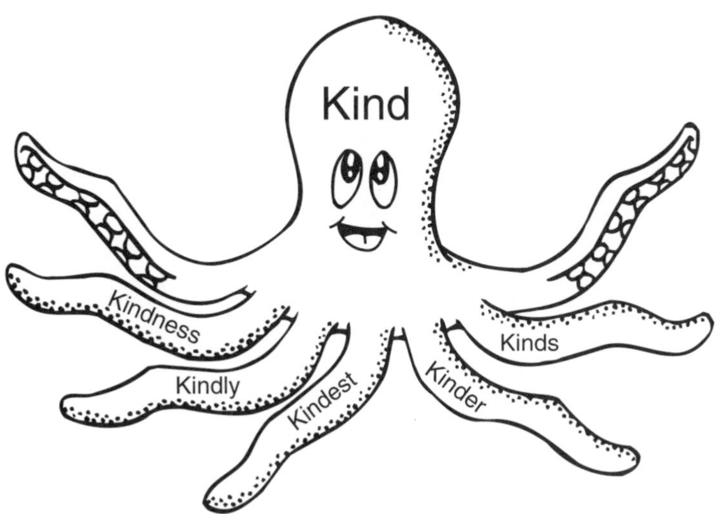

Six Steps for Identifying Difficult Words

Shanker and Ekwall (1988) offer a six-step strategy for students to use in identifying difficult words that they recognize when they hear them. According to Shanker and Ekwall, students who have learned to identify, syllabicate, pronounce, and blend affixes into entire words have already mastered the ability to decode many two- and three-syllable words, such as *voyage, wisdom,* and *historic.* However, the words that remain difficult for them are those that are not in their listening vocabulary. Students do not recognize these words when the teacher pronounces them and they are exceptionally long and difficult.

Before students can identify words that are not in their listening vocabulary, they must increase their meaning vocabulary. If the words are not in their meaning vocabulary, there is little point in pursuing the six generalizations that follow. The teacher must make a concerted effort to increase that vocabulary. Examples of long words to which the generalizations may apply are *ambiguous*, *dehumidify*, *benediction*, *standardize*, *fraudulent*, and *embezzlement.*

Here are the six generalizations:

1. Look for prefixes and suffixes.
2. Look for a known root word.
3. Read to the end of the sentence. Think of a word you know that makes sense that contains the same prefix, suffix, or root word.
4. If necessary, try making different divisions of the root word to form syllables.
5. Try different sounds, syllables, and accents until you form a word that makes sense.
6. If you still cannot figure out the word, consult a dictionary.

Generalization Strategy for Teaching Syllabication

Gunning (1996) suggested a *syllabication strategy* that is most useful with students in grade 5 and above who have little knowledge of the value of using syllables in decoding long, unknown words. These are usually students with reading or learning disabilities. Briefly, here is this strategy:

Step One: Auditory Perception of Syllables

Explain to students that many words have parts that are called *syllables.* Pronounce a group of words and have students clap or tap their pencils on their desks once for each syllable that they are able to hear: *di/vide*, *pil/grim*, *mer/chant*, *e/clipse*, *hu/man*, *de/gree*, *mod/el*, *pro/duct*, *per/cent*, *ju/ry*, *ex/ile*, *im/age*, *cli/mate.*

Step Two: Perception of Printed Syllables

Present one- and two-syllable words that contrast with each other so that students can understand printed syllables.

through	be	sun	a	ice	high
out	hold	stroke	bound	berg	light

Step Three: Perception of a Syllable Generalization

When students understand the concept of syllables, present words that illustrate a syllabic generalization. For example, the following words effectively illustrate the suffix *-ness* generalization (meaning state or quality of):

good	goodness
kind	kindness
dark	darkness
full	fullness
like	likeness

After you present these words, have the students read the words and contrast them. Encourage them to notice that the words in the first column have only one syllable, whereas those in the second contain two syllables. Read each word in the second column and have the students clap or tap their pencils on their desks as they hear each separate syllable in the word. Help them to discover that the *-ness* at the end of a word makes up a *separate syllable.* In later lessons help students discover other prefixes and suffixes and enlarge the generalization.

Step Four: Guided Practice

Have the students read selections of various kinds that contain words illustrating the target generalization. Have them complete review activities in which they *use syllabication clues and context together* to select the word that completes a sentence. The following sentences illustrate this activity:

Juana gave the homeless woman a dollar bill out of the good, goodness of her heart.

Harriet is an extremely kind, kindness person who always tries to help other people in need.

In the winter dark, darkness falls as early as half past four in the afternoon.

When I buy a quart box of strawberries in the summer, I want to get a full, fullness box.

Kathy's latest photograph is an excellent like, likeness of her.

Step Five: Application

Have students read all types of content and narrative materials that contain words with more than one syllable. Encourage them to apply the generalizations that they have learned.

Breaking Nonsense Words into Syllables

According to Heilman, Blair, and Rupley (1998), a knowledge of *vowel behavior* in words is an important aid in breaking words into syllables. However, the sounds of vowels and letter combinations are not as consistent as those of prefixes and suffixes. Nevertheless, many generalizations are helpful.

Although these examples are not words, the letter combinations can be broken into syllables to provide students with practice in this element of word structure: *binretion, flapratem, chumnish, dicten,* and *breeper.* The following is the most likely syllabication for each of these nonsense words: *bin/re/tion, flap/ra/tem, chum/nish, dic/ten,* and *breep/er.* Most able readers would pronounce these nonsense words in about the same way. Such readers probably would not think of the rules before pronouncing the words but undoubtedly would be influenced in some way by the rules they had learned.

Compound Word Game

The *Compound Word Game* is an interesting activity that intermediate-grade students enjoy completing independently or with a partner or partners. This activity requires students to form a new compound word but keep part of the old compound word. Students start off with a word and then add another word to form a compound word or a common two-word expression. Then they keep the last part of the compound word or expression and add a new word to form yet another compound word or expression.

Here is an example that begins with the word "ball":

ballpark . . . parkway . . . wayside . . . sidewalk . . . walkman . . . manpower . . . powerboat . . . boathouse. . . houseplant . . . plantlike . . . likewise . . . wisecrack . . . crackpot . . . potbelly

Compound Word Classification

To increase students' knowledge of compound words, construct a large wall chart with five headings—such as *Living Creatures*, *People*, *Things*, *Locations*, and *Food*—written across the top. Then ask the students to locate compound words that fit under these or other appropriate headings. Here is a sample list of compound words that students might include on such a list:

Living Creatures	**People**	**Things**	**Locations**	**Food**
grasshopper	milkman	postcard	downtown	peanut
blackbird	firefighter	fireplace	highway	cupcake
starfish	quarterback	flashlight	sidewalk	strawberry
seahorse	anchorperson	baseball	ballroom	grapefruit
bluebird	cowboy	snowplow	walkway	popcorn
goldfish	grandfather	haystack	uptown	watermelon
woodpecker	grandmother	wheelchair	turnpike	applesauce
bulldog	grandparent	spotlight	vineyard	oatmeal
mayfly	stepfather	folktale	backyard	seafood
rattlesnake	teammate	snowball	seacoast	pancake

Sentence Pair Accents

Heteronyms are words that are spelled the same but have different pronunciations, depending on where the accent is placed. Often the noun in the heteronym pair is accented on the first syllable, whereas the verb is accented on the final syllable.

Present this concept to students in the intermediate grades and then have them place the accent on the correct syllable depending on the word's use in sentence context. Here are some heteronyms that can be used in such an activity as well as several sample sentences demonstrating the correct placement of accent. For a comprehensive list of heteronyms, see again Fry, Kress, and Fountoukidis (2000, pp. 65–74).

affect (influence)—*affect* (pretend)
buffet (cabinet for dishes or self-serve meal)—*buffet* (strike)
commune (group of people living together)—*commune* (talk intimately)
console (cabinet)—*console* (ease grief)
content (things inside)—*content* (satisfied)
converse (opposite)—*converse* (talk)
contract (legal document)—*contract* (to bring on oneself)
entrance (going in)—*entrance* (charm)
invalid (disabled person)—*invalid* (not valid)
object (a thing)—*object* (to protest)
present (gift or not absent)—*present* (to introduce formally)
record (music disk)—*record* (write down)
refuse (waste, trash)—*refuse* (say no)

Here are some sample sentences:

My Victorian loveseat is a valuable and lovely *object* of art.
I really *object* to having to go to summer school this July.

Clare would like to have a classic Elvis Presley *record.*
I would like to be an archaeologist and *record* items found in an Egyptian tomb.

The windstorm will *buffet* my sailboat and may damage it.
I do not enjoy going to a *buffet* for lunch since I enjoy being served.

Reproducible Activity Sheets for Improving Word Structure Analysis Skills

The chapter now provides seven reproducible activity sheets to help students overcome specific difficulties in the various elements of word structure analysis. They can be duplicated in their present form or modified in any way you like based on the needs and interests of your own students. In addition, they can serve as models for you in constructing similar activity sheets to reinforce the various subskills of word structure analysis.

The seven reproducible activity sheets are as follows: Defining Made-up Words Using Word Root, Prefix, and Suffix Meanings—Sixth- to Eighth-Grade Level; Determining Word Etymologies—Seventh- to Twelfth-Grade Level; What's the Correct Prefix?—Sixth-Grade Level; What's the Correct Suffix?—Sixth-Grade Level; Dividing Content Words into Syllables—Fifth-Grade Level; Compound Word Game—Fifth- to Sixth-Grade Level; Determining the Correct Accent—Sixth- to Seventh-Grade Level.

Answer Key for Defining Made-up Words Using Word Root, Prefix, and Suffix Meanings

Note: The meanings of all the word roots, prefixes, and suffixes used in this activity sheet are found in Fry, Kress, and Fountoukidis (2000, pp. 85–113). The answers shown here are correct. However, approximations of these answers should be considered correct too: 1. fear of a sound(s); 2. good heat; 3. removal of a foot; 4. against a book(s); 5. bad water; 6. in favor of war; 7. small father; 8. excessive love; 9. state or quality of health; 10. state of quality of death; 11. bad marriage; 12. inflammation of an eye(s); 13. study of the moon; 14. false madness; 15. not alone; 16. relating to the law; 17. great (large) heart; 18. small lizard; 19. one who fights; 20. many women; 21. free water; 22. after birth; 23. all races; 24. under (the) earth; 25. across (a) city.

Answer Key for Determining Word Etymologies

1. *flect*, bend, Latin, to bend the knees; 2. *aqua*, water, Latin, water-bearing stratus of permeable sand, rock, or gravel; 3. *pater or patr*, father, Latin, a man who is father or founder of a group; 4. *gen*, birth or race, Greek, offspring of animals or plants; 5. *pod*, foot, Greek, doctor for foot problems; 6. *scop*, see, Greek, an instrument used to detect and study sounds in the body; 7. *trib*, give, Latin, a stream feeding a larger stream or lake; also, paying tribute to another; 8. *vol*, wish or well, Latin, marked by or disposed to doing good; 9. *sci*, know, Greek, having infinite knowledge; 10. *ambul or amb*, walk, go, Latin, to walk while asleep; 11. *psych*, mind or soul, Greek, sensitive to supernatural forces and influences; 12. *morph*, shape, Greek, occurring in various forms, styles, or characters; 13. *gram*, letter or written, Greek, a certain poem dealing

with a single thought or event and ending with an ingenious turn of thought; 14. *ortho*, straight or right, Greek, a dentist who straightens teeth; 15. *gyn*, woman, Greek, one who hates women; 16. *belli*, war, Latin, a person who has a fighting attitude; 17. *cosm*, universe, Greek, a little world; also, a man who is an epitome of the world; 18. *photo*, light, Greek, a camera lens that gives a large image of a distant object; 19. *biblio*, book, Greek, use of reading materials for helping in solving personal problems; 20. *san*, health, Latin, an establishment that provides therapy combined with diet and exercise for treatment; 21. *gam*, marriage, Greek, a mature male or female germ cell; 22. *anthr*, man, Greek, the study of human beings, their environments, races, cultures, and physical characteristics; 23. *hydr*, water, Greek, to remove water; also, to lose water in bodily fluids; 24. *ocu*, eye, Latin, involving only one eye; 25. *soph*, wise, Greek, an expert; also, a wise man or woman; 26. *opt*, best, Latin, the amount or degree of something that is most favorable; 27. *mut*, change, Latin, a significant and basic change; also, a change in hereditary material; 28. *surr or surg*, change, Latin, to raise from the dead; also, to bring to attention again; 29. *integ*, whole, Latin, any one of the natural numbers; 30. *gnos*, know, Greek, one who believes that the existence of God is unknowable

Answer Key for What's the Correct Prefix?

1. re-; 2. non-; 3. multi-; 4. anti-; 5. tri-; 6. tele-; 7. de-; 8. pre-; 9. ex-; 10. mid-; 11. in-; 12. non-; 13. micro-; 14. auto-; 15. trans-; 16. mis-; 17. in-; 18. sub-; 19. over-; 20. intra-

Answer Key for What's the Correct Suffix?

1. cheerful, f; 2. beggar, i; 3. terrify, a; 4. urban, d; 5. happiness, g; 6. smartest, k; 7. funny, m; 8. adulthood, h; 9. appendectomy, j; 10. combustible, o; 11. laryngitis, n; 12. joyous, l; 13. resident, e; 14. actor, b; 15. loyalty, c; 16. -less; 17. -age; 18. -ly; 19. -dom; 20. -ant; 21. -ist; 22. -ly; 23. -wise; 24. -ee; 25. -arium; 26. -en; 27. -ism; 28. -hood; 29. -man; 30. -ment

Answer Key for Dividing Content Words into Syllables

1. civ il; 2. bar ter; 3. da ta; 4. ba rom eter; 5. hu man; 6. di no saur; 7. or di nal; 8. re main der; 9. el e ment; 10. de fense; 11. block ade; 12. du ty; 13. vi rus; 14. so nar; 15. ep ic; 16. mo tive; 17. met a phor; 18. sur vey; 19. ex act; 20. cal cu late; 21. chem i cal; 22. hi ber nate; 23. sto ma; 24. tu mor; 25. sur plus

Answer Key for Compound Word Game

No answer key is possible for this activity sheet. However, consult Fry, Kress, and Fountoukidis (2000, pp. 330–332) for a comprehensive list of compound words.

Answer Key for Determining the Correct Accent

1. C, X; 2. C, X; 3. X, C; 4. C, X; 5. C, X; 6. X, C; 7. X, C; 8. C, X; 9. X, C; 10. X, C; 11. C, X; 12. C, X; 13. X, C; 14. C, X; 15. X, C

Name ______________________ Grade ___ Teacher ___________ Date _________

Defining Made-up Words Using Word Root, Prefix, and Suffix Meanings

Here are twenty-five *imaginary words.* Using your knowledge of common word roots, prefixes, and suffixes, try to determine *an approximate meaning* for each imaginary word and then write the meaning on the line beside the word. The first one has been done for you. You can work with a partner or partners if you like.

1. phonphobia ______ fear of a sound(s) ______
2. benetherm ______________________
3. podectomy ______________________
4. antibiblio ______________________
5. dysaqua ______________________
6. probelli ______________________
7. paterette ______________________
8. hyperphil ______________________
9. sanship ______________________
10. morthood ______________________
11. malgam ______________________
12. optitis ______________________
13. lunaology ______________________
14. pseudomania ______________________
15. imsol ______________________
16. judant ______________________
17. magnicard ______________________
18. microsaur ______________________
19. pugar ______________________
20. multigyn ______________________
21. liberhydr ______________________
22. postnat ______________________
23. pangen ______________________
24. subgeo ______________________
25. transurb ______________________

Name ________________________ Grade ___ Teacher ____________ Date __________

Determining Word Etymologies

Each of the words on this activity sheet has its origin in either a Greek or a Latin word root. Write the word root and its meaning, whether the word root is Greek or Latin, and an approximate meaning for the word. You can use a dictionary, book about word origins, or the Internet to help you complete this sheet. The first one has been done for you. If you want, you can work with a partner or partners.

Word	Word Root	Word Root Meaning	Greek or Latin	Meaning of the Root or Word
1. genuflect	flect	bend	Latin	to bend the knees
2. aquifer				
3. patriarch				
4. progeny				
5. podiatrist				
6. stethoscope				
7. tributary				
8. benevolent				
9. omniscient				
10. somnambulate				
11. psychic				
12. polymorphous				
13. epigram				
14. orthodontist				
15. misogynist				
16. bellicose				
17. microcosm				
18. telephoto				
19. bibliotherapy				
20. sanitarium				
21. gamete				
22. anthropology				
23. dehydrate				
24. monocular				
25. sophist				
26. optimum				
27. mutation				
28. resurrect				
29. integer				
30. agnostic				

Name ______________________ Grade ___ Teacher ____________ Date _________

What's the Correct Prefix?

Write in the prefix on the blank line that will give the correct meaning for the following root words.

1. ____________________ heat — to heat again
   pre- re- sub-

2. ____________________ stop — to continue an activity
   non- mis- im-

3. ____________________ colored — an article that has many colors
   ex- multi- post-

4. ____________________ war — to be opposed to war
   anti- pro- re-

5. ____________________ cycle — a toy that young children ride on
   contra- mon- tri-

6. ____________________ scope — a device for seeing the planets and stars
   tele- super- under-

7. ____________________ crease — to determine or become
   dys- de- milli-

8. ____________________ natal — before birth
   pre- pro- post-

9. ____________________ port — to send out or away
   post- im- ex-

10. ____________________ night — 12 A.M.
    micro- post- mid-

Write a prefix in front of the root word to make the correct word using the definition given.

11. ____________________ visible — unable to be seen
12. ____________________ fiction — literature that is not fictional
13. ____________________ wave — electromagnetic wave
14. ____________________ biography — a biography of a person written by him- or herself
15. ____________________ atlantic — crossing or extending across the ocean
16. ____________________ behave — act out in an unacceptable way
17. ____________________ accurate — faulty or wrong
18. ____________________ zero — a temperature below zero
19. ____________________ due — not paid when due
20. ____________________ mural — competitive *within* a student body

Name ______________________ Grade ___ Teacher ___________ Date _________

What's the Correct Suffix?

Underline the suffix *in each of the following words. Then draw a line to its correct meaning.*

1. cheerful	a. to make afraid
2. beggar	b. one who performs in the theater
3. terrify	c. one who is faithful
4. urban	d. relating to a city
5. happiness	e. one who lives in a certain place
6. smartest	f. a happy person
7. funny	g. the quality of joy
8. adulthood	h. the quality of being an adult
9. appendectomy	i. a person who asks other people for money
10. combustible	j. the surgical removal of an appendix
11. laryngitis	k. the most intelligent person
12. joyous	l. full of happiness
13. resident	m. humorous
14. actor	n. inflammation of the larynx
15. loyalty	o. can catch fire

Add a suffix to each root word to make a word with the meaning given.

16. thought	____________________	without consideration
17. pilgrim	____________________	the action (process) of going on a journey to a sacred place
18. mother	____________________	a person who is maternal
19. bore	____________________	the state or quality of being disinterested and tiresome
20. assist	____________________	a person who helps another in a superior position
21. capital	____________________	one who is a person of wealth and interested in business
22. lovely	____________________	beautiful
23. clock	____________________	the direction in which the hands of a timepiece move
24. pay	____________________	one who receives money
25. planet	____________________	a place to view and study astronomy (planets, stars, and other heavenly bodies)
26. length	____________________	to make longer
27. hero	____________________	the quality of being brave
28. false	____________________	an untruth
29. camera	____________________	a male who works in photography
30. amaze	____________________	a state of being surprised

Name ______________________ Grade ___ Teacher ____________ Date _________

Dividing Content Words into Syllables

Cross out the content word in each line that is incorrectly divided into syllables. Then write the correct syllable division of that word in the blank space provided.

1. doc u ment	ci vil	______________
2. cen tu ry	bart er	______________
3. dat a	can yon	______________
4. bar o meter	in ci sion	______________
5. hum an	e qua tor	______________
6. fer tile	din o saur	______________
7. ord i nal	fac tor	______________
8. pro duct	re ma in der	______________
9. elem ent	mul ti ply	______________
10. def ense	fed er al	______________
11. in va sion	blo ck ade	______________
12. man date	dut y	______________
13. vir us	vol ume	______________
14. tun dra	son ar	______________
15. con clu sion	e pic	______________
16. mor al	mot ive	______________
17. id i om	meta phor	______________
18. surv ey	mul ti ply	______________
19. car di nal	e xact	______________
20. mid way	cal cul ate	______________
21. che mi cal	gey ser	______________
22. chol rine	hi be rnate	______________
23. stom a	zy gote	______________
24. ha lo gen	tum or	______________
25. surp lus	con tour	______________

Name ______________________ Grade ___ Teacher ____________ Date __________

Compound Word Game

In this activity sheet you will need to *form a new word* while *keeping part of the old word.* Begin with one word and then add another word to *form a compound word.* Keep the last part of that compound word and then *add a new word* to form still *another compound word.* You can work with a partner or partners if you want. See how many compound words you can come up with and if you can beat the total number of words shown in the example (nine).

Example: *bird*

birdhouse . . . housefly . . . flypaper . . . paperback . . . backfire . . . fireside . . . sideboard . . . boardroom . . . roommate

Compound Word List One

______	______	______
______	______	______
______	______	______
______	______	______
______	______	______

Compound Word List Two

______	______	______
______	______	______
______	______	______
______	______	______
______	______	______

Compound Word List Three

______	______	______
______	______	______
______	______	______
______	______	______
______	______	______

Name ______________________ Grade ___ Teacher ____________ Date __________

Determining the Correct Accent

There are two content words in each row. On the line beside the word, write *C* if the word is correctly accented or *X* if the word is not correctly accented. The accent mark is placed *before* the accented syllable in each word.

1. 'nu mer al ________	quar 'tile ________
2. 'plate let ________	pro 'ton ________
3. tra 'che a ________	'i so tope ________
4. 'la ser ________	'in ert ________
5. 'fan ta sy ________	'sus pense ________
6. 'cli ché ________	'gen re ________
7. 'pa tri ot ________	'peas ant ________
8. in 'fla tion ________	'in den ture ________
9. har 'bor ________	ho 'ri zon ________
10. de 'com pose ________	de 'gree ________
11. 'hab i tat ________	hi 'ber nate ________
12. con 'cave ________	frac 'ture ________
13. 'vol ca no ________	'ret i na ________
14. 'ra dar ________	'me dul la ________
15. 'or gan ic ________	'hy brid ________

For Additional Reading

Allen, H., and Barbe, W. *Ready-to-Use Vocabulary, Word attack, and Comprehension Activities: Fifth-Grade Level* (pp. 47–86). Paramus, N.J.: Center for Applied Research in Education, 1998.

Allen, H., Barbe, W., and Levesque, M. *Ready-to-Use Vocabulary, Word Attack and Comprehension Activities: Sixth-Grade Level* (pp. 108–181). Paramus, N.J.: Center for Applied Research in Education, 1998.

Cooper, D. *Literacy: Helping Children Construct Meaning* (pp. 262–267). Boston: Houghton Mifflin, 1997.

Cunningham, P. *Phonics They Use: Words for Reading and Writing* (pp. 150–171). White Plains, N.Y.: Longman, 2000.

Fry, E., Kress, J., and Fountoukidis, D. *The Reading Teacher's Book of Lists* (4th ed.; pp. 85–99, 106–113, 330–332). San Francisco: Jossey-Bass, 2000.

Gunning, T. *Building Words: A Resource Manual for Teaching Word Analysis and Spelling Strategies* (pp. 199–224). Needham Heights, Mass.: Allyn and Bacon, 2001.

Miller, W. *Reading Skills Problem Solver* (pp. 123–169). San Francisco: Jossey-Bass, 2002.

Rasinski, T., and Padak, N. *From Phonics to Fluency* (pp. 59–74). White Plains, N.Y.: Longman, 2001.

Rinsky, L. *Teaching Word Recognition Skills* (pp. 87–108). Upper Saddle River, N.J.: Gorsuch Scarisbrick, 1997.

Tompkins, G. *Literacy for the 21st Century* (pp. 208–219, 248–258). Upper Saddle River, N.J.: Prentice Hall/Merrill, 2001.

Works Cited in Chapter Four

Carroll, J., Davies, P., and Richman, B. *The American Heritage Word Frequency Book.* New York: American Heritage, 1971.

Dale, E., and O'Rourke, J. *Students' Knowledge of Roots and Affixes.* Unpublished study. Columbus: The Ohio State University, 1964.

Fry, E., Kress, J., and Fountoukidis, D. *The Reading Teacher's Book of Lists* (4th ed.; pp. 85–99, 106–113, 330–332). San Francisco: Jossey-Bass, 2000.

Groff, P. "Teaching Reading by Syllables." *Reading Teacher,* 1981, *14,* 659–664.

Graves, M., and Hammond, H. "A Validated Procedure for Teaching Prefixes and Its Effect on Students' Ability to Assign Meaning to Novel Words." In M. Kamil and A. Moe (eds.), *Perspectives on Reading Research and Instruction* (pp. 184–188). Washington, D.C.: National Reading Conference, 1980.

Gunning, T. *Creating Reading Instruction for All Students* (pp. 134–135, 140, 142–143). Needham Heights, Mass.: Allyn and Bacon, 1996.

Heilman, A., Blair, T., and Rupley, W. *Principles and Practices of Teaching Reading* (p. 184). Upper Saddle River, N.J.: Prentice Hall, 1998.

Irvin, J. "Strategy for Teaching Word Parts." In M. Graves, C. Juel, and B. Graves (eds.), *Teaching Reading in the 21st Century* (pp. 207–208). Needham Heights, Mass.: Allyn and Bacon, 1998.

O'Rourke, J. *Toward a Science of Vocabulary Development.* Hawthorne, N.Y.: Mouton de Gruyter, 1974.

Shanker, J., and Ekwall, E. *Diagnosis and Remediation of the Disabled Reader* (pp. 180–182). Needham Heights, Mass.: Allyn and Bacon, 1988.

Tompkins, G., and Yaden, D., Jr. *Answering Students' Questions About Words.* Urbana, Ill.: Clearinghouse on Reading and Communication Skills and the National Council of Teachers of English, 1986.

Venezky, R. *The American Way of Spelling: The Structure and Origins of American English Orthography.* New York: Guilford, 1999.

White, T., Sowell, J., and Yanagihara, A. "Teaching Elementary Students to Use Word-Part Clues." *Reading Teacher,* 1989, *42,* 302–308.

5

Strategies and Activities for Improving Use of Context Clues to Identify New Words

Which word identification technique do you, as a competent reader, use most often? If you are a typical adult able reader, your answer to this question undoubtedly is: "Context clues, or the context in which the unknown word appears." There usually are a number of words whose approximate meaning you can determine from the context, even if you are unable to pronounce them correctly. However, pronunciation often is not important if their *approximate meaning* can be determined.

This chapter is designed to help classroom and special reading teachers, as well as learning disability teachers, learn how to present context clues most effectively to students in grades 5 to 12. The chapter opens by briefly explaining context clues and stressing their importance for effective reading in these grades. It also presents a useful classification scheme for context clues. The chapter then emphasizes that the use of context clues always is a *calculated estimate* of the meaning of unknown words. The next section of the chapter describes the advantages and limitations of using context clues.

The chapter then provides a number of classroom-tested strategies for using context clues while reading content material in grades 5 to 12, including wide reading of various kinds of materials; self-monitoring and self-correction while reading silently and orally; Dahl and Samuel's strategy for using context clues; Edwards and Dermott's method of teaching context clues; Gunning's strategy for teaching context clues; Harris and Smith's strategy for teaching context clues; variations of the cloze procedure; cryptology and mutilated messages; having students read past unknown words to the end of a sentence; using scrambled synonyms, "Help the Dragon Get Home," and musical cloze; and modeling the effective use of context clues. The chapter closes with seven reproducible activity sheets for improving general context clue usage and for improving context clues while reading various kinds of content material.

After reading Chapter Five, reading, special education, and content teachers should be well-prepared to teach context clue usage to all of their students in grades 5 to 12, including those with reading and learning disabilities.

USING CONTEXT CLUES TO IDENTIFY UNKNOWN WORDS IN CONTENT MATERIAL

Context clues can be defined as a word identification technique that readers use to determine the meaning, and sometimes the pronunciation, of an unknown word by examining the context in which it is located. The context can be the sentence, the surrounding sentences, the paragraph, or the entire passage. Context clues consist of both *semantic* (*word meaning*) and *syntactic* (*word order or grammar*) clues. They also are an excellent means of vocabulary development. The effective use of context clues requires some degree of abstract thinking. Context clues always are most helpful when *they are combined with word structure or phonic clues or both.*

Types of Context Clues

There are many different *classification schemes* for context clues. Some of them are credited to Herber (1967), Gunning (1996), Rinsky (1997), Tompkins (2001), and Lapp and Flood (1992). These classification schemes vary somewhat. The one chosen for this book was suggested by Burns, Roe, and Ross (1996, pp. 106–107).

Definition Clues

The word may be clearly defined in context. If the student has heard the word in oral form, he or she may be able to recognize it in print through the definition even though he or she may not be able to pronounce it correctly.

- Because Paul had a stroke and seems to be quite forgetful at this time, he may be suffering from *dementia.*
- An *ophthalmologist* is a medical doctor who specializes in treating diseases of the eyes, such as macular degeneration, diabetic retinopathy, and cataracts.

Appositive Clues

An appositive may offer a synonym or description of the word that will provide a clue to its recognition. Students may be taught that an appositive is a word or phrase that restates or identifies the word or expression it follows and that it usually is set off by commas, dashes, or parentheses.

- President Ronald Reagan was the victim of an attempted *assassination*, or murder, by John Hinckley, during his first term in office.
- *Chlorophyll*, the material in plants that makes them appear green, is manufactured by the process that is called photosynthesis.

Comparison Clues

A comparison of the unfamiliar word with a word that the student knows may offer a clue. In the examples, the familiar words *maker of maps* and *decaying* provide the clues for the less common words *cartographer* and *decomposing.*

- That *cartographer* surely is an excellent maker of maps.
- Because Wisconsin no longer removes deer that have been killed on its state roads, a driver may see a deer carcass *decomposing*, or decaying, nearly anywhere.

Contrast Clues

A contrast of the unknown word with a familiar word may offer a clue. In the examples, the familiar words *clean air* and *active* provide the clues for the less common words *smog* and *hibernate.*

- The thick *smog* of Los Angeles is unlike the beautiful *clean air* of the mountains that are located nearby.
- Deer do not *hibernate* in the winter as do bears; instead they are *active* trying to find the limited food that exists.

Common-Expression Clues

Familiarity with the word order found in many commonly heard expressions, particularly figurative expressions, can help students identify unknown words. Students with varied language and prior knowledge are more likely to be able to use figurative expressions to help them identify words than are students with less developed backgrounds.

- Searching for the *genealogy* of my family isn't my *cup of tea.*
- Raul was so *incensed* with me that he *jumped down my throat.*

Example Clues

Sometimes examples are given for words that may be unfamiliar in print, and these examples can provide the clues needed for identification.

- *Zoology* is the study of such animals as the rhinoceros, lion, hippopotamus, jackal, hyena, cape buffalo, leopard, and cheetah.
- A *cliché* is an overused phrase such as "whatever," "busy as a bee," or "old as the hills."

Since contemporary reading instruction views reading as a global, meaning-based process emphasizing comprehension from the initial stages, *context clues usually are the most effective word identification technique.* However, as already noted, context clues often are most helpful when they are used along with word structure and phonics and when there are only a few unknown words in the reading material. Usually there should not be more than *one* in *fifty* unknown words in the material if context clues are to be used effectively. Perhaps that is the main reason why an average reader can use context clues effectively only about *5* to *20%* of the time. Nevertheless, using context clues is an effective technique for identifying words and learning their meanings.

Students should understand that the use of context clues always is a *calculated estimate* of the meaning of the unknown word and that they should be more concerned with *meaning* than pronunciation. According to Schwartz (1988), Herman, Anderson, Pearson, and Nagy (1987), Nagy, Herman, and Anderson (1985), and Wysocki and Jenkins (1987), an average ten- to fourteen-year-old-student can learn *750* to *8,250* new vocabulary words through the *incidental learning* that is exemplified by context clues. In addition, it is estimated that students might learn *1,000* new vocabulary words a year from *thirty* minutes of daily free reading time in school, *providing* that the material is challenging and interesting but fairly easy to read. According to Nagy, Herman, and Anderson (1985), learning from context is the main mode of vocabulary acquisition throughout the school years, and this accounts for the positive relationship between wide reading and size of vocabulary. Learning from context, therefore, is a major factor in a student's reading development.

Students should be encouraged to be *risk-takers* while reading silently and orally. However, they should not make an excessive number of guesses about unknown words. In that case they may be called *context readers*. It is important to remember that below-average readers may rely too heavily on context clues, whereas good readers are more likely to use all the word identification clues. However, the use of context clues remains important for below-average readers too. A reading teacher or tutor usually should accept partial word knowledge, some uncertainty, and occasional misleading contexts with such students.

Students who read books at their level have only a *one in twenty chance* of learning the meaning of any word from context. Burns and Schell (1975) listed several traits associated with those who do not use context clues:

1. They stop when they meet an unknown word.
2. They rely too heavily on other skills, such as configuration and beginning or ending sounds.
3. They practice less effective analysis techniques, such as relying on signals from the teacher or picture clues.

At the intermediate-grade level and above, the preceding traits probably are most associated with students who have significant reading or learning disabilities.

Advantages and Limitations of Using Context Clues

Here are the main *advantag*es of using context clues:

- Most students can identify many words in context that they cannot identify in isolation. Some students with learning disabilities may be the exception, however.
- Students who have difficulties with phonic analysis may be able to identify words more effectively by using context.
- Readers who use context clues become independent decoders much more quickly than those who do not. They become competent at *predicting* what words might be. They then can confirm or reject their predictions depending on whether they make sense in the context of what they are reading. Then they continue reading rapidly.
- Words that do not have a consistent sound–symbol relationship may be more easily identified by using context clues.

Here are the main *limitations* of using context clues:

- Students who have limited reading skills find it very difficult to use context clues effectively.
- Context clues cannot be used successfully if there are a number of unknown words in the reading material.

- In many cases, the surrounding context may not be sufficient to provide accurate word identification or may provide misleading information about the unknown word.
- Because there are many synonyms in English that could make sense in different contexts, when context clues are used *alone*, they may not result in accurate word identification. When the *exact word* is required for some reason, a student also must use other word identification clues, such as word structure or phonic clues, along with context clues.

In summary, the use of context clues should be given the greatest emphasis, especially in grades 5 to 12, except perhaps with a few students at this level who have significant reading or learning disabilities. Such students often need to have more emphasis placed on other word identification techniques, especially word structure or phonics. However, even these students should understand the importance of context clues and use them when possible.

Strategies and Activities for Improving Use of Context Clues to Identify New Words

The chapter now provides a sampling of classroom-tested strategies for improving ability in general context clue usage and in context clue usage in the content fields of literature, social studies, and science. Although all of these strategies are useful in grades 5 to 12, you should modify any of them in light of the needs and interests of your own students.

Extensive Reading of a Wide Variety of Materials

Extensive reading of a wide variety of materials undoubtedly is the most effective and motivating way to improve ability in context clue usage. This reading should include varied materials, from fiction and nonfiction mass-market books at the independent or instructional reading levels to content textbooks, pamphlets, magazines and newspapers, reference books, and the World Wide Web.

Reading is a skill similar to any other skill—it improves with practice. An analogy can be drawn between reading and tennis, for example. A person who plays tennis often is usually a better player than one who rarely plays. Similarly, a student who reads extensively from all types of materials usually makes the best progress. In contrast, a student who does not read either for pleasure or for information often makes minimal progress. Such students often have reading or learning disabilities or are *reluctant readers*—students who can read adequately but choose not to unless required.

It is regrettable that a number of students in grades 5 to 12, often those with special needs, read as little as possible and therefore do not make much reading progress. Although it may be difficult, it is possible to motivate students to read for pleasure and information by providing them with easy, highly motivating material in which they are truly interested. I found this to be the case with Randy, an intermediate-grade boy I tutored for four summers. An activity sheet that I constructed for him about *kayaking* is a prime example of the kind of material that can truly interest a student. Randy was easily able to comprehend this material, which was on his own grade level. Yet at school he never could read near his grade level, presumably because his teachers did not provide him with material in which he had any interest.

You may be successful with students like Randy by encouraging them to read self-selected, fairly easy material that reflects their unique interests specifically. Such students often enjoy *informational books* about their special interests that build on their prior knowledge. You may be surprised at how effectively students in grades 5 to 12 can read material in which they have a special interest—material about a sport, racecars, boats, snowmobiles, fishing, hunting, unique animals, mysteries, space, or relationships between boys and girls (the latter is mainly interesting to girls), for example.

Self-Monitoring and Self-Correction While Reading

It is very important for students to learn both *self-monitoring and self-correction* while reading, both silently and orally. Students can be made aware of *miscues* (errors) that significantly interfere with their comprehension if the teacher has them listen to teacher- or tutor-read material or tape-recorded material, including oral reading samples of their own. Students should indicate when miscues occur and state why the miscues are not appropriate. When students have heard a disruptive miscue, they usually should finish listening to the entire sentence because it may provide additional information.

Self-monitoring is extremely important in improving context clue usage. Self-monitoring is a *mindset;* readers consistently think about what they are reading. If students cannot use context clues effectively and cannot comprehend what they read, they should learn to use the appropriate *fix-up strategies,* which include reading the material in the next paragraph or paragraphs. Usually the words *after the unknown word* provide more help than the words before it. A *place-holder* (a word that makes sense and is grammatically correct in the context) can be used until new information makes it necessary to try another response.

If neither strategy is successful, rereading the entire sentence containing the unknown word may be useful. However, before students do this, they should examine the unknown word by using word structure and phonic clues *along with context clues.*

One of the most important characteristics of an able reader is the awareness of disruptive miscues while reading silently or orally and quickly self-correcting these miscues for effective comprehension.

Dahl and Samuel's Strategy for Using Context Clues

One strategy that students may find useful while self-monitoring and self-correcting is *Dahl and Samuel's strategy* (1974):

1. Use information from the passage, prior knowledge, and language clues.
2. Predict which word is most likely to occur.
3. Compare the printed and predicted words to see if they match.
4. Confirm or disconfirm your prediction.

Edwards and Dermott's Method of Teaching Context Clues

Edwards and Dermott (1989) suggested that teachers select difficult words from content material that will soon be assigned, take a quotation from the material that uses each word in correct context, and provide written comments to the students to help them use appropriate context clues or other strategies, such as word structure or dictionary use, to figure out the difficult words.

The students then try to use the available clues to determine the meanings of the difficult words before they read the assignment. Class discussion may help them think through the most effective strategy to use to determine the word meanings.

Shanker and Ekwall's Strategy for Using Context Clues

Shanker and Ekwall (1988) provided the following strategy for helping students use context clues effectively to decode unknown words in their content material.

1. Have students preread material silently before reading orally. Discuss difficult, unknown vocabulary.

2. Have students set purposes for reading; they always should read for understanding and accuracy, not speed.

3. Use short, fairly easy, interesting selections if possible. Have students stop frequently to explain what they have read in their own words to ensure effective comprehension.

4. Use high-interest material, including student-authored material, as often as possible.

5. Encourage students to read *past* unknown words to the end of the sentence and then come back to the unknown words. As already noted, research has indicated that words that come *after* unknown words often are more helpful than those that come before.

6. Have students scan for important words. Have them guess the meaning and then decide if their prediction was accurate.

7. Encourage practice in the *act of reading.* There is no better way for students to learn to read for meaning. Provide time, appropriate materials, and an advantageous setting, and encourage silent and oral reading of age-appropriate, meaningful fiction and nonfiction materials.

Gunning's Strategy for Teaching Context Clues

Gunning (1996) suggested the following procedure for teaching context clues to students in grades 5 to 12.

Step One: Explain Context Clues
Show students the usefulness of context clues. Select five or six difficult, unknown words from a content assignment that students are going to read and show them how *context* could be used to derive the approximate meanings.

Step Two: Demonstrate Sternberg and Powell's (1983) Three-Step Process
Do this by asking the following questions:

What information in this selection will help me figure out what the unknown word means? (*selective encoding*)

When I put together all the information about the unknown word, what does the word apparently mean? (*selective combination*)

What do I know that will help me figure out the meaning of this word? (*selective comprehension*)

Step Three: Have Them Try Out the Tentative Meaning of the Unknown Word
Show students how to try out the tentative meaning of the unknown word by substituting the meaning they have guessed and reading the sentence to see if it fits. Explain that if the meaning does not fit the sense of the sentence, they should revise it.

Step Four: Model the Process
Model the process of using context clues with a variety of content words. Explain the thought processes involved in trying to figure out their meanings. Illustrate how examples, such as comparisons, contrasts, synonyms, appositives, prior knowledge, or a combination of strategies, might be used. Illustrate also how context and experience could be used to construct a *tentative meaning* for the unknown word, and then how the meaning could be tried out by substituting it in the sentence.

Step Five: Guided Practice
Have students use context clues to determine unfamiliar words in selected passages that provide meaningful clues. Go through one or two examples with the students. Then have them try to use the clues independently. Discuss the meaning of the unfamiliar words and the types of clues that they used.

Step Six: Apply the Process
Encourage students to use context clues in a selection they read. After the reading, have a class discussion. Ask how they went about deciding what the unknown word meant, what clues they used, and how they decided on their definition of the unknown word.

Reader-Selected-Miscue Strategy

Vacca, Vacca, and Gove (1995) suggested the *reader-selected-miscue strategy*, which they said could be adapted to a variety of reading situations. Here are the steps in this strategy:

1. Students are assigned to read a fiction or nonfiction selection silently and independently without interruption.

2. When they encounter a difficult word or a concept that does not make sense, they insert a bookmark or lightly mark the page, and then continue to read.

3. When they complete the reading, they then review the words or concepts that they marked and select the *three* that caused them the greatest difficulty.

4. The teacher asks the students to explain how they may have solved some of the problems or difficult words that they encountered on their own as they continued to read.

5. Finally, all the students examine the passage that contained the difficult words or concepts that they marked and help each other in clarifying them.

Gipe's Context Method

Gipe (1980) illustrated a *context method* in which students read new words in meaningful contexts, applying their prior knowledge. She then studied the effectiveness of that strategy in comparison with three other methods: an association method (in which an unknown word is paired with a familiar synonym), a category method (in which students place words in categories), and a dictionary method (in which students look up the word, write a definition, and use the word in a sentence).

The *expanded context method* was found to be the most effective of the four. The *application* of the new words may have been the most important part of the method. After students determined the meaning of the word from a variety of contexts, including a definition context, they *applied* it to their personal experiences in a written response. Therefore, the instruction followed a desirable technique for vocabulary—helping students to integrate the new words with their prior knowledge.

Variations of the Cloze Procedure

The *cloze procedure* is an effective strategy for students in grades 5 to 12 to improve context clue usage. Cloze was developed by Wilson L. Taylor (1953) and is based on the psychological theory of *closure*, which states that a person wants to finish an incomplete pattern. The cloze procedure is based on the *prediction aspect* of reading—that is, when a reader tries to predict the unknown words that he or she meets in a passage. Thus, the cloze procedure makes use of both context clues and grammar clues to help a reader identify unknown words.

Although cloze has a number of different variations, each of which can be useful in improving a student's context clue usage, it is constructed in the same overall way. Here's how to do it.

Construct a cloze procedure from a content textbook, a mass-market book, or any supplementary material. Select a passage of about *250* words from what you believe to be a student's instructional or high independent reading level. Type the first and last sentences with no deletions. Then, for the rest of the passage, type sentences omitting every *n*th word, unless the target word is a proper noun or a very difficult word. Normally every *eighth word* is omitted at the intermediate-grade level and every *fifth word* above the intermediate-grade level. The length of each blank space should be about *fifteen* typewritten spaces long.

When the cloze procedure is used to improve ability in context clue usage, *any word that makes sense in the passage* and satisfies the specific requirements of that particular cloze procedure should be counted as correct. Incorrect spelling that is decipherable is not penalized in any version of cloze.

A number of versions of the cloze procedure are most appropriate for grades 5 to 12. In one version for the intermediate grades each omitted word is replaced by a short typewritten space that is as long as the omitted word. For example, here is how the word *hydrogen* would look if it were deleted from this type of cloze procedure: _ _ _ _ _ _ _ _. In other versions of the cloze procedure, *entire sentences, several words at a time*, or *all the unimportant words in a passage* are deleted in a random way.

Selective word omissions may be useful variations of the cloze procedure in grades 5 to 12. In these variations, important nouns, verbs, adjectives, and adverbs are deleted. These words may carry the meaning of the author's writing. When selected nouns, verbs, adjectives, and adverbs are deleted, the emphasis is on the important information in the content passage and on the specialized vocabulary that is contained in it. These variations usually require considerable prior knowledge on the student's part about the subject on which the cloze procedure was constructed. Usually, deleted nouns and verbs are somewhat easier for students to determine than deleted adjectives and adverbs. The potential difficulty of these types of cloze procedure makes it desirable for students to complete them only *after* the target material has already been studied.

Again, remember that when any version of the cloze procedure is used to improve context clue usage, *any word that makes sense in context* and satisfies the requirements of that particular procedure should be considered correct even if it is not the exact word that was omitted.

Cryptology and Mutilated Messages

Many students in grades 5 to 12 enjoy figuring out codes and writing messages in code. When a message is written in code, something has been done to alter the graphic display and context clues are used to break the code.

Here are several examples of ways to alter or mutilate messages. You and your students will be able to think of many other ways. There are also mass-market books on cryptology that your students can consult for suggestions.

- No spaces are left between the words. For example:

  Astudentcanuseanumberofdifferentsearchenginestolocateaspecifictopiconthe WorldWideWeb.

- The bottoms of the letters are cut off. For example:

  Shamika currently is learning how to set up her own Web site in which she is trying to sell the beautiful custom-made jewelry that she creates.

- Numbers that stand for certain letters are substituted for the letters in the message. For example: a = 1; e = 2; i = 3; o = 4; u = 5; y (used as a vowel) = 6; w (used as a vowel) = 7. Here is the encoded sentence: Th3s S2p2mb2r 3 1m t1k3ng 1 t45r t4 Ch3n1 wh2r2 3 w3ll s22 th2 Gr21t W1ll, th2 T2rr1 C4tt1 W1rr34rs, 1nd th2 Y1ngtz2 R3v2r. (See Chapter Three for another example of this strategy.)

- Color names are added to the message and must be omitted for the message to make sense. For example: Next week green Joanne blue and I purple are pink going to white the Mall orange of America black in Minnesota brown to spend tan two lavender entire days turquoise doing maroon nothing but red shopping.

Scrambled Synonyms

This activity can be used in grades 5 and 6 to help students learn how to use contextual synonyms. Here is how: Construct sentences that use synonyms to introduce or define unfamiliar words. Do not include the new word in the sentence. Instead, construct a chart consisting of missing words and deceptive letters mixed up vertically, horizontally, forward, and backward (as in the following example).

Give each student a copy of the sentences and the word chart. The students then read the sentences, examine the chart, and select the missing synonyms from it. They then circle the synonyms and write them in the sentence.

1. This is a __________ of our new house. This representation is quite accurate.

2. That is a __________ package. It is very large.

3. A cat is a __________ animal. It must eat meat or fish products.

R	T	G	I	G	A	N	T	I	C	R	P	O	T	F
P	R	S	T	R	U	V	X	Y	C	P	P	Q	O	A
S	S	V	Y	R	R	O	P	S	T	Y	Z	T	S	C
T	R	Y	S	O	O	U	V	W	X	T	U	S	O	S
R	S	T	U	B	B	D	U	G	G	P	P	R	T	I
A	A	B	C	C	D	D	U	O	T	O	T	R	Y	M
Y	R	X	T	B	A	A	Z	X	Y	Z	T	R	X	I
A	B	D	U	T	X	T	O	P	P	U	O	T	T	L
S	R	R	S	U	O	R	O	V	I	N	R	A	C	E

Help the Dragon (Lion, Bear) Get Home

This game is most useful in grades 5 and 6. To construct the game, draw a game board with small squares on a large piece of poster board. At one end of the board draw a *dragon (or lion, or bear)* and at the opposite end draw a den. Make a set of three-inch by five-inch cards that offer detailed *descriptive statements.* A summary of each detailed statement is written in various squares on the game board. Obtain beans, corn kernels, or some other playing pieces for this game.

Here's how to play. First, have each student draw a descriptive card from the pack. After reading the descriptive statement, the student moves his or her playing piece to the square on the game board that has the correct summary statement. If the player cannot identify the summary statement, he or she returns her playing piece to the *dragon (lion, bear)* and waits for another turn. The first player who reaches the *dragon's (lion's, bear's) den* wins the game. If students select a descriptive card whose summary would move them in a reverse direction, they remain on their present place if they can identify the summary square. If they cannot identify the summary square, they should be helped to do so and then return to the *dragon (lion, bear).*

The diagram on the next page illustrates the game.

Musical Cloze

Mateja (1982) has suggested a strategy called *musical cloze.* Here's how it works. Select a song that is appropriate for your students and the content thematic unit that they are studying. Then make deletions in the lyrics—of selected parts of speech, words that fit into a particular category, words that show relationships, or any other category you wish.

Have students practice until they can sing the original song. Then have them sing it with the deletions, and have them suggest *alternatives* for the omitted words or phrases. Write these alternatives on the chalkboard in place of the original words. Later lead the students in a discussion of the appropriateness of their replacement choices and their reasons for choosing them.

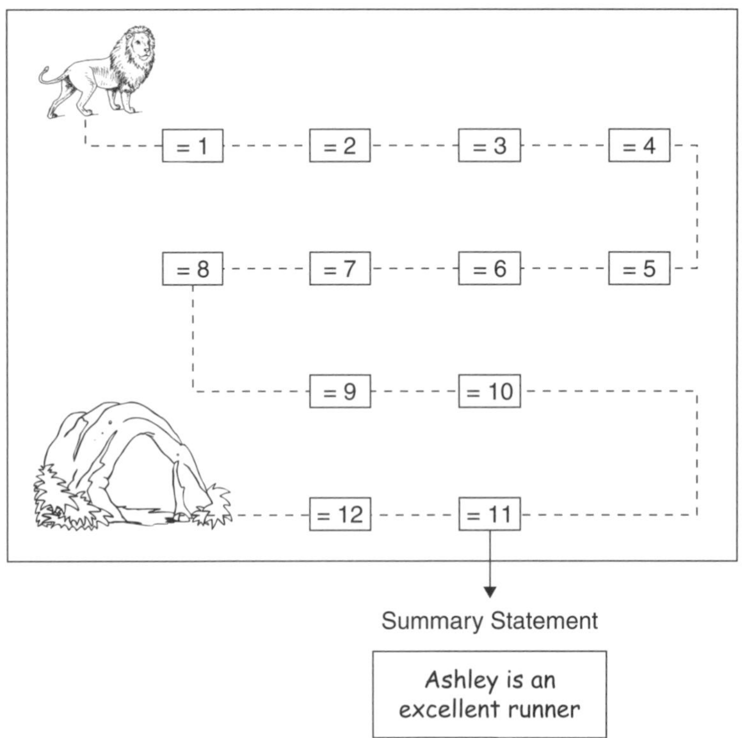

Teacher Modeling of Effective Use of Context Clues

May (1998) has discussed *teacher modeling of the use of context clues.* He stated that teachers should use a form of the direct teaching method by modeling the use of context clues. Teachers should demonstrate to students that the use of context clues while reading is very important. May suggested modeling in the following manner.

TEACHER: I want to show you what I think about when I meet a word whose meaning I don't know. I'll talk out loud to show you how I figure it out. [The teacher reads: "My beloved father and mother provided me with a *halcyon* childhood that included many pets, travel, and lots of love."] When I examine this sentence, I notice that the writer calls her father and mother *beloved.* This probably means that they were very nice people and that the writer still loves them. Then she says that her father and mother provided her with many pets, the opportunity to travel, and most importantly, lots of love. If the writer had all of those things and loved her parents too, then she probably had a very *happy* childhood. That's why I'm fairly certain that the word *halcyon* means *happy* or *very happy.*

Finally, the teacher sums it up:

TEACHER: So by thinking about all the clues that were provided in the sentence, I am able to determine that the word *halcyon* undoubtedly means *happy* or *very happy.*

Reproducible Activity Sheets for Improving Use of Context Clues

The chapter now provides seven reproducible activity sheets for improving general context clue usage and context clue usage while reading content material in literature, social studies, and science. You can duplicate these sheets in their present form or modify them any way you wish in light of the needs and interests of your own students. In addition, you can use them as models for constructing similar activity sheets for improving ability in context clue usage.

These are the activity sheets that follow: Choose the Correct Word in Sentence Context—Ninth- to Twelfth-Grade Level; What Word Is Missing?—Sixth- to Seventh-Grade Level; Select the Correct Definition of the Word in Context—Sixth-Grade Level; Write an Answer in Place of the Make-Believe Word—Fifth-Grade Level; Random Cloze Procedure—Fifth-Grade Level; Random Cloze Procedure from Social Studies—Sixth-Grade Level; Random Cloze Procedure from Science—Fifth-Grade Level.

Answer Key for Choose the Correct Word in Sentence Context

1. cygnet; 2. feral; 3. buffalo; 4. phoenix; 5. ferret; 6. farrier; 7. pride; 8. dark horse; 9. duck soup; 10. white elephant; 11. greenhorn; 12. lionize; 13. bovine; 14. lupine; 15. dogged; 16. bevy; 17. monkey business; 18. omnivorous 19. pecking order; 20. herbivorous

Answer Key for What Word Is Missing?

1. monkey; 2. hair; 3. paper; 4. house; 5. double; 6. sea; 7. sweet; 8. silver; 9. milk; 10. break; 11. silk; 12. master; 13. right; 14. string; 15. square

Answer Key for Select the Correct Definiton of the Word in Context

1. the inability to read; 2. on the percentage scale; 3. harmless; 4. female hormone; 5. make ready for reuse; 6. a person who exposes fraud; 7. middle; 8. drudge; 9. authorization; 10. are inactive; 11. traditional; 12. shed seasonally

Answer Key for Write an Answer in Place of the Make-Believe Word

Note: The answers included here are only for illustrative purposes. *Any answer that makes sense in sentence context should be considered correct:* 1. swimmer, pier, dock, loon, duck, raft; 2. car, automobile, stick, bicycle, skateboard, truck; 3. storms, stairs, cars, sounds, people; 4. swimming, boating, shopping, hiking, running; 5. dog, bear, man, coyote; 6. mountains, forests, trees, woods; 7. skiing, snowmobiling, sledding, tobogganing; 8. store, garage, restaurant, factory; 9. play, walk, swim, run, eat; 10. flowers, cacti, mountains, animals, birds; 11. jewelry, clothes, dresses, skirts, hats; 12. carpenter, runner, swimmer, craftsman, golfer

Answer Key for Random Cloze Procedure

Note: Any answer that makes sense in a blank space should be considered correct. The following answers are for illustrative purposes: population; packs; located; the; federal; and; caught; eyes; extremely; very; rose; with; ice; pounds; with; for; were; drug; minutes; signal; since; wolves; point; in; important; suited; about; must

Answer Key for Random Cloze Procedure from Social Studies

Note: Any answer that makes sense in a blank should be considered correct. The following answers are included only for illustrative purposes: most; slave; being; traveled; were; faith; were; they; escape; not; slaves; people; needed; ground; tiny; trap; shoveled; dug; cellar; safe; good; went; became; grass; land; cellar; years; knees

Answer Key for Random Cloze Procedure from Science

Note: Any answer that makes sense in a blank should be considered correct. The answers are included here only for illustrative purposes: hobby; her; clothes; hat, seem; person's; provide; boots; skid; spelunker, some, heavy; outfit; shirt; is; avoid; gloves; rope; clean; must; repairs; attached; light; on; carry; should; map; kit; some; bars; rule; cave; people; someone; not

Name ________________________ Grade ___ Teacher ____________ Date _________

Choose the Correct Word in Sentence Context

Each of the following *twenty terms* that are related to *animals* is used *once.* Fill in the most appropriate term to complete each sentence. You may use a dictionary if you wish.

feral	dogged	white elephant	bevy	cygnet
buffalo	monkey business	pecking order	farrier	herbivorous
lionize	ferret	dark horse	bovine	phoenix
lupine	greenhorn	duck soup	omnivorous	pride

1. A __________________ is the correct name for a baby swan.
2. Although Linda fed a __________________ cat who would come nowhere near her for a long time, it never became tame.
3. I hope you don't think you can ____________________ me with that story.
4. Shirley is a true survivor who, like a __________________, arose from the ashes of losing her leg in an accident.
5. Shandra's internist is trying to __________________ out the cause of her persistent acid reflux.
6. Rory already is a __________________ who shoes horses and is now trying to become a veterinarian.
7. When I was in Tanzania seven years ago, I saw an entire ____________ of lions, including males, females, and cubs.
8. Alejandro Gutierrez is a ______________________ candidate for the mayor of Tucumcari.
9. That geometry test yesterday certainly was __________________ for me, and I aced it.
10. The statue of Martha Washington looks like a __________________ to me and will not sell in a million years.
11. When my grandfather came from southern Sweden to the United States in 1910, he was called a __________________ by the Americans who already lived here.
12. There is not one Hollywood celebrity whom I really ________________.
13. Both cattle and oxen are members of the ___________________ family.
14. A ___________________ argument broke out between husband and wife.
15. Sarah is a tenacious, ___________________ person who never gives up once she has made up her mind.
16. When Ralph was hunting last week, he saw a ________________ of quails on the ground.
17. Josh and Jason caused trouble last weekend when they engaged in real ___________________.
18. An ___________________ animal feeds on both animals and plants.
19. In our class Matt always is at the bottom of the _________________.
20. Deer are ___________________ animals who eat only vegetable substances, sometimes including beautiful summer flowers and fresh vegetables from someone's garden.

Name ______________________ Grade ___ Teacher ____________ Date _________

What Word Is Missing?

Complete these *combinations of words* by filling in the *same word* that belongs with each word in the group. For each example, write the correct word in the spaces provided. The first example has been done for you. You may work with a partner or partners if you wish.

1. ______monkey______ business; ______monkey______ bars; ______monkey______ suit
2. ____________ brush; ____________ follicle; ____________ cell
3. ____________ birch; ____________ money; ____________ tiger
4. ____________ call; ____________ husband; ____________ rule
5. ____________ boiler; ____________ agent; ____________ cross
6. ____________ turtle; ____________ breeze; ____________ cucumber
7. ____________ potato; ____________ tooth; ____________ pea
8. ____________ fox; ____________ chloride; ____________ maple
9. ____________ shake; ____________ tooth; ____________ glass
10. ____________ up; ____________ even; ____________ camp
11. ____________ screen; ____________ gland; ____________ stocking
12. ____________ sergeant; ____________ race; ____________ plan
13. ____________ angle; ____________ field; ____________ wing
14. ____________ bean; ____________ along; ____________ quartet
15. ____________ dance; ____________ deal; ____________ knot

Name ________________________ Grade ___ Teacher ____________ Date _________

Select the Correct Definition of the Word in Context

Read the following sentences to yourself. *Circle the correct definition* for the underlined word in each sentence.

1. Ms. Marks has been crusading against illiteracy for all of her adult life.

   discrimination / the inability to read / homelessness

2. Shaundra scored in the ninety-first percentile on the verbal portion of the Graduate Record Examination.

   percent / quartile / number

3. My golden retriever has a benign tumor on her right side.

   dangerous / massive / harmless

4. Researchers now believe that a woman who takes estrogen after menopause may increase her risk of getting several kinds of cancer.

   vitamin E / female hormone / substance to thin the blood

5. Contemporary Americans always should recycle as much as possible.

   plan ahead / make ready for reuse / be careful with money

6. When Senator Jensen gave a speech about taxation, he sounded very much like a muckraker.

   bigot / a person who exposes fraud / patriot

7. My salary seems to be the median of all the salaries in our company.

   middle / highest / most popular

8. Abby acts like a *peon* on the job and this earns her no respect.

   drudge / superior person / friend

9. My mother received a mandate from the neighbors to pressure the alderman for a paved road in front of her house.

   reward / authorization / privilege

10. The bears in northern Wisconsin always hibernate for the winter.

    are inactive / are active / migrate

11. My father has believed in conservative principles for all of his life and has modeled them for all of his family.

    traditional / socialistic / progressive

12. I enjoy seeing the beautifully colored deciduous trees in the fall.

    alder / evergreen / leafy

Name ________________________ Grade ___ Teacher ____________ Date _________

Write an Answer in Place of the Make-Believe Word

Each of these sentences contains *one make-believe word.* Write in *any word* that makes sense in the sentence *in place of the make-believe word.* Write it on the line underneath the sentence. You can work with a partner or partners if you want.

1. When I went for a pontoon boat ride on Birch Lake this afternoon, I saw a *blager.*

   ____

2. The small child was hit by a *marmar.*

   ____

3. Jessie's dog always is frightened by *glab.*

   ____

4. Evie's favorite activity in the summer is *crade.*

   ____

5. Marsha was attacked by a *somding* while she was running last week.

   ____

6. The *wedde* in the West are very lovely in the fall.

   ____

7. A favorite wintertime activity of children in the Northeast is *rebke.*

   ____

8. To earn extra money last summer, my older brother worked in a *wach.*

   ____

9. A golden retriever always wants to *sanb.*

   ____

10. The most beautiful things in the desert are the *horps.*

    ____

11. My friend Kathy loves to buy *pepl.*

    ____

12. Jim Carlson is an expert *opat.*

    ____

Name ________________________ **Grade** ___ **Teacher** ____________ **Date** _________

Random Cloze Procedure

Read this passage about studying wolves in Wisconsin to yourself. Throughout the passage, words have been omitted in a random way. *Write a word on each blank line* that makes sense in the sentence. When you are done, *reread the entire passage* to make sure that it all sounds correct. You may work with a partner or partners if you want.

Tracking Wolves in Wisconsin*

The state of Wisconsin currently is attempting to place a radio collar and microchip on some of the state's wolf population to monitor their movements. The Wisconsin wolf _______________ has grown to 251 animals in sixty-six _______________ of 2 to 10 animals, each _______________ in fourteen northern counties. The Wisconsin wolf population remains listed as threatened by _______________ state, and endangered by the _______________ government.

One day in summer 2002 "Lena," the alpha female _______________ breeding matriarch of the Black Lake Pack, was _______________ in a live trap for study and tracking. Her amber _______________ told the biologists that she was _______________ unhappy and stressed to have been trapped. It also was _______________ dangerous for her as her temperature quickly _______________ to 107 degrees, 6 degrees above normal, after she was tranquilized _______________ ketamine/xylazine. The biologists used water, alcohol, and _______________ packs to try to lower her temperature to normal.

While she was tranquilized, she was weighed at seventy-two _______________ and measured at five feet three inches from nose-tip to tail-tip. She was fitted _______________ a radio collar vital to the state's monitoring efforts, and a microchip was implanted _______________ future identification. Blood was also collected, and wood tick and scat samples _______________ taken.

After all this was done, the _______________ yohimbine was administered to reverse the effects of the tranquilizer. Within sixty _______________ of receiving the reversal drug, Lena walked away with her radio _______________ being heard loud and clear. She joined fourteen Wisconsin wolves live-trapped _______________ spring and thirty-six _______________ transmitting via radio collars.

After resting near the capture _______________ for several days, Lena was on the move six miles from the place of capture. Lena, or Wolf 370F officially _______________ the study, was an _______________ part of the state wolf monitoring program.

The study has discovered that Wisconsin is well _______________ for wolves. However, some people still hold old prejudices _______________ wolves and feel they _______________ kill them. It would be wonderful if we would share our habitat with wolves as we do with other animals such as deer, bears, and many others.

---

* This is a true story.

Name _________________________ **Grade** ___ **Teacher** ____________ **Date** _________

Random Cloze Procedure from Social Studies

Read this passage about an *underground railroad station* in southern Wisconsin. Throughout the passage words have been omitted in a random way. Write a word in each blank space that makes sense in the sentence. When you are done, reread the entire passage to be sure that it all makes sense. You may work with a partner or partners if you want.

The Underground Railroad at Milton, Wisconsin

The "Underground Railroad" was not a railroad at all; instead, it was a group of people in several northern states who helped runaway slaves escape to Canada to gain freedom. One of the ________________ unusual stations on the Underground Railroad was the *Milton House Inn* in southern Wisconsin.

Andrew Pratt was a runaway ________________ from Missouri who had reached Illinois just before the Civil War, thinking he would be safe. However, he was thrown into jail there for the "crime" of ________________ black.

No one knows for sure how Pratt ________________ to Milton, but he simply arrived at that inn, which was owned by Joseph and Nancy Goodrich. They ________________ Christian people of deep ________________ who were known as *abolitionists:* people who ________________ wholeheartedly opposed to slavery.

Therefore, the Goodriches never asked if ________________ were going to help slaves ________________, but just how they were going to do it. They could ________________ figure out how they could keep runaway ________________ at a hotel in which ________________ came and went at any time. Fugitive slaves ________________ a secret entrance since they could not just knock on the hotel door.

Finally, Joseph Goodrich went under the ________________, just as the name suggested. There was a ________________ log cabin in back of the inn, and Joseph cut a ________________ door in the cabin floor and began to dig. He scraped, __________________, and hauled until he ________________ a tunnel fifty feet long and three feet high straight into the ________________ of the Milton House Inn.

Andrew Pratt hid in this tunnel, and when it was ________________, Joseph sent him to a friend who needed a ________________ farmhand. Later he ________________ into business for himself. Still later he ________________ a homesteader in southern Wisconsin, plowing acres of prairie ________________ to "prove up" or pay for government ________________ with hard work instead of money.

The underground tunnel to the ________________ of the Milton House Inn still exists today and is part of the Milton Historical Society Museum. One hundred fifty ________________ ago fugitive slaves crawled on hands and ________________ along a dirt passage barely wider than a man's shoulders. Today the tunnel has stone walls and a cement floor, but the chilly darkness is unchanged.

Name ______________________ **Grade** ___ **Teacher** ____________ **Date** _________

Random Cloze Procedure from Science

Read this passage about being a "spelunker." Words have been omitted from the passage in a random way. Write a word in each blank space that makes sense in that sentence. When you are finished, reread the entire passage to be sure that it all makes sense. You may work with a partner or partners if you want.

Being a Spelunker

A *spelunker* is a person who explores caves for recreation or as a hobby. It is a ________________ that you may want to pursue someday if you have the opportunity.

A spelunker selects his or ________________ outfit with an appreciation for the fact that caving is both dirty and hard on the ________________. A spelunker must have narrow-brimmed hard ________________ of the type worn by construction workers because cave ceilings are often lower than they ________________ and *stalactites* are a constant hazard to a ________________ head. A hat also should ________________ a bracket for holding a headlamp, and a strap under the chin to keep it in place when the spelunker climbs or crawls.

Most cavers prefer leather ________________ with tops high enough to support the ankles, but not so high as to cramp the calves. Since leather soles ________________ on smooth rocks and on mud, a ________________ should choose shoes with rubber soles and ________________ type of tread. Two pairs of socks should be worn: ________________ woolen ones over lightweight inner socks.

The best ________________ for caving is a moderately loose set of coveralls and a sweat ________________. In winter or when high in the mountains, insulated underwear ________________ very helpful. Most spelunkers ________________ zippers since they are too easily clogged by mud. Light, tough work ________________ protect the hands against cuts and possible ________________ burns, and they keep hands ________________ if the caver wants to use a camera.

Name ______________________ **Grade** ___ **Teacher** ___________ **Date** _________

Being a Spelunker (continued)

A spelunker always ________________ carry a light source, including spare parts for ________________. The primary light source usually is a carbide headlamp ________________ securely to a bracket on a hard hat. The lamp casts a broad, diffused ________________ by burning a gas produced by water dripping ________________ pellets of carbide. A spelunker also can ________________ a waterproof flashlight with spare batteries and a bulb.

Every spelunker ________________ bring a compass and a ________________ of the cave he or she is going to explore. Someone in the group should carry a first-aid ________________ for treating minor cuts and scratches. Each spelunker should bring ________________ high-energy food such as candy ________________, raisins, or peanuts and bottled water.

The single most important ________________ of spelunking is never to enter a ________________ alone. At least two, and preferably three, ________________ should be in every group. Always notify ________________ on the surface when the caving party is expected to return. If a party does ________________ return, someone can be sent to locate the spelunkers.

Spelunking is a fascinating hobby that always requires good judgment and care on the part of the spelunker.

For Additional Reading

Allen, H., and Barbe, W. *Ready-to-Use Vocabulary, Word Attack, and Comprehension Activities: Fifth-Grade Reading Level* (pp. 147–156). San Francisco: Jossey-Bass, 1998.

Burns, P., Roe, B., and Ross, E. *Teaching Reading in Today's Elementary Schools* (pp. 103–110). Boston: Houghton Mifflin, 1996.

Cheek, E., Jr., Flippo, R., and Lindsey, J. *Reading for Success in Elementary Schools* (pp. 122–126). Madison, Wis.: Brown & Benchmark, 1997.

Cooper, D. *Literacy: Helping Children Construct Meaning* (pp. 237–240). Boston: Houghton Mifflin, 1997.

Graves, M., Juel, C., and Graves, B. *Teaching Reading in the 21st Century* (pp. 200–205). Needham Heights, Mass.: Allyn and Bacon, 1998.

Miller, W. *The Reading Teacher's Survival Kit* (pp. 302–322). San Francisco: Jossey-Bass, 2001.

Savage, J. *Teaching Reading Through Literature* (pp. 152–155). Madison, Wis.: Brown & Benchmark, 1994.

Silver, J. *Real-Life Reading Activities for Grades 6–12* (pp. 37–70). San Francisco: Jossey-Bass, 2002.

Tompkins, G. *Literacy for the 21st Century* (pp. 240–243). Upper Saddle River, N.J.: Prentice Hall/Merrill, 2001.

Vacca, J., Vacca, R., and Gove, M. *Reading and Learning to Read.* New York: HarperCollins, 1995.

Works Cited in Chapter Five

Burns, P., Roe, B., and Ross, E. *Teaching Reading in Today's Elementary Schools* (pp. 106–107). Boston: Houghton Mifflin, 1996.

Burns, P., and Schell, L. "Instructional Strategies for Teaching Usage of Context Clues." *Reading World*, 1975, *15*, 89–96.

Dahl, P., and Samuels, S. "A Mastery-Based Experimental Program for Teaching Poor Readers High-Speed Word Recognition Skills." Unpublished paper, University of Minnesota, 1974.

Edwards, A., and Dermott, A. "A New Way with Vocabulary." *Journal of Reading*, 1989, *32*, 559–561.

Gipe, J. "Use of a Relevant Context Helps Kids Learn New Meanings." *Reading Teacher*, 1980, *33*, 398–402.

Gunning, T. *Creating Reading Instruction for All Children* (pp. 147–150). Needham Heights, Mass.: Allyn and Bacon, 1996.

Herber, H. *Teaching Reading in Content Areas.* Englewood Cliffs, N.J.: Prentice Hall, 1967.

Herman, P., Anderson, R., Pearson, D., and Nagy, W. "Incidental Acquisition of Word Meaning from Exposition with Varied Text Features." *Reading Research Quarterly*, 1987, *22*, 263–284.

Lapp, D., and Flood, J. *Teaching Reading to Every Child* (p. 241). New York: Macmillan, 1992.

Mateja, J. "Musical Cloze: Background, Purpose, and Sample." *Reading Teacher*, 1982, *35*, 444–448.

May, F. *Reading as Communication* (pp. 223–224). Upper Saddle River, N.J.: Prentice Hall/Merrill, 2001.

Nagy, W., Herman, P., and Anderson, R. "Learning Words from Context." *Reading Research Quarterly*, 1985, *20*, 233–253.

Rinsky, L. *Teaching Word Recognition Skills.* Upper Saddle River, N.J.: Gorsuch Scarisbrick, 1997.

Schwartz, R. "Learning to Read Vocabulary in Content Area Textbooks." *Journal of Reading*, 1988, *32*, 108–118.

Shanker, J., and Ekwall, E. *Diagnosis and Remediation of the Disabled Reader.* Needham Heights, Mass.: Allyn and Bacon, 1988.

Sternberg, R., and Powell, J. "Comprehending Verbal Comprehension." *American Psychologist*, 1983, *38*, 878–893.

Taylor, W. "Cloze Procedure: A New Tool for Measuring Readability." *Journalism Quarterly*, 1953, *30*, 415–433.

Tompkins, G. *Literacy for the 21st Century* (p. 242). Upper Saddle River, N.J.: Prentice Hall/Merrill, 2001.

Vacca, J., Vacca, R., and Gove, M. *Reading and Learning to Read.* New York: HarperCollins, 1995.

Wysocki, K., and Jenkins, J. "Deriving Word Meanings Through Morphological Generalizations." *Reading Research Quarterly*, 1987, *22*, 66–81.

6

Strategies and Activities for Improving Comprehension Skills While Reading Content Material

Which of these do you believe to be one of the main reading problems for students in grades 5 to 12: word identification or comprehension?

If you answered *comprehension*, you were correct. However, it is not merely comprehension but rather *higher-level comprehension*—specifically interpretive comprehension and critical reading—that is difficult for these students. Most students in grades 5 to 12 have adequate word identification skills and literal (lower-level) comprehension skills, with the possible exception of those with severe reading or learning disabilities. It is higher-level comprehension, especially in the content areas of literature, social studies, science, and mathematics, that causes most students difficulty. The strategies and materials contained in this chapter should help reading and learning disability teachers present comprehension skills, especially higher-level comprehension skills, effectively.

Chapter Six opens by briefly describing the elements of reading comprehension. It then explains the various levels of comprehension—textually explicit, textually implicit, and critical or evaluative. Next it presents myriad classroom-tested strategies for improving the various elements of comprehension. Some strategies for improving prediction are predictive QARs, the directed reading-thinking activity (DR-TA), and the anticipation-reaction guide. Strategies to improve ability in general comprehension include guided reading; semantic maps, webs, and weaves; comprehension mini-lessons; scaffolding, and think- and talk-alouds. Strategies for improving textually explicit comprehension include K-W-L, K-W-H-L, and teaching patterns of organization.

Implicit comprehension can be improved through textually implicit QARs, visual imagery, reciprocal questioning, the generating reciprocal inferences procedure (GRIP), providing students with the written characteristics of a job and having them guess which job it is; cybernetic sessions; and the investigative questioning procedure (InQuest). The chapter then explains strategies for improving ability in critical or evaluative reading, including critical QARs, discriminating between fact and opinion statements, and comparing material from different sources. Next, the chapter explains diagramming paragraphs to illustrate main ideas and significant details and the five-step strategy for locating the main idea. To improve ability in self-monitoring of reading comprehension, the following are suggested: the *click or clunk* strategy, fix-up strategies, and Davey and Porter's four-step instructional procedure for improving monitoring ability.

The chapter also explains strategies for improving ability in various other subskills of reading comprehension: writing directions for designs to be made on paper; completing the dialogue in whited-out comic strips; making a chain map; Brown and Day's rule for summarizing; providing a list of book titles and determining if the author was trying to inform, entertain, or persuade; and drawing impressions of a scene.

The chapter closes with seven classroom-tested reproducible activity sheets *constructed from the various content areas* that are designed to improve ability in general comprehension; textually explicit, textually implicit, and critical reading; comprehending the directly stated main idea and the implied main idea; reading and carrying out directions; placing items in correct sequence; summarizing material; and sensing the author's mood and purpose.

After reading this chapter, any classroom or reading, learning disability, or content teacher should be well-prepared to present and review the various elements of comprehension to all students in grades 5 to 12, whether or not they have special needs.

A Brief Description of Reading Comprehension

Reading comprehension is a complex process that is related to the *thinking process*. Very briefly, comprehension is *constructing meaning from the printed material.* It is an *interactive process* that requires readers to use their *prior knowledge* as well as the *printed material.* Based on this definition, a reading teacher or tutor, learning disability teacher, or content teacher must think about the characteristics of both the reader and the printed material. In the case of the reader, his or her prior knowledge of the material, interest in reading the material, purpose for reading the material, and ability to identify the words found in the material must be taken into consideration. As for the printed material, the number of hard words, the sentence length, and the format must be taken into account.

Although both the reader's prior knowledge and the features of the print material are important, usually the reader's prior knowledge and interest in the material are the most relevant. The greater prior knowledge the reader has, the less use he or she will have to make of the print material. That is the main reason why a specialist in a specific area—for example, chemistry, history, geology, economics—can often read material in that area much more rapidly and efficiently than a person who has less prior knowledge.

Also involved in comprehension is the process of *making connections* between what one knows and what one does not know, or between the old and the new (Searfoss and Readence, 1994). Shanklin and Rhodes (1989) wrote that comprehension often is an *evolving process*, beginning even before a book is opened, changing as the material is being read, and continuing to change even after the reading is completed. Because comprehension often improves when a reader interacts with others about aspects of the material read, classroom, group, or teacher-student discussions about reading materials can greatly improve comprehension.

Schema theory is based on contemporary research in comprehension. Schema theory attempts to explain how people store information in their minds, how the knowledge they possess is used, and how they acquire and add new knowledge to previous knowledge. Anderson, Wilson, and Fielding (1988) wrote that comprehension involves activating or constructing a *schema* that accounts for the elements in the text, similar to constructing the outline of a script. Therefore, a script outline for a reading about Egypt might contain the following categories (also called *slots*): *pyramid, tomb, mummy, mummification, camel, Nile River, Muslim, mosque, artifact, ushabti, pharaoh, Ramses II, deification*, and *temple*. Effective comprehension, then, means filling these slots with particular examples or instances.

Another focus of contemporary comprehension research is *self-monitoring (metacognition)*, which deals with readers' awareness of their own thinking as they try to understand the printed material. It is very important for readers to learn how to monitor their own reading comprehension. Research has consistently found that *good readers are much more competent at monitoring their comprehension than are poor readers.*

Finally, research has found significant relationships between comprehension and word identification skills (Adams, 1991). Therefore, if a student is having difficulty comprehending, the teacher must be sure that that student has a large sight word vocabulary and good word structure and phonic skills. Students with special needs in particular may need instruction and practice with word identification. In contrast, if good decoders have difficulty with comprehension, they may need help in language skills and listening comprehension.

Different Levels of Comprehension

In the past, comprehension skills were usually divided into several categories: *textually explicit, textually implicit, and critical (evaluative)*. Today, a number of researchers believe that comprehension is a language-based process that cannot be divided into arbitrary categories or levels. Instead, they believe that there are only two main categories of comprehension: *vocabulary knowledge (word meaning)* and *understanding the material.*

Because they believe that comprehension cannot be divided into discrete categories, they also believe that it cannot be taught as separate skills to students. However, I believe that it is helpful to teach the most important parts of comprehension separately, especially to students with special needs, so that they may truly understand and use them.

Here are several levels of comprehension and the more important skills required for each level (Miller, 1999). (For comprehensive descriptions of the various skills needed in textually explicit and implicit comprehension and critical reading, consult *Reading Skills Problem Solver* [Miller, 2002], pp. 202–207, 266–270, 321–325.)

Textually Explicit (Literal or Factual: "Right There") Comprehension

- Answering "right there" questions in the reading material (questions for which answers are found directly in the material).
- Locating directly stated main ideas and topic sentences.
- Locating significant and irrelevant details.
- Placing items in correct sequence or order.
- Reading and following directions.
- Interpreting abbreviations, symbols, and acronyms. (For a complete list of abbreviations, symbols, and acronyms, see *The Reading Teacher's Book of Lists* [Fry, Kress, and Fountoukidis, 2000], pp. 136–137, 419–427, 428–431, and 437).
- Understanding explicitly stated cause–effect relationships classifying information such as single words.
- Understanding the types of expository (content) textbook structure—enumeration/description, time sequence, explanation/process, comparison/contrast, problem/solution, explicit cause and effect.

Textually Implicit (Interpretive or Inferential: "Think and Search") Comprehension

- Answering "think and search" ("putting-it-together") questions. (The reader must *deduce* the answers from reading the material—the answers are not directly found in the material.)
- Answering questions that call for interpretation. (Again, the answers are not found right in the material.)
- Drawing conclusions and generalizations from the reading material.
- Predicting outcomes and material content.
- Summarizing what was read.
- Sensing an author's mood and purpose.
- Locating implied main ideas. (The main idea of a paragraph must be inferred from thinking about all the material in the paragraph—it is not directly stated.)
- Constructing visual images.
- Understanding implicitly stated cause–effect relationships.
- Classifying or categorizing that involves implied relationships.
- Recognizing analogies.
- Weaving together the ideas in a passage.
- Interpreting figures of speech.

Critical (Evaluative: "Think and Search") Reading

- Responding to questions calling for critical or evaluative answers.
- Discriminating between real and make-believe.
- Distinguishing between fact and opinion.
- Verifying factual statements.
- Comparing different sources of information.
- Critically analyzing persuasive language.
- Critically analyzing advertisements.
- Evaluating slanted writing.
- Detecting assumptions.
- Detecting propaganda techniques, including those we name *bandwagon*, *testimonial*, *name calling*, *plain folks*, *card stacking*, and *transfer*.

Strategies for Improving Prediction Skills

In the following sections, the chapter presents a sampling of classroom-tested strategies for improving ability in prediction skills, general comprehension skills, and the most important comprehension subskills. Although all of them are helpful in grades 5 to 12, I encourage you to modify any of them in light of the abilities, needs, and interests of your own students. We begin with strategies for improving prediction skills.

Predictive QARs

Using *predictive QARs* or *predictive questions* is one of the easiest and most effective ways to improve comprehension. This simple strategy requires no special materials but rather a *mindset* on the part of readers. If students ask themselves prediction questions about the content of the material both *before* and *during* reading, their comprehension greatly improves. Predictions can be made from the title of a narrative story, an expository story, or a content textbook chapter or section.

Before reading any material, students can ask themselves questions such as these: What do I think this book (or chapter, or section) will be about? What do I think will happen in this book? What would I like to have happen in this book? What do I think will be the most important concepts in this chapter or section?

While reading the material, students can ask themselves questions such as the following: What do I think will happen next in this book (or chapter, or section)? What would I like to see happen next in this book? What do I think (the main character) will do next in this book? What do I think (the main character) should do next in this book? What do I think are the most important concepts so far in this chapter or section? What do I want to remember from what I have read up to this point in this chapter or section?

These kinds of questions help students to *read purposefully.* All reading should be purposeful, because reading done with specific purposes is likely to result in effective comprehension. Teachers and tutors can help students set important purposes for reading. Students with special needs in particular often read a book or a content assignment in a meaningless manner with no purpose except to finish it. Some purposes for reading in grades 5 to 12 are to understand the directly stated and implied main ideas, to locate significant details, to read and carry out specific directions, to place a number of items into correct sequence, to create visual images, and to find patterns of organization, among others.

If students have well-formulated purposes for reading a passage, book, or content assignment, they can apply themselves to a specific and manageable task. Cunningham and Wall (1994) stated that when teachers establish a purpose for reading, they always should (1) provide a precise statement of what students are to focus on, or (2) provide a clear preview of the task the students will be asked to perform when they are finished reading. This helps them use the formulated purpose to choose the appropriate comprehension strategies.

Blanton, Wood, and Moorman (1990) recommended having students set a *single purpose* for reading, rather than multiple purposes. A single purpose may be especially necessary for students with special needs, such as learning disabled students, because it helps them avoid the confusion that is possible with several different purposes.

Students should set their own purposes if possible. When teachers set a purpose for reading narrative or content material, they should *think aloud* how they developed the purpose, thus modeling purpose-setting for students. After students have finished reading a book or content assignment, their purposes should be discussed to ensure that they were met. Also, it is crucial that tests or quizzes reflect the purposes for which the reading was done. For example, students are often asked to read for important concepts rather than for specific details; but if the test evaluates significant details rather than ability to locate concepts, then students will become discouraged and will not effectively set purposes in their future reading, as well as perform poorly on the test.

The Directed Reading-Thinking Activity (DR-TA)

The *Directed Reading-Thinking Activity (DR-TA)* is a prediction strategy that was developed by the late Russell G. Stauffer of the University of Delaware (1975, 1980). The DR-TA is useful because it involves *prediction* and reading with specific purposes. DR-TA encourages *active involvement* with the reading material by having students make predictions about the material and then check the accuracy of their predictions. This is the main reason why DR-TA improves understanding and remembering so effectively.

Here are the basic steps of the process:

1. Have students read the title of the narrative, informational book, content textbook chapter, or major section. Then, on the basis of this title and their own prior knowledge, have them make predictions about the content of the material. If you want, either you or your students can write down the predictions.

2. Tell the students they should read the material to determine if it confirms or disconfirms the predictions they made. Then have them read the material one section at a time.

3. After the reading is completed, have the students discuss each of their predictions, indicating which ones were confirmed and which ones were not. Help students to determine which criteria should be used to decide whether or not the predictions were confirmed. This portion of the DR-TA can be written down too if you wish.

4. If the material is not read at one time, alternate periods of reading and discussion until the entire book or content assignment has been completed. In each case, stress the *validity* of the student's thinking, not the correctness of the predictions.

The Anticipation-Reaction Guide

The *anticipation-reaction guide*, developed by Readence, Bean, and Baldwin (1981), is an excellent strategy to use to improve students' prediction abilities and as a follow-up to reading. It is effective because it *activates* a student's prior knowledge before reading by using *statements* instead of *questions* to get them more involved in their reading. It uses the same statements after reading to encourage students to reflect on what they have learned from the reading and how their knowledge about the material has changed. *Statements* require students to recognize and respond, whereas questions only require students to give a response. As a result of using this strategy, students should be able to produce their own questions and statements more effectively. This is an extremely helpful strategy for all students in grades 5 to 12, whether or not they have special needs, and especially when they are reading content material.

Here is a brief description of how the anticipation-reaction guide can be constructed and used:

1. *Identify major concepts.* First, as the teacher or tutor, you should identify the main concepts in the reading selection by reading the material carefully yourself, and reading the teacher's guide as well if one is available.

2. *Determine students' knowledge of these concepts.* Attempt to determine how the main concepts in the reading material support or refute what the students already know about the material.

3. *Create statements.* Create a number of statements about the content material that can be used both for prediction before reading and follow-up afterward. Students should have sufficient knowledge to understand what the statements mean, but not enough knowledge to understand them completely. These statements also should reflect the important concepts in the material.

4. *Decide statement order and presentation style.* Usually, the order of the statements should follow the order of the material. The guide can be presented on a computer-generated sheet or the chalkboard. The set of directions and blanks for the students' responses should be included.

5. *Present the anticipation-reaction guide.* When you present the guide to your students, have the students read the directions and statements silently. Tell them that they will share their thoughts and opinions about each statement by defending their agreement or disagreement with the statements. Students can work individually or with a partner or partners in making their responses.

6. *Discuss each statement briefly.* First, ask for a show of hands to indicate the students' agreement or disagreement with each statement. Then tally the responses. Encourage students to evaluate their own views based on the views of other students.

7. *Have students read the material.* After the prediction aspect of the guide, have the students read the material with the purpose of determining what the author says about ideas in each statement. As they read, students should keep two things in mind: (1) their own thoughts and beliefs as well as those held by other students, and (2) how what they are reading relates to what was discussed earlier.

8. *Conduct follow-up discussions.* After reading the material, students can *respond again* to the statements. Here, the anticipation guide serves as an excellent basis for a post-reading discussion in which students share the new information that they learned from reading and how their previous concepts may have been altered by what they now believe the material stated. Students should understand that they do not have to agree with an author as long as they have logical evidence for their own beliefs.

You will find a reproducible copy of an anticipation-reaction guide in the content area of social studies in the last section of this chapter.

Questionnaire-Inventories for Activating Prior Knowledge and Encouraging Prediction

Here are several other ways to activate students' prior knowledge and encourage prediction before they read a narrative or content selection. (These prediction strategies were adapted from *Teaching Reading Comprehension: From Theory to Practice* [Devine, 1986, pp. 79–81]).

1. *Simple questionnaires and inventories.* Have students complete a twenty- to thirty-item activity sheet of questions, including true–false items, fill-in-the-blank-items, and incomplete sentence items (give only the first part of the statement from the material they are to read).

2. *Open-ended inventories.* Have students write responses to such questions as these: *What do you know about the Battle of Chattanooga in the Civil War?* Or, *What do you know about the process of photosynthesis in plants?*

3. *Informal content checks.* This activity helps you and your students determine how much they already know about a specific subject before they read about it.

4. *Informal concept activity.* Have students list words on the chalkboard that label the concepts or the sentences containing the concepts that the teacher has selected for their importance. This technique will help you locate students who have inaccurate prior knowledge (schemata) in a particular subject matter area.

5. *Synonym and definition activity.* In this activity, you list words and concepts on the chalkboard or an activity sheet with a parallel list of synonyms placed in incorrect order. The students draw lines from each word to the correct synonym.

Strategies for Improving General Comprehension Skills

These strategies will help you improve your students' general comprehension skills.

Extensive Reading

Extensive reading of motivating, relevant, and fairly easy material usually *is the single most effective way* to improve reading comprehension.

As stated earlier, comprehension usually improves most significantly if the student has a specific purpose for reading. Such reading can take place in narrative and informational mass-market (trade) books, poetry, student and appropriate adult magazines and newspapers, content textbooks, and materials on the World Wide Web, among others. Students always should have a purpose for reading, monitor their comprehension as they read, and be prepared to demonstrate in some way that they have understood the material.

Reading Poetry

Reading *poetry* is an enjoyable way for students in grades 5 to 12 to improve their comprehension skills. Because poetry is a condensed form of writing, every word included is important to understanding it. Poetry also encourages visual imagery because it has sensory descriptions and introduces interesting material. In addition, poetry provides opportunities for students to learn new words, concepts, and attitudes and to experience life through the eyes of the poet. Finally, it has form and usually is easy to learn.

Here are some types of poetry:

- *Lyric*—descriptive poetry that usually has a song quality.
- *Narrative*—poetry that tells a story or describes an occurrence.
- *Limerick*—poetry with five lines of verse set in a specific rhyming pattern that usually is humorous.
- *Free verse*—poetry that does not rhyme.
- *Haiku*—an ancient form of Japanese verse, popular with contemporary students, that contains three lines consisting of seventeen syllables and often dealing with the topic of nature. Students in grades 5 to 12 usually enjoy constructing their own haikus and sharing them with classmates.
- *Nonsense*—poetry that is ridiculous and whimsical.

Poetry can be used for the following purposes, all of which have as an ultimate goal to improve comprehension: improving the understanding of rhyming; improving comprehension at higher levels because it may require interpretation; improving visual imagery and students' imaginations; and enhancing students' self-concept and self-confidence.

The following are some books of poetry that you may want to use with your older students. The interest level *by age* is indicated in parentheses after each citation. Of course, there are many other books that are equally useful.

Burdett, L. *Macbeth for Kids.* Westport, Conn.: Firefly Books, 1996. (10–12)

Crew, G. *Thompson's Excellent Poetry Book.* Edinburgh, Scotland: Lothian Books, 2002. (10–12)

Dakos, K. *The Goof Who Invented Homework and Other School Poems.* New York: Dial Books for Young Readers, 1996. (10–12)

DiYanni, R., and Rompf, K. *The McGraw-Hill Book of Poetry.* New York: McGraw-Hill, 1993. (12+)

Ferguson, M., Stallworthy, J., and Salter, M. *Norton Anthology of Poetry.* New York: W. W. Norton, 1996. (10+)

Gage, A., and Thatch, N. *We Are a Thunderstorm.* Kansas City, Mo.: Landmark Editions, 1990. (10–12)

Glenn, M. *Jump Ball: A Basketball Season in Poems.* New York: Dutton Children's Books, 1997. (12+)

Glenn, M. *Who Killed Mr. Chippendale?* New York: Penguin, 1999. (12+)

Honeycutt, I. *Waiting for the Trout to Speak: Poems.* Charlotte, N.C.: Novello Festival Press, 2002. (14–18)

Hopkins, L. (ed.). *Best Friends.* New York: HarperCollins, 1986. (10–12)

Janeczko, P. *Poetry from A to Z: A Guide for Young Readers.* New York: Simon & Schuster, 1994. (12+)

Kennedy, X., and Kennedy, D. (eds.). *Knock at a Star.* Boston: Little, Brown, 1982. (10+)

Larrick, N. *Piping Down the Valleys Wild.* New York: Dell, 1968. (10+)

McCord, D. *One at a Time.* Boston: Little, Brown, 1986. (10+)

Merriam, E. *The Inner-City Mother Goose.* New York: Simon & Schuster, 1969. (10–12)

Meyer, J. *Teen Ink 2: More Voices, More Visions. Vol. 2.* New York: Heath Communications, 2001. (12+)

Nye, N. (ed.). *The Tree Is Older Than You: Bilingual Poems from Mexico.* New York: Simon & Schuster, 1999. (10–12)

Rylant, C. *But I'll Be Back Again.* New York: Orchard, 1989. (12+)

Silverstein, S. *A Light in the Attic.* New York: HarperCollins, 1981. (12+)

Strickland, D., and Strickland, M. *Families: Poems Celebrating the African-American Experience.* Honesdale, Penn.: Wordsong/Boyds Mills, 1994. (10–12)

Viorst, J. *If I Were in Charge of the World and Other Worries.* New York: Atheneum, 1981. (12+)

Young, N. *The Innermost Explosion: An Anthology of Poetry by Students at the Augustineum School, Windhoek.* Namibia, Africa: New Namibia Books, 1993. (12+)

Guided Reading

Guided reading helps focus students' attention on certain concepts and ideas as they read. Guided reading can be used effectively with both content and narrative reading. Some students read materials from beginning to end without stopping to reflect on what they are reading. However, especially with content materials, it is very helpful to *guide students' reading* so that they focus on, comprehend, and learn from certain aspects of the material.

Guided reading can be used in the following ways, among others:

- To encourage interpretive and critical thinking by having students notice examples of fact and opinion, interpret, draw conclusions, or predict outcomes
- To help students manipulate the material in ways that will help them to understand and remember the important concepts better—writing main ideas and significant details, outlining, summarizing, and making graphic organizers
- To help students monitor their understanding of what they read

Students may understand and enjoy a story more if they focus their attention on certain aspects of character, setting, plot, or theme. They can be made aware of interesting, colorful language. They may also benefit from making personal responses to what they are reading, making predictions about what they will read, or thinking about how book or story characters may feel. These are all useful outcomes of guided reading activities for narrative reading.

Therefore, guided reading activities for narrative material can include the following:

- Reading with a partner or partners and then sharing reactions to the reading
- Writing informally, as in keeping a reading journal or dialogue journal
- Using reading guides—that is, answering questions or completing charts or outlines on character, plot development, point of view, or aspects of style or language

The guided reading procedure is designed to help students think about and use the concepts and ideas in the material in a way that will help them understand it, enjoy it, and remember it better.

Semantic Maps, Webs, and Weaves

Semantic maps, webs, and *weaves* are strategies that students in grades 5 to 12 can use with a partner or partners, or independently, to organize ideas and graphically demonstrate their relationships. The map or web is a visual representation of the main concept and related concepts in a narrative or content reading assignment. Semantic maps or webs are sometimes graphic organizers that look like a spider web—thus, the name. However, a number of students have difficulty completing a semantic web because the material they want to include does not fit inside the circles in a previously constructed web. If students are allowed to construct their own web completely, they usually like it better.

Because a semantic map or web is a visual representation of the main concept and related concepts, it can be used *before, during,* or *after reading* to improve comprehension. Students can formulate their own maps or webs while they are reading a selection or after they have finished it. Because this is a fairly difficult skill for many students to master, they first should be given direct instruction and a partially completed map to finish. Subsequently, they can be given an unfinished map with only the main idea or concept included. Only after considerable practice with partially completed maps should students be required to construct their own maps.

Similar to a semantic map or web, a *semantic weave* is a visual display of information and how it is related. The semantic weave differs from the web in that it indicates *comparisons.* A weave enables students to focus on the similarities and differences between characters, incidents, events, or concepts. Aspects of reading are placed together for comparison in a semantic weave.

Semantic maps, webs, and weaves all improve comprehension by providing a *framework* for focusing on important points, rather than myriad unimportant details. Students also have a written record of their thoughts, thus enabling them to analyze, synthesize, and remember them.

Here is an example of a completed semantic map on the topic of *China*. There are many other ways in which such a semantic map could be organized.

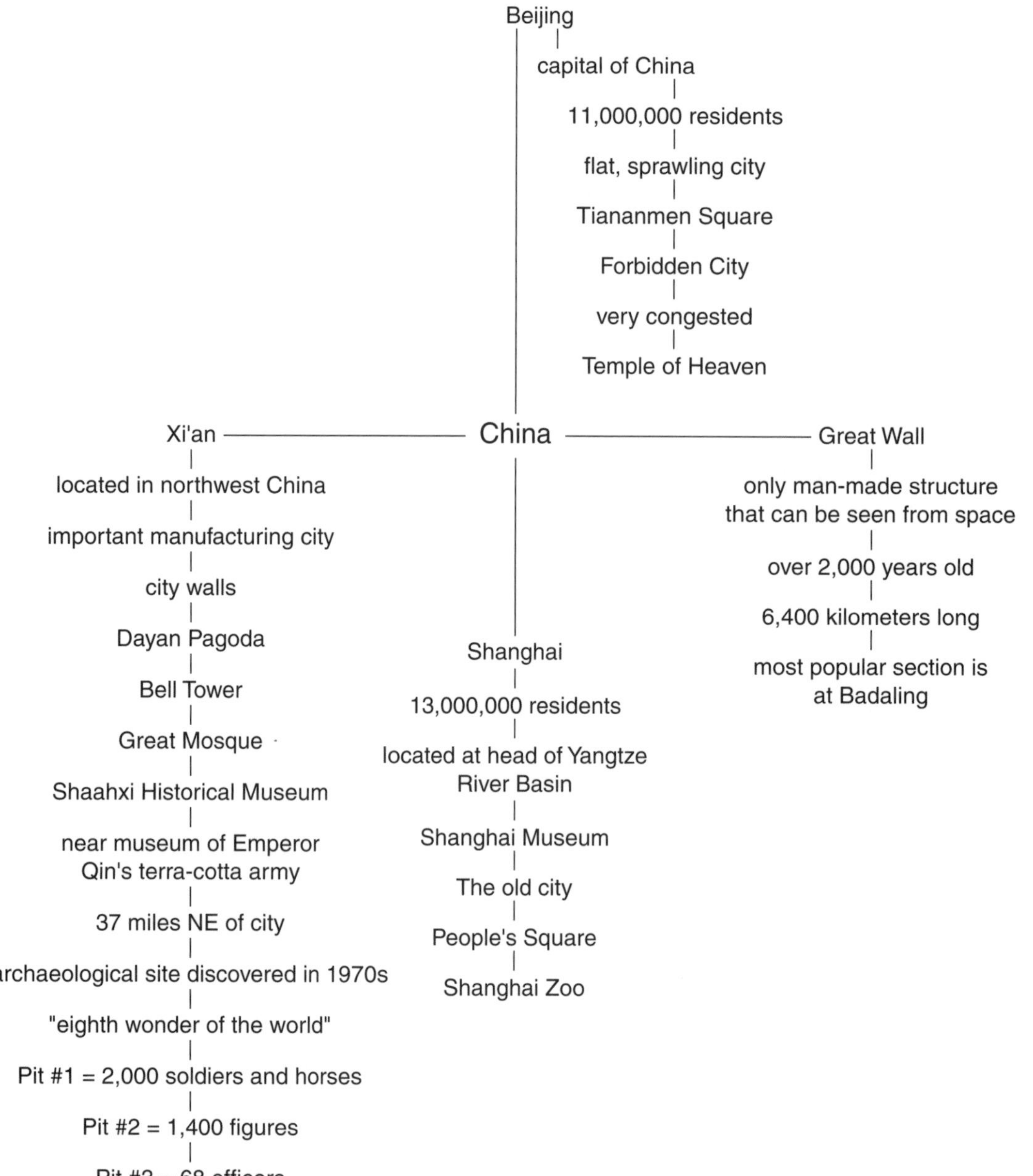

Here is an example of a *semantic weave* that is designed to illustrate the differences between the countries of *China* and the *United States.*

	China	United States
ancient	yes	no
democracy	no	yes
communist	yes	no
Judeo-Christian country	no	yes
Buddhist country	yes	no
Shopping	yes	yes
Beautiful	yes	yes
Most populated country	yes	no
Polluted	yes	in some places
Dollar	no	yes
Renminbi (RMB)	yes	no
Mandarin language	yes	no
English	not often	yes
Shares border with 16 countries	yes	no
In shopping — "Buyer beware"	yes	sometimes

Mini-Lessons for Comprehension Improvement

Mini-lessons (Atwell, 1998) are fifteen to thirty-minute *direct instruction lessons* designed to help students learn various comprehension skills and become more strategic readers and writers. In these lessons the teacher or tutor and the students focus on a single goal, and students are made aware of why it is important to learn that skill or strategy. They also are taught how to use a particular skill or strategy through *modeling*, *explanation*, and *practice.* Then they apply the skill or strategy independently by using authentic content reading materials. Mini-lessons usually have the following five steps:

1. *Introduce the skill or strategy.* The teacher or tutor names the strategy or skill and explains why it is useful. He or she also shares examples of how and when the skill or strategy should be used.

2. *Demonstrate the skill or strategy.* The teacher explains the steps of the skill or strategy and models how to use it with authentic reading and writing activities.

3. *Practice using the skill or strategy.* With the teacher's or tutor's guidance, the students then practice the skill or strategy. The teacher or tutor provides feedback to the students about how well they are doing.

4. *Review the skill or strategy.* The teacher or tutor and the students review the steps of the skill or strategy. Students reflect on what they have learned and how they would apply it in comprehension activities. Students also may construct a poster about the skill or strategy to be put up in the classroom.

5. *Apply the skill or strategy.* Students use their newly learned skill or strategy in authentic content comprehension activities.

Through such five-step mini-lessons, responsibility for learning comprehension skills is transferred from teacher to students, thus increasing the likelihood that they will learn and actually use the target skills and strategies (Bergman, 1992; Duffy and Roehler, 1987; Pearson and Gallagher, 1983).

Scaffolding

Scaffolding is an effective way to improve comprehension skills. Scaffolding in reading is loosely based on the technique that house painters or carpenters use in their work. Usually these workers do not stand on a ladder but rather construct a *scaffold*—placing a wooden plank between sawhorses or something similar. Then these workers stand on the scaffold. This makes the job both safer and easier for them.

In the same way, scaffolding helps students, instead of requiring them to complete a task independently. For example, if students are to learn how to construct a semantic map, the following are helpful steps in scaffolding the skill for them:

- Explain the purpose and general format of a semantic map.
- Place a completed semantic map from a content area assignment on a transparency or a large sheet of chart paper.
- Give students a partially completed semantic map based on a content assignment and have them finish it either independently or with a partner or partners.
- Provide students with a semantic map from a content assignment with only the main headings completed and have them finish it either independently or with a partner or partners.
- Have students completely construct a semantic map from a content assignment either independently or with a partner or partners.

Using Talk-Alouds and Teachable Moments

Teachers and tutors can use *talk-alouds* with students so that they describe the steps they use to apply a strategy or skill as they complete a task (Baumann and Schmitt, 1986). Then they ask questions to guide students through the steps of the talk-aloud.

In this instructional technique the teacher or tutor shares with students the thought processes they go through as they use a reading skill or strategy (Davey, 1983; Wade, 1990). In comprehension, students can use think-alouds on activating prior knowledge, making predictions, and monitoring reading comprehension, among many others (Bergman, 1992).

Teachers and tutors also should take advantage of *teachable moments* in the classroom or during tutoring sessions to share information about reading skills and strategies. They can introduce, review, or extend a skill or strategy in these very brief sessions. As they listen to students read aloud or talk about the processes they use in reading, they often have opportunities to teach a specific skill or strategy (Atwell, 1998). In their conferences with students about their reading, they can informally share information about relevant reading skills and strategies too. Meanwhile, students can ask questions about reading skills and strategies or volunteer information about how they solved a reading problem. Teachers and tutors who are careful observers of students and listen carefully to their students are able to take advantage of teachable moments effectively.

The Five-Phase Instructional Sequence

The *five-phase instructional sequence* (Roth, Smith, and Anderson, 1984) can help students comprehend and retain content information. This strategy consists of the following five steps:

1. *Preparation.* Begin this instructional strategy by presenting an overview of the content material and some background information. Activate the students' prior knowledge and clarify any misinformation they may have about the content material they are going to read.

2. *Exploration.* Help the students explore the topic and become more aware of their prior knowledge. Activities that can be included in this step of the instructional sequence are demonstrations, experiments, discussions that encourage creative or divergent thinking, use of the World Wide Web, models, pictures, videotapes, and independent reading. Tell the students that they should share their own thoughts and ideas. Ask them critical questions with the goal of creating "mental conflict" in order to stimulate their thinking.

3. *Acquisition.* Discuss any conflicts in the concepts that students currently hold. Present relevant material from the content textbook or other sources, such as informational and narrative mass-market (trade) books, the World Wide Web, and magazines and newspapers. Also have students read for a specific purpose and conduct a follow-up discussion to the reading. It may be necessary to reread the textbook and other material.

4. *Practice-application.* To be sure that students remember the new knowledge and concepts they have learned, give them many opportunities to work with the ideas: conducting experiments, preparing demonstrations, holding class or small-group discussions and small-group problem-solving sessions, and so on.

5. *Synthesis.* Help students to synthesize the new information to be sure that the new ideas and concepts are related to their other concepts and prior knowledge. Some activities to use in this step are applying new concepts, explaining new concepts, and constructing a concept map to demonstrate the relationships.

Providing Sufficient Wait Time to Respond

Providing sufficient wait time for students to answer comprehension questions was researched by Rowe (1974) during science lessons. Her research focused on the length of the *interval* between the time a teacher asked a question and then expected an answer, asked the question of another student, or rephrased the original question. She called this interval *wait time.*

Rowe found that the average teacher wait time was only *0.9 seconds*. However, Rowe found that when teachers allowed at least a *3-second wait time*, both teacher questioning characteristics and student answering behavior improved greatly. Improved teacher questioning characteristics included asking fewer but higher-quality questions, and accepting more divergent answers. Teachers also had higher expectations for below-average readers. Student responses too were affected in a positive way by the increased wait time. Shy and below-average readers answered more questions, students' answers to questions were more elaborate, and students showed more confidence while answering questions as reflected by their vocal inflection.

In summary, providing a wait time of at least *three seconds* after asking comprehension questions should improve both teacher questioning and student question-answering behavior. Probably the main difficulty in doing this is a teacher's feeling of unease when a student does not respond immediately. It is important, however, to try to overcome this feeling in order to ensure better student answers to comprehension questions.

Flow Charts

Flow charts that students follow, much as they might follow a road map, can help them comprehend both narrative and content material. In narrative material students can chart the structure of a story, whereas in content reading they can chart the main ideas in a content passage.

Here is a sample flow chart constructed from science.

Flow Chart
The Life of Melvin the Muskie

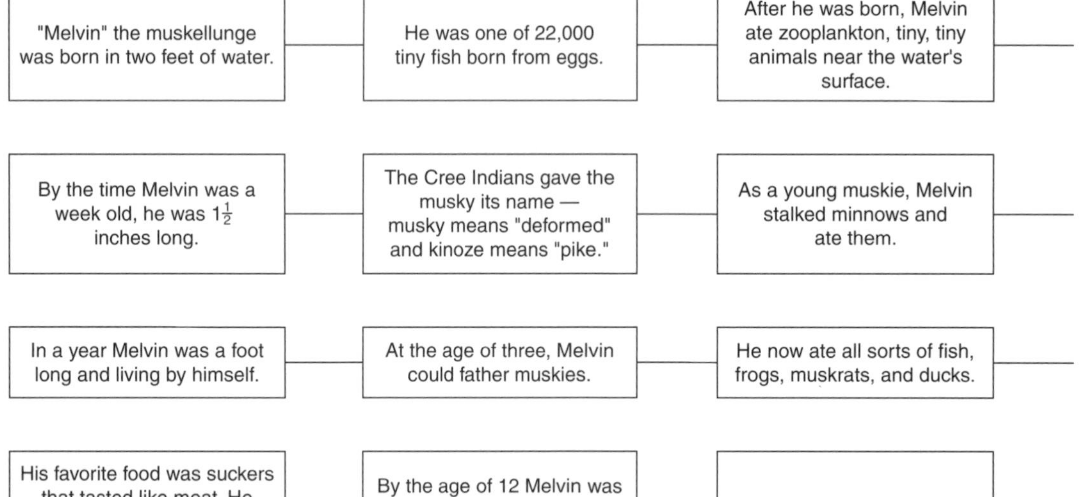

Using Thematic Units to Improve Comprehension in Literature, Social Studies, Science, and Mathematics

Many classroom and content teachers wonder how they should best help students who simply cannot understand the required textbook. This may happen because many content textbooks are written above the grade level of the students who are to read them; they contain difficult specialized vocabulary and organizational patterns that are different from those found in narrative materials.

Therefore, a good alternative to using traditional content textbooks is to use *thematic units* to present and review target content. Students usually enjoy thematic teaching units much more than traditional teaching approaches that emphasize content textbooks only.

If you decide to use thematic units to present and practice subject matter, you must first select a topic that is appropriate for the needs and interests of your students. Theoretically, students should select their own topics to study because they have the greatest interest in such topics, but this usually is not possible when target topics have been previously chosen.

For example, if a sixth-grade class is to study the topic *Life on the American Frontier*, get some help from the school librarian or media specialist and bring in many resources related to this topic. Although various content textbooks also can be used, other resources such as informational and narrative trade books, videotapes, and resource people can be used, as well as the World Wide Web and relevant computer software. Then divide the students into *cooperative learning groups*. Usually, you will assign each group a topic to research, and then you will act as a *facilitator*, not a director of learning.

Each group then conducts its own research on the topic. They can use any of the resources already presented or other resources not found in the classroom or even in the school. For example, for this particular subject, a group might take a field trip to a museum to view artifacts from the American frontier. In addition, all of the instruction in literature, social studies, science, and mathematics is related to the theme. Each group then presents summaries of what it has learned to the rest of the class in a variety of creative ways.

In sum, thematic unit teaching is *integrated teaching with active student involvement* at each stage of the process. In this process, each student reads materials that he or she is able to understand, is motivated to learn about, is actively involved in learning, and displays independence in learning. Therefore, the topic of the unit usually is more *relevant and meaningful* than in traditional teaching.

Here are the *main advantages* of using thematic units to present and reinforce content learning:

- Each student normally reads at his or her independent or instructional reading level and therefore can experience success.
- Students learn to work cooperatively with their classmates even if they have different reading abilities.
- Strategies for improving comprehension skills can be taught and practiced effectively in thematic units.
- Students develop independent work habits.
- Students see the relevance of what they are learning and can easily relate it to their own lives.

- The process enhances a student's self-esteem. This is especially important for students with special needs.
- The process effectively integrates learning in all of the content fields.
- The process promotes active student involvement and critical and creative thinking skills, which are very important in our contemporary democratic and technological society.

Here are the *main limitations* of using thematic units in content teaching:

- The process requires an experienced teacher who is knowledgeable, well organized, flexible, creative, and nonjudgmental.
- It requires extensive cooperation among subject matter teachers in a middle school or junior high school.
- A few students may not be independent and mature enough to handle this degree of freedom successfully. Some students with special needs may need more direct instruction and guidance. However, even such students can learn to function in this type of curriculum with sufficient preparation and guidance.

Strategies for Improving Textually Explicit Comprehension Skills

These strategies will help you improve your students' textually explicit comprehension skills.

K-W-L and K-W-H-L

The *K-W-L* and *K-W-H-L* strategies are valuable in the intermediate grades and above for content material in social studies and science. All students at this level should have instruction and practice in using both of these strategies because they improve the comprehension and retention of content material.

K-W-L is the acronym for *What I Know—What I Want to Learn (Know)—What I Have Learned.* Developed by Ogle (1986, 1989), K-W-L activates students' prior knowledge, encourages them to construct questions to read to answer, directs students to search for answers to these specific questions while reading, and helps them effectively summarize what they learned from the reading. This strategy is very helpful because it encourages students to use their prior knowledge while reading and gives them specific purposes for reading.

This strategy may be presented in a whole-class, small-group, or individual setting to those students who seem able to benefit from using it. Here's how to do it. First, identify the most important concepts in the material and ask students to state what they already know about these concepts. Write these concepts on the chalkboard or a large sheet of chart paper under the heading titled *What I Know.* Second, provide motivation by focusing on what students want to learn about these concepts. Write these questions under the column titled *What I Want to Learn (Know).* When students have determined their purposes for reading, ask them to read the material specifically to locate the answers to their questions.

In the last step, have the students orally or in writing summarize what they learned from the material. They can complete this column of the K-W-L activity sheet independently or with a partner or partners. In either case, have students complete this portion of the activity sheet without referring to the material that they have read. If you want, you can have your students then use the material contained in the third column to construct their own semantic map. This map can serve as an outline for writing a brief summary of the material, which is considered the *Plus* part of the strategy, making it *K-W-L Plus.*

K-W-H-L adds one more step before the final step called *How Can I Find Out.* In this step, with your help, students brainstorm about resources they could use to locate the needed information. Some of these resources are content textbooks, informational mass-market (trade) books, newspapers and magazines, print reference materials, the World Wide Web, computer software, videotapes, and classroom visitors.

Here is how you might create a K-W-L activity sheet on how to answer questions from a restaurant menu. First, provide students in grades 5 to 8 with copies of a *restaurant menu.* You can use an actual restaurant menu from a local restaurant or create a sample menu specifically for this activity.

Then ask students questions about the menu. These should be detailed questions that emphasize textually explicit comprehension skills and provide students practice with answering at that level. Here are some sample questions: What meals does this restaurant serve—breakfast, lunch, dinner, or all three of them? What kind of appetizers does this restaurant have? What is the price for a cup of coffee? What kinds of potatoes are available at this restaurant? What is the name of your favorite food that is found in this restaurant? What desserts are served at this restaurant? What is the price of the most expensive entrée at this restaurant?

Here is an example of a K-W-L activity sheet.

Name____________________ Grade_____ Teacher________________ Date_____

K-W-L WORKSHEET

K	W	L
What I Know	What I Want to Learn	What I Have Learned

Twenty Questions

The oral game *Twenty Questions* can be used to help students practice focusing attention on details. Select an object and have students try to discover the object by asking detailed questions.

This game is most appropriate for students in grades 5 and 6 and with students who have special needs.

Text Lookbacks

In a text lookback, students look over the material to search for the answer to a question or to review the material to remember it better.

A text lookback can consist of any of the following: rereading the chapter headings; rereading the topic sentences of each paragraph; skimming through the entire reading material; scanning for a specific detail such as a name, place, or date; or rereading a specific paragraph or a few sentences.

The text lookback is a very useful strategy for most students with special needs, such as learning or reading disabled students. Such students often do not think of using this strategy unless it is specifically pointed out to them and they are given practice in using it.

Retelling

Retelling is an excellent way both to evaluate and to improve comprehension skills. Retelling means having students retell the main concepts and important details in a reading assignment after they have read it. It can be used as an *alternative* to textually explicit comprehension questions when students have finished reading. Retelling and explicit comprehension questions should not be used together because that puts too much focus on evaluating or improving comprehension.

Retelling has been used since the 1920s for evaluating comprehension skills. It was the primary way of evaluating comprehension on the first standardized reading tests. However, it fell out of favor for many years, being replaced by comprehension questions. Today retelling is enjoying renewed popularity, and it is recommended as an alternative way to improve comprehension skills as well as to assess them.

When and Where?

This game is appropriate for use in grades 5 and 6. It is designed to help students develop an understanding of time and place. Here's how to do it. On a sheet of paper, type a series of short stories that involve various times and places. On another sheet, construct a crossword puzzle with questions about time and place. For example, "The second story takes place in the state of ____________________." You can provide a separate answer sheet for self-correction if you wish.

Chunking Clues

Chunking clues, sometimes called *phrase training,* attempts to focus students' attention on meaningful *units of language* by breaking up sentences into phrases or ideational chunks. For example, the following sentence would be "chunked" this way:

> The World Wide Web/ is an excellent tool/ to use/ in researching material/ for a term paper/ although/ it always should be read/ critically/ since it may contain/ some errors.

Training in chunking material can direct attention to wording, concepts, and sequencing, but it must be accompanied by discussions about comprehension, which is the main reason for chunking. Asking students where they would place phrase markers in reading material stimulates discussion about meaning in a relevant way.

Stevens (1981) found that chunking procedures were helpful to tenth-grade male students. However, Brozo, Schmelzer, and Spires (1983) discovered that although chunking training helps below-average readers, few studies have found that it helps other students. Therefore, chunking probably is most useful with students who have special needs such as reading or learning disabilities. It *may* be one way of helping them improve comprehension, but it must be used along with many other strategies.

Teaching Patterns of Organization

To become proficient readers of content materials, students must have direct instruction in the common *paragraph patterns of organization* that are used in the materials they read. This instruction should be emphasized in the middle school and continue through the secondary school. It always should use students' own content materials and be related to their current topics of study.

There are several different schemes for organizing paragraphs. Here is one of them:

- *Main idea plus examples.* The main idea is placed at the beginning of the sentence in a topic sentence. The remainder of the sentences in the paragraph then clarify, explain, or expand on the main idea.
- *Time order.* The paragraph is organized in a chronological manner, usually proceeding from the earliest events to the most contemporary.
- *Compare and contrast.* The material in the paragraph illustrates either a comparison or a contrast with the main idea (that is, the topic sentence).
- *Cause and effect.* The paragraph explains how the effects are the result of the cause described in it.
- *Climax.* The paragraph begins with a problem that culminates in a climax near or at the end of the paragraph.

Here is another way to classify a paragraph pattern of organization:

- *Enumeration.* A topic is immediately followed by information that expands on it; that is, a main idea is followed by descriptive details.
- *Relationships.* These include the *cause–effect relationships* often found in social studies textbooks and the *compare–contrast relationships* often found in science textbooks. In addition, relationships may be *classifications.*
- *Problem solving.* The problem presented has to be solved by the reader in order to demonstrate understanding of a concept. This pattern of organization often is found in science and mathematics textbooks.

Manzo and Manzo (1993) presented the following common twelve paragraph patterns of organization:

1. Introductory
2. Definition
3. Transactional *(shift attention from a previous pattern)*
4. Illustrative
5. Summary
6. Main idea and supporting details
7. Chronological ordering
8. Compare–contrast
9. Cause–effect
10. Problem–solution
11. Descriptive *(attempting to evoke a mental picture or visual image)*
12. Narrative *(containing a sequence of storylike events)*

Using Expository Paragraph Frames for Improving Comprehension and Retention of Content Reading

Expository story frames can be used as sentence starters that include *signal words* or *phrases* to fit the paragraph organization. The *sequential pattern of organization* is one of the easiest for students in the middle grades and students with special needs to use.

Here is how to do it. First, write a paragraph about content material that uses such *cue words* as *first, next, then, after that, later,* and *finally.* Then copy the sentences onto strips of paper, discuss the sequential order of the material, place the sentence strips in random order, and have students arrange the sentence strips in sequential order in a pocket chart. Then, as a group, have the students read the arranged sentences. After that, they can arrange the sentences individually and copy them onto their papers in paragraph form. If you wish, they can illustrate the information that was found in the paragraph.

After this procedure has been used several times, this strategy can be placed on an activity sheet that uses a passage containing *sequentially ordered paragraphs.* Have students read this passage silently. Then give them an activity sheet that provides an *expository passage frame* that indicates *sequence* for them to complete. This paragraph frame should emphasize the sequential nature of the content passage that the students just read. This frame then provides students with a summary of the content passage that should help them to understand and remember it better.

Here is an example of an expository passage frame:

Name __________________ **Grade** _____ **Teacher** _____________ **Date** ______

Expository Passage Frame

First this passage ____

____

Next this passage ____

Then this passage ____

After that this passage ____

Later this passage ____

____

____

Finally this passage ____

____

____

Strategies for Improving Textually Implicit Comprehension Skills

These strategies will help you improve your students' implicit comprehension skills.

Textually Implicit QARs

Questioning strategies can be used both for assessment and for improving comprehension. In several research studies Raphael (1982, 1986) taught students three kinds of QARs or questioning strategies. QAR instruction encourages students to think about both their prior knowledge and their reading material when they answer questions. The relationship between questions and their answers that require information from a number of sentences or paragraphs in the material is called *think and search.*

Most of the comprehension questions that students are asked in grades 5 to 12 should be of the think-and-search type. It is important that teachers ask all students, including those with reading and learning disabilities, mainly these kinds of questions—that is, textually implicit or interpretive questions. If students have not been asked many such questions, they are unlikely ever to attain competence in answering questions at this level.

In studies on QARs, researchers found that *modeling the decision* about the kind of QAR that questions constituted was an important part of teaching students about the concept. *Supervised practice* following a teacher's modeling also was important. According to the research, average and below-average students made the greatest improvement after training in use of QARs.

The following diagram shows the think-and-search element of the QARs that Raphael studied.

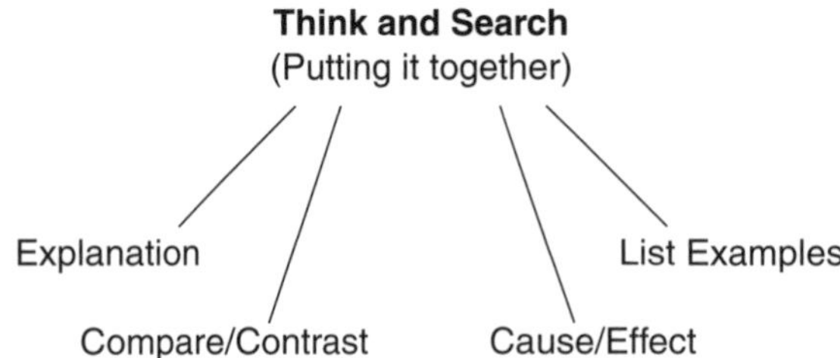

Reciprocal Questioning

Reciprocal questioning (the *ReQuest procedure)* is a useful strategy for helping students in the middle school and above, especially those with special needs, to become active questioners at the textually implicit level of comprehension. Although Manzo (1969) developed the original ReQuest procedure, it has been revised by many other reading specialists. It is one of the most useful strategies for improving ability in textually implicit comprehension. My teacher-trainees have used it very effectively with hundreds of students in different teaching and tutoring settings over the years.

The main steps of this procedure are as follows. However, you should modify them based on the needs and interests of your own students.

1. Tell the students to ask several textually implicit questions about each sentence in a selection that they think you might ask.

2. Next, answer each question as fairly and completely as you can and tell the students that they must subsequently do the same.

3. You and your students then silently read the first sentence.

4. Close the book. Have a student ask you questions about that sentence. Answer them.

5. Next have the students close the book, and you ask them questions about the material. You should provide an excellent model for their questions. Your questions always should be at the textually implicit (interpretive) level.

6. After a number of additional sentences, the procedure can be modified to reflect an entire paragraph rather than individual sentences if the students seem able to do so.

Visual Imagery

Formulating *visual images*, also called *mental images*, is a very good strategy for improving textually implicit comprehension. It is especially effective if students are reading narrative material that lends itself well to formulating visual images while they are reading. Many students do not think about using this strategy as an aid to comprehension unless they have direct instruction and practice in it. Creating visual images enhances the use of prior knowledge and improves the ability to make inferences about what is read, an important aspect of textually implicit comprehension. In addition to improving comprehension, mental imagery can help students remember what they read.

Visual imagery is so effective because it is an active, generative process. For example, in a research study comparing fourth-grade students who read a story without illustrations and formulated their own image while reading with fourth-grade students who noticed the illustrations included in the story, the group that formulated its own images remembered the story better (Gambrell and Javitz, 1993). Apparently, formulating one's own images is more effective than using someone else's illustrations. Visual imagery is an easy strategy to present, and students usually enjoy creating their images while reading.

You can easily create activity sheets as guides. Students read a passage that lends itself to imaging and then draw one or more illustrations reflecting the material. This type of activity sheet probably is most appropriate in grades 5 and 6. Most older students may find it too "juvenile."

A good way to improve visual imagery is to have students read interesting, descriptive mass-market books and ask them to try to picture the books' main characters, setting, or events. The following are some trade books that can be used for this purpose, but countless additional ones also can be used. The *interest level by age* is indicated after each book.

Alexander, L. *The Arkadians.* New York: Dutton, 1995. (11–13)

Almond, D. *Kit's Wilderness.* New York: Bantam/Doubleday/Dell Books for Young Readers, 2001. (12+)

Burnett, F. *The Secret Garden.* New York: Penguin/Putnam Books for Young Readers, 1986. (10–12)

Burnett, F. *A Little Princess.* New York: Barnes & Noble Books, 1998. (10–12)

Chetwin, G. *Jason's Seven Magical Night Rides.* New York: Bradbury, 1994. (11+)

Curtis, C. *Bud, Not Buddy.* New York: Random House Books for Young Readers, 2002. (10–12)

Dahl, R. *The Vicar of Nibbleswicke.* New York: Penguin/Putnam Books for Young Readers, 1994. (10–11)

Dahl, R. *The Witches.* New York: Penguin/Putnam Books for Young Readers, 1998. (10–11)

Dahl, R., and Blake, Q. *The Twits.* New York: Viking Penguin, 1998. (10–12)

Duane, D. *A Wizard Abroad.* Orlando: Harcourt Brace, 2001. (10)

Erickson, J. *The Original Adventures of Hank the Cowdog.* New York: Penguin/Putnam Books for Young Readers, 1999. (10–12)

Farrell, J., and Mayall, B. *Middle School: The Real Deal: From Cafeteria Food to Combination Locks.* New York: William Morrow, 2001. (10–12)

George, J. *My Side of the Mountain.* New York: Penguin/Putnam Books for Young Readers, 2001. (10–12)

Hill, K. *The Year of Miss Agnes.* New York: Aladdin Paperbacks, 2002. (10–12)

Hobbs, W. *Downriver.* New York: Bantam/Doubleday/Dell Books for Young Readers, 1996. (12+)

Holt, K. *My Louisiana Sky.* New York: Bantam/Doubleday/Dell Books for Young Readers, 1999. (12+)

Holt, K. *When Zachary Beaver Came to Town.* New York: Bantam/Doubleday/Dell Books for Young Readers, 2001. (10–12)

Kaye, M. *Missing Pieces.* New York: Bantam/Doubleday/Dell Books for Young Readers, 2001. (10–12)

Klause, A. *Alien Secrets.* New York: Delacorte, 1993. (10+)

L'Engle, M. *Amy of the Starfish.* Bantam/Doubleday/Dell Books for Young Readers, 1981. (12+)

Mackel, K. *From the Horse's Mouth.* New York: HarperCollins, 2002. (10–12)

Morris, G. *The Squire's Tale.* New York: Bantam/Doubleday/Dell Books for Young Readers, 1999. (12+)

O'Dell, S. *Island of the Blue Dolphins.* New York: Bantam/Doubleday/Dell Books for Children, 1971. (12+)

O'Dell, S. *Sing Down the Moon.* New York: Bantam/Doubleday/Dell Books for Young Readers, 1992. (12+)

Pullman, P. *The Golden Compass.* New York: Bantam/Doubleday/Dell Books for Young Readers, 2001. (10–12)

Renmison, L. *Knocked Out by My Nunga-Nungas: Further Confessions of Georgia Nicholson. Vol. 3.* New York: HarperCollins, 2002. (10–12)

Rowling, J. K. *Harry Potter and the Prisoner of Azkaban.* New York: Scholastic, 2001. (10–12)

Sachar, L. *Holes.* New York: Bantam/Doubleday/Dell Books for Young Readers, 2000. (10–12)

Sebestyen, O. *Words by Heart.* New York: Bantam/Doubleday/Dell Books for Young Readers, 1981. (10–12)

Snyder, Z. *Libby on Wednesday.* New York: Bantam/Doubleday/Dell Books for Young Readers, 1991. (10–12)

Taylor, M. *The Road to Memphis.* New York: Penguin/Putnam Books for Young Readers, 1992. (10–12)

Taylor, M. *Roll of Thunder, Hear My Cry.* New York: Viking Penguin, 1997. (10–12)

Taylor, M., and Ginsburg, M. *The Friendship.* New York: Penguin/Putnam Books for Young Readers, 1998. (9–12)

Whelan, G. *Homeless Bird.* New York: HarperCollins, 2001. (10)

White, R. *Belle Prater's Boy.* New York: Bantam/Doubleday/Dell Books for Young Readers, 1998. (10–14)

Generating Reciprocal Inferences Procedure (GRIP)

Reutzel and Hollingsworth (1988) stated that one important aspect of comprehension is the ability to *formulate inferences.* A two-stage approach used to help students develop this ability is called the *Generating Reciprocal Inferences Procedure (GRIP).* First, the teacher or tutor models exactly how an inference is made by reading, and then he *highlights key or clue words* in the material. For example, the teacher or tutor may read aloud the following passage, in which he highlights certain clue words, as illustrated:

> Ann and Rosemary went on a *trip* last Wednesday evening. They *boarded a large paddle-wheel boat* that was docked in the city of LaCrosse, Wisconsin. As the *paddle-wheel boat cruised,* Ann and Rosemary ate a delicious dinner of salad, fried chicken, meatballs, red potatoes, and cake. When the paddle-wheel boat reached Lock and Dam Number 7, *it was raised* several feet higher. After cruising for about three hours, the paddle-wheel boat *returned* to the *dock* in LaCrosse. During the cruise, Ann and Rosemary saw many interesting sights, such as *barges, motorboats,* and *fishing boats.*

Where were Ann and Rosemary? This passage requires the reader to make a certain type of slot-filling inference—*a location inference.* The teacher or tutor makes this inference after highlighting the clues in the text that led to that conclusion. After making the inference, the teacher justifies the inference by pointing out how each passage clue, combined with prior knowledge, supported the inference that Ann and Rosemary were on a paddle-wheel boat cruise on a river—the Mississippi River as inferred from the location of LaCrosse, Wisconsin.

The GRIP lesson continues with four additional paragraphs. These paragraphs are needed to release the responsibility for inferencing gradually from the teacher to the students. In the next paragraph, the teacher highlights the words, the students make the inference, and the teacher justifies the inference the students made. The third paragraph is then read, and the students justify the inference. In the fourth and last passage, the students highlight the key words, make the inference, and justify the inference all by themselves.

After students are capable of assuming full responsibility for finding key words, inferencing, and justifying the inference, they are able to *generate reciprocal inferences.* Students are paired to write their own inference paragraphs. This is done by generating a list of five or more key words and writing the text, incorporating the clues without giving away the inference to be made. After writing, the students in each pair exchange paragraphs, mark key words, make the inference, and justify their inferences to the author. This process may continue as long as necessary and as long as the students' interest stays high. Variations on this approach include placing the paragraphs written by students on transparencies and asking them to locate the key words, make an inference, and justify their own inferences in writing. In another variation, a game board activity includes directions for playing the game; see the next section for more on this version.

GRIP has been shown to increase students' abilities to make inferences across a variety of measures and under different conditions (Reutzel and Hollingsworth, 1988). GRIP is an example of a gradual release in comprehension instruction that improves textually implicit (interpretive) comprehension.

Playing the GRIP Board Game

Students play the *GRIP board game* in pairs. Before playing the game, each student must understand the rules for playing the game and follow them carefully. Here is how the game is played. (This section has been adapted with permission from Reutzel and Hollingsworth, 1988. See the Works Cited section for complete information on this work.)

1. This game requires two players.
2. Write four sentences that go together to formulate a story. Underline the clue words in each sentence.
3. Select a marker.
4. Place the marker on START.
5. Throw the die, allowing the player with the highest score to begin the game.
6. Each player moves his or her marker the number of spaces indicated on the die.
7. If a player lands on STATION, the other player reads a sentence.
8. If a players lands on MAGNIFYING GLASS, he or she moves to the nearest STATION, and the other player reads a sentence.
9. A different sentence is read at each STATION.
10. A player must be on STATION to guess, and he or she is allowed only one guess.
11. If a player lands on STOP SIGN, he or she should go back to the space on which he or she started the turn.
12. One player can be on the same space as the other player.
13. If a player lands on SIDETRACKED, he or she must follow the feet.
14. If a player lands on SQUAD CAR, he or she should follow the road.
15. Whoever guesses what the story is about is named the winner, and the game is over.

To introduce the GRIP board game, the teacher or tutor can play it with one student while the other students watch. This makes the transition from discussing the rules to playing the game simpler.

Phase In–Phase Out Strategy

This strategy is designed to encourage *active student questioning* on the textually implicit (interpretive) level. The teacher or tutor phases in the questioning process by taking the first step in modeling implicit questions that are appropriate to the content. He or she then offers additional information about the content to be read or about the topic.

Some knowledge of the material to be read is necessary in order to generate the appropriate questions. Once students have an idea of the kinds of questions that can be asked about the different types of content, they are placed into groups to ask each other questions on the material to be read. The final phasing out occurs when the students ask and answer implicit questions on their own.

Having Students Infer the Correct Job or Profession

Provide each student with a slip of paper on which you have written characteristics of a job or profession. Have each student read the material on the slip of paper and write down the job or profession that the characteristics suggest.

Here are several examples:

This is one of the medical specialties.
It is related to the diagnosis of injuries and diseases of the bones and joints.
This specialist performs operations on human bones and joints.
Several of the operations that this specialist performs are hip replacement, knee replacement, and shoulder replacement.
What is the name of this type of medical specialist?
Answer: *Orthopedic surgeon*

This person has studied animals extensively.
He or she often has majored in the science of zoology at college.
Therefore, this person understands the basic characteristics of most animals.
This person may provide suggestions about how to alter an animal's behavior or may actually work with an animal to improve its behavior so that it is more acceptable to humans.
What is the name of this professional?
Answer: *Animal behaviorist*

Cybernetic Sessions

In *cybernetic sessions*, small groups of students respond to preplanned implicit (interpretive) questions during a limited period of time. In the *preplanning phase*, the teacher or tutor writes a question on each of several poster boards or sheets of butcher paper and hangs them up around the classroom. He should use thought-provoking questions that may elicit misconceptions. During the *response-generating phase*, students are placed in groups of five or six around each of the poster questions. Students are asked to contribute as many answers as possible to each poster question while the group recorder writes them down on a separate sheet of paper. After the allotted time, each group moves to another question station, and the process is repeated. Each time, a new recorder is selected.

The next phase involves *data synthesizing*, where the groups all pool their answers to each question. This phase occurs after each group has had the chance to circulate around the room and answer all the poster questions. At this point, the teacher writes all the responses under each posted question.

In the *final presentation phase*, the teacher can place posters on bulletin boards, type them up as handouts, or re-read them as a form of review. This strategy is effective when questions related to a content assignment are used or before reading a narrative mass-market (trade) book.

Investigative Questioning Procedures (InQuest)

Investigative Questioning Procedures (InQuest) is a creative concept that improves students' interaction with narrative material. It was developed by Shoop (1986) and can be used in instructional groups. The group stops reading at a crucial place in a trade book or story. One student assumes the role of a major character; others become "on-the-scene" investigative reporters who ask the character questions about events in the book or story. The emphasis in InQuest is to develop students' ability to formulate and answer textually implicit (interpretive) comprehension questions.

Jeopardy Using Analogies

This *game-like activity* is designed to help students in grades 5 to 8 evaluate analogies. Here's how to make the board. On a large piece of tag board, attach twenty-five small envelopes in five rows each. On each envelope write a dollar amount: $10, $20, $50, $100, and $250. Then attach headings to each column, such as *Rock Groups*, *Movie Stars*, *Sports Figures*, *Computer Terms*, and *Historical Figures*. In each envelope, insert cards with an analogy involving the words that fit under the category. Write the correct answer on the back. Here are several examples of analogies; the answers are shown in parentheses:

Touchdown is to football as home run is to ___________________. *(baseball)*

Thomas Jefferson is to the Declaration of Independence as Abraham Lincoln is to the ________________________. *(Gettysburg Address)*

Clark Gable is to Rhett Butler as Vivien Leigh is to ____________________. *(Scarlett O'Hara)*

The Beatles are to Liverpool, England, as Elvis Presley is to ________________. *(Memphis, Tennessee)*

A Web site is to an encyclopedia article as electronic mail (e-mail) is to _______________________. *("snail" mail)*

The game is played much like the television version. Choose one student to play the role of the emcee, and choose two or three others to play the game. Students take turns selecting the envelope of questions they want to answer. The emcee reads the analogy, and if a player can complete it correctly, he or she accumulates that amount of money and has another turn. If the student is wrong, another player has the chance to answer. The player who has the most money when all the envelopes have been chosen wins the game.

Dyadic Learning

In this strategy students work in *dyads* (pairs) to read and learn content material. One partner assumes the role of "rememberer" and orally summarizes the material that was read while the other partner becomes the "listener-facilitator," correcting mistakes and adding information. Students are told to read a selected number of paragraphs and then switch roles. They may work together to draw pictures or diagrams or make outlines illustrating the main concepts in the selection.

Strategies for Improving Critical (Evaluative) Reading Skills

These strategies will help you improve your students' evaluative reading.

Critical (Evaluative) QARs

Students in grades 5 to 12 must have numerous opportunities to answer *questions at the critical (evaluative) level of comprehension.* If students are not asked questions that call for evaluative responses, they will never learn to respond at this level. Yet the future of our democratic society greatly depends on the ability of our citizens to think and read critically. Far too many students in grades 5 to 12—and many adults—have never learned to analyze critically what they read but rather take it at face value.

Critical thinking and reading require some degree of abstract intelligence. All students, however, including those with learning and reading disabilities, can make good progress in learning to read critically within the limits of their intellectual capabilities. All students can improve their critical reading ability if they are given instruction and frequent opportunities to respond at this level.

Some critical reading skills that can be incorporated into critical QARs are as follows:

- Discriminating between fact and opinion
- Comparing different sources of information
- Critically analyzing persuasive language
- Detecting assumptions
- Evaluating slanted writing
- Analyzing editorials and letters to the editor

Critical QARs cannot be given a yes or no answer. If students try to answer a question this way, they should then expand on that answer by explaining why they believe as they do. A simple *yes* or *no* does not constitute critical evaluation.

Because critical reading often involves *controversial issues*, it is not always welcomed in public or private schools. However, at the present time more reading teachers and tutors are allowing students to voice their own opinions on a variety of controversial topics, such as premarital sex, abortion, legalization of marijuana and other drugs, the legal drinking age, and contraception.

The following are several examples of critical QARs from the content area of social studies.

- Do you believe that the words "under God" should be included in the Pledge of Allegiance when it is recited in classrooms in the United States? Why do you believe as you do?
- Do you think that security screeners should use *racial profiling* at airport security checkpoints? Why do you believe as you do?
- Do you think that all incoming college freshmen should read the Quran (Koran) in order to understand the Muslim religion better? Why do you believe as you do?

Discriminating Between Fact and Opinion

Discriminating between fact and opinion is an important element of critical or evaluative reading. Students in grades 5 to 12 can be given a series of written statements and asked to determine if they are fact or opinion. These statements may be written on an activity sheet for students to complete either independently or with a partner or partners.

Students can learn *key words* that *may* signal opinions. Some of these key words are *think, believe, surmise, feel, assume, imagine, deem, suppose, best, worst, prettiest, friendliest, nicest,* and *ugliest,* among many others.

Here are several statements that call for students to indicate whether they are fact or opinion.

Xcel Energy stock was trading at 9.78 at 1:00 P.M. on Tuesday, August 20, 2002. *Fact.*

The stock market downturn during the summer of 2002 was entirely caused by the terrorist attack against the United States on September 11, 2001. *Opinion.*

President George W. Bush was born in Midland, Texas, a son of George H. W. and Barbara Bush. *Fact.*

If a person votes for a Republican candidate, he or she must hold conservative views. *Opinion.*

The major news organizations report the national news in a manner that has a liberal bias. *Opinion.*

Verifying Factual Statements

Students should learn how to *verify factual statements* found in printed material as one important aspect of critical reading instruction. Some ways of doing this are by using content textbooks, informational trade books, experts in the field, reference books of various types, the World Wide Web, newspapers, magazines, movies, and videotapes.

However, all of this material must be evaluated *critically.* Although content textbooks, informational books, and reference works can contain errors, the World Wide Web, movies, and videotapes may be more likely to contain significant errors. The World Wide Web especially is prone to contain significant errors because Web sites are not evaluated by experts in various fields as are most other resources. Students should be made aware that all material found on Web sites is subject to error and must be evaluated very carefully.

Inquiry Charts

Inquiry charts can be constructed in order to promote critical reading skills (Hoffman, 1992). To begin the class or group, choose a topic and construct questions that will be the basis of the inquiry. Then record these questions on a large chart. Materials such as content textbook passages, informational and narrative trade books, encyclopedia articles, material from the World Wide Web, and newspaper or magazine articles that pertain to the topic also may be gathered and listed on the inquiry chart.

Then ask the students questions to determine their prior knowledge about the topic and enter their responses, whether they are correct or incorrect, on the chart under the target questions. Information that students have that is not related to the target questions is recorded in the column titled *Other Interesting Facts and Figures.* If students have other questions that have not been identified, you can list them under *New Questions.* The students then either read the resource materials independently, with a partner, or in a group, or you can read it to them. Each resource is discussed, and students determine if the information is appropriate to answer the target questions. Information relevant to the questions is recorded in the proper spaces on the inquiry chart. More *Interesting Facts* and *New Questions* also can be added to the chart.

After all the resource materials have been read and the information learned from them has been recorded, students write summary statements to answer each question, using information from all the resources. Students also summarize the *Interesting Facts.* Then they compare what they listed as prior knowledge with the newly learned information and determine the differences. They also clarify any misconceptions previously held. Individual students or small groups of students further research the appropriate sources of information and report their findings to the class or group.

Here is a sample American history inquiry chart.

Inquiry Chart: Guiding Questions

Topic: The Battle of Little Bighorn, June 1876	1. Who fought in the Battle of Little Bighorn?	2. Where was the Battle of Little Bighorn fought?	3. How many fought and were killed in the Battle of Little Bighorn?	4. What is known about General Custer?	5. Other interesting facts and figures:
What we know:	There were Sioux and Cheyenne Native Americans under Sitting Bull,	It was fought in the Black Hills near Montana,	There were 4,000 Native Americans in the battle	Custer was a brave, experienced Indian fighter.	The Native Americans stripped and mutilated the uniformed dead soldiers.
www.ibiscom.com/custer.htm.	and three columns of the United States Army commanded by Custer, Benteen, and Reno.	near the Sioux village along the Rosebud River,	and 400 Army members;	He was perhaps too rash and thoughtless.	Custer's body was not scalped or mutilated.
www.hillsdale.edu/academics/history/War/America/Indian/1876-Bighorn-Times.htm	The Native Americans vastly outnumbered the Army men.	near the upper valley of the Little Bighorn River.	300 soldiers were killed.	He was the youngest general in American history.	The Battle of Little Bighorn was the worst American military disaster ever.
Summary	It would have been virtually impossible for the Army to win the Battle of Little Bighorn because of the difference in the numbers.	The Cheyenne and Sioux forced 210 of Custer's men to a long high ridge north of the Little Bighorn River.	The Native Americans achieved their greatest victory.	He wore buck-skins and his hair was cut short for battle.	By 1877 the Sioux nation had been defeated in spite of their victory.

Comparing Different Sources of Information

Students in grades 5 to 12 should learn how to *compare different sources of information* as one important element of critical reading. Some of these sources may be content textbooks; informational or narrative trade books; reference books of various types such as encyclopedias, almanacs, and atlases; the World Wide Web; newspapers; magazines; movies; videotapes; and experts in the field who come to the classroom to make a presentation.

For example, students may notice significant differences in emphasis in the material on a certain topic as presented in a content textbook and on the World Wide Web. They should learn how to evaluate which of the two sources probably is more accurate.

Cooperative Learning

Cooperative learning is an excellent strategy for improving critical reading skills. The small-group work of cooperative learning encourages *active participation* in situations in which students can extend their knowledge with others of different ability levels and diverse backgrounds. As they share ideas, students create a forum to present issues and responses and clarify their thinking. As they share planning and responsibilities, it encourages a sense of commitment to the group and to learning.

Uttero (1988) discovered that when students incorporated *critical learning strategies* into cooperative learning groups, these positive effects were found:

- Students were enthusiastic about the learning and expressed enjoyment about working together.
- Below-average readers saw themselves as valuable contributors and developed more positive attitudes about school and learning.
- By working actively and cooperatively in their groups, students began to internalize critical reading strategies and to use some of them.

Recognizing Propaganda Techniques

Propaganda is a deliberate attempt to use words and nonverbal cues to persuade people to accept an idea, take a position, or adopt an attitude. Politicians often use propaganda (political "spin") to win elections on the basis of emotion rather than critical thought. Advertisers use it to influence people to buy a certain product or use a specific service, and medical professionals use it to influence patients to use or abstain from a specific drug or action. There also are many other examples of how propaganda is used.

Here are the most common propaganda techniques.

- *Bandwagon:* People are encouraged to become part of a specific group by buying the target product or taking a certain action.
- *Testimonial:* Well-known personalities, primarily in the entertainment or sports fields, endorse a product with the idea that other people will follow their testimonial. Many products and services of all types are sold in this way.
- *Plain folks:* To inspire admiration and confidence, a wealthy or powerful person attempts to convince people that he or she is an ordinary person just like them.
- *Name calling:* Words and terms that have unpleasant connotations are used to try to influence people. The following are some of them: *redneck, trailer trash, liberal, conservative, miser, lazy, poor white trash, out of touch,* and *ivory tower,* among countless others.
- *Card stacking:* All of the *good points* or *advantages* of a product or service are listed, but none of the bad points or disadvantages are mentioned.
- *Transfer:* The favorable feeling that people have for a *symbol* is carried over or transferred to an idea or product that someone is trying to sell. For example, after September 11, 2001, the *American flag* was found on a wide variety of products. The positive feeling that people had for this nation's flag was "transferred" to the product that was to be sold.

Detecting Assumptions

Assumptions are statements that are not proven or supported. They may be directly stated or merely implied. Students who do not read critically may accept them as facts. A paragraph similar to this example can be used to introduce this element of critical reading.

> The New York Stock Exchange really took a hit during the summer of 2002. Many people lost most of their retirement funds. This financial loss was the direct result of the fiscal policies of President George W. Bush and his financial advisers. Our country enjoyed economic prosperity under President Bill Clinton, but our entire economic structure collapsed under the Bush presidency. That is why he will not be reelected to the presidency in 2004.

Locating Directly Stated and Implied Main Ideas and Significant Details

In order to read critically, it is essential for students to know how to locate the main idea and supporting details in what they read. Here are several strategies to teach them how to do so.

Diagramming Paragraphs to Illustrate Main Ideas and Significant Details

To diagram a paragraph, list the main idea as well as the supporting details, as illustrated by the following paragraph.

> Sir Isaac Newton is considered by many mathematicians and scientists to be one of the most superior intellects the world has ever known. Newton was born on Christmas Day in 1642 to a farm family living in Lincoln County, England. He was a premature baby who seemed frail and sickly. Because he had poor health, he could not play the games that other children played. Instead he invented such perfectly constructed toys as waterwheels, a mill, and a wooden clock.

Main idea: Sir Isaac Newton is considered by many mathematicians and scientists to be one of the most superior intellects the world has ever known.

Supporting details: Newton was born on Christmas Day in 1642 to a farm family living in Lincoln County, England. He was a premature baby who seemed frail and sickly. Because he had poor health, he could not play the games that other children played. Instead he invented such perfectly constructed toys as waterwheels, a mill, and a wooden clock.

To illustrate the relationship between the main idea and the supporting details in a paragraph, you can draw the paragraph in a diagram such as the following:

Sir Isaac Newton is considered by many mathematicians and scientists to be one of the most superior intellects the world has ever know.
Newton was born on Christmas Day in 1642 to a farm family living in Lincoln County, England.
Isaac was a premature baby who seemed frail and sickly.
Since he had poor health, he could not play the games that other children played.
Instead he invented such perfectly constructed toys as waterwheels, a mill, and a wooden clock.

Other paragraphs have two main ideas:

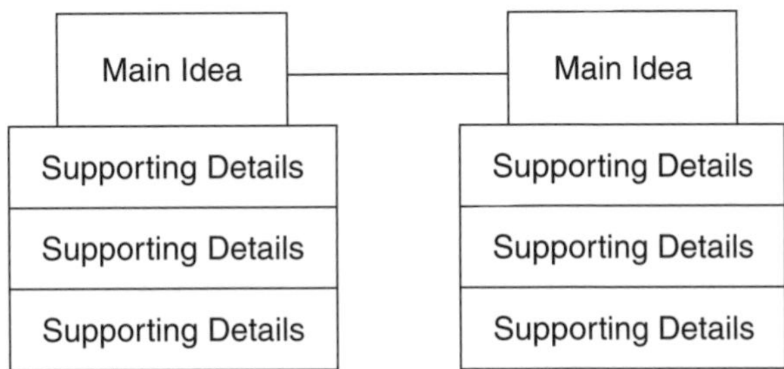

Paragraphs can take other forms, too, such as the following.

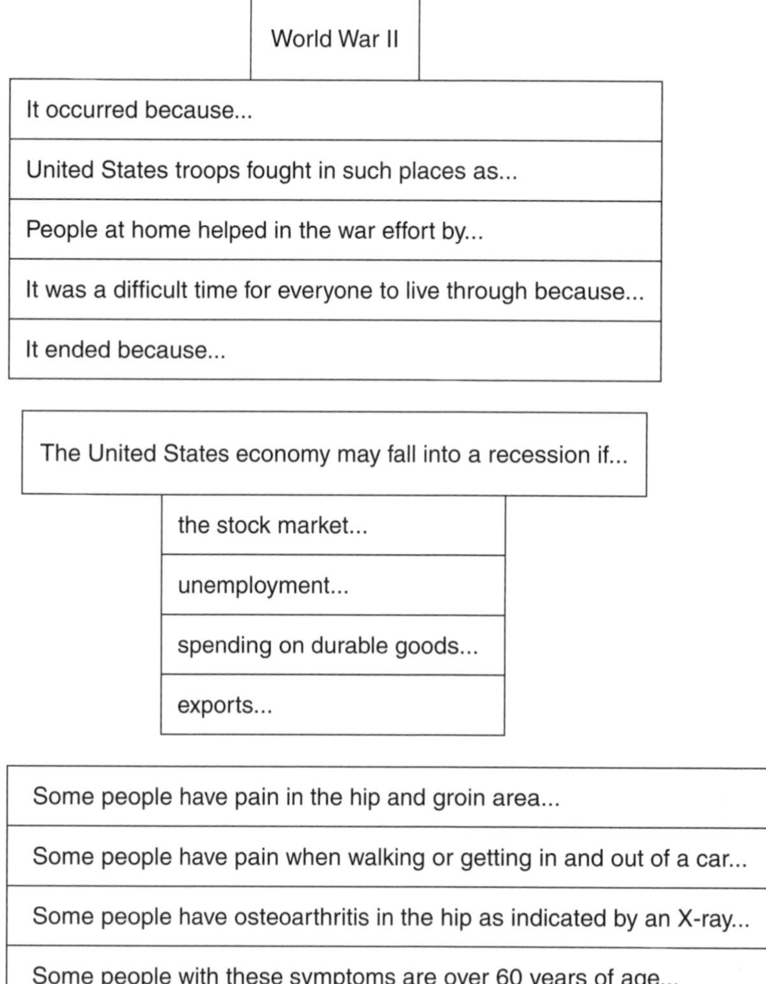

World War II
It occurred because...
United States troops fought in such places as...
People at home helped in the war effort by...
It was a difficult time for everyone to live through because...
It ended because...
The United States economy may fall into a recession if...
the stock market...
unemployment...
spending on durable goods...
exports...
Some people have pain in the hip and groin area...
Some people have pain when walking or getting in and out of a car...
Some people have osteoarthritis in the hip as indicated by an X-ray...
Some people with these symptoms are over 60 years of age...
The result is that...

Five-Step Strategy for Locating the Main Idea

It may be helpful to provide students with a specific strategy for finding the main idea in a paragraph or selection. If students have mastered the prerequisite skills of decoding the words, understanding the vocabulary, and remembering and understanding the details of a paragraph, the following steps may help them locate the main idea (Shanker and Ekwall, 1988):

1. Read the entire paragraph.
2. Study each sentence and then restate it in your own words.
3. Ask yourself which one thing most of the sentences were about.
4. Find or state the main idea.
5. Check your answer.

The final step is very important. To check their answer students need to review *each sentence* and ask themselves: "Does this sentence tell about or support the main idea?"

To teach this strategy, follow these steps:

1. Introduce the steps.
2. Demonstrate or model the use of the steps with a sample paragraph that all students can follow. One way to do this is to write it on a large chart.
3. Provide considerable guided practice. For example, give students a series of short paragraphs and go through all the steps together.
4. Provide independent practice only after students have demonstrated ability to complete the steps with teacher guidance.
5. Provide review when needed.

If students are going to master this skill, they must follow each of the steps listed. Present the strategy on the chalkboard or chart paper so students can see it. Tell the students that you are going to show them how it works. It is important to show students what you are doing by thinking out loud as you proceed through each step. Then, when you work with students to practice these steps on sample paragraphs, it is a good time for students to discuss their interpretations of the sentences and main ideas. The independent practice and later review will help them learn the new skill if the previous instruction was effective. A similar strategy can be used to teach other specific comprehension skills.

Selecting and Writing a Statement of the Implied Main Idea

Locating an *implied main idea* in a paragraph is a very difficult skill for most students in the middle school and beyond to master. To do so they must read a paragraph and synthesize the concepts to deduce the main idea that is merely implied. This requires abstract thought and prior knowledge. Students also must have considerable direct instruction and meaningful practice using their own narrative and content materials. The skill of locating an implied main idea in a paragraph often requires much time and experience before a student masters it.

One strategy that can be used for this purpose is for the teacher or tutor to provide students with several paragraphs that have an implied main idea. Then have them read each paragraph independently or with a partner and place an X or check mark in front of the sentence provided by the teacher that contains a statement of the implied main idea. The activity sheet should contain three or four options and should be fairly simple at the beginning and gradually become more difficult.

A subsequent strategy requires students to read a paragraph that contains an implied main idea. Have them read the paragraph either independently or with a partner and then formulate a statement of the implied main idea. They then should write down this statement. Although the statements of different students may vary slightly, each should be an approximation of the implied main idea.

Using Newspaper Articles for Formulating and Locating Main Ideas
You can collect newspaper articles and cut off the headlines. Then have students formulate headlines using the information found in the lead paragraph. Show them how to do this before you ask them to work on this project independently.

You can also collect old newspapers and cardboard for mounting them. Cut out a number of articles from the newspaper that you think will interest the students, and cut the body of each article from its headline. Mount each article and title on cardboard. Have the students read each article and locate the most appropriate title for it. Have the students discuss the reasons for their choices and make the activity self-checking by coding articles and headlines. As a follow-up, have students match advertisements to pictures or captions to cartoons.

Writing a Fictional Newspaper Article
Have students in grades 5 to 8 write a fictional newspaper article in which the most important information is found in the introductory paragraph. This paragraph should contain a clearly defined main idea and important details. The remainder of the newspaper article should expand on and clarify the information found in the first paragraph.

Self-Questioning About the Main Idea
Self-questioning about the main idea (Andre and Anderson, 1979) may improve the comprehension and retention of content materials at the middle-grade level and beyond. In this strategy students are taught to identify the *main idea of each paragraph* as they are reading and then are shown how to *formulate and answer a question* about the main idea. They then repeat this procedure with the next paragraph.

Very briefly, here are the main steps in this strategy.

- *What:* Students are told they will be learning how to ask and answer questions about the main ideas of paragraphs as they read content material.
- *Why:* Students are told this is important because they then will have better comprehension and retention of the content material that they are studying.
- *How:* The teacher models how to identify main ideas in a paragraph. Next the teacher decides on one or two words that state the topic of the paragraph. Then a main idea sentence about the paragraph is formulated. The teacher then provides several examples of possible main idea sentences for a particular paragraph as well as several unacceptable main idea sentences. She then shows students how to generate and answer a question about the main idea, and provides them with several examples of possible questions that could have been formulated for a particular paragraph. Several unacceptable questions also are discussed.
- *When:* Students should be told that they may employ the self-questioning strategy whenever they are reading content material that seems very difficult to understand and remember. They should begin again identifying main ideas for the paragraphs and formulating and answering questions about these main ideas.

Strategies for Improving Self-Monitoring or Metacognition of Reading Comprehension

Here are some strategies for improving self-monitoring.

"Click" or "Clunk"

The act of *self-monitoring one's own comprehension* is also called *metacognition* or *metacomprehension.* The ability to plan, check, monitor, revise, and evaluate one's unfolding comprehension is very important in reading. If students do not detect comprehension breakdowns, then they will not take action to correct misinterpretations of the material. However, if they expect that reading material should make sense and if they have the ability to self-correct comprehension problems, then they can make reading progress.

To help students develop the ability to monitor their own comprehension processes, Carr (1986) proposed a strategy called *click or clunk.* This strategy encourages readers to *reflect after reading* each paragraph or section by stopping and asking themselves if the meaning or message *clicks* for them or just goes *clunk.* If it *clunks*, what do they think is wrong? What can be done to make sense of it?

Fix-up Strategies

If students have determined from self-monitoring that they do not understand what was read, they should apply the appropriate *fix-up strategies.* Here are several useful fix-up strategies:

- *Sound and sense strategy.* This strategy (*Sound and Sense Strategy*, 1981) can be a good step in helping students, especially those with special needs, to identify unknown words and self-monitor their reading. As students apply this strategy, they focus on making sense out of print so reading is meaningful. They then use *phonics* and *context* to identify the unknown word. Here are the steps that students take:

  Skip the unknown word and read to the end of the sentence.
  Return to the unknown word and associate appropriate sounds for initial and final letters of the word.
  Return to the beginning of the sentence and reread, attempting to identify the word.
- *Suspending judgment.* Students need to practice suspending judgment. Often a new specialized vocabulary term is introduced in content reading, but a clear definition is not developed in the sentence. The student must continue reading, searching for additional clues to provide clarity to resolve the comprehension problem. Frequently authors present additional information later in the material to clarify the unknown concept. If additional information is not presented or comprehension cannot be constructed, students need to stop and use other tools such as a dictionary or ask for assistance.
- *Asking for assistance.* Students should ask for assistance when they need it unless it is used as a "crutch" that stops them from gaining independence. This assistance can be obtained from classmates as well as the teacher, teacher's aide, or tutor.

Monitoring Cards

Babbs (1984) suggested that students use nine monitoring prompt cards as they read. They are as follows:

1. *Click*—I understand.
2. *Clunk*—I don't understand.
3. Read on.
4. Reread the sentence.
5. Go back and reread the paragraph.
6. Look in the glossary.
7. Ask someone.
8. What did it say?
9. What do I remember? *(to check comprehension at the page level)*

These should be used only *after* students have thought about the reading with these goals is mind.

- What is reading?
- What is my goal?
- How difficult is the material?
- How can I accomplish my goal?
- How can I check on whether I have achieved my goal?

Davey and Porter's Four-Step Instructional Procedure for Improving Monitoring Ability

Davey and Porter (1982) developed a four-step instructional procedure for improving the comprehension-monitoring ability of students with special needs. This procedure is designed to help students understand the purpose of print, focus their attention on meaning while reading, evaluate their comprehension while reading, and develop fix-up strategies to improve comprehension and retention. Here are the main steps in this monitoring procedure:

How

1. *The first step involves teacher demonstration and modeling.* By using the cloze procedure, the teacher or tutor can show students that they usually can understand a passage even if they do not understand every word in it. *Fix-up strategies* such as rereading, or using meaning clues, using a dictionary or glossary also can be introduced. The teacher or tutor can model comprehension monitoring while reading aloud to students.

2. *The second step involves focusing attention during reading or comprehension and consists of a comprehension-rating task.* Students are given *sentences* to read and then to rate for comprehension. Some should make sense and some should not. Working first in small groups and later independently or with a partner, students rate their comprehension of each sentence using a + for sentences that they understand and a – or 0 for sentences they do not understand. Later they are given *paragraphs* to read and rate for understanding using the same format as the sentences.

3. *The third step is to help students establish their criteria for understanding, which involves a three-point rating task.* First working in groups and then working independently or with a partner, students rate sentences, paragraphs, and longer print material in the following way: *I understand this very well; I understand this somewhat; I don't understand this at all.* The teacher and students then discuss their rating for various sentences, paragraphs, and longer passages, and discuss their reasons for the ratings. Students then should be shown how to find sources of difficulty in content material.

4a. *The fourth step is to improve fix-up strategies and is used when students have developed competence in the first three steps.* Some of the *fix-up strategies are as follows:*

Skip the word if you think it will not interfere with comprehension.
Use context clues to predict or decode the word. Usually an approximate meaning and pronunciation is acceptable.
Use word structure such as base or root words, prefixes, suffixes, and syllable units or chunks within the word to help determine its approximate meaning.
Use graphophonic (phonic) clues to sound out the word.
Use a textbook glossary or a dictionary to locate the meaning and pronunciation of a word.
Ask your teacher, aide, tutor, classmate, family member, or friend for help.

4b. Some *concept-level fix-up strategies* are the following:

Read on in the content passage.
Reread the part that you did not understand.
Ask yourself questions about the material as you read.
Examine the titles, headings, pictures, and graphic aids carefully.
Visualize the concepts in your mind as you read.
Relate the concepts in the material to your own prior knowledge.
Ask someone to help you understand the passage.
Change your rate of reading by slowing down for difficult parts and speeding up if the material is easy.
Hypothesize by thinking to yourself: I think the author is trying to say ______________________________.
Suspend judgment in the hope that the author may add more information later.

What, Why, and When

To be sure that middle- and upper-level students will actually use this method of monitoring their comprehension while reading content materials and then employ appropriate fix-up strategies, it is important for teachers and tutors to do the following:

> *What:* Tell students they will be learning how to monitor or evaluate their own comprehension.
>
> *Why:* Tell them this is important because the *sole purpose of reading is understanding and sometimes remembering what is read.*
>
> *When:* Tell students they should monitor their own comprehension *every time* they read. They should pause at regular intervals and ask themselves if they are really understanding what they are reading. If they are not, they should employ the appropriate fix-up strategies.

Strategies for Improving Reading and Carrying Out Directions

Here are strategies for understanding and carrying out directions.

Become Aware of Key Words

Help students to become aware of *key words* that indicate a set of directions, such as *first, second, third, next, then, later,* and *finally.* As students read directions, have them review this knowledge by having them make lists of words that were used to indicate the steps.

Make Designs

Write directions for making designs to be drawn on a sheet of paper. As an example, you can write the following directions:

1. Draw an A on your paper 5½ inches from the top and bottom and 4¼ inches from each side.
2. Draw a B in the upper right-hand corner 5 inches from the A.
3. Draw a C in the lower right-hand corner 5 inches from the A.
4. Draw a D on the lower left-hand corner 5 inches from the A.
5. Draw an E in the upper left-hand corner 5 inches from the A.
6. Make an F in the upper middle 5 inches from the A.
7. Draw a G in the lower middle 5 inches from the A.

Following Directions to Apply for a Driver's License

Students in middle school and junior high school usually are greatly anticipating receiving their first driver's license. Therefore, one of the most motivating strategies for improving reading and carrying out directions may be related to applying for one. To apply for a driver's license, students need to read the application blank very carefully and follow the directions exactly while completing it.

Here are some sample items from such an application form. Of course, this form can be varied in any way you wish.

Application for Driver's License

Print in block letters:

Full Name ____

(Last) (First) (Middle)

____

Number and Street Address City Zip Code

______________________ M F

Social Security Number Sex (Circle One)

______________________ ______________________

Date of Birth (mo/day/year) Place of Birth

__________ __________ __________ __________

Eye Color Hair Color Weight Height(ft. in.)

Check condition of your health:

Excellent ________ Fair ________ Poor ________

Explain any physical disabilities that you have:

____

In the event of my death, I wish to be an organ donor.

Yes ____________ No ____________

______________________ ______________

Signature Date

Strategies for Improving Ability in Placing Items in Correct Sequence

Here's how to help improve sequential ability.

Arrange Age-appropriate Comic Strips in Correct Sequence

This activity probably is the most appropriate for students in grades 5 and 6. Locate *age-appropriate comic strips* and cut them apart by frames. Then laminate the frames to make them more durable and long-lasting. Have students try to reassemble each comic strip by placing it in the correct sequence. If you want, each comic strip that is to be used for this purpose can be placed in a large envelope. If you want to make this activity self-checking, place the correct sequence number on the back of each comic strip frame before laminating it.

Complete the Dialogue in Whited-out Comic Strips

As an alternative to the preceding activity, white out some of the balloons of dialogue in a comic strip and have students infer and write in the appropriate dialogue. You can also delete the ending frame and have students infer and write an ending for the strip.

Other Strategies for Improving Sequential Ability

After students have become adept at placing six or seven steps in sequential order, they can apply this skill to stories and articles. To help them become aware of the sequence of a story (or book), have them map out the main events indicating how the story progresses to its climax and the resolution of the problem. Help students create causal links between the events in the story, because this may help their retention (McNamara, Miller, and Bransford, 1991). A literary technique that may make a story more interesting but cause the sequence to be more difficult is *flashback*. When a flashback occurs, point it out and discuss why the author used it. Students may understand this technique better if they try it in their own writing.

With biographies and historical accounts, show students how to use dates to keep events in order. Encourage them to make a time line to keep track of the sequence of events. If your students read about the steps in a process, have them notice the sequence. Show them how they could use a graphic organizer to display a process or chain of events. A chain map is a graphic organizer that can be used to demonstrate sequence. The following is an example of a *chain map* from the area of science.

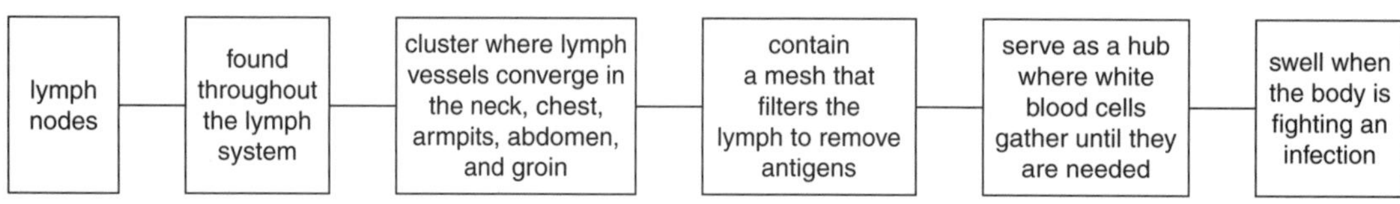

Using a Story Frame to Practice Sequence

A variation of a *story frame* can be used to provide students practice with sequence when reading a story or narrative trade book. The following illustrates how a story frame can be used for this purpose.

In this story, the problem begins when ________________.
After that, ________________. Next ________________. Then ________________.
The problem is solved when ________________. The story ends ________________.

Strategies for Improving Ability to Summarize Material

Here are some strategies for summarizing material.

Brown and Day's Rules for Summarizing

This strategy encourages students to determine what is important and then to condense and put it into their own words. Brown and Day (1983) offered these rules for summarizing:

- Delete trivial or irrelevant information.
- Delete redundant information.
- Provide a superordinate term for members of a category.
- Find and use generalizations the author has made.
- Create your own generalizations when the author has not provided them.

Idea Maps

Idea maps can be used to summarize content material, and they may be easier to compose than traditional summaries. Have students lay down an 8½- by 11-inch sheet of paper horizontally; then have them write the title or heading of the chapter or section they are reading in the middle of it. Have them use subheadings or skim the material to locate major topics, and then number them and place the numbers in blocks arranged clockwise around the title. After reading each section, they fill in the appropriate block with the most important details, stated in a concise manner. Emphasize that each student's map will be a little different because each student will have his or her own ideas about which details are most important (Taylor, 1986).

Other Strategies

Here are some other helpful strategies.

Improving Ability in Sensing an Author's Mood and Purpose

Provide a list of book titles for students and ask them to consider the titles and decide whether the author was trying to *inform, entertain, or persuade.* Here are several titles that can be used for this purpose.

Clements, A. *Frindle.* New York: Simon & Schuster Children's Press, 1997. (Entertain)

Corwin, M. *And Still We Rise: The Trials and Triumphs of Twelve Gifted Inner-City High School Students.* New York: HarperCollins, 2001. (Persuade)

Spinelli, J. *Stargirl.* New York: Knopf, 2000. (Entertain)

Wightwick, J., and Gunn, W. *Way-Cool Spanish Phrase Book.* New York: McGraw-Hill, 1998. (Inform)

Yates, J. *The Ins and Outs of Prepositions: A Guidebook for ESL Students.* Hauppauge, N.Y.: Barron Educational Series, 1999. (Inform)

You can also play an *instrumental CD* and have students draw how they feel as they listen to the CD.

Improving Ability in Visual Imagery

One strategy for improving visual imagery is to have students draw pictures of concepts or topics rather than use words to describe or talk about them. This is very effective with students who have difficulty expressing their ideas through words alone.

Using drawings as a springboard and integrating them with discussions before reading the content material, students can activate their prior knowledge, set a purpose or purposes for reading, and create a framework for organizing new knowledge. McConnell (1992–93) stated that drawings provide "a visible and explicit record of learning which can be reflected upon, altered, and developed" (p. 269). In addition to helping students explore prior knowledge and develop purposes for reading, drawings also foster comprehension and language use and help clarify concepts that are easily misunderstood.

Students also can visualize a scene from a narrative book to enhance their comprehension of the scene. Often students' own visualizations are more effective than the illustrations contained in the material.

Reproducible Activity Sheets for Improving Comprehension Skills While Reading Content Material

Chapter Six now provides seven reproducible activity sheets for improving comprehension skills while reading content material in such areas as literature, social studies, and science. They can be duplicated in their present form or modified in any way you want based on the needs and interests of your students. In addition, they can serve as models for you to construct similar activity sheets for improving comprehension skills while reading content material.

The seven reproducible activity sheets are as follows: Anticipation-Reaction Guide—Seventh- to Eighth-Grade Level; Partial Headlines from Social Studies—Sixth-Grade Level; Drawing Conclusions—Seventh- to Ninth-Grade Level; Determining Which Is the Better Invention—Seventh- to Ninth-Grade Level; Completing a Job Application Form—Ninth- to Twelfth-Grade Level; Summarizing a Passage from Science—Sixth- to Eighth-Grade Level; What Was the Author Trying to Do: Inform, Entertain, or Persuade?—Seventh- to Ninth-Grade Level

Answer Key for Anticipation-Reaction Guide

1. Yes; 2. No; 3. Yes; 4. Yes; 5. No; 6. Yes; 7. No; 8. Yes; 9. Yes; 10. No; 11. Yes; 12. No; 13. Yes; 14. Yes; 15. Yes; 16. No; 17. Yes; 18. No; 19. Yes; 20. Maybe

Answer Key for Partial Headlines from Social Studies

A N AA II; B K DD JJ; C P U HH; D L BB EE; E M V FF; F O W NN; G Q Y KK; H R Z LL; I S CC MM; J T X GG

Answer Key for Drawing Conclusions

Someone had cut the purse in the hope that money or other valuables would fall on the ground so they could be stolen; Egypt; orthopedic surgeon; World War II veterans are becoming older and will be dying in the near future so all their war experiences will be lost forever if they are not shared now.

Answer Key for Determining Which Is the Better Invention

Note: The answers shown are for illustrative purposes only. Any answer that a student can justify using logical analysis should be considered correct. *1. polio vaccine*—it prevents crippling among children; it saves family members from worry; it allows children to live long, healthy lives; *heart transplant*—it saves lives of adults with life-threatening heart problems; it restores normal activity; it restores families; *2. jet airplane*—passengers can travel rapidly; it flies mail and freight; it makes the world easily accessible; it makes the world "smaller"; *spacecraft*—formulates weather data; is the source of many products used on earth; can fly to space stations and other planets; *3. dishwasher*—saves time washing dishes; makes dishwashing easy and hygienic; *microwave*—cooks food quickly; may add to the taste of foods; very easy to use—even children can use it; *4. barbed wire*—keeps animals such as cattle inside a fence; keeps prisoners in jail; protects property; *steel plow*—makes cultivating and planting easier; won't wear out or break like a wood plow; *5. electricity*—operates appliances; provides light; *telephone*—provides instant communication; people can talk across states or countries; *6. television*—is a source of entertainment, news, current events, weather, sports, advertisements; *radio*—is a portable source of news, weather, entertainment, sports; *7. computer*—saves times in writing; keeps excellent records, saves time and effort in business; makes record keeping simple and accurate; *camera*—can record family photographs for later use; preserves historical images; provides visual images for television, books, magazines, and newspapers; *8. antibiotics*—cures illnesses, prevents infection, prevents death, shortens time of illness; *anesthetics*—enables painless surgery; enables painless childbirth; enables painless dental procedures; *9. air conditioning unit*—cools home or automobile; makes living in hot weather more comfortable; prevents heat exhaustion and heat stroke; *furnace*—makes cold temperatures safe and comfortable; enables people to live comfortably in cold climates; *10. washing machine*—avoids washing on a washboard; gets clothes very clean; saves time and effort; *clothes dryer*—avoids hanging clothes on a line; saves time and effort.

Answer Key for Summarizing a Passage from Science

2; 1; 2; 3; 1; 2

Answer Key for What Was the Author Trying to Do?

Colin L. Powell—inform; *Vote for Our Children*—persuade; *School on the Road for Circus Kids*—entertain.

Name ________________________ Grade ___ Teacher ____________ Date __________

Anticipation-Reaction Guide

As you read this passage about the *Yangtze River and its three gorges*, you will learn a number of interesting facts about them and how they are being changed by the construction of the Three Gorges Dam. Before you read this passage, write *Yes*, *No*, or *Maybe* on the line under the word *Before* to show what you believe to be true at this time. After you have read the passage, write *Yes*, *No*, or *Maybe* on the line under the word *After* to indicate what you now believe to be true.

Before **After**

_______ _______ 1. The Yangtze River is called the Long River by the Chinese people.

_______ _______ 2. The Yangtze River is the longest river in the world.

_______ _______ 3. The Three Gorges Dam will change the beautiful scenery along the Yangtze River forever when it begins full operation in 2009.

_______ _______ 4. The Yangtze River is a widely used waterway for commerce today, as it has been for centuries in the past.

_______ _______ 5. The fertile land along the Yangtze River feeds about 10% of the people in China.

_______ _______ 6. Fengdu, China, located along the banks of the Yangtze River, is called the "city of ghosts."

_______ _______ 7. The river channel widens at the first gorge along the Yangtze River.

_______ _______ 8. The small boat that takes visitors into the three lesser gorges is called a *wupan*.

_______ _______ 9. When the Three Gorges Dam is completed, only the tops of the mountain peaks in the three lesser gorges will be visible.

_______ _______ 10. The middle gorge is called the Wusan Gorge.

_______ _______ 11. Currently boats enter the locks of the Gezhou Dam, which opened in 1989.

_______ _______ 12. Between the Gezhou Dam and Wuhan, China, the river banks are steep, and the river is very narrow.

_______ _______ 13. The Three Gorges Dam on the Yangtze River was begun in 1993 and is scheduled to be completed in 2009.

_______ _______ 14. When the Three Gorges Dam is completed, many cities along the Yangtze River will be flooded forever.

_______ _______ 15. Already most of the people in these cities have been relocated to higher ground.

_______ _______ 16. The dam and the relocation of the people will cost about $10 billion in U.S. money.

_______ _______ 17. When the Three Gorges Dam is completed, it will be the world's largest dam and hydroelectric station.

_______ _______ 18. The dam is being built only to control flooding and improve navigation.

_______ _______ 19. When the dam is completed, large ships will be able to go from the East China Sea to Chongquing, China.

_______ _______ 20. A Yangtze River cruise is fascinating to everyone.

The Yangtze River and Its Three Gorges

The Chinese people call it the Long River, or *Changjiang.* To travelers from the West it is known as the Yangtze. It is the third longest river in the world, flowing from its source in the high Tibetan range below the snowcapped peaks of the Himalayas to the East China Sea, a distance of thirty-nine hundred miles.

Soon the magnificent scenery along the Yangtze River will be changed forever when the Three Gorges Dam is completed. As the water behind the new dam rises and the lower portion of the mountain walls becomes submerged, the visual height of the majestic walls that frame the river will be lessened and much of the river's beauty will be lost forever.

However, at the present time, the Yangtze River remains the same as it has been for centuries—a waterway for commerce with barges and fishing boats, a fertile breadbasket that feeds one-third of China, and an inspiration for poets and painters who find its craggy mist-shrouded peaks magical and awe-inspiring.

I recently took a cruise downstream from Chongquing to Wuhan, China, and found it fascinating and unique. The first stop on this voyage was Fengdu, the thirteen-hundred-year-old Tang Dynasty "city of ghosts." There I took an exciting chair lift to visit a ghost palace where clay figures are used in various scenes, including one that presents a vision of torture in hell.

Then the boat entered the first gorge on the Yangtze River—the Qutang. As the boat approaches the gorge, the river channel narrows. The gorge is called the "Windbox" by many westerners because the rock face of the walls has been carved by erosion into a shape that resembles a giant bellows.

In between the first and second gorges, I took a smaller boat called a *wupan,* which holds about twenty-five passengers. It traveled from Wushan into three little gorges on the Daning River. Once the Three Gorges Dam is completed, the water level will be 573 feet above sea level, and an existing bridge at the entrance to these three lesser gorges will barely remain above the water level. In these lesser gorges I saw holes that had been chiseled high into the rock face of the canyon walls. Once, they supported poles that held planks that formed a walkway high above the river. Unfortunately, all but the tops of these peaks will be submerged once the new dam is completed.

The middle gorge on the Yangtze is called the Wu Gorge, and the third gorge is called the Xiling Gorge. After passing through these two gorges, the cruise boat entered the Gezhou Dam, which opened in 1989. A contest was held onboard to guess the exact time when the huge doors of the locks would open, and the winner earned 250 yuan—about $30.

Between the Gezhou Dam and the city of Wuhan, the river banks are low and fairly flat. Along the banks of the Yangtze River, 25% of China's fertile land lies. After Wuhan, the Yangtze River flows on to Shanghai, where it empties into the East China Sea.

The Three Gorges Dam project began in 1993 and is scheduled to be completed in 2009. By the time it is finished, many of the cities along its banks will be flooded forever. Already most of the people have been moved to buildings much higher above the river, and the old buildings are now being demolished. The dam and the relocation of the people will cost about 204.9 billion yuan, or $25 billion. When it is completed, it will be the world's largest dam and hydroelectric station. It is being built to supply electricity, control flooding along the river, and improve navigation by providing a deep water pathway from the East China Sea to Chongquing.

I found my Yangtze River cruise fascinating, and I'm sure that you also would enjoy it.

Name ______________________ Grade ___ Teacher ____________ Date _________

Partial Headlines from Social Studies

At the end of this activity, *write the letters of the phrases that complete the sentences started in Group One* about historical events that occurred in the early West. *Take one phrase from each group* (Groups Two through Four) *to complete the sentences.* You may work with a partner if you wish.

Group One

A. Wyatt Earp,

B. The Battle of Little Big Horn

C. Jesse Woodson James,

D. John B. Stetson,

E. Bat Masterson (William Bartholomew Masterson),

F. Annie Oakley (Phoebe Ann Moses),

G. James Butler ("Wild Bill") Hickok,

H. The gunfight

I. Geronimo died

J. Samuel Colt,

Group Two

K. was fought

L. who made the famous western hats,

M. the legendary western figure,

N. who fought at the OK Corral,

O. the legendary frontierswoman,

P. the famous outlaw,

Q. marshal of Abilene, Kansas,

R. at the OK Corral took place

S. at age eighty

T. the maker of the revolver named after him,

Name ________________________ Grade ___ Teacher ____________ Date _________

Partial Headlines from Social Studies, continued

Group Three

U. died in St. Joseph, Missouri,

V. was born in County Rouville, Quebec, Canada,

W. was born in Darke County, Ohio,

X. was born in Hartford, Connecticut,

Y. was born in Troy Grove, Illinois,

Z. in Tombstone, Arizona,

AA. was born in Monmouth, Illinois,

BB. was born in Orange, New Jersey,

CC. on the reservation

DD. in Wyoming

Group Four

EE. on March 5, 1830.

FF. on November 26, 1853.

GG. on July 19, 1814.

HH. on April 3, 1882.

II. on March 19, 1848.

JJ. on June 25, 1876.

KK. on May 27, 1837.

LL. on October 26, 1881.

MM. at Fort Sill, Oklahoma.

NN. on August 13, 1860.

____

____

Note: Students can research the answers for this activity sheet at www.burger.com/westdate.htm.

Name ________________________ Grade ___ Teacher ____________ Date _________

Drawing Conclusions

Read each selection silently. Then answer the question following it after by *drawing a conclusion* from the material.

In September 2002, I was walking one morning in Tiananmen Square in Beijing, China. However, I had become separated from my tour group and was trying in vain to catch up with them while being jostled by throngs of people. Suddenly a Chinese man said to me in English: "You're dropping things out of your purse." I looked down on the ground and saw a number of papers there, including my trip itinerary. I was puzzled as to why the papers had fallen out because I was sure my purse was zipped, but I picked them up and put them back in the purse. Imagine my surprise when I noticed that they fell out again! I then examined the purse and noticed a vertical cut about one inch in length and a horizontal cut about ten inches in length.

What do you think had happened to my purse at Tiananmen Square in Beijing, China?

____

____

____

____

Kathy had always wanted to visit this country because it was so important to the civilization of the ancient world. However, she never believed that her dream of visiting it would become a reality. The security Kathy saw at this predominantly Muslim country nearly overwhelmed her. Soldiers carrying AK-47 rifles were stationed at all the main tourist sites throughout the country. Kathy saw the world-famous Aswan Dam in the part of the country called Nubia. The people who live there, the Nubians, are darker-complexioned than the people in the northern part of the country. Kathy also saw the tombs in the Valley of the Kings, where mummification was practiced. It was believed that a person needed a physical body in order attain life after death. Perhaps the most unique artifacts that Kathy viewed were the objects that were taken from the tomb of King Tut by Howard Carter in 1927.

What country do you believe Kathy visited?

____

Name ________________________ Grade ___ Teacher ____________ Date _________

Drawing Conclusions, continued

My mother began having a pain in her groin area in July, especially when she was walking. For several weeks, she thought that it was a pulled muscle, but the pain did not go away. Finally my mother had X-rays and an MRI and was diagnosed with *avascular necrosis*, a disease in which the hip joint dies due to a lack of blood, develops small cracks, and eventually collapses. As the disease progressed, my mother had pain in her hip, her thigh, her knee, her calf, and her foot. Often the pain was excruciating. There is only one surgical intervention that can correct this problem—total hip replacement, sometimes called total hip arthoplasty. My mother's surgery is scheduled for December 3 at the local hospital.

What kind of medical doctor do you think will perform this surgery?

____

World War II was a very difficult time for the servicemen and servicewomen who fought so bravely. Some served in Europe where many bloody battles were fought, such as the D-Day invasion at Normandy. Others served in the Pacific at places such as Iwo Jima and Guadalcanal, and others flew dangerous missions, many of whom were shot down. Although many World War II veterans were unable to share their war experiences for many years, they are now speaking about them more often, especially to students in middle school, high school, and college.

Why do you think it is important for World War veterans to speak about their experiences at this time?

____

____

____

____

Name ______________________ **Grade** ___ **Teacher** ___________ **Date** _________

Determining Which Is the Better Invention

In your opinion, which are the greatest inventions and discoveries ever made? Can you value one invention or discovery more than another? What criteria can be used to determine the value of an invention or discovery? For each pair of inventions or discoveries listed here, underline the one that you believe is more important for the world. Then, in the blank space provided, write the reasons why you think one is more beneficial than the other.

1. polio vaccine, heart transplant surgery ______________________________

   ____
2. jet airplane, spacecraft ______________________________________

   ____
3. the dishwasher, the microwave ______________________________

   ____
4. barbed wire, steel plow ______________________________________

   ____
5. electricity, the telephone ______________________________________

   ____
6. television, radio ____

   ____
7. the computer, the camera ______________________________________

   ____
8. antibiotics, anesthetics ______________________________________

   ____
9. air conditioning unit, the furnace ______________________________

   ____
10. the washing machine, the clothes dryer ______________________________

    ____

Name ________________________ **Grade** ___ **Teacher** ____________ **Date** _________

Completing a Job Application

Fill out this job application form to the best of your ability. You can make up the answers to the questions about education and employment history if you want.

It is our policy to comply with all applicable state and federal laws prohibiting discrimination in employment on race, color, sex, age, religion, national origin, or other protected classification.

Instructions: Type or print clearly in black or blue ink. Answer all questions.

Date: __________

Name: ____

Last First Middle

Address: ____

Street City State and Zip Code

Telephone: _____________________ Social Security Number ________________

Position Desired: ____________________ Full-time ___Part-time ___Temporary ___

Have you worked for this company before?

Yes ___ No ___

If you are a minor under age 18, do you have a certificate of age? Yes ___ No ___

Are you a U.S. citizen or otherwise authorized to work in the U.S. on an unrestricted basis?

Yes ___ No ___

Are you willing to work overtime as required?

Yes ___ No ___

Education Name and Address of School Degree/Diploma

High School ____

College ____

Trade, Business, Vocational, Technical ____

Special Skills and Qualifications: List job-related skills, training, honors, awards, and special accomplishments.

____

____

Name ______________________ Grade ___ Teacher ____________ Date _________

Completing a Job Application, continued

Employment History: Start with current or last position.

Employer: ____

Address: ____

Supervisor: ____

Telephone Number: ____

Job Title: ____

From: __________________ To: ___________________

Duties: ____

Salary: ____

(beginning) (ending)

Reason for Leaving: ____

Employer: ____

Address: ____

Supervisor: ____

Telephone Number: ____

Job Title: ____

From: __________________ To: ___________________

Duties: ____

Salary: ____

(beginning) (ending)

Reason for Leaving: ____

May we contact your current employer? Yes ___ No ___

References: Do not include relatives or former employers.

Name/Title Address and Telephone Number Occupation

1. ____

2. ____

3. ____

I certify that the information contained in this job application is true and complete to the best of my knowledge and understand that any false information on this application may be grounds for not hiring me.

Signature ______________________________________

Name ______________________ Grade ___ Teacher ___________ Date _________

Summarizing a Passage from Science

This passage is about the *Eurasian milfoil,* a type of aquatic vegetation that is found in a number of lakes in this country. At the end of each paragraph you will find *three summary statements* about that paragraph. *Place an X in front of the best summary of each paragraph.* If you want, you can reread the entire passage when you have finished.

The Eurasian Milfoil

Aquatic life is changing rapidly in a number of the lakes in the United States. The past several years have seen major developments of aquatic vegetation known as the *Eurasian milfoil,* which has produced giant beds. These weedbeds are found in every bay that is part of a main lake basin. The Eurasian milfoil is an extremely fast-spreading vegetation and can rapidly take over a lake.

_____ 1. Weedbeds are found in nearly every lake.
_____ 2. The Eurasian milfoil is rapidly taking over the aquatic life in many lakes.
_____ 3. Eurasian milfoil is usually found in giant beds.

Eurasian milfoil was introduced into the United States from Europe in the early 1900s. It is now found from mid-America eastward and on the West Coast. It is a perennial aquatic plant that blooms from June to August.

_____ 1. Eurasian milfoil is an aquatic plant that is not native to the United States but is now often found in lakes here.
_____ 2. Eurasian milfoil is a perennial plant.
_____ 3. Eurasian milfoil first came to the United States in the early 1900s.

Eurasian milfoil grows very rapidly and forms dense mats that will grow to the surface. The plants have a long thin reddish stem about one-eighth of an inch in diameter with twelve to twenty small green leaflets in each leaf section. They occur in groups of four down the length of the stem.

_____ 1. Eurasian milfoil is found on the surface of the water.
_____ 2. Eurasian milfoil grows rapidly and forms dense mats of plants with a long reddish stem and small green leaflets.
_____ 3. Eurasian milfoil has a long thin stem.

Name ________________________ Grade ___ Teacher ____________ Date _________

The Eurasian Milfoil, continued

As with most organisms introduced into an unnatural environment, Eurasian milfoil can wreak havoc once established. Also, once established, it can be very difficult to control or remove. Because it grows so rapidly and creates such thick mats, it can wipe out native plants by blocking sunlight and eventually killing them off completely. The method Eurasian milfoil uses to reproduce is what makes it so prolific. Plant fragments are its main source of reproduction because tiny pieces can create an entire new plant once they come in contact with a suitable substrate.

_____ 1. Eurasian milfoil is not native to the lakes of the United States.

_____ 2. Eurasian milfoil often is able to kill native water plants by blocking their sunlight.

_____ 3. Eurasian milfoil is difficult to control or remove from lakes because it grows very rapidly and uses plant fragments as a main source of reproduction.

Government agencies are trying a number of methods to control the spread of Eurasian milfoil, including hand and mechanical harvesting, water manipulation, and aquatic herbicides. Aquatic herbicides are considered a last resort because of the adverse effects on the ecosystem. Aquatic insects such as the milfoil weevil are also being used in some places because they are less expensive and have a limited environmental impact.

_____ 1. Government agencies are trying a number of different ways to control the spread of Eurasian milfoil.

_____ 2. Aquatic herbicides may have adverse environmental effects.

_____ 3. The milfoil weevil may be helpful in controlling the spread of Eurasian milfoil.

At this time anglers can help to control this swift-spreading vegetation. They should not run boat motors through weeds because this chops up the weeds, and fragments will quickly root themselves in other areas of a lake. They also should check their boats and boat trailers after leaving a body of water that has the Eurasian milfoil. Currently many boat landings contain posters about the Eurasian milfoil and reminders to remove it from boats and trailers before leaving the boat landing.

_____ 1. Anglers should not run their boat motors through weedbeds.

_____ 2. Anglers are being encouraged to stop the spread of Eurasian milfoil in several different ways.

_____ 3. Boat landings should contain posters about the Eurasian milfoil.

Name ________________________ Grade ___ Teacher ____________ Date _________

What Was the Author Trying to Do: Inform, Entertain, or Persuade?

On the line under each passage, write either *inform*, *entertain*, or *persuade*, describing what the author was trying to do in that passage.

Colin L. Powell

Colin L. Powell was born in New York City on April 5, 1937, and he graduated from Morris High School in 1954. He received a bachelor's degree in geology from City College of New York in 1958 while being active in the ROTC program and achieving the rank of cadet colonel.

Powell began his military career by accepting a second-lieutenant commission in the U.S. Army. In 1962 he served as military adviser in South Vietnam. He became a division operations officer in Vietnam in 1968.

Powell earned an MBA degree from George Washington University in 1971. From 1972 to 1973 he served as an assistant to the deputy director of the Office of Management and Budget. In 1973 he became a battalion commander in South Korea.

Powell graduated from the National War Congress in 1976 and soon became commander of the Second Brigade of the 101st Airborne Division at Fort Campbell, Kentucky. Some of his later military positions were deputy commander at Fort Leavenworth, Kansas, and military assistant to the U.S. Secretary of Defense. He became chairman of the Joint Chiefs of Staff, the highest military command in the United States, in 1989. In this position, Powell gained international recognition as one of the chief architects of the successful 1991 Gulf War against Iraq. Powell retired from the Joint Chief of Staffs in 1993.

In 1995 Powell wrote his memoirs, entitled *My American Journey*, and embarked on a nationwide tour to promote the book. Powell is active as a guest lecturer and in 1996 was named to the board of trustees at Howard University, a predominantly African American university.

During his tenure in the military, Powell received several service medals, and he also received the Ronald Reagan Freedom Award in 1993. As the capstone of a distinguished career, on January 20, 2001 he was sworn in as the first African American Secretary of State by President George W. Bush.

____

Name ________________________ Grade ___ Teacher ____________ Date _________

What Was the Author Trying to Do: Inform, Entertain, or Persuade?, continued

Vote for Our Children

I could make many sound arguments in favor of supporting the school bond referendum next Saturday. However, perhaps the most important point I can make is this: How can we adults look the children of our community in the eye and tell them that the schools they now have are the best that we can give them?

Can we look our children in the eye and try to explain the leaky roofs, the exposed wiring, the broken plumbing, the use of trailers as classrooms, the standing water on the classroom floors? Can we look them in the eye and tell them why their classrooms cannot handle the technology of the twenty-first century? Can we look them in the eye and tell them that these horrific conditions are the best that the adults of this community can do for them?

Of course, the answer is a definite *no!* We must decide that we will give the children of Loda the kind of schools that they deserve and need. We can do that at a cost of about $30 a year for the average homeowner.

How can we tell our children that they are not worth less than sixty cents a week? How can we tell our children that the overcrowded, rundown, and shoddy schools that we now have are all they deserve?

There are other arguments in favor of the school bond issue too—our area's ability to compete for new jobs, the importance of education for economic development, and many more. However, the strongest argument of all is this: we must give our students the quality schools that they deserve.

Let's all go out and vote *yes* next Saturday on the school bond referendum for the sake of our children—our country's future!

____

Name ________________________ Grade ___ Teacher ____________ Date __________

What Was the Author Trying to Do: Inform, Entertain, or Persuade?, continued

School on the Road for Circus Kids

The children of acrobats, trapeze artists, animal keepers, and others who travel the country with the Ringling Brothers and Barnum and Bailey Circus make up the *school on the road for circus kids.* Life on the road can be an education in itself because these children are able to visit sites that most others only read or dream about.

On most days the school on the road comes in the form of a teacher like Brenda Shaw, the teacher for the Ringling Brothers *Red Unit,* one of the two that crosses the country. In many cities the "school" is often cramped, small, and windowless, with folding chairs and a large wooden box on rollers to carry the school supplies from place to place. However, the teacher and students try to brighten up their makeshift classroom with student art.

Older kids attend school in the morning, while younger ones attend in the afternoon, and there are not many children in either class. However, the kids attend school on any day that the circus has shows scheduled, so that means that they often go to school six or seven days a week. Circus kids take standardized tests to track their progress, as well as subject matter tests, just like all other students.

Ms. Shaw says that she has noted a positive aspect of circus life: it teaches adaptability and exposes kids to people from all walks of life. She says that all of the children she teaches are mature for their age and very bright. Although they may argue with each other, they are a tight-knit group—very good-natured and willing to help. They also are very verbal, because they are used to being around adults.

But circus kids sometimes talk about missing friends and family and the homes they go to during the brief December off-season. Circus officials say that the adjustment can be difficult for the teacher too, who lives in one small classroom on the circus train and on any one day can find a herd of elephants or zebras passing by her doorway. So far, however, Ms. Shaw seems to love it, because she gets to know the students and their parents in a way she never would in a more traditional setting. She plans to stay on for a few more years because she very much enjoys the children, their parents, and the opportunity to see the country.

____

For Additional Reading

Allen, H., Barbe, W., and Levesque, T. *Ready-to-Use Vocabulary, Word Attack, and Comprehension Activities: Sixth-Grade Reading Level* (pp. 192–231). San Francisco: Jossey-Bass, 1998.

Buettner, E. "Sentence by Sentence Self-Monitoring." *Reading Teacher,* 2002, *56,* 34–44.

Heilman, A., Blair, T., and Rupley, W. *Principles and Practices of Teaching Reading* (pp. 238–296). Upper Saddle River, N.J.: Prentice Hall/Merrill, 1998.

May, F. *Reading as Communication* (pp. 107–139). Upper Saddle River, N.J.: Prentice Hall/Merrill, 1998.

Miller, W. *Ready-to-Use Activities and Materials for Improving Content Reading Skills* (pp. 188–292). San Francisco: Jossey-Bass, 1999.

Miller, W. *The Reading Teacher's Survival Kit* (pp. 354–405). San Francisco: Jossey-Bass, 2001.

Miller, W. *Reading Skills Problem Solver* (pp. 201–355). San Francisco: Jossey-Bass, 2002.

Newman, G. "Comprehension Strategy Gloves." *Reading Teacher,* 2001, *55,* 329–332.

Pira, J. "The Picture of Reading: Deriving Meaning in Literacy Through Image." *Reading Teacher,* 2002, *56,* 126–154.

Reutzel, R., and Cooter, R., Jr. *Teaching Children to Read* (pp. 174–221). Upper Saddle River, N.J.: Prentice Hall/Merrill, 2000.

Silver, J. *Real-Life Reading Activities for Grades 6–12* (pp. 1–28). San Francisco: Jossey-Bass, 2002.

Tompkins, G. *Literacy for the 21st Century* (pp. 269–303). Upper Saddle River, N.J.: Prentice Hall/Merrill, 2001.

Works Cited in Chapter Six

Adams, M. *Beginning to Read: Thinking About Learning About Print.* Urbana-Champaign, Ill.: Center for the Study of Reading, 1991.

Anderson, R., Wilson, P., and Fielding, L. "Growth in Reading and How Children Spend Their Time Outside of School." *Reading Research Quarterly,* 1988, *23,* 285–303.

Andre, M., and Anderson, T. "The Development and Evaluation of a Self-Questioning Strategy." *Reading Research Quarterly,* 1979, *14,* 605–623.

Atwell, N. *In the Middle: About Writing, Reading, and Learning.* Portsmouth, N.H.: Heinemann, 1998.

Babbs, P. "Monitoring Cards Can Help Improve Comprehension." *Reading Teacher,* 1984, *38,* 200–204.

Baumann, J., and Schmitt, M. "The What, Why, How, and When of Comprehension." *Reading Teacher,* 1986, *39,* 640–647.

Bergman, J. "SAIL—A Way to Success and Independence for Low-Achieving Readers." *Reading Teacher,* 1992, *45,* 598–602.

Blanton, W., Wood, K., and Moorman, G. "The Role of Purpose in Reading Instruction." *Reading Teacher,* 1990, *43,* 486–493.

Brown, A., and Day, J. "Macrorules for Summarizing Text: The Development of Expertise." *Journal of Verbal Learning and Verbal Behavior,* 1983, *22,* 1–14.

Brozo, W., Schmelzer, R., and Spires, H. "The Beneficial Effect of Chunking on Good Readers' Comprehension and Expository Prose." *Journal of Reading,* 1983, *26,* 442–445.

Carr, H. *Developing Metacognition Skills: The Key to Success in Reading and Learning.* MERIT Chapter 2 Project. Philadelphia: School District of Philadelphia, 1986.

Cunningham, A. *The Guinness Book of World Records.* New York: Time Warner, 2003.

Cunningham, J., and Wall, L. "Teaching Good Readers to Comprehend Better." *Journal of Reading,* 1994, *37,* 480–486.

Davey, B. "Think Aloud: Modeling the Cognitive Processes of Reading Comprehension." *Journal of Reading,* 1983, *27,* 44–47.

Davey, B., and Porter, S. "Comprehension-Rating: A Procedure to Assist Poor Comprehension." *Journal of Reading,* 1982, *30,* 197–202.

Devine, T. *Teaching Reading Comprehension: From Theory to Practice* (pp. 79–81). Needham Heights, Mass.: Allyn and Bacon, 1986.

Duffy, G., and Roehler, L. "Improving Reading Instruction Through the Use of Responsible Elaboration." *Reading Teacher,* 1987, *20,* 548–554.

Fry, E., Kress, J., and Fountoukidis, D. *The Reading Teacher's Book of Lists* (4th ed.; pp. 419–427, 136–137, 430–431, 437, 428–429). San Francisco: Jossey-Bass, 2000.

Gambrell, L., and Javitz, P. "Mental Imaging Text, Illustrations, and Children's Story Comprehension." *Reading Teacher,* 1993, *28,* 264–276.

Hoffman, J. "Critical Reading/Thinking Across the Curriculum: Using I-Charts to Support Learning." *Language Arts,* 1992, *69,* 121–127.

Manzo, A. "The ReQuest Procedure." *Journal of Reading,* 1969, *13,* 123–126.

Manzo, A., and Manzo, U. *Literacy Disorders: Holistic Diagnosis and Remediation.* Fort Worth, Tex.: Harcourt Brace, 1993.

McConnell, S. "Talking Drawings: A Strategy for Assisting Learners." *Journal of Reading,* 1992–93, *36,* 260–269.

McNamara, T., Miller, D., and Bransford, J. "Mental Models and Reading Comprehension." In R. Barr, M. Kamil, P. Rosenthal, and P. Pearson (eds.), *Handbook of Reading Research* (vol. 2; pp. 490–511). White Plains, N.Y.: Longman, 1991.

Miller, W. *Ready-to-Use Activities and Materials for Improving Content Reading Skills* (pp. 189–190). San Francisco: Jossey-Bass, 1999.

Miller, W. *Reading Skills Problem Solver* (pp. 201–355). San Francisco: Jossey-Bass, 2002.

Ogle, D. "K-W-L: A Teaching Model That Develops Active Reading of Expository Text." *Reading Teacher,* 1986, *29,* 564–570.

Ogle, D. "The Know, Want to Know, Learning Strategy." In D. Muth (ed.), *Children's Comprehension of Text* (pp. 205–223). Newark, Del.: International Reading Association, 1989.

Pearson, P., and Gallagher, M. "The Instruction of Reading Comprehension." *Contemporary Educational Psychology,* 1983, *8,* 317–344.

Raphael, T. "Question-Answering Strategies for Children." *Reading Teacher,* 1982, *36,* 186–190.

Raphael, T. "Teaching Question-Answer Relationships, Revisited." *Reading Teacher,* 1986, *39,* 516–522.

Readence, J., Bean, T., and Baldwin, R. *Content Area Reading: An Integrated Approach.* Dubuque, Iowa: Kendall/Hunt, 1981.

Reutzel, D., and Hollingsworth, P., "Get a GRIP on Comprehension." *Reading Horizons,* 1988, *29,* 71–78.

Roth, K., Smith, E., and Anderson, C. "Verbal Patterns of Teachers: Comprehension Instruction in Content Areas." In G. Duffy, L. Roehler, and J. Mason (eds.), *Comprehension Instruction: Perspectives and Suggestions.* White Plains, N.Y.: Longman, 1984.

Rowe, M. "Wait Time and Rewards as Instructional Variables, Their Influence on Language, Logic, and Fate Control: Part I—Wait Time." *Journal of Research in Science Teaching*, 1974, *11*, 81–94.

Searfoss, L., and Readence, J. *Helping Children Learn to Read.* Needham Heights, Mass.: Allyn and Bacon, 1994.

Shanker, J., and Ekwall, E. *Diagnosis and Remediation of the Disabled* (p. 239). Needham Heights, Mass.: Allyn and Bacon, 1988.

Shanklin, N., and Rhodes, L. "Comprehension Instruction as Sharing and Extending." *Reading Teacher*, 1989, *42*, 496–500.

Shoop, M. "InQuest: A Listening and Reading Comprehension Strategy." *Reading Teacher*, 1986, *39*, 670–674.

Sound and Sense Strategy. Boston: Houghton Mifflin, 1981.

Stauffer, R. *Directing the Reading-Thinking Process.* New York: HarperCollins, 1975.

Stauffer, R. *The Language Experience Approach to the Teaching of Reading.* New York: HarperCollins, 1980.

Stevens, K. "Chunking Material as an Aid to Reading Comprehension." *Journal of Reading*, 1981, *25*, 126–129.

Taylor, K. "Summary Writing by Young Children." *Reading Research Quarterly*, 1986, *21*, 193–208.

Uttero, D. "Activating Comprehension Through Cooperative Learning." *Reading Teacher*, 1988, *41*, 390–395.

Wade, S. "Using Think-Alouds to Assess Comprehension." *Reading Teacher*, 1990, *43*, 442–453.

7

Strategies and Activities for Improving Study Skills in Content Areas

I was an excellent student in high school, college, and graduate school, but I was never taught study strategies during my school career. Therefore, when I was a student, my only study strategy was to read content assignments over and over, trying to remember all the important concepts and details that they contained. Although this technique enabled me to earn good grades, it was very inefficient. I can only imagine what I could have learned with less effort if I had been taught effective study skills such as those discussed in this chapter. Reading and content teachers should present effective study skills to students in the intermediate grades and higher, using their content materials in literature, social studies, science, and mathematics.

Chapter Seven presents numerous strategies and activity sheets for improving study skills in the content areas. The chapter opens by describing the basic study skills, which may be classified as selecting and evaluating, organizing, following directions, locating information, using graphic aids, reading rate and flexibility, and test-taking strategies. Then the chapter provides a multitude of classroom-tested strategies for improving these study skills. Using these strategies should save students time and effort in reading and remembering the important information from their reading assignments.

Next, the chapter presents a variety of classroom-tested strategies for improving study skills while reading in the four content areas of literature, social studies, science, and mathematics. Many of these specialized strategies are unique and highly motivating. They should be helpful to all students, including those with reading and learning disabilities.

The chapter closes with seven classroom-tested reproducible activity sheets for improving ability in various elements of general and specialized study skills. After reading this chapter, all teachers should be well prepared to teach basic and content study skills to all their students in the intermediate grades, middle school, and secondary school.

The Basic Study Skills

The basic study skills can be classified in several ways. The system I have chosen to include here is reader-friendly and usable. The subskills included are selecting and evaluating, organizing, following directions, locating information, using graphic aids, reading rate and flexibility, and test-taking.

Selecting and Evaluating

Selecting and evaluating is a skill that includes the following subskills: locating a directly stated main idea in a paragraph; locating an implied main idea in a paragraph; locating the main idea in a longer selection; finding the significant details in a paragraph; locating the irrelevant details in a paragraph; locating the topic sentence in a paragraph; finding the answer to a specific question; recognizing the author's purpose for writing a selection; and evaluating the accuracy of the information.

Because all of these skills were described in detail in Chapter Six, they will not be discussed again here. Refer to Chapter Six for information on effectively presenting and reinforcing any of these selection and evaluation skills.

Organizing

Organizational skills include the following: outlining a paragraph; outlining an entire chapter; taking notes; placing items in correct sequence; summarizing a paragraph; and summarizing a longer selection.

Outlining

Outlining is a study skill that helps students comprehend and retain the material in their reading assignments by helping them to organize it. Although students usually are taught outlining in the intermediate grades, many do not attain competency and usually dislike outlining. Therefore, most never outline content assignments unless they are required to do so. Although outlining is a difficult skill to present and to master, it may help some students understand and remember the important concepts in a content assignment. The basis for success in outlining is the ability to *grasp relationships* among the ideas involved. The foundation for outlining can be found in the primary skills of classifying (grouping ideas) and summarizing.

Friedland and Kessler (1980) stated they were successful in teaching outlining to intermediate-grade students by using a practical exercise. They introduced the concept of outlining without naming it by asking students how they could best arrange the contents of a messy drawer. The next exercise was to prepare and organize a classroom inventory. Later, students advanced from classifying items to classifying ideas—from the simple and concrete to the complex and abstract.

Students can develop the concept of outlining naturally if you make a list of related ideas in a simple format. Such lists may have the more important ideas set off by numerals and the supporting ideas indicated by letters. Move first to the use of main ideas, with supporting details indented, and then add letter and number designations.

As you teach formal outlining, present its basic principles, as illustrated in this brief outline form.

Topic

I. A major idea
  A.
    1.
      a.
        (1)
          (a)
          (b)

To present traditional outlining, first construct a brief outline from one of the content area textbooks that your students are using. Then place the outline on the board, showing students either in a large or small group how the main ideas in each paragraph often turn into the main points in an outline. Demonstrate to students how significant details in each paragraph usually become the minor points in an outline. Usually an outline uses Roman numerals for the major headings, uppercase letters for the first subheading under the major headings, and then numerals for the minor points or details in the outline.

You may want to construct a partially completed outline from a chapter in a content textbook, duplicate it, and have students finish it. Later all the students should share their responses to the outline. Only after they have had considerable instruction and practice in completing partially finished outlines should they be expected to construct their own outlines based on a reading assignment. Indeed, it may be beneficial to continue supplying students with a partially completed outline for each content reading assignment that they are to outline. If you do not provide such assistance, it may be extremely difficult for you to motivate them to ever construct their own outlines of reading assignments.

Alternative Outlining: Semantic Maps or Webs

A *semantic map or web* is an excellent alternative to the traditional outline. Constructing a map or web as after reading a content assignment can help students discriminate between the major and minor points in the material and help them remember the important concepts.

Clustering is a strategy that students use as they gather and organize information they are learning in a learning log or on a chart or poster (Rico, 1983). A *cluster* is another name for a semantic map or web. Clusters are weblike diagrams with the topic or nuclear word written in a circle centered on a sheet of paper. Main ideas are written on rays drawn out from the circle, and branches with details and examples are added to complete each main idea.

Most students would much rather construct their own version of a semantic map or web than a traditional outline, which is much more structured. Therefore, I recommend that reading and content teachers consider providing students with instruction and practice in constructing semantic maps or webs to supplement, if not supplant, the traditional outlines that they would otherwise require. For detailed information about how to construct semantic maps and webs, refer to Chapter Six.

Taking Notes

Taking notes is another organizational skill. Most students in the middle school and high school are not adept at taking notes either from their content reading assignments or from teacher presentations. Effective note taking may facilitate comprehension and retention through "encoding" of material. It requires locating directly stated and implied main ideas and significant details. It may consist of taking notes on index cards or highlighting the content textbook. In each case, many students take such extensive notes that they become virtually useless.

In your initial presentation on note taking, take paragraphs from your students' content textbooks and make notes from them on the board or on a handout. Later have students take notes on index cards from one section of a chapter in their textbook. Initially, note taking always should occur under your direction in class so that you can help your students if they have difficulty.

Students should make notes on only one part of a topic and from one source on each note card. They should label each note card's topic and write on only one side of the card. They should also place their note cards in alphabetical order using the topic labels of each. They also should paraphrase the words from each source unless they are certain that the author's exact words will be quoted directly in the research paper that they will write later. They should put their own ideas on the topic on special note cards or within brackets on each regular note card.

The first two sample note cards on the next page were constructed from a social studies text on the life of former President Jimmy Carter. The third note card contains the student's own views on the topic.

When a student in a content class is taking notes in his or her textbook, he or she can highlight the main idea in each paragraph with a highlighter of one color, such as red, then underline the significant details in each paragraph with a highlighter of a different color, such as blue. The student can also write the important specialized vocabulary terms found in each paragraph in the margin or underline them with a highlighter of yet a different color. However, if you do not emphasize *limiting* the use of highlighting, most students will highlight numerous items in each paragraph. The excessive use of highlighting then makes this technique meaningless.

Placing Items in Correct Sequence

See Chapter Six for detailed information on this.

Summarizing

Summarization is an organizational study skill that also was presented in Chapter Six as an element of interpretive comprehension. When students summarize content reading material, they review the most important information they gained by reading and studying a single paragraph or longer selection. To be sure that they understand the material, they should summarize it in their own words. Summarizing requires identifying main ideas, locating significant details, omitting irrelevant details, putting the information gained into proper sequence, and paraphrasing the author's own words.

A reading or content teacher can present the study skill of summarizing to all students or to a group of students. For the initial presentation, place a paragraph or a section of a content textbook on the board or a transparency so that all students can read it silently. Then have them summarize the material orally or in writing and subsequently share their summaries. Because summarization is a fairly difficult study skill to master, students should have considerable instruction and supervised practice before attempting to do it independently.

Jimmy Carter's Early Life
Jimmy Carter (James Earl Carter Jr.) was born October 1, 1924 in the small farming town of Plains, Georgia. He grew up in the nearby community of Archery. His father was a farmer and his mother was a nurse.

www.ibiblio.org/lia/president/carter library/generalmaterials/biographies/ jimmy

Jimmy Carter's Education
Jimmy Carter attended Plains, Georgia public schools, Georgia Southwestern College, the Georgia Institute of Technology, and received a Bachelor of Science degree from the United States Naval Academy in 1946. He did graduate work in nuclear physics at Union College.

Ibid.

What I Learned About Jimmy Carter
Jimmy Carter was a farmer who became president in 1977. After the presidency, he became active in many humanitarian causes such as building houses for Habitat for Humanity, human rights, and eliminating poverty. As a result of his efforts, he received the Nobel Peace Prize in October 2002.

Following Directions

To follow directions, students must be able to determine the relevance of the directions; follow a one-step direction; and follow a number of directions in correct sequence

Following directions, an element of literal comprehension, was discussed in detail in Chapter Six. Please refer to Chapter Six for information on how to present this important reading skill.

Locating Information

Locating information includes the following subskills: *using the school or public library* (the Dewey Decimal System, Library of Congress System, library card catalogue, subject card, author card, title card, cross reference card, on-line card catalogue); *using the World Wide Web* (search engines, on-line databases); *using content textbook parts* (title page, copyright page, preface and introduction, table of contents, index, glossary, appendices, footnotes, bibliographies); *using reference materials* (dictionaries, encyclopedias in print and on CD-ROM, atlases); *using the Reader's Guide to Periodical Literature;* and *using other sources* (the *New York Times Index*, almanacs, government publications, and the *Guinness Book of World Records).* These resources are described in the following paragraphs.

Using the Library

School libraries and media centers are essential to the effective teaching of content study skills, whether the teacher uses thematic units of instruction or traditional content teaching. Reading and content teachers and librarians and media specialists all must work together as a team to help students develop the skills they need to use these resources effectively.

Students should first be taught appropriate library behavior, with the teacher emphasizing that such behavior is respectful of others. Library users should be fairly quiet (not silent) to ensure that everyone in the library can read and study without distractions.

Because libraries have different types of organization, it is most effective to plan your lessons based on your own school library. Some common organizational patterns include arranging books in the following categories:

- Fiction (sometimes subdivided further into picture books, hardcover books, and paperback books)
- Nonfiction
- Biographies
- Reference books
- Periodicals (magazines and newspapers)

Most libraries in the United States are organized according to either the Dewey Decimal System or the Library of Congress System. Most school libraries use the less complex Dewey Decimal System, whereas university libraries and the main libraries in major cities use the Library of Congress System. The Library of Congress System normally is used when there is a need to classify a broader range of topics and a wider range of materials.

Melvil Dewey developed the system for organizing nonfiction books on the shelves of libraries that is named after him. The *Dewey Decimal System* consists of *ten primary classes*, with each one organized using a set of numbers. Novels and biographies usually are classified separately. The ten primary classes are intentionally very broad so that each can be divided into subclasses. Each subclass then can be further divided by using a decimal point and a number. The use of the decimal point means that the Dewey Decimal System has endless possibilities to make more subdivisions and can be expanded to classify books on any topic.

Using the Dewey Decimal System, students locate books in the library by their call numbers. The call number is obtained from the card catalogue. The call number appears on the spine of the book, and it identifies the specific location of the book on the library shelf. The numbers on the spine of the book are a code; the code reveals certain things about the book and helps students locate it.

Here are the ten primary classes of the Dewey Decimal System.

000–099: Generalities	500–599: Pure science
100–199: Philosophy and related	600–699: Technology (applied science)
200–299: Religion	700–799: The arts
300–399: The social sciences	800–899: Literature and rhetoric
400–499: Language	900–990: General geography, history, and so on

If you want a listing of the Dewey Decimal System that contains the *major subdivisions* in each main category, you can consult, among others, Strichart and Mangrum's, *Teaching Study Strategies to Students with Learning Disabilities* (pp. 129–131). (See Works Cited for complete publishing information.)

The Library of Congress, one of the world's largest libraries, is located in Washington, D.C. The special system developed to organize this library is known as the *Library of Congress System.* Students who will be using college and university libraries or other large libraries should be familiar with it. Here are the nineteen primary classes in the Library of Congress System. These twenty letters are combined with numbers and decimals to generate call numbers for books.

Primary Classes	**Call Numbers Start with Letter**
General works	A
Philosophy, psychology, religion	B
Auxiliary sciences of history	C
History: General and Old World	D
History: America	E–F
Geography, anthropology, recreation	G
Social sciences	H
Political sciences	J
Law	K
Education	L
Music	N
Language and literature	P
Sciences	Q
Medicine	R
Agriculture	S
Technology	T
Military science	U
Naval science	V
Bibliography, library science	Z

Students should be taught that the *card catalogue* is like the index of a book, and that books are located in four ways in most of them: by the *author card*, the *subject card*, the *title card*, and the *cross-reference card.* Students should learn how to read each type of card and develop an awareness of the type of card to look for, depending on the information that they have or need. The following figures illustrate four types of cards. Visiting a library and using a card catalogue should enable students to understand that cards are arranged alphabetically by author, subject, or title, and that author, subject, and title cards all contain the same information.

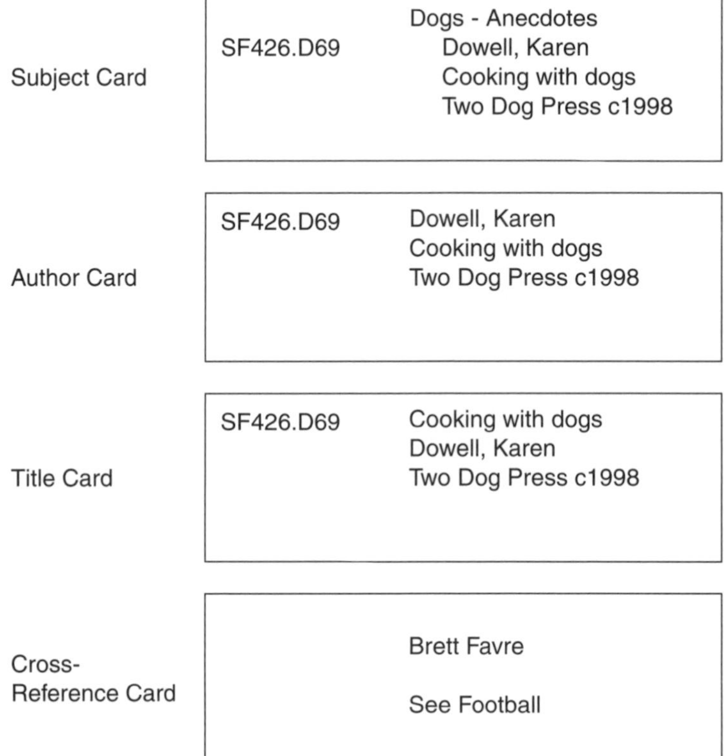

A number of contemporary libraries have *on-line card catalogues.* These automated systems enable students to go to the Web site of an appropriate library and search its catalogue for a specific book or subject matter area. Many on-line card catalogues enable students to search using the book title, author, subject, call number, ISBN, or keywords. The on-line card catalogue is a database of all the materials found in a library and is similar to a traditional card catalogue.

The Library of Congress has an on-line card catalogue that can be used both for searching and browsing. A group of libraries—public, academic, school, and corporate—also may share an automated system of on-line databases; this enables students to search the catalogues of a number of different libraries to locate a specific book or subject.

Using the World Wide Web (Internet)

The *World Wide Web* is an excellent research tool for students in the intermediate grades, middle school, and secondary school. Many of them probably already use this resource at home. However, if students are not familiar with using a *search engine* to expedite their research, they should be taught how to do so and then provided with practice in researching a topic from one of their own content topics. Several of the most useful search engines are *Yahoo*, *Lycos*, *Google*, *AOL Search*, *MSN Search*, *SearchEducation*, and *Thunderstone Website Index.*

To use a search engine for research, a student should access its homepage and type in the keywords for the search that he or she wants to do. As an example, if the student wanted to research the Civil War's Battle of Chattanooga, he should type in the term "Battle of Chattanooga"; a listing of appropriate Web sites will then appear on the computer. A student may need practice before being able to log on to the *best site* for the information he needs, because some of the sites located by a search engine may not be particularly relevant.

When students have located what appears to be a useful Web site, they should be aware that some of the material contained in it may not be accurate. Students should be taught to examine who prepared the material shown. For example, a Web site that was prepared by the American Kennel Club on this organization is likely to be accurate, whereas a Web site constructed by an individual may or may not be. Students should attempt to verify the information found with another source, such as another Web site or print material. When using the World Wide Web as a research tool, it is extremely important for a student to be a critical reader. However, it is a very useful tool because it is as handy as the student's computer at school or at home.

On-line databases use computer technology to acquire information through an on-line search. In an on-line search, a computer is used to retrieve information from databases long distances from the library where the student begins the search.

On-line databases are available for a variety of subjects and provide information in the form of indexes and abstracts covering such sources as periodical articles, books, and research reports; complete text of newspapers and periodicals; and directories of various types.

Here are several databases that may be useful to students in grades 5 to 12: *Magazine Index* is an index of more than four hundred popular magazines; *GPO Monthly Catalog* is a database that indexes the publications of the Government Printing Office; *National Newspaper Index* is a database that indexes the *Christian Science Monitor*, the *New York Times*, and the *Wall Street Journal.*

A comprehensive listing of specific subject on-line databases is contained in *Books, Libraries, and Research* (Hauer, Murray, Dantin, and Bolner, 1987).

Using Content Textbook Parts

Content textbooks are composed of similar sections: usually a title page, copyright page, preface or introduction, table of contents, index, glossary, appendices, footnotes, and bibliography. In addition, each chapter usually contains a title, introduction, headings, subheadings, conclusions, questions, and references. Although not all content textbooks have these parts, most social studies and science books, as well as some literature and mathematics textbooks, do.

If students understand the information presented in each part of a content textbook, they can understand the material. For example, the copyright page indicates whether the information contained in the book is up to date or out of date, although this depends somewhat on the content area. For example, a science textbook may become outdated much sooner than a book containing classic literature. The preface may point out the purposes for which the book was written, and the table of contents presents an outline of what material the book contains and helps set expectations about what will be found when reading it. Each book part contains information that can be helpful to a reader.

To assess a student's ability to use textbook parts, a reading or content teacher can design informal content inventories that will indicate whether the student is competent in the textbook aids that the inventory is evaluating. These inventories may take the following forms.

One variation attempts to determine if a group of students can use the *various aids* that are included in the selected content textbook. This inventory usually is given at the beginning of a course or semester. To formulate such an inventory, construct about twenty questions on the use of textbook aids, such as table of contents, index, diagrams, maps, italicized words, tables, and graphs. The students complete the inventory using their textbook to answer the questions.

Another content reading inventory is designed to determine if students can understand a selected content textbook. To construct this type of inventory, choose a passage of one thousand to two thousand words from the middle of the content textbook. Have the students silently read the passage. Each student then answers an open-ended question, such as: *What was this passage about?* Each also answers some objective questions about the passage. These questions evaluate their competency in such reading skills as literal comprehension, interpretive comprehension, critical reading, specialized vocabulary, and finding the directly stated and implied main ideas, significant details, and irrelevant details.

Another content reading inventory is based on *one specific chapter* of a selected content textbook. This also is an open-book evaluation that is given near the beginning of a class or semester. It is designed to determine if students possess the unique reading skills that are required to comprehend the selected content textbook effectively. This content inventory includes a matching vocabulary exercise composed of some of the specialized vocabulary terms found in the chapter. It also can include literal, interpretive, critical, and creative questions, as well as questions about the main idea and important details from the chapter.

For models of several types of content inventories, consult *Alternative Assessment Techniques for Reading & Writing* (Miller, 1995; pp. 223–225).

Using Reference Materials

There are four types of *dictionaries* with which students in grades 5 to 12 should become familiar. *Unabridged dictionaries* contain entries for most of the common words in the English language. Although they do not contain all the words, they usually contain between 250,000 and 500,000 entries. Several common unabridged dictionaries are *Webster's Third New International Dictionary of the English Language, Unabridged*, and *The Random House Dictionary of the English Language.* The most comprehensive dictionary of the English language is the *Oxford Dictionary of the English Language.* It contains more than one million entries and is continually being revised because new words are added to our language each day.

Abridged dictionaries are shortened forms usually containing between fifty thousand and a hundred thousand entries. Their main advantage is their smaller size and portability. Most are published in paperback form, which makes them relatively inexpensive, and they probably can be purchased by any student.

Special dictionaries also are available. These are devoted to various technical fields. Complete definitions are provided for the specialized vocabulary in a field such as medicine, psychology, education, business, and technology. Students should determine if there are special dictionaries for the subjects they are studying. *Electronic dictionaries* are handheld dictionaries so small they fit in a shirt pocket. Those electronic devices that provide only synonyms or antonyms are actually *electronic thesauruses.* Some of the most useful electronic dictionaries have a "sounds like" function that is useful for students who spell words phonetically and need this function to locate the correct spelling of words.

To use a dictionary effectively, students must know about entries, guide words, root words, and how to locate a word quickly using alphabetical order. An *entry* is a word, term, abbreviation, or affix that appears in alphabetical order in the dictionary. Entries are printed in boldface type to make them stand out from the other information provided. The *opening guide word* is the first word listed in the alphabetical sequence of entries on a page in a dictionary. The *closing guide word* is the last entry on the page. Both the opening and closing guide words appear at the top of the page to show all the entries that alphabetically fall between these guide words. The *root* of any word is a word without prefixes and suffixes. Students need to be able to identify the root word and the prefix or suffix separately so they can learn the definition of the word. Students also need to use their knowledge of *alphabetical order* to locate entries quickly.

Dictionary usage is a fairly difficult skill for students to learn, and its use is best motivated if students use a dictionary to search for definitions of words that they really need to know for their content assignments.

An *encyclopedia* is a special type of reference book that contains articles on a wide variety of subjects written by experts. The articles found in an encyclopedia provide students with the opportunity to gain information on a subject quickly. Because an encyclopedia contains so much information, it usually is published in a number of volumes. The volumes are arranged in alphabetical order so that a student who wants to obtain information about "the Gettysburg Address" would look for this topic in the *G* volume. Letters are stamped on the spine of each volume to indicate the alphabetical range of information included. Guide words are printed at the top of each page to help students quickly find the target topic.

Students should learn that an encyclopedia is a good place to begin learning about a topic. It also may provide a recommended outline for preparing a paper on that topic. Many articles contain a bibliography at the end listing authoritative books on the topic. Encyclopedias also have an index that can be used to locate information. The index cross-references students to many other related topics of which they might not otherwise be aware.

An encyclopedia also can be found in CD-ROM form for use on the computer. Entire sets of encyclopedias are available on disks. One of these is the *1998 Grolier Multimedia Encyclopedia, Deluxe Edition.* An encyclopedia on CD-ROM may be more motivating for some students to use than a print encyclopedia.

Here are several tips for students who use CD-ROM encyclopedias:

- Be sure to spell the topic correctly so that it can be located.
- Because keywords are very important, be sure to have a list of related general and specific topics to use when keyword searching.
- Once the program has started, look for direction words such as "search" or "find" with an empty rectangular box nearby. This usually is the place to type in the topic or keywords.
- Scan the list of results and click on the topic or topics that seem most relevant. Go back to the results list to view other articles as needed.

Very briefly, here are the advantages of using a print or CD-ROM encyclopedia:

Print	**CD-ROM**
Because of the multivolume format, several students can use a single set at the same time.	Programs on computer do not depend as heavily on student's alphabetizing skills.
Book format allows students to view the entire article without scrolling.	Articles and pictures can be retrieved and printed.
Books can be used without electricity and can be moved anywhere, including being checked out of the library to take home.	Articles often include multimedia information such as sound, video, and animation.
Books can sometimes be used more quickly because they are not dependent on being turned on and loaded on a computer.	Boolean searching allows a student to search more than one keyword at the same time.
Print encyclopedias usually contain more information than online encyclopedias.	Most libraries can update CD-ROM encyclopedias more often because of their lower price.

An *atlas* is a book of maps. There are different types of maps, each serving a different purpose. A geographical atlas provides maps that show the features of the earth's surface, such as oceans, lakes, rivers, mountains, and plateaus. A political atlas provides maps that show how the earth is divided into different countries, states, and important cities and other political regions. A road atlas contains maps that help people drive from one place to another. Many different types of atlases are available in a school or public library.

Using the *Reader's Guide to Periodical Literature*

Students in grades 5 to 12 often need to use periodicals to locate information for content assignments. The *Reader's Guide to Periodical Literature* is the best reference for this purpose. It is a guide to 175 of the most popular magazines published on a variety of topics. This resource is often referred to by its shortened title: *Reader's Guide.*

Because magazines are published on a frequent basis, *Reader's Guide* is updated every two weeks. At the end of every three months, a separate volume of *Reader's Guide* is published, and an annual bound edition is published once each year. Because *Reader's Guide* is published so often, it enables students to obtain current information on a topic.

Articles in *Reader's Guide* are arranged alphabetically by subject and author. Part of the information found in entries is in the form of *abbreviations.* Students will need to become familiar with the basic abbreviations used in entries. Entries sometimes contain a "See" or "See also" reference to help students locate more information on a topic.

To locate information using *Reader's Guide*, students should follow this procedure:

1. Select a topic on which they want information available in periodicals.
2. Locate *Reader's Guide* in the library.

3. Gather the issues and bound volumes of *Reader's Guide* for the years to be included in the search.

4. Locate magazine articles on the topic.

5. Use the "See" and "See also" references to locate additional articles.

6. Prepare a bibliography card for each reference to be used.

To find the magazines containing the articles they want, students should follow the following procedure:

1. Look in the card catalogue by the title of the magazine to determine if the library has that magazine. In some cases, they will have to go to a larger library to locate a specific magazine.

2. Locate the section of the library where the magazines are stored and look for the selected magazine by its title. Magazines usually are filed in alphabetical order on the shelves. The most recent issues often are found in the magazine section of the reading room of the library.

3. Use the volume number to locate the specific issue needed. Then use the page numbers to locate the article.

4. Students should ask for help if they need it.

Using Other Sources

The *New York Times Index* is the most comprehensive and widely available newspaper index. Most libraries that have the *New York Times Index* also have a microfilm collection of this newspaper going back to 1913. The *New York Times Index* is organized according to subject, not by author or title. Each entry for an article includes a brief summary.

Several other common newspaper indexes are the *Wall Street Journal Index*, *Washington Post Newspaper Index*, and *Index to the Christian Science Monitor.*

An *almanac* is a reference book that provides summaries, tables, charts, statistics, and other useful information on a wide range of subjects. Some of the topics that may be included in an almanac are world affairs, current scientific developments, maps and illustrations, sports, history, religion, taxes, cities and states, calendars, celebrities, and travel, among others.

Almanacs are updated yearly. They contain an enormous amount of information presented in a variety of formats. Students must learn how to use the index included in an almanac as well as how to interpret the graphs, tables, charts, diagrams, and maps that appear in it.

Government publications are distributed at no cost to designated libraries and institutions. The thirteen hundred libraries receiving documents from the Government Printing Office (GPO) are called *depository libraries*. Depository libraries house government publications as separate collections, organized by the Superintendent of Documents (SuDocs) classification system. The SuDocs system is an alphanumeric system used by the GPO to assign call numbers to documents. When this is not the case, students should refer to the *Monthly Catalog of United States Government Publications* to locate documents.

The 2003 Guinness World Records is an excellent source of information for students in grades 5 to 12. This resource is highly motivating, especially to students with reading or learning disabilities who do not want to use other sources for information. It is available from Time Incorporated Home Entertainment.

Using Graphic Aids

There are five kinds of *graphic* or *visual aids* used by authors to explain and compress information or concepts: maps, graphs, tables, charts, and diagrams.

Maps

Maps are representations of the earth's surface designed to indicate relationships. Many maps appear in social studies textbooks although they may also be found in science, mathematics, and literature books. The first step in map reading is to *examine the title* to determine what area is being presented and what type of information is being given about that area. The content or reading teacher should emphasize the importance of determining the information provided by the title before moving on to a more detailed study of the map. To understand a map, students need to know about the map legend, compass, and scale. The *legend* usually is found near the bottom of the map and provides the symbols necessary for interpreting the information found on the map. The *compass* tells the directions for the map, and the *scale* is used to tell distances in miles or kilometers. Because it is impractical to draw a map to the actual size of the area represented, maps must be greatly reduced in size. The scale shows the relationship of a given distance on the map to the same distance on the earth. Students in middle school and above also should learn to understand such map concepts as *latitude and longitude, the Tropic of Cancer and Tropic of Capricorn, the north and south poles*, and *the equator*.

A *weather map* is similar to those that students see in newspapers or on television. A weather map shows the main weather systems for a geographical area. Symbols are used to indicate clear skies, cloudy conditions, rain, snow, temperatures, and weather fronts. A *physical map* is used to show the features of the earth's surface such as mountains, plateaus, deserts, and important bodies of water. No political boundaries are shown on a physical map. A *political map* is used to indicate political or government boundaries. Different countries that make up a continent as well as their sizes and locations are shown on a political map. A *road map* contains the primary and secondary roads for a geographical area. Major highways usually are identified by dark lines, and secondary roads often are indicated by lighter lines. Numbers are printed inside symbols to identify highways and roads. Sometimes students will encounter maps that combine features from several different types of maps.

The following figures show a weather map of North America, a political map of the western United States, a physical map of the western hemisphere, and a road map of Vilas County, Wisconsin.

Weather Map

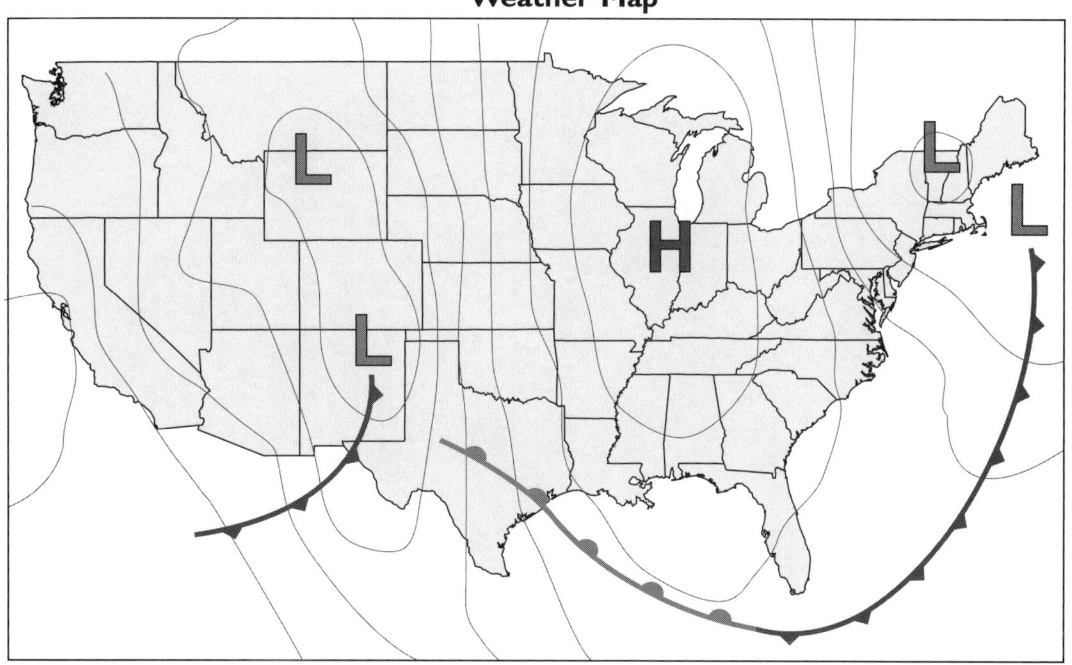

Political Map of the Western United States

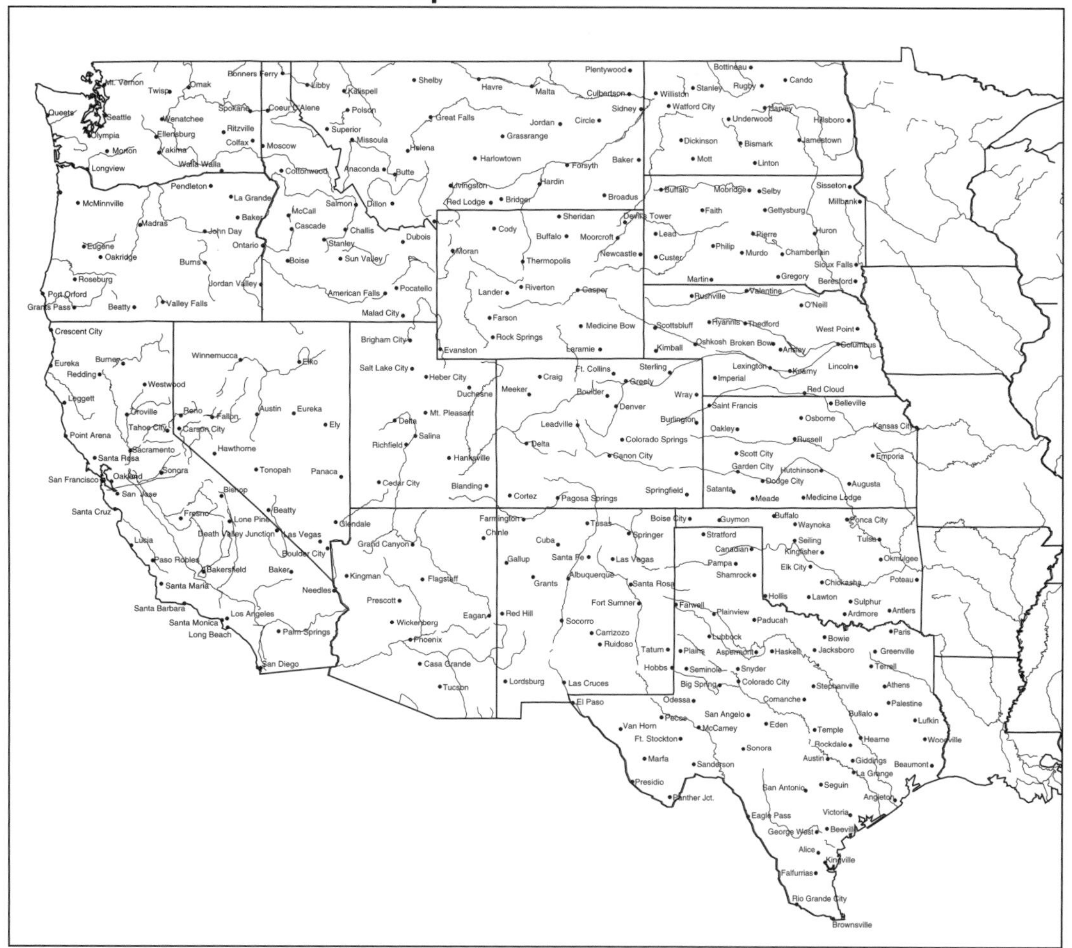

Physical Map of the Western Hemisphere

Road Map of Vilas County, Wisconsin

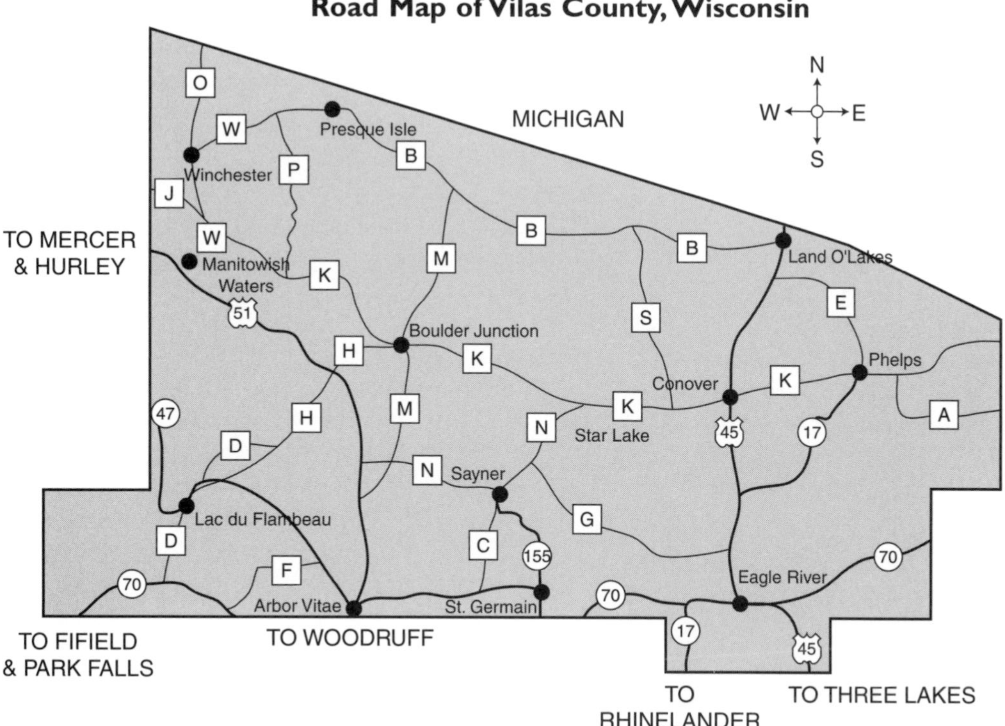

Graphs

Graphs illustrate facts that are difficult to understand when presented in text only. There are many different types of graphs, and the form used depends on the type of information that the author wants to present. Here are the four common types of graphs that are used in social studies, science, and mathematics.

- *Pictographs* or *picture graphs.* In this type of graph, each picture stands for a quantity of an entity. To understand a pictograph, students must read the title and refer to the key. This type of graph expresses *quantities* through pictures.
- *Circle or pie graphs.* This type of graph uses the circle design to indicate the relationships between parts and a whole. Each part indicates the amount or percentage of the whole it represents. All the parts must equal the total and add up to 100%.
- *Bar graphs.* This type of graph uses bars to indicate how one set of facts compares to another. A bar graph has a title at the top, labels on the left side and at the bottom, and a number line. To understand a bar graph, students must read the title and all the labels, and examine the length of each bar in relation to the number line. By comparing the length of the bars, students can draw conclusions from the facts shown by the bars.
- *Line graphs.* This type of graph usually is used to demonstrate trends over a period of time. It has a title at the top and labels at the left side and the bottom. On the left side there also is a number line. Dots show the quantity of what is illustrated by the graph. The dots are connected by a line to demonstrate a trend or show how the item is changing. To understand a line graph, students should begin by reading the title, then read the label at the bottom to determine what the

dots represent. Then they should read the label at the left to learn what the numbers represent. Next they must look at any one dot if they want to learn about a specific item. Finally, they should look at the line connecting the dots to determine the trend or how the items are changing.

Here are examples of these four types of graphs:

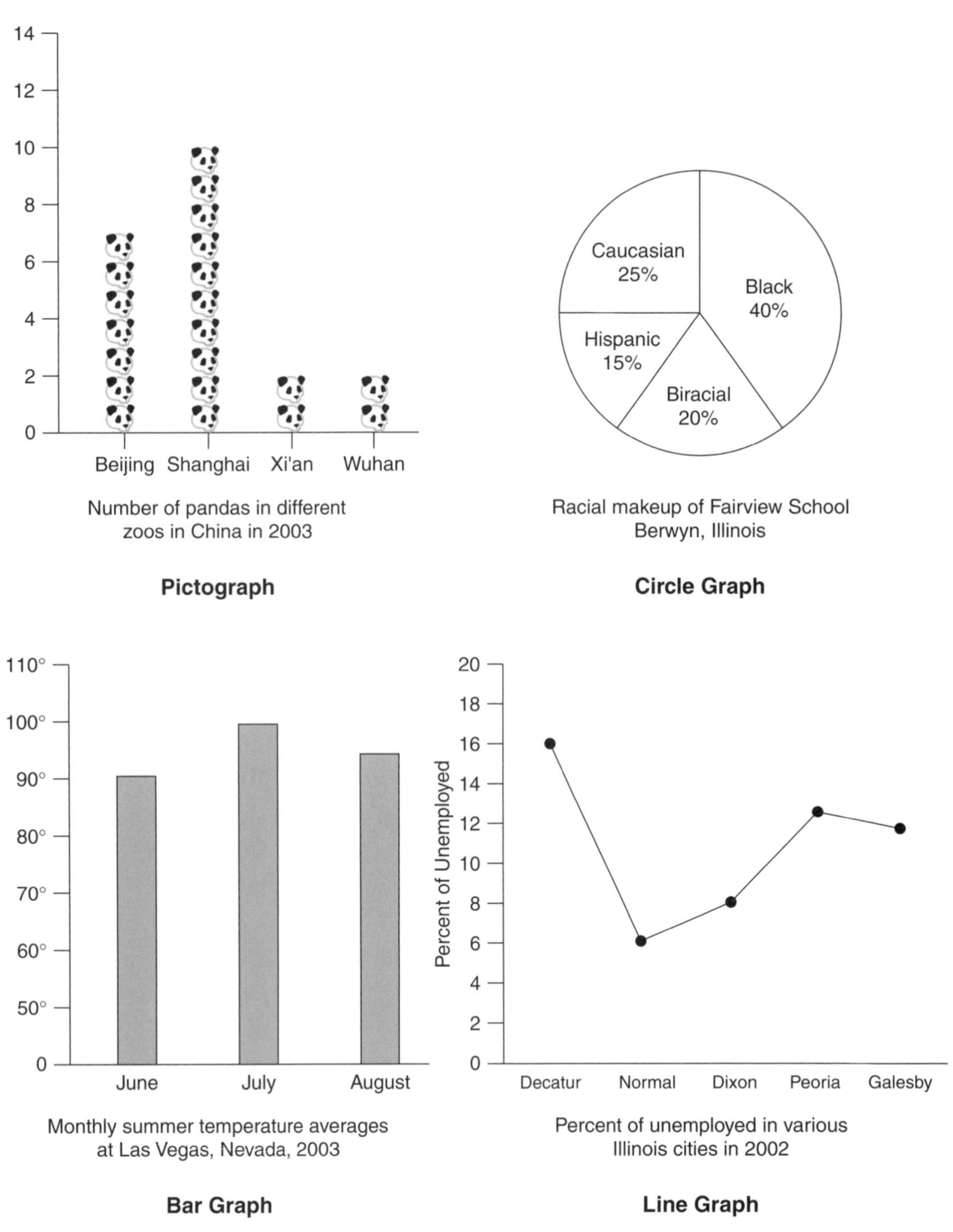

Number of pandas in different zoos in China in 2003

Pictograph

Racial makeup of Fairview School Berwyn, Illinois

Circle Graph

Monthly summer temperature averages at Las Vegas, Nevada, 2003

Bar Graph

Percent of unemployed in various Illinois cities in 2002

Line Graph

Tables

The *tables* that appear in social studies and science reading materials may be problematic for students. Tables are used to illustrate facts that would be difficult to understand quickly and accurately if they were presented in text alone. The overwhelming amount of information presented in a small amount of space in a table may confuse students unless they are given instruction and practice in reading tables.

Tables are divided into columns. A table should have a heading that explains its purpose, and each column also should have a heading that explains its purpose. In each column there may be numbers or words or a combination of both to illustrate the information the author wants to present.

To understand a table, students should first read the title to learn what the table is designed to present. Then they should look at each column heading to learn what information the table contains. Next they should look in each column to obtain the specific facts. A reading or content teacher should model how to read tables, verbalizing the mental processes involved in locating the information from them. Then students should be required to read a table and answer related questions about them.

Charts

Charts are used to show organization or a process by which a product works. In some charts the information is presented in boxes, and lines are used to illustrate how the boxes are related. By studying the chart, the student can determine how the items to which the chart is devoted operates.

A *flow chart* or *time line* is used to illustrate a process by which something occurs. It usually illustrates the flow, organization, or sequence of a social studies or science concept in some way. Either of these may be easier to interpret than traditional charts found in content textbooks. Information is presented with drawings and a series of arrows. Statements usually are found next to the drawings to show what is occurring at that point. The arrows demonstrate the direction or order in which the process occurs. An example of a flow chart is shown on the next page.

Flow Chart for House Painting

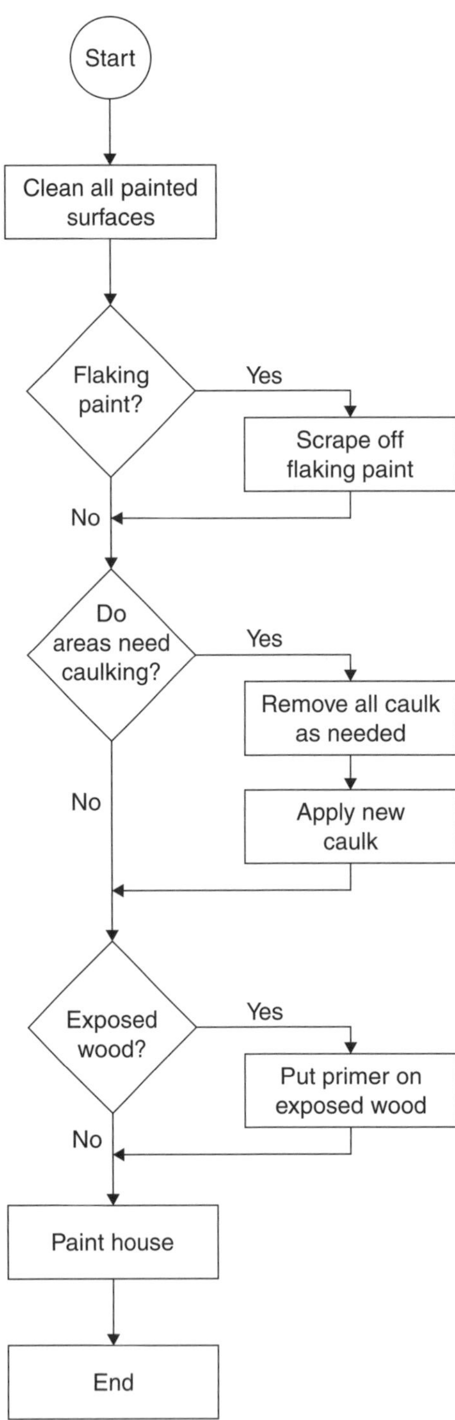

Diagrams

Diagrams are used to illustrate the parts of an object. Diagrams also may be used to demonstrate how parts go together or how the object works. Next to the diagram the student will find a key that explains the information contained in the diagram. Students need to use both the diagram and the key to interpret the diagram correctly. Here is a sample diagram.

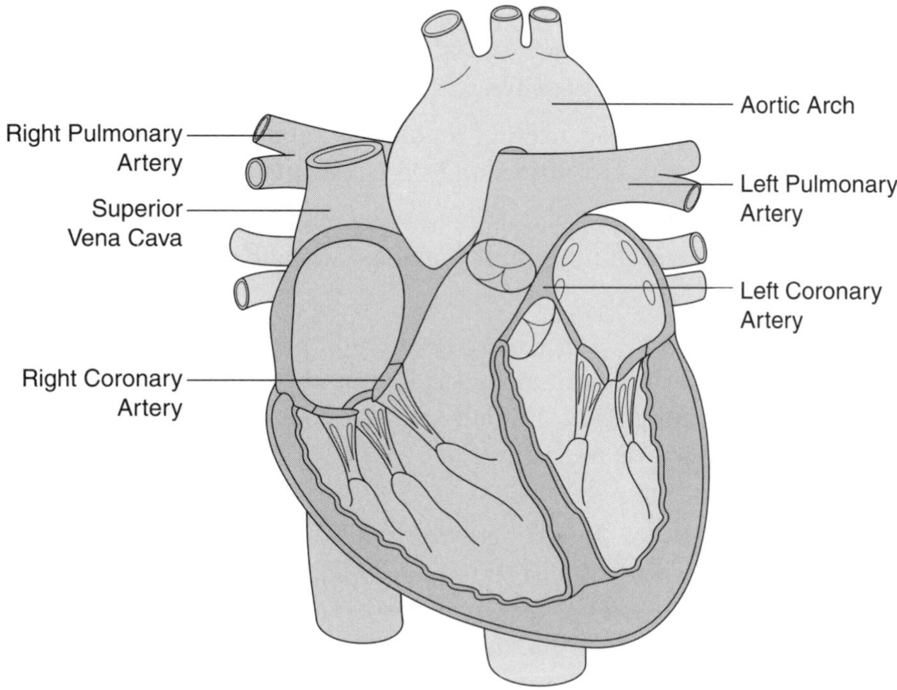

This is a diagram of the human heart. There are 2 main sides of the heart, the right and the left. The right part of the heart receives blood from the body and pumps it to the lungs to get oxygen. From the lungs, the blood goes to the left side of the heart. The left side of the heart then pumps the blood out to the rest of the body. The heart has valves inside that make sure that blood can only go one direction and cannot go backwards. The heart is made of muscle and to contract, it needs oxygen and nourishment as well. This is supplied by the arteries to the heart which supply blood to the heart. This is a diagram of the heart with the coronary arteries. There is a right coronary artery and a left coronary artery. The left coronary artery almost immediately divides into two big branches, the LAD and the circumflex. So the normal heart usually has 3 main vessels.

Flexibility of Reading Rate

When *reading rate* and *flexibility* improve, a student's comprehension and retention of reading material also may improve, especially in the middle school and above. This should be emphasized *only* for those students who have good word identification skills and adequate comprehension. The concept of reading flexibility should be pointed out to average and above-average readers as one important way to improve their comprehension and retention of reading materials.

A student's rate of reading always should depend on the *difficulty of the reading material, her purpose for reading it, and her prior knowledge about the topic of the reading material.*

Here are the reading rates that students in grades 5 to 12 should have:

- *Skimming.* Skimming is reading for a general impression of the reading material. It is a reading rate of more than a thousand words per minute. It usually is most applicable in the survey or preview portion of a study technique, when reading very easy material, such as a "light" novel or some parts of the newspaper, or when gaining a general impression.

- *Scanning.* Scanning is moving one's eyes very rapidly across print to locate a specific detail such as a name, place, or date. Because all of the words are not perceived in scanning, it is not possible to estimate the rate of scanning.
- *Rapid reading.* Rapid reading is used in reading material such as a novel for main ideas. It usually is a rate of four hundred words per minute or more.
- *Study-type reading.* Study-type reading is reading mainly for facts and details in content areas such as social studies and science. It usually is at a rate of 250 to 350 words per minute.
- *Careful analytical reading.* Careful analytical reading is reading and rereading very carefully for details. It is perhaps best illustrated by reading mathematical verbal problems and reading very difficult scientific material. It is probably at a rate of about 75 to 150 words per minute.

Students in grades 5 to 12 should be given opportunities to learn to vary their reading rate depending on the difficulty of the material and their purpose for reading. If students are not taught to read *flexibly,* they may read every type of content material in a word-by-word manner even though sometimes, as with an easy novel, they should read much more rapidly. Students should be encouraged to read easy, interesting material where comprehension is not a problem, in *thought units* or groups of words, skipping unimportant portions of the material instead of reading in a word-by-word manner.

Effective Test-Taking Strategies and "Testwiseness"

Although *test-taking skills* and *testwiseness* are somewhat similar, they also have some important differences. Test-taking skills are long-term study strategies, whereas testwiseness refers to a set of strategies students can use while taking tests. Some test-taking skills are frequent reviews of content material, class notes, and other assigned materials. In addition, numerous short study sessions are more effective than long cramming sessions.

Testwiseness refers to some principles that can be applied to content exams independently of subject knowledge. To be "testwise" is to be able to make use of the flaws that commonly are found even in good teacher-made tests and to apply logic, common sense, and good organization skills in any test-taking situation. Obviously, testwiseness alone will not result in good grades in middle school or high school. There is no substitute for studying regularly using effective study strategies. However, testwiseness skills can help students do better on classroom content tests. Although some educators do not approve of teaching testwiseness to students, it is logical that if all students are equally testwise, no student has an unfair advantage, and differences in performance should be attributable only to different degrees of knowledge.

Therefore, both test-taking skills and testwiseness should be taught to all students in grades 5 to 12. Not to do so unfairly penalizes those students who have not discovered both of these skills independently through logic and trial and error.

Specialized Skills Needed While Reading Literature

The content area of *literature* requires students in grades 5 to 12 to master certain specialized skills. A literature program should encourage students to learn about their literary heritage; expand their imagination; evaluate different kinds of literature; increase awareness of different types of language; develop a love for literature; develop preferences for different types of literature; and grow intellectually, emotionally, and socially.

Literature teachers can organize instruction by genre, literary elements, or topics in order to vary the students' experiences. Reading and literature teachers also should introduce students to the specialized vocabulary and skills they need to develop an appreciation of the different types of literature.

Literature consists of a number of different genres or forms, including realistic fiction, historical fiction, biographies, autobiographies, poetry, plays, information books, fantasy and folklore, novels, short stories, and essays. Students should be able to recognize and evaluate all of these different genres or forms. Historical fiction, biographies, autobiographies, and informational books all may help students to solve problems in their own lives as well as to understand the problems of others better.

To understand literary passages, students must be able to recognize and analyze plots, themes, characterization, settings, and authors' styles. The *plot* is the overall plan for the book or story; the *theme* is the main idea the writer wishes to convey; and *characterization* is the way in which the writer makes the reader aware of the characteristics and motives of each person in the story. The *setting* consists of time and place, and the *style* is the author's mode of expressing thoughts.

Figurative language is one aspect of literature that is difficult for many students to understand. Most students need considerable instruction if they are to understand figurative language well. Some figures of speech that may cause students in grades 5 to 12 difficulty are as follows:

- *Simile:* a comparison using *like* or *as*
- *Metaphor:* a direct comparison *without* the words *like* or *as*
- *Personification:* giving the attributes of a person to an inanimate object or abstract idea
- *Hyperbole:* an extreme exaggeration
- *Euphemism:* substitution of a less offensive term for an unpleasant term or expression

Although literature has a specialized vocabulary, understanding it may not be as crucial as in social studies or science. However, students should be aware that knowing these terms will help them recognize the use of certain elements in literature. A few of these terms are as follows: *antithesis*, *cliché*, *imagery*, *moral*, *onomatopoeia*, and *stanza*. For a comprehensive list of literary terms, see Fry, Kress, and Fountoukidis, *The Reading Teacher's Book of Lists* (2000; pp. 155–158).

In addition, the content area of English requires an awareness of different types of language, including listening, speaking, reading, and writing. English also has a specialized vocabulary. Students in grades 5 to 12 should be knowledgeable about the following terms: *noun*, *pronoun*, *determiner*, *verb*, *adverb*, *adjective*, *manuscript*, *cursive*, and *parliamentary procedure*, among others.

Specialized Skills Needed While Reading Social Studies

Social studies consists of the study of history, geography, political science, sociology, and economics. It is important that students in grades 5 to 12 master the most important elements of these content areas in order to have a productive and satisfying life. However, much of the material in social studies textbooks is very difficult for them because it is often written on a higher reading level than the grade level for which it is designed. For example, a sixth-grade social studies textbook may be written at the seventh-grade reading level or above. Thus, often only the above-average readers in a class can understand it effectively.

Therefore, one of the most important specialized skills for students reading social studies materials is to understand the important technical terms. For example, such technical terms as *apartheid, filibuster, monopoly, referendum, secede, sovereignty,* and *totalitarian* in political science and *cartographer, deciduous, equinox, meridian, precipice, steppe,* and *topography* in geography are required for effective comprehension. In addition, some social studies terms differ from their use in general conversation. For example, when a student hears the word *boom, cabinet, bill, strike,* or *recall,* it may have a different meaning than the one that he already knows. This is why social studies teachers always should ensure that students clearly understand the concepts represented by these terms.

For comprehensive lists of elementary and intermediate social studies vocabulary and elementary and intermediate geography vocabulary, see *The Reading Teacher's Book of Lists* (Fry, Kress, and Fountoukidis, 2000; pp. 138–142).

Social studies teachers should help students evaluate the accuracy and authenticity of the material they read. Although *fictionalized* biographies and diaries are very helpful in teaching students about historical figures and events, teachers should make sure students understand that these stories are not completely factual. Students can consult reference books or the World Wide Web, among other sources, to find out if dates, places, and names are accurate. Sometimes an author's foreword or postscript may offer clues to the fictional aspects of a story. Students also should know that authors sometimes use first-person narrative accounts to make the action seem more personal, but in reality the supposed speaker is not the one who did the writing.

Students need to search for an author's biases, and if a bibliography is provided, check to see how much the author depended on *actual sources.* Actual or firsthand sources usually are more authoritative than secondary sources. Newspaper editorials and letters-to-the-editor also are good sources for material for teaching students to search for author biases.

Students must be able to recognize cause-and-effect and comparison–contrast relationships and understand chronological order. Social studies materials usually are written in a very precise and compact expository style; many ideas are expressed in very few lines of print. For example, an author may discuss a span of several hundred years in a single page or even a single paragraph, or may cover complex issues in a few paragraphs even though entire books instead could be devoted to these issues.

Specialized Skills Needed While Reading Science

A number of special skills make the learning of science a very difficult content area for many students. One of the science and reading teachers' most important tasks is to enable students to identify and understand the technical vocabulary found in most science textbooks. For example, a typical science textbook may include such specialized vocabulary terms as *carcinogen, diffraction, embryology, halogen, invertebrate, malleable, nucleolus, pituitary, rarefaction, seismograph, thermocouple, valence electron,* and *zygote.* Because science contains many words with unique meanings, science or reading teachers should teach specific scientific concepts and terms *before* students meet them in their reading. Although context clues often help students to identify unknown scientific vocabulary, context is not particularly useful with technical scientific terms.

In addition, some scientific vocabulary terms have more common meanings: for example, *control, power, rate, root, wave, host,* and *hammer.* Science also has several symbol sets. The symbols and subscripted numbers used in the following formulas all must be mastered to read scientific material accurately.

Compound	**Formula**	**Phase of Matter**
Sodium bicarbonate	$NaHCO_3$	Solid
Isopropyl alcohol	C_3H_8O	Liquid
Methane	CH_4	Gas

Science is based on several different disciplines. It contains numerous words with either Greek or Latin *morphemes.* Therefore, the study of the meaning of prefixes, suffixes, and word roots may be very helpful for students in learning the meaning of unknown scientific terms.

One of the most important reading skills required is *reading to follow directions.* This is very important in laboratory exercises, for example, where even a minimal variance from directions can result in an improperly conducted experiment. Experiments that must be read and written also have a text structure that is different from that found in other materials. Much scientific writing is presented in strict categories with understood requirements for what is acceptable in each. Here is a typical problem-solving paradigm:

I. Statement of the problem
II. Hypotheses
III. Procedure
IV. Observation
V. Collection of the data (results)
VI. Conclusion(s)

Many students are not familiar with this structure before encountering it in reading scientific materials, so it should be presented to them. Reading scientific material requires organizing ideas so that relationships are clear and so that inferences can be drawn on the basis of the relationships. In addition, readers always must be able to understand the purpose of an experiment, read the list of materials to determine what must be obtained in order to perform the experiment, and determine the order of steps to be followed while conducting the experiment. Before they perform an experiment, students should try to predict its outcome based on their prior knowledge. Later they must compare their predicted conclusions with the actual conclusions.

Reading scientific material also requires such comprehension strategies as *recognizing main ideas and important details, drawing conclusions, recognizing cause-and-effect relationships,* and *understanding sequential order.* It also is important for students to read scientific material very *critically* and to check the copyright dates of scientific material to ensure that it is current. Students should use the *scientist's inquiring attitude* when reading scientific material. These materials usually are written in a very compact, expository style that often involves explanations, classification, and cause-and-effect relationships. Students usually must be able to interpret such *reading aids as tables, charts, diagrams, and graphs.* Such visual aids are often difficult for students to understand, so they may skip over them while reading.

Finally, scientific material must be read slowly and deliberately with rereading often necessary to understand fully the information presented. This is called *careful analytical reading,* with a reading rate of about 75 to 150 words per minute.

Science textbooks are often written at a significantly higher reading level than the grade level for which they are designed; a sixth-grade science textbook may well be written at the seventh-grade reading level or perhaps even at a higher level. Therefore, the textbook is difficult for all but the above-average readers in a class and much too difficult for those reading at the upper primary-grade level or lower. One solution is to provide average and below-average readers in a class with alternative materials to use for science instruction. These alternative materials can be an easy-to-understand series of science textbooks or various types of supplementary science materials, so students can read about the topic from another source. Furthermore, science can be very effectively taught in thematic units, where students can read a variety of materials from different sources such as informational trade books, reference books, the World Wide Web, magazines, and newspapers, among others.

Specialized Skills Needed While Reading Mathematics

To understand mathematics, students must face a number of inherent difficulties and have some specialized skills. Mathematics has a specialized vocabulary that students in grades 5 to 12 must learn. Examples include *cosine, deviation, histogram, inverse, micron, probability, axis, quartile,* and *theorem.* In addition, mathematics contains a number of words with multiple meanings, such as *altitude, scale, plot, exact,* and *odd.* However, some mathematical terms have prefixes, suffixes, or word roots that students can use to determine their meaning. As an example, the word *millimeter* is a thousandth of a meter.

To improve mathematical vocabulary, teachers can assign a mathematical term each day that the students must identify and subsequently use in a sentence. The teacher can ask questions about the terms being studied or ask students to dramatize the meaning of mathematical terms. The meanings of prefixes, suffixes, and word roots and their application to mathematical terms can be studied. An excellent source of prefixes, suffixes, and word roots and their meanings is *The Reading Teacher's Book of Lists* (Fry, Kress, and Fountoukidis, 2000; pp. 85–113).

In addition to difficulties with mathematical terms, students often have difficulty with the unique symbol system. Students must be able to interpret such symbols as +, *X*,

=, <, >, @, :, /, #, %, ( ), *a + b = c, a · b, a (b − c), and (a + b + c + d)*, among many others. They also may be able to interpret such abbreviations as *cm., mm., pd., lb., qt., pt., km.*, among many others. Symbols often may be difficult for students because some symbols have different meanings in other contexts; for example, "–" means *minus in mathematics*, but is a *dash in regular print.*

In addition, to read numbers effectively students must understand *place value.* They must understand that the number *758.92* has three places to the left of the decimal point and two places to the right of it (which they must differentiate from a period). This indicates that the left-most numeral indicates a precise number of *hundreds*, the next numeral indicates how many *tens*, and the next numeral indicates how many *ones.* In this example, the number is seven hundreds, five tens, and eight ones, or *seven hundred fifty-eight.*

To determine the value to the right of the decimal point, students should understand that the first place is *tenths*, the second place is *hundredths*, and so forth. In this example there are *ninety-two hundredths*; therefore, the entire number is *seven hundred fifty-eight and ninety-two hundredths.* Because this procedure consists not merely of reading from left to right, as is usually the case, but also reading back and forth, it is easy to see why it can be difficult for students.

Reading mathematical sentences also presents problems. For example, students should recognize numerals and symbols and then translate them into verbal sentences that make sense—as in reading *144 ÷ 12 = 12* as *one hundred forty-four divided by twelve equals twelve.*

Mathematics material is very concise and abstract and involves complex relationships. A high density of ideas per page appears in this type of material and understanding *every word* is crucial because just *one word* may be the key to understanding an entire section or verbal problem. Another problem that affects students' ability to solve difficult mathematical verbal problems is the three-level translation of each problem's vocabulary. Students must be able to translate from the *general* to the *specialized* to the *symbolic* vocabularies. The ability to translate among the vocabularies is essential to the conceptualization of the message contained in that word problem. Briefly, here is one procedure students can follow to solve word problems:

1. Learn all the word meanings.
2. Determine exactly what the problem is asking for.
3. Decide what facts are needed to solve the problem.
4. Determine which mathematical operations must be performed.
5. Determine the order in which the operations should be performed.

Graphs, maps, charts, and tables often occur in mathematical materials. Students need specific instruction and practice in using these visual aids in order to perform well on many mathematical assignments.

In summary, mathematics presents countless challenges for students, even otherwise good readers. Verbal math problems present an especially significant problem for many. The strategies and materials provided in the next section of this chapter should help mathematics and reading teachers present the important reading skills for all types of mathematical materials much more effectively.

STRATEGIES FOR IMPROVING STUDY SKILLS IN THE CONTENT AREAS

Chapter Seven now provides a sampling of classroom-tested strategies for improving ability in study skills in the content areas. Although all may be helpful in grades 5 to 12, you should modify them in light of the abilities, needs, and interests of your own students.

Strategies for Improving Organizational Skills

Here are some strategies for improving organizational skills.

The EEEZ Strategy

The *EEEZ strategy* is a general organizational study strategy that encourages students to elaborate mentally on new content information to facilitate long-term retention. The acronym *EEEZ* (*take it easy, explain, explore, expand*) refers to a set of strategies that can be used as a postreading experience to "help anchor the content in memory" (Dana, 1989, p. 32–33).

According to Dana, after reading, students should review what they have read in light of the purpose that was set for the reading assignment. They should be told that after reading they should *take it easy* (EEEZ) and make an attempt to *explain* (E) the content in a manner commensurate with the purpose set for reading. They might have to answer questions, define a concept, or provide a summary. They should then *explore* (E) the same content material as described by authors in different textbooks. These comparisons often help students to clarify important ideas. They then *expand* (E) the subject matter by reading other textbooks that go beyond the content covered in the original textbook.

After expanding, students should respond to the original purpose for reading the assignment given by the teacher, embellishing their responses with additional content discovered during the EEEZ process.

Note Taking

Here are some general suggestions for note taking. Students should include keywords and phrases in their notes; enough context to make the material understandable when they review it; and a bibliographic reference with each note. They should also copy direct quotations exactly as they are found in the content material.

Gunning's (1996) strategy for taking notes consists of the following steps:

- Write the name of the topic on the top line of an index card. For example: *The terra-cotta warriors—the people who discovered them.*
- Turn the topic into a question: *What were the people doing when they discovered the terra-cotta warriors?*
- Search for information that answers that question. You can skim through the material to locate the relevant facts.
- Take notes on details that answer your question. Write the notes in your own words. The most effective way to do this is to read a brief section and then write the important facts from memory.
- To save time and space, leave out unimportant words such as *the*, *a*, and *an*, and write in phrases instead of sentences.

- Check back over the section. Make sure that you have taken all the notes that answer your question and that you have put them into your own words.
- Fill in identifying information. At the bottom of the card write the page number where you obtained the information. At the top write the author's name, the title of the article, title of the book or periodical, volume number if it has one, publisher's name, place where the publisher is located, and date of publication.

According to Flippo (1988) note taking and "note making" are important study skills. Note taking is useful to students as they listen to information presented in lectures and discussions. But students must be taught to take notes that are appropriate to the demands being placed on them (Caverly and Orlando, 1991). Notes are helpful to the extent that they contain information that will be tested, but what students do with their notes is equally important. Students must cognitively process the information, encoding it in the same way that they will need to do on a test (Anderson and Armbruster, 1991).

Flippo recommended that students develop skill in condensing their study notes by rewriting them several times. Each time they condense the notes further, they have to determine what is most important and synthesize the information. Flippo also described note-taking and note-making strategies such as organizing class notes into topic cards, lists, outlines, and diagrams, and organizing class lecture notes.

Kiewra (1984) suggested a sequence of steps to facilitate note-taking success: (1) using effective techniques during class lectures and discussion; (2) taking extensive notes at first; (3) employing paraphrasing or summarizing note-taking procedures; (4) revising notes as quickly as possible after they are taken; (5) reviewing notes before the next class; and (6) incorporating externally provided notes on all note-taking and reviewing procedures.

Palmatier's Unified Notetaking System

Palmatier's Unified Notetaking System (PUNS) (1971, 1973) is a strategy that encourages students to review lecture notes immediately after class and supplement them with textbook information. The note-taking format also provides a built-in study system by separating keywords from the body of the notes. Here are the basic steps in this system:

- *Step One: Record.* Use only one side of 8½-inch by 11-inch notebook paper with a 3-inch margin on the left side. Record lecture notes to the right of the margin. Use a modified outline form to isolate the main topics. Leave space where information seems to be missing. Number each page as you record the notes.
- *Step Two: Organize.* As soon after class as possible, add two sections to the notes. First place labels inside the left margin. These notes should briefly describe the information in the recorded notes. Next, insert *important textbook information* directly into the recorded notes. If you need more space, use the back of the notebook paper.
- *Step Three: Study.* Remove the notes from the loose-leaf binder, and lay them out so that only the left margin of each page is visible. Use the labels as memory cues to recite as much of the information on the right as you can recall. The labels can be turned into question stems: *What do I need to know about (*insert the label*)?* Verify your recall immediately by lifting the page to read the

information recorded to the right of the label. As you master the material on each page of notes, set that page aside in an *I already know* stack. For objective tests, the labels can be approached at random, simulating the format of multiple-choice, true–false, and matching tests. For essay tests, group information into logical units, formulate predicted essay questions, and practice writing answers. Teachers should help students to process material to higher levels by exposing them to several different means of annotating, critiquing, and responding to what they read and hear.

Strategies for Improving Ability to Locate Information

Here are some strategies for improving ability to locate information.

Library Hunts

Each week, pose a problem that requires your students to use their reference skills in the school library or media center. Ask questions such as these:

- What is the Dewey Decimal System number for information books about the Seine River in France?
- Where would you find a book about Tom Brokaw, the television news anchor?
- Where would you find the book *The Lovely Bones* by Alice Sebold?
- What are the titles of all the books contained in this library that were written by Stephen King?
- What are the titles of one fiction book and one nonfiction book that are located in this library?

Reference Match

After discussing and demonstrating various types of reference materials, provide a list of reference materials and a separate list of information found in those materials. Have students match the information to the source. Here is an example:

a. almanac	_____	1. contains synonyms for commonly used words
b. atlas	_____	2. provides summaries, tables, charts, statistics, and other useful information on an extensive range of subjects
c. encyclopedia	_____	3. contains articles on a wide variety of subjects written by experts
d. thesaurus	_____	4. computerized source of information on a wide variety of topics
e. encyclopedia	_____	5. a book of maps on CD-ROM

Atlas Information

Have students use an atlas to locate information such as states sharing borders, the capital of each state, the name of the largest city in a state, the numbers of the major highways in a state, among many others.

Topic Sort

Write a number of relevant topics on 3-inch by 5-inch index cards and place them in a box. On the chalkboard or an activity sheet, draw the spines of a set of encyclopedias.

Have each student select a topic and state or write which volume they would use to locate information on that topic.

Creative Vocabulary
This activity is designed to help students understand the purpose of a glossary. You can use this activity either during a group storytelling activity or as part of a creative writing activity. In either case, have students make up words that fit their story no matter how ridiculous they may be.

Have students write a glossary for the "new" or "unfamiliar" words. Students can then exchange these glossaries and compare and discuss their definitions.

Card Catalogue Search
Visit the library or media center after having discussed the library card catalogue. Then present a two-column list with information needed in one column and the type of card in the other column. Have students match the columns. Then have them use the library card catalogue to locate the needed information. Here is a very brief example:

a. Author card	_____ 1. You want to find out a book that describes life in the United States during the Vietnam War.
b. Subject card	_____ 2. You want to locate a book by General Colin Powell.
c. Title card	_____ 3. You want to locate the book *The Greatest Generation.*

Looking It Up
Spiegel (1990) recommended the book *Looking It Up* (Foster and Foster, 1989) as a resource for teaching library skills to students in grade 5, especially if they have special needs. This reproducible workbook contains eight units on a variety of topics related to library skills.

On-Line Card Catalogues
If a school library has a computerized card catalogue, students will be able to search for books by title, author, and subject, much as they do with the manual card catalogue. They should choose the type of search they need, type in the keywords necessary for the search, and view a list of the available books on the monitor. For example, a student could choose an author search, then type in the name *Judy Blume.* The on-line catalogue then lists all of the books housed in the library that were authored by Judy Blume.

Strategies for Improving Ability to Locate Information on the World Wide Web

Students can use the extensive information resources available on the World Wide Web as they research written and oral reports (Harvey, 1998). Displays at Web sites include text information, pictures, sound, video, and animated graphics, and also provide connections to related information using hypertext links. Although most Web sites have been developed by adults, some have been created by students during thematic units, and students especially enjoy visiting these sites.

The World Wide Web is easy to use. Students locate Web sites with information related to their topics using search engine software. One of the most effective search engines for students is *Yahoo for Kids* (www.yahooligans.com). On the search engine's homepage, students type in the topic for the search, and the software program searches for related sites. A list of Web sites with their URL addresses and brief annotations then appears on the homepage.

Students review the list and then click on an address to connect to that Web site. They look at the site and if it seems useful, they "bookmark" it or add it to their list of favorites so they can return to it easily. They can print out copies of all the information available on the site, but they usually are most interested in printing photographs, diagrams, maps, and other graphics to incorporate into their reports. Using the World Wide Web enhances students' content area learning and their computer literacy.

Because of possible difficulty with certain Web sites and Internet access, reading and content teachers should preview all sites before students use the Internet for research. Many teachers prefer to give their students a list of appropriate sites related to the topic rather than give them free access to the World Wide Web. Teachers mark these sites with bookmarks or prepare a written handout for students listing the appropriate URL addresses.

You may wish to check the following resources for more information on using the World Wide Web:

Heide, A., and Silborne, L. *The Teacher's Complete and Easy Guide to the Internet.* New York: Teachers College Press, 1999.

Leu, D. J., and Leu, D. D. *Teaching with the Internet: Lessons from the Classroom.* Norwood, Mass.: Christopher Gordon, 1998.

Strategies for Improving Content Textbook Use

Lessons that teach students about the parts of content textbooks and how they can be helpful should be included in both reading and content instruction. Most social studies and science textbooks contain a title page, copyright page, preface, table of contents, bibliography, index, and glossary. In addition, each chapter usually contains a title, introduction, headings, subheadings, conclusions, questions, and references. Students need to learn about the various content textbook parts, the information that each contains, and their uses.

- Have students predict the specific information that may be found in various chapters by using the table of contents. Write the predictions on the chalkboard. Then have students locate the appropriate pages in the content textbook to check their predictions.
- On the day you distribute a new textbook, lead students in an examination of its table of contents. They should learn that the contents lists the topics the book discusses and the pages on which they appear, making it unnecessary to search through the entire book to locate a specific section. You can help your students discover information about their new textbooks by asking questions such as these: *What topics are presented in this book? What is the first topic discussed? How many chapters does this book contain? On what page does the discussion about ______________ begin?*
- Have students look at several copyright pages and tables of contents from books in the same subject area (either social studies or science textbooks). Using the

table of contents, have students compare differences in topics. Then, using the copyright dates, have students attempt to match the copyright dates to the correct tables of contents. You may have to guide students by pointing out topics that may be relatively new to that field and would not have been included in earlier textbooks.

- Give students a list of specific items found in various chapters, sections, and subsections. Have students match the items on the list with the titles shown in the table of contents. Discuss reasons why the matches were made and check the appropriate sections to determine if they were correct.
- Students in grades 5 to 12 should become familiar with indexes. They should understand that an index is an alphabetical list of items and names mentioned in a textbook and the pages where these items or names appear. Some books contain one general index and some contain subject and author indexes as well as other specialized indexes. Most indexes contain both main headings and subheadings, and students should be given opportunities to use these headings to locate information in their textbooks. Teachers can help students examine the index of a book and make inferences about the importance the author gives to various topics based on the amount of space devoted to them.
- Compare pages in an index and a glossary of a content textbook. Have students discuss the differences and write them on the chalkboard. Discuss the purposes of each one.
- Discuss the differences between a glossary and a dictionary. A glossary contains definitions for specialized vocabulary terms that appear in that content textbook, whereas a dictionary includes definitions of both specialized and general vocabulary terms. Locate sentences in the textbook that contain content-specific vocabulary terms and have students look up their meanings in the glossary. Then have them read the paragraph that contains the term to determine if the definition is appropriate.
- Students should be shown that the appendices contain supplementary information that may be helpful, such as tables or charts. There may be times when students need to use this material, but they will not use it if they have never been exposed to it.
- Footnotes and bibliographies refer students to other sources of information on the subject being discussed, and you should encourage students to turn to these sources for clarification, additional information on a topic for a report, or their own interest. A bibliography that appears at the end of a chapter or at the end of the entire textbook is a list of references that the author consulted when researching the textbook. Or it may contain additional information.

Strategies for Improving Ability in Using Reference Materials

An *encyclopedia* contains articles on a wide variety of subjects written by experts. These articles provide students with the opportunity to gain information on a subject quickly. An encyclopedia usually is published in a number of volumes arranged in alphabetical order so that a student who wants to locate information about *the Salem witch trials*, for example, would look for this topic in the *S* volume. Letters are stamped on the spine of each volume to indicate the alphabetical range of information contained in it. For example, if a volume is stamped with the letters *M–N*, it contains articles about subjects beginning with the letters *M* and *N*. Guide words are printed at the top of each page to help students quickly locate the target topic.

Students can be given an activity sheet containing a listing of a number of content subjects that they can research in a print or on-line encyclopedia. Ask them to write down five or ten facts that they learned from reading the target encyclopedia article or articles.

When it comes to *atlases*, use the following procedure:

- Give students a copy of the road map for your state that is contained in a road atlas. Have them locate target cities, interstate highways, state highways, and county roads.
- Have students answer questions such as these about atlases: What are the major types of atlases? (*Geographical, political, road.*) What information can you expect to get from a political atlas? (*Political boundaries of different countries, states, and perhaps towns and villages.*) What information can you expect to get from a geographical atlas? (*Features of the earth's surface such as oceans, lakes, rivers, land masses, mountains, and plateaus.*) What information can you expect to get from a road atlas? (*Maps showing the road system for a specific area. A United States road map will show the major highways across the fifty states.*) What atlas should you use to locate the major rivers in a country? (*Geographical atlas.*) What atlas indicates the location of the fifty state capitals in the United States? (*Political atlas.*) What atlas should you use to plan an automobile trip from Duluth, Minnesota, to Seattle, Washington? (*Road atlas.*) Which of these atlases would you like to own? Why?

To locate information in the *Reader's Guide to Periodical Literature*, students may follow this procedure:

1. Select a topic on which they want information available in periodicals.
2. Locate the *Reader's Guide* in the library.
3. Gather the issues and bound volumes of the *Reader's Guide* for the years to be included in the search for information.
4. Locate magazine articles on the topic.
5. Use the *See* and *See also* references to locate additional articles.
6. Prepare a bibliography card for each reference to be used.

Students can complete an activity sheet that uses the *Reader's Guide* containing questions such as the following:

1. Select a page from the March 2003 *Reader's Guide to Periodical Literature.* Then write the names of three topics found on this page in which you might be interested.

   ____

2. For the topic *computer programming* write the names of the topics listed under *See also.*

   ____

   ____

3. What topics are listed as *See also* for *computer input—output equipment?*

   ____

   ____

4. For the topic *computer graphics* select three magazine bibliographic references and write them on these lines.

   ____

   ____

   ____

The most effective way for students to learn how to use the *Reader's Guide* is when researching the answer to a real-life problem or researching information for use in a thematic unit that the class is studying.

The *New York Times Index* is the most comprehensive and widely available newspaper index. Most libraries that have this index also have a microfilm collection of this newspaper going back to 1913. The *New York Times Index* is organized according to subject, not by author or title. Each entry for the article includes a brief summary.

Here is an entry that follows the *New York Times Index* format from 2002:

[1]**Travel**
[2]•*Italy*
[3]Jay Goeldi's article on travel attractions in Italy
[4]illustrations [5](M) Je 14[6] 18:2[7]

1. **Travel** is the heading and can be identified as such because it is printed in boldface.

2. *Italy* is a subdivision under **Travel**. This subdivision is identified by the dot in front of the word *Italy,* which is printed in italics.

3. This is an abstract or short comment on the article.
4. This shows that the article contains illustrations.
5. (L) indicates a long article of two columns or more, (M) a medium-length article up to two columns, and (S) a short item (usually a half-column or less in length).
6. This indicates the month and date when the newspaper containing this article was published.
7. This indicates the paper number and column number where the article appears.

It should be noted that Roman numerals are used to indicate section numbers for Sunday editions of the paper. A "p" in an entry stands for "page."

Students can be asked questions such as these about this article:

1. What is this article about? *travel in Italy*
2. Who wrote the article? *Jay Goeldi*
3. Under which heading does this article appear? *Travel*
4. Under which subdivision does this article appear? *Italy*
5. How long is this article? *one page*
6. When did this article appear? *June 14, 2002*
7. On what page would you look for this article? *18*
8. In what column would you look to locate this article? *2*

Almanacs, which provide summaries, tables, charts, statistics, and other useful information on an extensive range of subjects, are updated daily or yearly and contain an enormous amount of information in a variety of formats. You can even find almanacs on the World Wide Web. One interesting example is *Wilsons Almanac* at www.wilsonsalmanac.com/copyright.html. This almanac is updated daily by Pip Wilson and originates in Sydney, Australia. A student can subscribe to this on-line almanac by e-mail: *WilsonsAlmanac-subscribe@yahoogroups.com.* It summarizes some of the more interesting events that occurred on that date in history.

Here is a sample of events that occurred on July 19 along with some questions for students that can be constructed from reading these events:

64 A.D.—Rome's great fire begins: History records that Rome burned for six days and that threatening groups of men who claimed to be "acting under orders" prevented people from extinguishing this tragic fire. Nero is said to have enjoyed watching the fire and played the lyre, a musical instrument, as he did so. He might have set the fire for his own amusement or as an excuse to expand his palace.

164 A.D.: A dragon more than one hundred meters long was found dead on Yehwang Mountain in Henan province in China. According to Chinese lore, this was a bad omen for Emperor Huan, who ignored it, and died at age thirty-five in 167 A.D. Xiang Kai, who had warned of the omen, was released from the prison in which the emperor had placed him and was called a hero.

1333: The Battle of Halidon Hill between the Scots and the English took place.

1692: Five women were executed for practicing witchcraft in Salem, Massachusetts.

1825: The Times of London reported that hundreds of the townspeople of Wickham-Skeith, Suffolk, England, put Isaac Stebbings to the ancient witchcraft test of "swimming." He would have drowned had not the local minister intervened.

1848: The first women's rights convention opened at Seneca Falls, New York.

1971: British comic Marty Feldman appeared for the defense in the "Oz Trial." He called the judge "a boring old fart."

Here are some questions:

1. What musical instrument is Nero said to have played during Rome's six-day fire in 64 A.D.? *the lyre*

2. What emperor ignored the dragon that was found dead in 164 A.D. in Henan province, China? *Emperor Huan*

3. What two countries fought the Battle of Halidon Hill in 1333? *Scotland and England*

4. How many women were executed for practicing witchcraft in Salem, Massachusetts, in 1692? *five*

5. Who intervened to save Isaac Stebbings from drowning in Wickham-Skeith, England, in 1825? *the local minister*

6. Where was the first women's rights convention held in 1848? *Seneca Falls, New York*

7. What British comic appeared for the defense in the "Oz Trial" in 1971? *Marty Feldman*

As for *government publications*, students can complete an activity sheet to assess and improve their knowledge of the government publications that are available to them for research purposes. Teachers might include the following information on this kind of activity sheet:

> The United States government publishes materials on many subjects. Your school library may have a special section where government publications are kept. Visit your library and ask the librarian the following questions to help you learn more about the government publications that are available for your use.

1. Where are the United States government publications kept in your school or city library?
2. Which librarian (if any) is assigned to help students use government publications?
3. Place a check mark in front of each government publication that is found in your school or city library?
   Guide to U.S. Government Publications
   American Statistics Index: A Comprehensive Guide and Index to the Statistical Publications of the U.S. Government Publications Reference File
   List of Classes of United States Government Publications Available for Selection in Depository Libraries
   Statistical Abstract of the United States
   Congressional Information Services Indexes to Publications of the United States Congress
   Government Reports Announcements and Index
   Monthly Catalog of United States Government Publications
4. Write a brief description of the information contained in the publications of those found in your school or city library.

Guinness World Records (Cunningham, 2003) is an excellent source of interesting facts for most students in grades 5 to 12. Most students very much enjoy researching many different types of world records from this book. The following sample text and questions are based on facts about baseball from the 2001 *Guinness World Records.* However, it is most motivating if students themselves decide what records they want to search for.

Baseball World Records

Biggest contract: The biggest baseball contract was an average of $15 million per year for seven years. It was signed by Kevin Brown of the Los Angeles Dodgers on December 2, 1998. Brown's contract will be worth a total of $105 million.

Fastest base runner: The record for the fastest time for circling the bases is 13.3 seconds, set by Ernest Swanson of Columbus, Ohio, in 1932. His average speed around the bases was 18.45 miles per hour.

Fastest pitch: The greatest reliably recorded speed at which a baseball has been pitched is 100.9 miles per hour by Lynn Nolan Ryan (California Angels) at Anaheim Stadium in California on August 20, 1974.

Longest home run: The record for the longest measured home run in a major league game is 634 feet by Mickey Mantle for the New York Yankees against the Detroit Tigers at Briggs Stadium in Detroit, Michigan, in September 1960.

Longest throw: Glen Gorbous of Canada threw a baseball 445 feet and 10 inches on August 1, 1957.

Longest throw by a woman: Mildred "Babe" Didrikson threw a baseball 296 feet on July 25, 1931.

Most spectators: An estimated 114,000 spectators watched an exhibition game between Australia and an American service team during the Olympic Games in Melbourne, Australia, on December 1, 1956.

Attendance for a single game in the United States: 92,706 for a game between the Los Angeles Dodgers and the Chicago White Sox on October 6, 1959.

Highest season's attendance ever in all major league baseball games: 70,372,221 in 1998.

Here are the questions:

1. What baseball player signed the largest contract in the history of baseball? *Kevin Brown*
2. What was the average speed of Ernest Swanson as he circled the bases in 13.3 seconds in 1932? *18.45 miles per hours*
3. What pitcher threw the baseball at the fastest recorded time in 1974? *Lynn Nolan Ryan*
4. Who threw the longest measured home run in a major league game in 1960? *Mickey Mantle*
5. What baseball player from Canada threw a baseball 445 feet 10 inches in 1957? *Glen Gorbous*
6. Who made the longest baseball throw by a woman in 1931? *Mildred (Babe) Didrikson*
7. How many people watched an exhibition game between Australia and an American service team during the Olympic Games in 1956? *114,000*
8. What is the record attendance for a single game in the United States? *92,706*
9. What is the record for the highest season's attendance in all major league baseball games? *70,372,221*

Strategies for Improving Ability in Using Graphic Aids

Here is how to improve ability with maps, graphs, tables, charts, and diagrams.

Maps

One of the most important graphic skills is *map reading.* Many maps appear in social studies textbooks, and they also may be found in science, math, and literature books.

Students can self-assess their basic map-reading concepts, vocabulary, and symbol interpretation. The reading or content (or most likely the social studies) teacher should provide all the students with a self-assessment sheet and have them complete it. Some questions that can be included are as follows:

What is a map? ______________________________

What are the four cardinal directions? ______________________________

What is a map scale? ______________________________

What is a map key or legend? ______________________________

What are the symbols used in a map key or legend? ______________________

____

What is a map grid? ____

What does *parallel* mean?

____

What does *perpendicular* mean?

____

What are map coordinates? _______________________________________

What is a physical map? ____

What is a political map? ____

What is a road map? ____

What is a boundary? ____

What are contour lines on a map? _________________________________

What is a demographic map? ______________________________________

Name three things you can learn from a physical map. _________________

____

Name three things you can learn from a political map. _________________

____

Name three things you can learn from a road map. _____________________

____

Here are several suggestions for teaching map-reading skills. As with most reading skills, these are taught most effectively when students must read maps for real purposes in one or more of their classes. In any case, map skills always should be immediately applied to *authentic materials* soon after instruction has taken place.

- To teach students to apply a map's scale, help them construct a map of their classroom or their neighborhood to a specified scale.
- To teach students directions on maps, provide them with pictures of directional indicators that are tilted in different ways with *north* indicated on each one. Model the location of other directions based on the knowledge of where north is for one of the indicators. Then let students fill in *S* for *south*, *E* for *east*, and *W* for *west* on each of the other indicators.

- Demonstrate the use of a map's legend. Then have students practice using the map's legend by asking them questions such as these: In what city is the state capital of South Dakota located? Near what cities in Wisconsin do you see a symbol for a state park? What is the name of one national forest in Washington State? What is the name of the marine base that is located near San Diego, California? What is the name of one river in Illinois?
- Give students a map of their city and have them locate the approximate location of their home or apartment on the map. An alternative is to do this activity on the computer using a program such as *Street Atlas USA*, Version 7.0. Using a computer program may be more motivating for students than using a typical map.
- Have students look at a map in their social studies textbook and ask them questions such as the following, which are based on a physical map of the United States.

  What is the name of one mountain range that is found near Tucson, Arizona?
  What is the name of the river that divides the states of Minnesota and Wisconsin?
  What city is located near the Badlands of South Dakota?
  What is the name of the mountain range that is located near the city of Asheville, North Carolina?
  What is the name of the very large lake in south-central Florida near the city of Clewiston?
  What is the name of the river that divides the United States and Mexico near the city of Mission, Texas?
  What is the name of the large lake east of Milwaukee, Wisconsin?
  What two rivers converge near Cairo in extreme southern Illinois?
  What is the name of the mountain range that is near Salt Lake City, Utah?
  What is the name of the body of water that is south of the state of Mississippi?

- Have students demonstrate that they understand terms such as *peninsula, isthmus, gulf, delta,* among many others by locating these features on a map.
- Use the MAP (Make-A-Place) activity, originated by L. B. James, to develop map-reading skills (Hayes, 1992). Here's how: Each student draws a map of an imaginary place. As this activity continues, students find names for the earth's surface features, discover how the earth's surface features are represented on maps, and learn the important features of maps, such as directional indicators and legends. They also learn how these features affect land use and cultural development.
- Ask students to compare information from two (or more) maps and to note relationships between the two maps.
- Discuss the importance of captions on maps.
- Provide activities that require students to analyze climates, trade routes, currents, and topography.

Graphs

Teachers can enhance students' skill in reading and using graphically displayed information by working with the graphs in their content textbooks. These displays, which are sometimes ignored by both teachers and students, can make content materials more interesting and meaningful for students. Students also can be encouraged to do their own meaningful research and develop their own graphic displays to share their research findings. Doing so helps students understand better how to use graphic materials and what the relationships are. Flippo (1997) also presents several ideas for developing graph-reading skills and strategies by using student-generated questions and research.

One of the most effective ways to help students learn to read graphs is to have them construct meaningful graphs (Hadaway and Young, 1994). Here are some examples of such activities:

- Create a pictograph (picture graph) showing the number of boys and girls in each class in a specific grade of middle school. One picture of a boy or girl can represent five boys or girls.
- Create a circle graph that illustrates the percentage of each school day that a student spends in school, studying at home, eating, watching television, playing sports, using the computer, sleeping, among other things.
- Create a bar graph showing the number of Democrats, Republicans, and Independents in the United States Senate in 2003.
- Create a line graph showing the number of books read by students in a certain class outside of school for pleasure or information over an eight-week period.

Lapp and Flood (1992) suggested an activity to help students understand picture graphs that can be used in grades 5 to 8. The teacher should help students collect data about the areas surrounding their homes or school. Getting information from the library, chamber of commerce, weather station, or state house, they can locate the amount of rainfall in different areas, the location of natural resources, or elevations, among others. Based on the information gathered, they should select a color code representing the various elevations, amounts of rainfall, and so on. Then, using the color code, they can design a picture graph showing amounts of precipitation, elevations, among many other characteristics.

Tables, Charts, and Diagrams

Students should learn that a unique type of information can be found in *tables*, and that this information can be used comparatively. Teachers should model how to read tables, verbalizing the mental processes involved. As noted earlier, tables may be difficult for students because they present an overwhelming amount of information in a condensed form.

Ask students to read a table and answer related questions about it. The most effective way for intermediate-grade and middle-school students to learn to interpret tables is to use those found in their own social studies, science, and mathematics textbooks. Students at these reading levels can learn to make comparisons from different types of data and draw valid conclusions from the data. Tables may be used in social studies textbooks to present information such as total campaign spending, average temperature, and heights above sea level. In science textbooks there may be tables that differentiate chemical elements, illustrate distances in space, and compare the characteristics of freshwater lakes. In mathematics, tables may show various mathematical elements such as multiplication facts or square roots of numbers.

Both *diagrams* and *charts* are commonly used in social studies and science textbooks to clarify new vocabulary terms or illustrate concepts. A diagram contains labels designed to help the reader interpret it. Often a diagram shows how parts go together or how an object operates. Diagrams may also be used in science when a scientific concept, such as various organs of the body, like the eyes or ears, are diagrammed so that they can be easily analyzed.

Either a *flow chart* or *time line* is a graphic aid that illustrates the flow or sequence of content material in some way. Either may be easier to interpret than the traditional chart found in content textbooks.

Strategies for Improving Reading Rate Flexibility

Reading flexibility can be emphasized with students at the middle-school level and above. As noted earlier, students at these levels with good basic word identification and comprehension skills always should be given opportunities to learn to *vary their reading rate depending on the difficulty of the material and their purposes for reading it.* If students are not taught the importance of reading content materials *flexibly,* they are likely to read every type of content material in the same word-by-word manner, even though some types should be read much more rapidly.

Here are several strategies to use to improve reading rate and flexibility with students who have good word identification and comprehension skills.

- Vary reading rate depending on the purpose for reading and the difficulty of the material.
- Read easy interesting material where comprehension is not a problem in *thought units* or groups of words.
- Skip unimportant words and unimportant portions of the material if comprehension will not be affected by these omissions.
- Read fairly easy and motivating material for twenty to thirty minutes each day as rapidly as possible while retaining a 70% or better comprehension level.
- Eliminate word-by-word reading except when reading exceedingly difficult material such as verbal math problems. Word-by-word reading may improve reading comprehension in such cases.
- Eliminate audible whispering, lip movements, and subvocalizations, because these habits can greatly slow reading rate. In a few instances, such as when reading very difficult scientific material or verbal math problems, these strategies may improve comprehension to some extent.
- Eliminate finger-pointing as this habit also can slow reading rate considerably. Finger-pointing only can be recommended for beginning readers of any age who need the "crutch" that this action supplies.
- Eliminate head movements because these movements often slow reading rate; the eyes can move across a page much more rapidly than the head can move from left to right.

Harris and Sipay (1990) suggested the following drill for students to improve reading rate and to learn skimming and scanning:

1. Select an easy novel for beginning practice. (*Note to teacher:* In a class or group it is helpful for all students to read the same book.)

2. Read about ten pages, underlining each line with a finger or keeping pace with the eyes.

3. "Practice-read" the same ten pages, using a finger pattern to guide the eyes. The first three times are done at twelve seconds per page, the fourth time at six seconds per page, and the fifth time at four seconds per page. After the first practice read, write down any words or ideas that you recall. After each subsequent practice read, add to the notes. Have someone count the seconds until you establish the rhythm.

4. Repeat Steps 2 and 3 with consecutive sections of the book for about a half hour daily. Marked improvement in the rate of reading and in recall should be noticed within one or two weeks. Practice should be continued until you are satisfied with your performance.

In summary, using motivated timed reading with comprehension checks seems to be the most effective way to improve reading rate and flexibility. In terms of transfer, procedures that most closely resemble normal reading conditions probably are the most effective, and flexibility of reading rate always should be emphasized.

Strategies for Improving Test-Taking and "Testwiseness"

Very briefly, here are some of the most useful test-taking strategies that either reading or content teachers may wish to present to students.

- *When you are first told about a test:* Ask your teacher as much about the test as you can. Find out the exact day on which the test will be given. Ask your teacher to tell you how many items will be on the test and what type of items these will be: multiple choice, true–false, matching, completion, or essay. Ask your teacher to provide you with some sample items similar to those on the test if he or she is willing to do so.
- *The evening before the test:* Study only for a short time and do not cram for the test because this additional study will only confuse you. Make sure you have all the supplies you will need to take the test, such as sharpened pencils, paper, a watch, and a calculator if it is needed and allowed. If possible, get a good night's sleep and don't worry about the test.
- *The day of the test:* Eat a good breakfast. Think positively and tell yourself that you will do well on the test. Double-check that you have all the materials needed for the test. Do not cram the last few minutes before the test; this can cause you to forget information that you have already learned. Cramming also may increase your test anxiety.

Here are a few suggestions for improving performance on various types of tests. Additional information can be found in *Ready-to-Use Activities & Materials for Improving Content Reading Skills* (Miller, 1999; pp. 440–442).

Multiple-Choice Tests

- Read and follow all of the directions carefully.
- Decide what you think the answer might be before you read any of the options.
- Read the question again, this time with the answer you selected to see if it sounds correct.
- When one of the options is "all of the above," it usually is the correct option.
- Options with the qualifier "most" usually are correct.
- Options with absolute qualifiers such as "all" or "none" usually are incorrect.
- Omit any items you are not sure of and come back to them when you have finished the test; this way you avoid not finishing the entire test.
- Always make a calculated guess if you are not sure of the right answer unless there is a penalty for an incorrect answer. Never leave a multiple-choice question blank.
- You may be able to find the answer to one multiple-choice question in the stem of another multiple-choice question.
- The longest or most complete option is likely to be the correct one.

True–False Tests

- Read all of the directions carefully.
- Always make a calculated guess if you do not know the correct answer. Never leave a true–false item blank unless there is a penalty for an incorrect answer.
- Longer statements are more likely to be true than shorter ones.
- Be aware of such words as *all*, *none*, *always*, and *never*. These words usually indicate the statement is false.
- Be aware of such words as *usually*, *generally*, *sometimes*, and *seldom*. These words usually indicate the statement is true.
- Assume absolute statements are *false* while qualified statements are *true*.
- Assume an answer is true unless it can be proved false.
- Be certain *all* parts of the statement are correct before marking it true.

Matching Tests

- Read all of the items in both columns before answering.
- Determine if you can use a choice more than once.
- Begin by marking the easiest matches.
- Make all the correct matches before guessing at any of the other matches.
- Cross out items in both columns as they are used.

Completion or Fill-in-the-Blank Tests

- Read the entire sentence or paragraph.
- Decide which word could best fit in the blank.
- Write an answer that grammatically fits the blank.

- Use the length of the blank as a clue unless all of the blank lines are the same length.
- Read the entire sentence again, including your choice, to be sure it fits and sounds correct.

Essay Tests

- Read and restate the question or statement in your own words before trying to answer it. If you cannot do so, ask the teacher if he or she can explain it.
- Budget your time so that you are certain to complete the test.
- Make a brief outline before you write your answer to help you organize it more effectively.
- Consider carefully the meanings of the following essay test directions before and during the writing. *List, outline:* List tells you to present the information in an item-by-item series; outline tells you to provide the main points in a specific format. *Critique* tells you to summarize and evaluate. *Discuss, describe, explain:* All of these direction words tell you to write as much as you can about a question or statement. *Diagram, illustrate:* These two direction statements tell you to make a drawing with each part labeled. *Compare, contrast:* Compare tells you to indicate how two or more items are connected. Contrast tells you to indicate how they are different. *Criticize, evaluate, justify:* These direction words require you to reach a conclusion about the value of an item. Criticize and evaluate both require you to think about the positive and negative aspects of an item before reaching a decision about it. Justify requires you to give reasons for an action or decision. *Relate, trace:* Relate tells you to indicate how two or more items are connected. Trace tells you to state a series of items in logical order. *Summarize:* This tells you to write a brief statement that indicates something about all of the important ideas.
- Unless the directions state otherwise, never write a minimal answer. Teachers expect you to elaborate and provide full explanations and details of essay answers.

Five-Day Test Preparation Plan

Very briefly, here is the five-day test preparation plan.

Part One: Getting ready: Here are some things that all students can do to prepare to take any test: Ask the teacher what kind of information will be included on the test. Ask the teacher what types of questions will be included on the test. Use a study strategy such as Survey Q3R and take appropriate notes from the reading materials. Use appropriate note-taking techniques.

Part Two: Preparing for the test:

- *Day Five.* Students should review their textbook notes for all of the assigned chapters in the textbook that will be included on the test. They also should review their written class notes from lectures and discussions, and ask their teacher to explain any concepts that are still unclear.
- *Day Four.* Students should study the information in their textbook notes and class notes. They should begin to memorize this information by reviewing it at least three times during the day.

- *Day Three.* Students should rewrite both their textbook notes and their class notes in a briefer form. Teachers should encourage students to use abbreviated language while rewriting their notes. The rewriting provides students with a multimodal review of the information they have to learn.
- *Day Two.* Students should write questions they think might be on the test. They should then write answers to these questions using their rewritten textbook and class notes as necessary.
- *Day One.* This is the day the students take the test. They should briefly review their rewritten textbook and class notes before the school day begins, such as at breakfast or on the school bus.

The SCORER Strategy

The *SCORER Strategy* is a test-taking strategy that may enable students to obtain higher scores on content tests than otherwise would be the case. The acronym stands for *schedule, clue, omit, read, estimate, review.* It consists of these steps (adapted from Carmen and Adams, 1972):

- Students *schedule* their time while taking a test.
- Students identify the *clue* words to help them answer questions. Usually the directions should contain the clue words.
- Students *omit* the hardest items at first.
- Students *read* carefully to be sure they understand and fully answer each question.
- Students *estimate* what should be included in the answer, perhaps by writing down some notes or an outline for the answer.
- Students *review* their responses before turning in the test.

STRATEGIES FOR IMPROVING STUDY SKILLS WHILE READING IN THE CONTENT AREAS

Strategies are presented here for the content areas of literature, social studies, science, and mathematics.

Strategies for Improving Study Skills While Reading Literature

Here are a number of strategies to use with students who are reading and studying literature in grades 5 to 12. Modify any of these strategies in light of your own students' needs, abilities, and interests.

Survey Q3R

The general steps of the study strategy Survey Q3R are *survey, question, read, recite,* and *review* (Robinson, 1961). To use Survey Q3R in reading literature, you must vary it somewhat from its traditional format. For example, the *survey step* can be used effectively with a novel, a short story, an essay, and poetry. Because few of these literary genres contain subheadings, students usually must formulate their own purposes for reading based on their prior knowledge and the genre. In addition, the final step in the process, *review,* may be useful for summarizing what was learned from the reading.

The Extendi-Character Strategy

The objective of this strategy is to promote identification of particular qualities of characters in short stories and to extend imaginative thinking. It is most applicable with middle-school students and above. Before the activity is attempted, students should have read a variety of short stories with various characters and have had classroom instruction in characterization.

Because it may be difficult for students to obtain a clear picture of a particular character in a novel or short story, you can ask them to *extend* the scope of their awareness of the character through their imagination by composing fictitious circumstances into which students can project these characters. Here are some examples of the situations you can create for your students:

- Your character has been involved in an automobile accident because he ran a stop sign. He has a severe head injury and has injured an adult and a child in the other car. He is now in the hospital and probably will be given a ticket for "failure to yield." How will your character adjust to these new circumstances?
- Your character's younger sister has just been diagnosed with leukemia. How will she react to this situation?
- Your character has just witnessed one of her best friends shoplifting an article of clothing from a store in the mall. What will your character do about this situation?
- Your character has just been rejected at the college of his choice that he has planned to attend for many years. How will he adjust to this situation?
- Your character's father has just won the state lottery. How will your character react to this change in her family's circumstances?

Have the students match the situation you've created with a character they have read about recently. Then have them compose two or three paragraphs to answer each question.

The Efficient Reading Strategy

Reutzel and Cooter (2000) have suggested an *efficient reading strategy* that appears to be comprehensive and helpful with both narrative and expository materials with the exception of mathematics. It is effective while reading many literary selections as well as with social studies and perhaps science materials. The strategy is a combination of previewing and skimming. Here are its basic steps:

1. Read the first two paragraphs of the selection to obtain an overview of the material.

2. Next read the first sentence of each successive paragraph. Then skim the remainder of the paragraph to obtain important supporting details for each topic sentence.

3. Read the final two paragraphs of the selection to review the main ideas.

According to Reutzel and Cooter, this procedure has improved comprehension efficiency up to 80% with mature readers, but requires only about one-third the time of normal reading. Note, however, that some literature materials should be read simply to be *enjoyed.* This procedure may spoil a reader's enjoyment of the selection and in such cases should not be used.

Teaching Figurative Language in Literature

Here are several strategies for teaching such figurative expressions as *similes, metaphors, personification, hyperbole,* and *euphemism.*

- Show a metaphor such as "Becky is sly as a fox" together with the more explicit simile "Becky acts sly like a fox" and explain that metaphors have missing words that link the things being compared (such as "acts like"). Other sentence pairs also can be shown and explained.
- Ask students to find the missing words in metaphors, such as "Kersti is as meek as a lamb." Students can provide their guesses and explain their reasons aloud.
- Show students pictures of possible meanings of figurative expressions found in their reading materials and ask them to accept or reject the accuracy of each picture. For example, if you illustrate the sentence "Sarah is as deaf as a doorpost" with a picture of Sarah standing by a doorknob, students should reject the accuracy of the picture.
- Have students write an actual meaning for a number of idiomatic expressions such as the following:

  Mario *bent over backwards* to please his father.

  My father's new executive assistant does not *know the ropes,* and there seems to be no one who is willing to help her.

  That orthopedic surgeon is *wet behind the ears.*

  Kathy *drove a hard bargain,* and ended up with a beautiful 1920s dress at the vintage clothing sale.

  Everyone in the office *coughed up $10,* and we bought Morgan a wedding gift.

  Emanuel was *down in the dumps* after his soccer team lost an important game.
- Provide each student with a copy of a poem that contains figurative language and have the class compete to determine who can locate all the figures of speech first. You may require students to label all figures of speech properly and then explain them.
- Have students participate in an "idiom search" in which they look in all types of reading materials and try to locate as many examples of idioms as they can. They then must define each one in a way that corresponds with its usage.
- Find a cartoon that contains a figure of speech and have students answer questions about the cartoon to determine if they understand it.

You also can have students look for other examples in newspaper comics with figurative language and ask them to cut out the examples and bring them to school for discussion.

Literature Response Groups

In *literature response groups* the reading or literature teacher selects several books for which multiple copies are available, introduces each one, lets students choose which books to read, presents the books to the students if they are unable to read them independently first, holds discussions about the books, may have students respond in reading logs, and allows students to decide about ways to share their experience of the book (Egawa, 1990).

In these groups students initiate and continue discussion topics, connect literature selections to their own lives, compare literature selections and authors with each other, note authors' styles, and consider authors' purposes. The structured book choices lead students to try books in a variety of genres and by a variety of authors.

The Clued-in Strategy

The *clued-in strategy* is designed for literature students in middle school and above. It requires students to retrieve pieces of information from their reading and then apply them in a new way. This skill should help students to sort facts from their reading and locate a common element among those facts to encourage new learning. Based on the reading background of the class, select some common elements such as characters, theme, author, or any others that are significant to the selections. Place each clue verse in an envelope and mark the envelopes beginning with number one.

Divide the class into groups and give each group several envelopes marked in sequence beginning with number one. Each envelope should contain a clue or a problem. When that problem is solved and the correct answer has been written on it, each group is allowed to open envelope number one. If the problem cannot be solved, provide the answer to the group on request and give them a two-minute penalty. Because this is a timed race, it is possible that the winning group may be the last group to finish if it did not need to ask for an answer and thus be penalized. Allow five minutes for each clue during a forty-minute period.

Here are several examples of clues that can be used for this activity.

1. This well-known author planned her entire series of books while traveling on a train in England. *(J. K. Rowling)*

2. This poet wrote the unique poem entitled "The Cremation of Sam McGee." *(Robert Service)*

3. This famous playwright from Stratford-on-Avon in England wrote the play entitled *Romeo and Juliet. (William Shakespeare)*

4. This well-known author of young people's books wrote the book entitled *Are You There, God? It's Me, Margaret. (Judy Blume)*

5. This famous black poet wrote the well-known poem entitled *One Way Ticket. (Langston Hughes)*

Strategies for Improving Study Skills While Reading Social Studies

Here are a number of classroom-tested strategies to improve students' study skills while reading social studies materials. You should modify any of these in light of the needs, abilities, and interests of his or her own students.

Thematic Units of Instruction

Social studies should be taught in *thematic units of instruction* as much as possible. Thematic unit teaching in social studies is an attempt to integrate other content areas such as literature, science, mathematics, and often art, music, and drama into learning social studies materials. A true middle school with its integrated, team-teaching approach best illustrates thematic unit teaching.

When thematic unit teaching is used in social studies, the social studies teacher, in consultation with the literature, science, and mathematics teachers, selects one important *theme* or *unit* that is going to be studied for a specified time period such as four weeks. One topic for a middle school class might be *Life in Ancient Egypt.* Then the entire important content about life in ancient Egypt would be learned by the students with teachers primarily acting as *facilitators of learning* instead of presenters. Some, if not all, of the content and strategies to learn this content is selected by the students with teacher guidance if necessary. The students use all the various content areas in the implementation of learning about the subject. Much of the learning involves the students' active participation working independently, in groups, or with the entire class using material from all the different content areas when appropriate.

Social studies material learned in thematic units usually is much more relevant and meaningful to students than that learned in traditional textbook teaching. Students are encouraged to read appropriate materials on their own level instead of being required to read material that is too difficult for them, as may be the case in traditional teaching. Reading materials such as content textbooks at different reading levels, informational trade books, newspapers, magazines, and reference books of various kinds such as print encyclopedias and encyclopedias on CD-ROM are used. Therefore, students are encouraged to work cooperatively with other students who have varying reading levels; this helps below-average readers avoid the stigma of reading only with other below-average readers.

A Web site that teachers may find helpful in formulating thematic units in social studies is www.education-world.com.

Survey Q3R

Survey Q3R helps students understand and remember content material. It is especially effective in helping students comprehend and retain important information from social studies textbooks. Here is how to use Survey Q3R in social studies (adapted from Robinson, 1961):

- *Survey or preview.* Have the student survey an entire social studies textbook chapter to gain an overall impression of the material. In this survey or preview, the student may read the introduction and summary and the first sentence in each of the paragraphs. He or she also may examine the pictures, maps, graphs, diagrams, tables, and other aids. It should be noted that the survey or preview portion of this technique *always should be used* while reading social studies materials even if no other part of Survey Q3R is used; this part alone greatly adds to a student's comprehension and retention of the material.
- *Question.* Have students pose questions they want to read to answer during this step. They turn each subheading in the social studies textbook chapter into a question and also formulate additional questions to read to answer.

- *Read.* Students then read the social studies chapter *on a selective basis,* trying to answer the questions that they have posed. In this selective reading, they fill in the gaps in their reading by capitalizing on their prior knowledge. This step helps the student to become *more involved in the reading.*
- *Recite.* This step applies only to one section at a time. After the students have read a section purposefully, they recite the important information gained from that section either in an oral or written form, depending on which is more efficient for them.
- *Review.* This is done after the students have finished the entire chapter. They review the important concepts, generalizations, and facts that were learned from this chapter. They can use the written notes they have made in the fourth step (*Recite*) of this procedure if desired.

The Newspaper

A local or national *newspaper* is one of the most versatile sources of reading material that either social studies or reading teachers can use. Newspapers have a number of unique advantages not found in any other type of reading material for students in grades 5 to 12. For example, when students read a newspaper, they learn to read for different purposes than with other reading materials. They also are able to read relevant material that appears adult-like, which is especially motivating for students with special needs.

Here are some sections of the newspaper and the unique reading skills that are required for effective understanding of each:

- *Local and national news stories:* Locating main ideas and important details (who, what, where, when, why, and how), recognizing sequence, making inferences and drawing conclusions, recognizing cause–effect relationships and recognizing comparison–contrast relationships.
- *Editorials and letters-to-the-editor:* Discriminating between fact and opinion, recognizing an author's biases, recognizing an author's purposes, identifying various propaganda techniques, making inferences, and drawing conclusions.
- *Sports section:* Reading for pleasure, locating main ideas and important details, and recognizing sequence.
- *Classified advertisements:* Locating main ideas and important details and detecting propaganda techniques.
- *Advertisements:* Detecting propaganda devices, discriminating between fact and opinion, making inferences, drawing conclusions, and improving critical reading skills.
- *Weather:* Interpreting maps, charts, and tables.
- *Entertainment section:* Interpreting the TV schedule (reading for important details), critical reading, detecting propaganda techniques, and reading to follow directions.

Student newspapers such as the *Weekly Reader* and *Know Your World* are most often used in elementary and middle-school classrooms. *Know Your World* is designed for students who are ten to sixteen years old but are reading on a second- to third-grade reading level, whereas *Weekly Reader* has a separate publication for each grade level.

Here are several activities that may motivate students in grades 5 to 12 to read newspapers more effectively:

- Have students choose news stories from a local, regional, or national newspaper. Then have them locate the *who, what, where, when, why,* and *how* in these news stories.
- Place a number of news stories with the headlines cut off and the headlines themselves into a large brown envelope. Then have students match the correct headline with the correct news story. This activity can be made self-checking.
- Provide students with copies of news stories about the same event from two different newspapers. Have them find the similarities and differences between the two news stories and discuss in what ways they are alike and different.
- Have students compare a news story and an editorial on the same topic. Discuss the similarities and differences.
- Select editorials and letters-to-the-editor that have divergent opinions on the same topic. Have students locate the emotional language and propaganda techniques in each editorial or letter-to-the-editor and mark it.
- Have students locate newspaper advertisements that illustrate the various types of propaganda techniques.
- Have students use the index of a newspaper to locate the page on which various items such as the obituaries, the weather, the letters-to-the-editor, the comic strips, the quotes from the New York Stock Exchange, the sports, and the local news are found.
- Have students examine a newspaper for possible typographical errors and have them discuss the effect of these errors on the material in which they appeared.
- Have students write their own classified advertisements following the abbreviated model language found in the classified ads in a newspaper.

Study Guides and Pattern Guides

Study guides are flexible classroom-tested devices that help students during and after reading. They can be used effectively both in social studies and science in grades 5 to 12. Study guides can take many forms, such as asking students to respond mentally or in writing to a series of questions about a reading assignment, complete a time line, construct a semantic map or a structured overview, formulate a comparison–contrast chart, list the steps of a process, or solve a crossword puzzle. The most effective guides help students organize information and reflect on it.

Briefly, here is a procedure to follow when constructing a study guide.

1. Analyze the selection to be read. Notice the major concepts or principles for your students to learn. Make a note of the sections that students must read to understand the concepts. Indicate those pages that students may skip because they do not contain important concepts.

2. Consider elements of the assignment that may pose problems for students, such as difficult vocabulary, figurative language, complex organization, or difficult to understand explanations.

3. Assess the organizational patterns of the chapter, such as sequential, process–explanation, cause–effect, comparison–contrast, or enumeration–description.

4. Notice the strategies or skills that students might need to understand the material most effectively.

5. Construct a study guide that helps students learn the important content, helps them understand the material effectively, and helps them use the most effective strategies and skills.

Noticing the pattern of writing in a content assignment improves understanding and remembering (Herber, 1970). A *pattern guide* may be a partially completed outline in which the main ideas are included or it may involve matching causes and effects of a comparison–contrast pattern. A pattern guide helps students obtain important information from a content assignment and organize the information so they can notice the main ideas and see how the details relate to them.

Cause-and-Effect Radio Show

This activity is most effective in grades 5 to 9. One group of students prepares a radio script or newscast to present to the class. The news can be either serious or humorous. Several possible topics are student elections in the school, upcoming school events, local or national current events, or real-life stories about students or teachers. A microphone from a tape recorder can be used. The student audience listens to the "newscast" and makes a cause–effect chart, noting five effects of five causes. The group of newscasters determines if they are correct or not.

The Mnemonic Method

Mnemonics are artificial memory devices, such as using verses to remember various concepts and facts in a content area such as social studies. Mnemonics are helpful when it is not possible to create more meaningful connections. One especially useful mnemonic device is the keyword technique.

The *keyword technique* uses visual images to build associations. To use the keyword technique, students create a keyword that sounds like the item they want to remember. For example, to remember the name *General Colin Powell*, the former head of the Joint Chiefs of Staff, students might select the word *pound.* Then they create an interactive image that involves both the keyword and the person's accomplishment. For General Powell, the interactive image might be General Powell *pounding on the table* during a meeting of the Joint Chiefs. The keyword technique may aid memory because when students see the name *Powell,* they think of the word *pound.*

Many traditional rhymes were written primarily to help students remember concepts and facts. Here is an example: *Thirty days hath September, April, June, and November. All the rest have thirty-one except February, which has twenty-eight and twenty-nine in a leap year.*

Words made from the first letter of a series of words are often used to help memory. They are called *acronyms* and here are some examples:

ATM: Automated teller machine
CEO: Chief executive officer
DOA: Dead on arrival
IQ: Intelligence quotient
MIA: Missing in action
NAACP: National Association for the Advancement of Colored People
SAT: Scholastic Aptitude Test
TBA: To be arranged
VCR: Video cassette recorder
UN: United Nations

In *acrostics* a phrase is used to learn a series of unrelated words or letters. For example, *Every Good Boy Does Fine* has been used for many years as a help in memorizing the letters of the musical scale (*E, G, B, D,* and *F*). Acrostics and acronyms work effectively because they provide a way to organize information whose natural organization is random.

However, the most effective mnemonic devices are those that students create for themselves. The teacher can help students create rhymes or other devices for remembering important dates, names, rules, or other items that must be remembered. It should be noted that all of the strategies for using graphic aids described earlier in this section are appropriate for improving study skills in social studies because that is the content area in which they are most applicable.

Strategies for Improving Study Skills While Reading Science

Reading and science teachers can use a number of strategies to improve students' study skills while reading science materials. You should modify any of those presented here based on the needs, abilities, and interests of your students.

Thematic Units of Instruction

It is very helpful to teach science in *thematic units.* Thematic or unit teaching helps students understand more easily the relationships between science and the other content areas. Thematic unit teaching in science is less common at the secondary-school level than in the middle school. It is an attempt to integrate other content areas such as literature, social studies, mathematics, art, music, and drama into the learning of science material.

When thematic unit teaching is used in science, the science teacher, in consultation with the literature, social studies, and mathematics teachers, selects one important *theme* or *unit* to be studied for a particular time period, such as four weeks. One possible middle-school science topic is *the immune system.* The important content about the immune system is learned by the students with the teachers mainly acting as *facilitators of learning* instead of lecturers or presenters. The students use the content areas of literature, social studies, science, and mathematics, and perhaps art, music, and drama, to learn about the immune system. Most of the learning involves active participation by the students working independently, in groups, or with the entire class, and using material from all the different content areas when appropriate.

To summarize, in thematic unit teaching all of the material the students learn usually is relevant and encourages students' active involvement. They also are encouraged to read appropriate material on their reading level, which is especially helpful to those with special needs. All types of materials are employed in thematic unit teaching, such as content textbooks at various levels, informational trade books at different levels, and reference books of various types such as print encyclopedias and encyclopedias on CD-ROM.

Exclusion Brainstorming

Exclusion brainstorming can be used in prereading to activate and build students' background knowledge before reading. A reading or content teacher can distribute a list of words, most of which are related to the main ideas presented in the reading assignment. Then the teacher can ask students to mark words that they think are related to the main ideas presented in the reading assignment. Students then read the assignment to note if they marked the correct words (Johns, Van Leirsburg, and Davis, 1994).

Survey Q3R

Survey Q3R can usually be employed in its original form with science material. As stated earlier, Survey Q3R consists of the following main steps: *survey, question, read, recite, review.* When Survey Q3R is used in reading scientific material, the final or review step may be enhanced if you have students summarize what they have read by constructing a semantic map or writing a brief summary. Either of these follow-up strategies can help them firmly fix in their minds the important technical vocabulary and concepts that they learned from the reading. Thus, this final step should enable them to be better prepared for a test on a chapter or unit.

The Inquiry Method

The *inquiry method* is a questioning strategy that is applicable in science classes. It encourages students to ask questions abut the content assignment in the form of *hypotheses.* The teacher then answers only *Yes* or *No* to each of the questions. If students formulate enough correct question hypotheses, they should arrive at the correct conclusion. In addition, the reading or science teacher always should encourage students to ask questions about their science textbook assignments in order to be critical readers. For example, a teacher might ask students to read a science assignment as if they were scientific investigators trying to research a particular problem. They should determine what kind of questions they would ask and why they would ask them.

The Directed Reading Inquiry

The *Directed Reading Inquiry (DIA)* is based on the Directed Reading-Thinking Activity (DR-TA). This strategy is applicable for study reading in scientific material. The DR-TA strategy includes the following main steps:

- Make predictions from title clues.
- Make predictions from picture clues.
- Read the material.
- Assess the accuracy of the predictions, adjusting the predictions as needed.
- Repeat the procedure until all parts of the lesson have been covered.

DIA suggests that students preview a part of a science reading assignment and predict responses to the questions *who*, *what*, *where*, *how*, and *why*. The reading or content teacher then records the answers on the chalkboard. After class discussion of the ideas, students read to confirm or change their predictions. The predictions provide a purpose for reading, and along with class discussion, provide the mindset needed for approaching the reading of scientific material.

Science Dominoes

This gamelike activity can be used in grades 5 to 8 for analyzing the word derivations of scientific terms. To construct it, cut rectangular dominoes measuring 1 inch by 1½ inches from stiff cardboard. On one domino write two derivatives of the same scientific term on both ends. This double derivative is to be used as the beginning domino. For the remainder, write two words with different derivatives on each domino.

The game begins by having the players turn all the dominoes face-down, with each player drawing five dominoes. The student who has the double domino should place it on the table. If no player has the double domino, all the dominoes are returned face-down to the middle, and the players draw again. In turn, each player tries to match one end of the domino to an open end of another domino already played. The player who cannot make a match draws up to five dominoes from those remaining. If a match is not possible, the player loses a turn. The game ends when one player has used up all of his or her dominoes or no one can play. In this case, the player with the fewest number of dominoes is the winner.

Here are examples of scientific terms that can be used in this activity:

cardiac	cardiology	cardiogram	cardiovascular	cardiologist
microscope	telescope	periscope	stethoscope	telescopic
psychiatry	podiatry	pediatrician	geriatrics	psychiatrist
optician	optometrist	optic	optical	optically
analysis	paralysis	electrolysis	catalyst	analyst

Is There a Correct Answer?

This activity is designed to develop the skills of problem solving and predicting. The teacher prepares copies of incomplete fictitious events that relate to some concept in science and to students' extracurricular experiences as well as three or four different endings to the event. The students then decide which of the endings the character in the story would most likely select and try to justify their answers. After each student has made a selection, he or she joins classmates who have chosen the same answer. The group then prepares a rationale for their response and presents it to the class. Here are several examples of incidents that can be used in this activity:

> Even though there is a recycling bin for aluminum soda cans in Eisenhower Middle School, a student sees one of his classmates throwing a soda can into a trash barrel. Which of the following actions does the first student take?
>
> a. He says nothing about it to the other student.
> b. He explains in detail the importance of recycling aluminum soda cans to the second student.
> c. He removes the soda can from the trash barrel himself and places it in the recycling bin.

During an experiment in chemistry class, a student notices that her lab partner has put the wrong chemical into a glass beaker. Which of the following actions does the first student take?

a. She does nothing.
b. She tells the student that he has put the wrong chemical in the beaker for this experiment.
c. She throws away all the chemicals in the beaker so that the experiment cannot take place.

Do You Know the Meaning?

This game can be used in grades 5 to 8 for the purpose of improving scientific vocabulary knowledge. To construct the game, draw circles with scientific vocabulary written in each of them on a large piece of cardboard. Here are some examples of scientific terms: *mitosis, igneous, hematocrit, lava, stratosphere, radiation, hydrocarbon, deciduous, estrogen.*

The game board is placed on a table, and players sit about three feet away. Using small plastic disks, the players aim for any scientific term. They must give the technical meaning of whatever word a disk lands on. A student judge decides if the definitions are acceptable. Players receive ten points each time they know the correct meaning of a term. The game ends when each word has been given a correct definition, and the winner is the player with the most points.

Strategies for Improving Study Skills While Reading Mathematics

Reading and mathematics teachers can use several strategies to improve their students' study skills while reading mathematics materials. You should modify any of those presented here based on the needs, abilities, and interests of your students.

Thematic Units of Instruction

It is helpful to teach mathematics in *thematic units* as much as possible. Thematic unit teaching in mathematics enables students to use what they have learned as a tool for solving important, meaningful problems. When thematic unit teaching is used in mathematics, the mathematics teacher, in consultation with the reading, social studies, and science teachers, selects one important theme or unit (often from social studies or science) that is going to be studied for a time period such as four weeks. Much, if not all, of the content about the theme is selected by the students themselves with teacher direction if necessary. Most of the learning about the theme or topic involves active participation by the students themselves working independently, in groups, or in the entire class.

Mathematical word (verbal) problems are a very important part of thematic unit teaching in mathematics. In this type of teaching, the mathematical verbal problems that are used always should evolve between the collective efforts of teachers and students. These word problems should be integrated with literature, social studies, science, music, art, and drama whenever possible.

In a variation of thematic unit teaching, the reading or mathematics teacher identifies a curricular topic in mathematics, and students then identify real-life problems. Students can formulate their own word problems that are related to the unit and then either solve them on their own or "publish" them for other students to solve. They also can formulate new word problems from old problems, which enhances their understanding of mathematics and integrates prior knowledge with new knowledge. A student can formulate a topic for a mathematics word problem from his or her own related interests.

Understanding Mathematical Materials and Solving Mathematics Word Problems

According to Collier and Redmond (1974), mathematics material is very concise and abstract and involves complex relationships. They suggested the following procedure to help students understand mathematical materials and solve mathematics word problems.

1. Read the material rapidly or at a normal rate in order to get an overview and to determine the main points.
2. Read the material a second time, this time "more slowly, critically, and analytically," and determine the details and relationships involved.
3. Read some parts of the material a number of times if it is required, varying the purpose each time.
4. Determine the relevant operation or operations.
5. Decide which operations must be performed to solve the problem.
6. Determine whether all of the needed information is given to solve the problem.
7. Read the numerals and operation symbols needed to solve the problem.
8. Adjust the reading rate to the difficulty of the material. Mathematical word problems must be read at a slow, analytical rate.

SQRQCQ

A plan similar to Survey Q3R has been developed especially for mathematical word problems; it is called *SQRQCQ*. As with Survey Q3R, the reading or mathematics teacher should model SQRQCQ for the class and conduct whole-class practice before expecting students to try the strategy independently. In addition, the teacher must remind students to use this strategy regularly before they can be expected to use it consistently. Here are the steps of this study strategy (adapted from "Reading Study Skills: Math and Science," Fay, 1965):

- *Survey*: Read through the mathematical word (verbal) problem quickly to get an overall impression of what the problem is about.
- *Question*: Ask yourself general questions relating to problem solving such as: "What is the problem to be solved?" "What do I need to find out?" "What important information is provided in this word problem?"
- *Read*: Read the problem again carefully, paying close attention to details and relationships that will help in the problem-solving process.

- *Question*: Answer the question: "What mathematical operation or operations are needed to solve this problem?"
- *Compute:* Do the computation decided on in the previous step.
- *Question*: Answer the question: "Does this answer make sense?" If not, then you may need to repeat some or all of the process.

How Is Your Stock Doing?

This activity is designed for students in grades 5 to 8. Help students choose a particular stock and keep track of its gains and losses by reading the report in the newspaper. Students then can graph the daily fluctuations by putting the date on the x-axis and the gains or losses on the y-axis. The class can have a car wash or bake sale and buy several shares of their own stock.

Find the Treasure

This activity can be used in grades 5 to 8. Hide a small "treasure" somewhere in the classroom. Place clues around the room that describe tasks to be completed in order to locate the object. The clues may say: "Measure 19 feet 5 inches from the desk" or "Divide 144 by 12 and walk that number of feet to find the clue." Construct a different set of clues for each player.

Add It in Your Head

This activity is designed to provide practice in the skill of *estimating* in an everyday situation. Have the students go shopping with a family member or friend when a number of items are being purchased in a grocery store, a drug store, discount department store, or hardware store. Without using paper and pencil, have the students keep a running estimate of items as they are placed into the shopping cart. Have them include an estimate of the sales tax and then round off.

After the shopping has been completed, the student should tell their companion their estimate, which is then written on the back of the cash register receipt. Then, on a chosen date, discuss with the class what type of estimation errors were made most often and why. Then collect the cash register slips to study the errors and identify students who need additional help with this skill.

Reproducible Activity Sheets for Improving Study Skills in the Content Areas

Chapter Seven now provides seven reproducible activity sheets for improving study skills in the content areas of literature, social studies, science, and mathematics. You can duplicate them in their present form or alter them in any way you wish based on the needs and interests of your own students. In addition, they can serve as models for you in constructing similar activity sheets for improving study skills while reading content material.

The seven reproducible activity sheets are as follows: Organizing Material—Seventh- to Eighth-Grade Level; The Dewey Decimal System—Fifth-Grade Level; Interpreting Two Bar Graphs—Sixth-Grade Level; Interpreting an Air Flight Chart—Sixth- to Eighth-Grade Level; Skimming for Specific Purposes—Seventh- to Eighth-Grade Level; Using the Newspaper Effectively—Sixth- to Eighth-Grade Level; Roman Numeral "Brain Teasers"—Sixth- to Eighth-Grade Level.

Answer Key for Organizing Material

Note: The following answers are for illustrative purposes only; evaluate each student's answers in light of the information presented in the passage. I. Nova Scotia, a Maritime Province: A. Comprises the peninsula of Nova Scotia, Cape Breton Island, and several small islands; B. Bounded by a number of different bodies of water; C. Population is about one million; D. Main industries are fishing, shipbuilding, and transatlantic shipping. II. Halifax: A. Capital of Nova Scotia; B. Modern port city; C. Has many museums, galleries, restaurants, and gardens; D. Charming seaside towns are located nearby. III. The Climate of Nova Scotia: A. Owes its climate to the sea; B. Abundant snowfall and thick fogs; C. Cape Breton Island is wettest section; D. Winter storms can be fierce; E. Halifax is a foggy and misty city. IV. Minerals of Nova Scotia: A. Many top-quality minerals inland and by the seashore; B. Bay of Fundy has excellent zeolites. V. History of Nova Scotia: A. Region first visited by the Vikings in 1000 A.D.; B. Micmac Native Americans were original inhabitants; C. French settlers named the region Acadia; D. Treaty of Utrecht awarded area to England in 1713 after conflict with France; E. Many English Loyalists emigrated to region after American Revolution; F. Joined Dominion of Canada in 1867.

Answer Key for The Dewey Decimal System

1. 400–499; 2. 500–599; 3. 100–199; 4. 800–899; 5. 900–999; 6. 700–799; 7. 600–699; 8. 200–299; 9. 000–099; 10. 900–999; 11. 000–099; 12. 600–699; 13. 400–499; 14. 200–299; 15. 300–399; 16. 500–599; 17. 900–999; 18. 600–699; 19. 700–799; 20. 800–899

Answer Key for Interpreting Two Bar Graphs

1. b; 2. c; 3. a; 4. d; 5. b; 6. a; 7. b; 8. a; 9. b; 10. d

Answer Key for Interpreting an Air Flight Chart

1. SE 990; 2. US Air 1650; 3. US Air 1820; 4. AA 316; 5. AA 316; 6. AA 221; 7. AA 751; 8. AA 1425; 9. SE 990; 10. SE 427

Answer Key for Skimming for Specific Purposes

Note: The facts and details included here are only for illustrative purposes. Examine your students' answers to determine if each fact or detail is correct as stated in the passage. 1. When a person has sickle cell anemia, the red blood cells are crescent shaped. 2. Sickle cell anemia is caused by an abnormal type of hemoglobin. 3. Sickle cell anemia is inherited as an autosomal recessive trait. 4. Sickle cell anemia is most common in African Americans and to a lesser degree in Hispanic Americans. 5. The disease can be life-threatening when damaged red blood cells break down or bone marrow fails to produce blood cells. 6. Genetic counseling is recommended for all carriers with the sickle cell trait. 7. Sickle cell anemia can be treated with a bone marrow transplant. 8. Persons with sickle cell anemia can live relatively normal lives even without a bone marrow transplant. 9. Medicines can be given to control the pain, and penicillin can help prevent infection. 10. Although hydroxyurea is a new drug that may help patients with sickle cell anemia, it has not been approved for use in children.

Answer Key for Using the Newspaper Effectively

Note: Some of the questions on this activity sheet can only be answered by the students themselves. Here are the other answers that you may want to use in evaluating this activity sheet: 6a. This section summaries the activities in the city or region that people can use for entertainment or to view art or cultural exhibits. Movie descriptions and reviews, theater descriptions and reviews, descriptions and reviews of art exhibits are some of the features that can be found in this section. 6b. This section provides a description of a deceased's life. Usually people who have died recently in the community, region, or nation are included here. 6c. These are several words placed at the beginning of a news story or article that very briefly describe its contents. 6d. This is the name of the person who wrote the news story or article. 6e. This is the Associated Press, a wire service that provides news for local newspapers. 6f. This is United Press International, a wire service that provides news for local newspapers. 6g. This section includes interesting articles about the lives of people whom readers may identify with. Several examples might be an article about a local quilter, a birdwatcher, a jogger, among many others. 6h. These are statements of opinion written by the management of the newspaper. 6i. These are paid or unpaid endorsements for local or national politicians. 6j. This is a person who writes an opinion column that is distributed on a nationwide or regional basis. 6k. These are short advertisements that are paid for by people who may or may not be subscribers to a newspaper. They are in a large variety of categories such as Help Wanted Ads, Automobiles for Sales, Pets for Sale, Garage Sales, among many others. 6l. This is the newspaper listing of owner, address, and so on. 6m. These are both personal advice columns. 6n. This is a line giving the date in a newspaper. 6o. This is a service that provides up-to-the-minute news for newspapers. 7a. A10; 7b. A12; 7c. A2; 7d. B8; 7e. C1; 7f. B1; 7g. D1; 7h. D5; 7i. B5; 7j. A5; 7k. A1; 7l. B3.

Answer Key for Roman Numeral "Brain Teasers"

1. L + END = LEND; 2. M + AID = MAID; 3. L + OAF = LOAF; 4. D + ATE = DATE; 5. M + ALL = MALL; 6. V + AT = VAT; 7. L + AND = LAND; 8. D + ON = DON; 9. C + ASK = CASK; 10. V + ICE = VICE; 11. L + INK = LINK; 12. C + ALL = CALL; 13. M + OLD = MOLD; 14. D + ILL = DILL; 15. V + OMIT = VOMIT; 16. D + RIP = DRIP; 17. C + HIP = CHIP; 18. M + EAT = MEAT; 19. D + RUM = DRUM; 20. M + ANGLE = MANGLE

Name ________________________ Grade ___ Teacher ____________ Date __________

Organizing Material

Read this passage about the Canadian province of *Nova Scotia* and *complete the partially finished outline* about the material.

Nova Scotia

Nova Scotia, Canada, is one of the Maritime Provinces. It comprises the peninsula of Nova Scotia, Cape Breton Island, and a few small adjacent islands. It is bounded by the Northumberland Straits, the Gulf of St. Lawrence, the Atlantic Ocean, the Bay of Fundy, and New Brunswick. The population of Nova Scotia is approximately one million, and its economic mainstays are fishing, shipbuilding, and transatlantic shipping.

Halifax, the capital of Nova Scotia, is a modern port city that has a unique culture and heritage. It offers an impressive array of entertainment, museums, galleries, historic sites, fine restaurants, colorful gardens, and lively nightlife. Near to Halifax are a number of charming seaside towns, sun-drenched beaches, sparkling coves, and miles of rugged shoreline guarded by graceful lighthouses.

Nova Scotia owes its climate to the sea. It has beautiful winters with lavish snowfalls, misty sunlight, thick fogs, and expansive sea ice. The highlands of Cape Breton Island are the wettest part of Nova Scotia, but there is a good supply of precipitation over all of it. Storms frequently pass close to the Atlantic Coast of Nova Scotia, and winter storms are especially devastating. Halifax has a reputation as a foggy and misty city with an average of 122 foggy days at the Halifax International Airport.

Nova Scotia is a mineral collector's paradise. A wide range of top-quality minerals can be found at many sites, both inland and along the seashore. The Bay of Fundy region offers world-class zeolites, and the world's highest tides are continually exposing new material.

The region was first visited by the Vikings in 1000 A.D., and it was inhabited by the Micmac Native Americans when John Cabot claimed it for England in 1497. In 1605 French settlers adopted the Micmac name *Acadia* for the region. English and Scottish colonists arrived by 1621. The conflict between France and England over control of the area was ended by the 1713 Treaty of Utrecht, which awarded it to England. In the 1750s the British expelled most of the French settlers. After the American Revolution, many Loyalists who had supported England in the war emigrated there. Nova Scotia joined the Dominion of Canada in 1867 as one of the original members.

Name ________________________ Grade ___ Teacher ____________ Date __________

Organizing Material, continued

Outline of "Nova Scotia"

I. Nova Scotia, a Maritime Province

A.

B.

C.

D.

II. Halifax

A.

B.

C.

D.

III. The Climate of Nova Scotia

A.

B.

C.

D.

E.

IV. Minerals of Nova Scotia

A.

B.

V. History of Nova Scotia

A.

B.

C.

D.

E.

F.

Name ______________________ Grade ___ Teacher ____________ Date _________

The Dewey Decimal System

Using this table, write the numbers for the library classifications for the book titles that are found under it.

000–099	Generalities
100–199	Philosophy and related
200–299	Religion
300–399	The social sciences
400–499	Language
500–599	Pure science
600–699	Technology (applied science)
700–799	The arts
800–899	Literature and rhetoric
900–999	General geography and history, and so on

1. ________________ *The Relationship Between the Finnish and Hungarian Languages*
2. ________________ *The Benefits of Joint Replacement Surgery*
3. ________________ *Philosophers of the Twentieth Century*
4. ________________ *The Poetry of Robert Frost*
5. ________________ *The History of Ancient China*
6. ________________ *George Gershwin's Music*
7. ________________ *Growing a Bonsai Tree*
8. ________________ *The Quran (Koran)*
9. ________________ *The Encyclopedia Britannica*
10. ________________ *Taking a Barge Cruise on the Seine River*
11. ________________ *The Farmer's Almanac*
12. ________________ *The International Space Station*
13. ________________ *Thompson's Latin Grammar*
14. ________________ *The Gods of Ancient Egypt*
15. ________________ *Native American Legends*
16. ________________ *Advanced Calculus*
17. ________________ *The Battle of Vicksburg*
18. ________________ *The Boston Terrier*
19. ________________ *The Art of Picasso and Other Cubists*
20. ________________ *See How They Run* (a stage play)

Name ____________ Grade ___ Teacher ____________ Date ________

Interpreting Two Bar Graphs

Examine the following two bar graphs carefully. They illustrate the *monthly* and *annual average temperature* and *precipitation* in the desert city of *Tucson, Arizona.* After you have studied the two graphs carefully, answer the questions on the next sheet. You may work with a partner or partners if you wish.

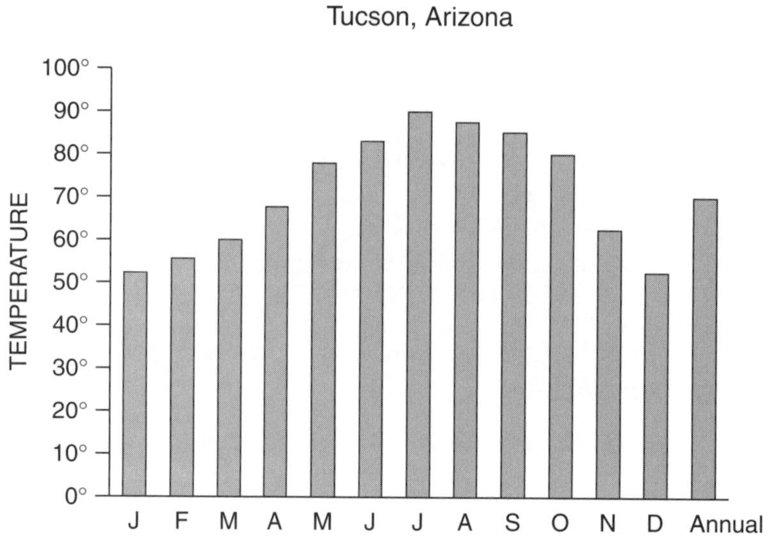

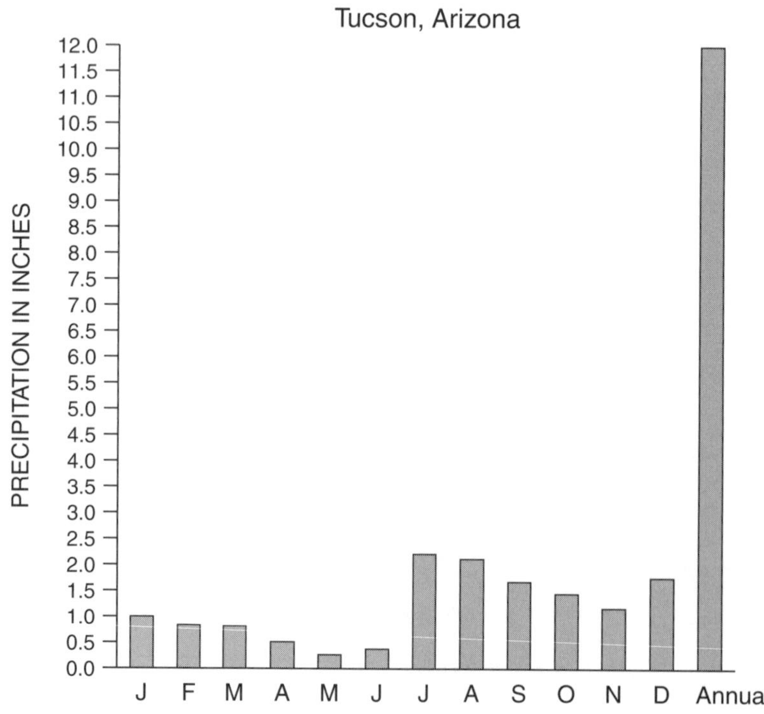

Name ____________________ Grade ___ Teacher ____________ Date _________

Interpreting Two Bar Graphs, continued

1. What is the mean temperature in Tucson, Arizona, for the month of July?

   a. 79.2 b. 86.5 c. 66.0 d. 80.9

2. What is the coolest month of the year in Tucson, Arizona?

   a. February b. December c. January d. November

3. What is the annual mean temperature for Tucson, Arizona?

   a. 68.6 b. 59.1 c. 74.2 d. 58.8

4. What is the mean temperature in Tucson, Arizona, for the month of March?

   a. 54.6 b. 70.7 c. 80.9 d. 58.8

5. What is the hottest month in Tucson, Arizona?

   a. June b. July c. August d. September

6. What is the annual total precipitation in inches for Tucson, Arizona?

   a. 11.65 b. 9.80 c. 10.01 d. 13.4

7. What is the driest month in Tucson, Arizona?

   a. May b. June c. January d. April

8. What is the wettest month in Tucson, Arizona?

   a. September b. July c. October d. December

9. What are the three driest months in Tucson, Arizona?

   a. April, May, June
   b. January, February, March
   c. October, November, December
   d. February, March, April

10. What are the three wettest months in Tucson, Arizona?

    a. January, February, March
    b. July, August, September
    c. September, October, December
    d. August, September, October

11. What is the amount of precipitation in inches for the month of September in Tucson, Arizona?

    a. 1.91 b. .96 c. 2.20 d. 1.38

Name ____________________ Grade ___ Teacher ____________ Date _________

Interpreting an Air Flight Chart

Read this *air flight chart* carefully and then answer the questions below.

Flights to Tampa, Florida, from Las Vegas, Nevada

Depart	Arrive	Flight Number
6:00 A.M.	9:15 A.M.	AA 751
7:15 A.M.	10:30 A.M.	US Air 1650
9:30 A.M.	12:45 P.M.	SE 880
11:45 A.M.	1:50 P.M.	AA 221
2:30 P.M.	6:00 P.M.	SE 427
3:05 P.M.	6:40 P.M.	AA 316
5:10 P.M.	8:25 P.M.	US Air 1820
7:10 P.M.	10:40 P.M.	SE 990
8:20 P.M.	11:55 P.M.	AA 1425

1. What flight arrives in Tampa at 10:40 P.M.?

   ____

2. What flight arrives in Tampa at 10:30 A.M.?

   ____

3. What flight leaves Las Vegas at 5:10 P.M.?

   ____

4. What flight arrives in Tampa at 6:40 P.M.?

   ____

5. What flight leaves Las Vegas at 3:05 P.M.?

   ____

6. What flight leaves Las Vegas at 11:45 A.M.?

   ____

7. What flight arrives in Tampa at 9:15 A.M.?

   ____

8. What flight arrives in Tampa at 11:55 P.M.?

   ____

9. What flight leaves Las Vegas at 7:10 P.M.?

   ____

10. What flight arrives at Tampa at 6:00 P.M.?

   ____

Name ________________________ **Grade** ___ **Teacher** ____________ **Date** _________

Skimming for Specific Purposes

Read the following passage about *sickle cell anemia.*

Sickle Cell Anemia

Sickle cell anemia is a chronic disease in which the red blood cells that normally are *disc-shaped* become *crescent shaped.* As a result they function abnormally and break down, causing painful episodes.

Sickle cell anemia is caused by an abnormal type of *hemoglobin,* the oxygen-carrying pigment in the blood. It is inherited as an *autosomal recessive trait,* which means it occurs in someone who has inherited hemoglobin *S* from both parents. A person who inherits hemoglobin *S* from one parent and normal hemoglobin from the other will have the *sickle cell trait.* A person with the sickle cell trait will usually have only mild symptoms or no symptoms of sickle cell anemia.

Sickle cell anemia occurs in *eight* out of *one hundred thousand* persons. However, it is much more common in certain populations, affecting *one* out of *six hundred* African Americans and *one* out of *a thousand* to *fourteen hundred* Hispanic Americans. This disease may become life-threatening when damaged red blood cells break down or bone marrow fails to produce blood cells. Repeated crises can cause damage to the kidneys, lungs, bones, liver, and central nervous system. These painful crises, which occur in 70% of patients, can last hours to days. Some patients have one episode every few years, whereas others have many episodes per year. The crisis can be severe enough to require admission to the hospital for pain control and intravenous fluids.

Because sickle cell anemia can result when two carriers with the sickle cell trait have a child together, genetic counseling is recommended for all carriers of the sickle cell trait.

General health visits to a physician are recommended to ensure that patients are receiving adequate nutrition and proper vaccinations and are maintaining proper activity levels.

Sickle cell anemia can be treated with a bone marrow transplant, which is a complicated procedure. To qualify, a patient needs a bone marrow donor providing a match with a low risk of being rejected. Even without a cure that is provided by a bone marrow transplant, persons with sickle cell anemia can live relatively normal lives. Medicines can be used to manage the pain, and daily doses of penicillin can help prevent infection. Most doctors prescribe daily doses of vitamin supplements as well. Folic acid in particular can help produce new red blood cells. Patients who develop complications from sickle cell anemia may receive regular transfusions of red blood cells. *Hydroxyurea* is a relatively new drug for people with sickle cell anemia, but the U.S. Food and Drug Administration has not approved it for use in children.

Now, on another sheet of paper, briefly list ten facts or details you remember about sickle cell anemia.

Name ________________________ Grade ___ Teacher ____________ Date _________

Using the Newspaper Effectively

Read the material on this activity sheet about *using the newspaper* effectively. Then *answer each question.* You may work with a partner or partners if you wish.

1. What are the names of the newspaper or newspapers that come to your home?

   ____

2. Put a check mark in front of the parts of the newspaper that you read regularly.

   _____ National news section
   _____ Local news section
   _____ Sports section
   _____ Editorials
   _____ Letters-to-the-editor
   _____ Features
   _____ Comic strips
   _____ Entertainment/arts section
   _____ Obituaries
   _____ Advertisements
   _____ Classified advertisements
   _____ Other sections (write their names on the back of this sheet)

3. Where is the index in the newspaper that you read?

   ____

4. Where is the weather in the newspaper that you read?

   ____

5. How do you locate the part of the newspaper that you read? Check one.

   _____ Use the index.
   _____ Turn to each page and look for it.

6. Write a brief description for each of the following newspaper terms.

   a. Entertainment/arts section

   ____

   b. Obituaries

   ____

   c. Headline

   ____

   d. Byline

   ____

   e. AP

   ____

   f. UPI

   ____

Name ________________________ Grade ___ Teacher ____________ Date _________

Using the Newspaper Effectively, continued

g. Features section

____

h. Editorials

____

i. Political endorsements

____

j. Syndicated columnist

____

k. Classified advertisements

____

l. Masthead

____

m. "Dear Abby" or "Ann Landers"

____

n. Dateline

____

o. Wire service

____

7. Read the following newspaper index and then answer the questions:

Index

National news: A1
Birthdays in the news: A2
Local news: A3
International news: A5
Regional news: A7
Obituaries: A10
Letters-to-the editor: A12
Bill O'Reilly's syndicated column: A13
Bill Flick's column: B1
Anniversaries and weddings: B3
Health news: B5
Food/eating out section: B8
Sports: C1
Business news: D1
Classified advertisements: D5

Name ________________________ **Grade** ___ **Teacher** ____________ **Date** _________

Using the Newspaper Effectively, continued

a. Where would you look to find out who has died in the city or surrounding areas?

____

b. Where would you look to find a letter to the editor about a sewer bond referendum?

____

c. Where would you look to see which celebrities are celebrating a birthday today?

____

d. Where would you look for a restaurant review by a restaurant critic?

____

e. Where would you look to see who won a Green Bay Packers–Chicago Bears football game?

____

f. Where would you look to find Bill Flick's column?

____

g. Where would you look to find the latest stock market quotes?

____

h. Where would you look to find a kennel that sells Boston Terriers?

____

i. Where would you look to find an article on the benefits of exercise?

____

j. Where would you look to find a news story about the conflict between Israel and Palestine?

____

k. Where would you look to find an article about the budget crisis in Washington, D.C.?

____

l. Where would you look to find an article about your sister's recent wedding?

____

Name ______________________ Grade ___ Teacher ___________ Date _________

Roman Numeral "Brain Teasers"

This activity sheet contains some brain teasers using Roman numerals. Read each one and then substitute the correct Roman numeral for its Arabic equivalent. You can use the chart of Roman numerals on this activity sheet if you wish. Then think of a word for the definition given in the equation. Combine the Roman numeral with the word to formulate a *new word* for each example. An example has been provided for you. You may work with a partner or partners if you wish.

Roman Numerals	
I =1	C = 100
V = 5	D = 500
X = 10	M = 1000
L = 50	

Example: 500 + a piece of cloth = PULL

D + RAG = DRAG

1. 50 + STOP = to give the use of for a time

   _______ + ______________ = ________________________

2. 1000 + HELP = servant

   _______ + ______________ = ________________________

3. 50 + DOLT = shaped as bread

   _______ + ______________ = ________________________

4. 500 + PAST TENSE OF EAT = a social engagement

   _______ + ______________ = ________________________

5. 1000 + EVERYONE OF = an enclosed shopping center

   _______ + ______________ = ________________________

6. 5 + A PREPOSITION = a large vessel or tank

   _______ + ______________ = ________________________

7. 50 + SIGNIFIES ADDITION = a solid portion of the earth's surface

   _______ + ______________ = ________________________

8. 500 + TO AND TOWARD THE SURFACE OF = to put on clothing

   _______ + ______________ = ________________________

9. 100 + TO REQUEST = a barrel of any size

   _______ + ______________ = ________________________

Name ________________________ Grade ___ Teacher ____________ Date _________

Roman Numeral "Brain Teasers," continued

10. 5 + WATER FROZEN SOLID BY COLD = an action or habit

    ______ + ____________ = _________________________

11. 50 + A COLORED LIQUID USED FOR WRITING = a loop or ring of a chain

    ______ + ____________ = _________________________

12. 100 + EVERYONE OF = to telephone

    ______ + ____________ = _________________________

13. 1000 + ADVANCED IN YEARS = a fungus producing a furry growth

    ______ + ____________ = _________________________

14. 500 + NOT IN GOOD HEALTH = an edible hardy annual herb

    ______ + ____________ = _________________________

15. 5 + TO LEAVE OUT = to throw up

    ______ + ____________ = _________________________

16. 500 + TO CUT OR TEAR APART = to fall in drops

    ______ + ____________ = _________________________

17. 100 + EITHER SIDE OF THE BODY BELOW THE WAIST AND ABOVE THE THIGH = to strike small pieces from the surface of

    ______ + ____________ = _________________________

18. 1000 + TO CHEW AND SWALLOW = the flesh of animals used as food

    ______ + ____________ = _________________________

19. 500 + AN ALCOHOL DISTILLED FROM FERMENTED SUGARCANE JUICES = a percussion instrument

    ______ + ____________ = _________________________

20. 1000 + THE POINT FROM WHICH LINES OR SURFACES CONVERGE = to mutilate by cutting roughly

    ______ + ____________ = _________________________

For Additional Reading

Allen, H., Barbe, W., and Levesque, T. *Ready-to-Use Vocabulary, Word Attack, and Comprehension Activities* (pp. 192–267). San Francisco: Jossey-Bass, 1998.

Barbe, W., Allen, H., and Sparkman, B. *Reading Skills Competency Tests: Advanced Level* (pp. 110–121). San Francisco: Jossey-Bass, 1999.

Donovan, E., and Smolkin, L. "Considering Genre, Content, and Visual Features in the Selection of Trade Books for Science Instruction." *Reading Teacher*, 2002, *55*, 502–520.

Miller, W. *Ready-to-Use Activities & Materials for Improving Content Reading Skills* (pp. 325–462). San Francisco: Jossey-Bass, 1999.

Reutzel, R., and Cooter, R. *Teaching Children to Read* (pp. 526–564). Upper Saddle River, N.J.: Prentice Hall/Merrill, 2000.

Rice, D. "Using Trade Books in Teaching Elementary Science: Facts and Fallacies." *Reading Teacher*, 2002, *55*, 552–565.

Roser, N., and Keehn, S. "Fostering Thought, Talk, and Inquiry: Linking Literature and Social Studies." *Reading Teacher*, 2000, *55*, 416–426.

Strichart, S., and Mangrum, C. *Teaching Study Strategies to Students with Learning Disabilities*. Needham Heights, Mass.: Allyn and Bacon, 1993.

Tompkins, G. *Literacy for the 21st Century* (pp. 456–487). Upper Saddle River, N.J.: Prentice Hall/Merrill, 2001.

Umstatter, J. *Brain Games!* San Francisco: Jossey-Bass, 1996.

Works Cited in Chapter Seven

Anderson, T., and Armbruster, B. "The Value of Taking Notes During Lectures." In R. Flippo and D. Caverly (eds.), *Teaching Reading and Study Strategies at the College Level* (pp. 166–194). Newark, Del.: International Reading Association, 1991.

Carmen, R., and Adams, W. *Study Skills: A Student's Guide to Survival.* New York: Wiley, 1972.

Caverly, D., and Orlando, V. "Textbook Study Strategies." In R. Flippo and D. Caverly (eds.), *Teaching Reading and Study Strategies at the College Level* (pp. 86–165). Newark, Del.: International Reading Association, 1991.

Collier, C., and Redmond, L. "Are You Teaching Kids to Read Mathematics?" *Reading Teacher*, 1974, *27*, 804–808.

Dana, C. "Strategy Families for Disabled Readers." *Journal of Reading*, 1989, *33*, 30–35.

Egawa, K. "Harnessing the Power of Language: First-Graders' Literature Engagement with *Owl Moon.*" *Language Arts*, 1990, *67*, 582–588.

Fay, L. "Reading Study Skills: Math and Science." In J. A. Figurel (ed.), *Reading and Inquiry.* Newark, Del.: International Reading Association, 1965.

Flippo, R. *Test Wise: Strategies for Success in Taking Tests.* New York: Fearon Teacher Aids/Simon & Schuster, 1988.

Flippo, R. *Reading Assessment and Instruction: A Qualitative Approach to Diagnosis.* Orlando: Harcourt Brace, 1997.

Foster, M., and Foster, P. *Looking It Up: Learning Library Skills.* Glencoe, Ill.: Lake, 1989.

Friedland, J., and Kessler, R. "A Top (to Bottom) Drawer Way to Teach Outlining." *Teacher*, 1980, *98*, 110–111.

Fry, E., Kress, J., and Fountoukidis, D. *The Reading Teacher's Book of Lists* (4th ed.; pp. 155–158; 138–142; 85–113). San Francisco: Jossey-Bass, 2000.

Gunning, T. *Creating Reading Instruction for All Children* (pp. 324–326). Needham Heights, Mass.: Allyn and Bacon, 1996.

Hadaway, N., and Young, T. "Content Literacy and Language Learning: Instructional Decisions." *Reading Teacher*, 1994, *47*, 522–527.

Harris, A., and Sipay, E. *How to Increase Reading Ability* (p. 652). White Plains, N.Y.: Longman, 1990.

Harvey, S. *Nonfiction Matters: Reading, Writing, and Research in Grades 3–8.* York, Me.: Stenhouse, 1998.

Hauer, Murray, Dantin, and Bolner. *Books, Libraries, and Research.* Dubuque, Iowa: Kendall/Hunt, 1987.

Hayes, D. "Initiate Cartographic Literacy with the MAP Activity." *Journal of Reading*, 1992, *35*, 659–661.

Herber, H. *Teaching Reading in Content Areas.* Englewood Cliffs, N.J.: Prentice-Hall, 1970.

Johns, J., Van Leirsburg, P., and Davis, S. *Improving Reading: A Handbook of Strategies.* Dubuque, Iowa: Kendall/Hunt, 1994.

Kiewra, K. "Students' Note-Taking Behaviors and the Efficacy of Providing the Instructor's Notes for Review." *Contemporary Educational Psychology*, 1985, *10*, 378–386.

Lapp, D., and Flood, J. *Teaching Reading to Every Child* (pp. 401–402). New York: Macmillan, 1992.

Miller, W. *Alternative Assessment Techniques for Reading & Writing.* Paramus, N.J.: Center for Applied Research in Education, 1995.

Miller, W. *Ready-to-Use Activities & Materials for Improving Content Reading Skills* (pp. 440–442). San Francisco: Jossey-Bass, 1999.

Palmatier, R. "Comparison of Four Notetaking Procedures." *Journal of Reading*, 1971, *14*, 235–240, 258.

Palmatier, R. "A Notetaking System for Learning." *Journal of Reading*, 1973, *17*, 36–39.

Reutzel, R., and Cooter, R. *Teaching Children to Read* (pp. 549–550). Upper Saddle River, N.J.: Prentice Hall/Merrill, 2000.

Rico, G. *Writing the Natural Way.* Los Angeles: Tarcher, 1983.

Robinson, F. *Effective Study.* New York: HarperCollins, 1961.

Spiegel, D. "Materials for Integrating Science and Social Studies with the Language Arts." *Reading Teacher*, 1990, *44*, 162–165.

Street Atlas USA, Version 7.0. Freeport, Me.: Delorme, 2003.

Strichart, S., and Mangrum, C., II. *Teaching Study Strategies to Students with Learning Disabilities* (pp. 129–131). Needham Heights, Mass.: Allyn and Bacon, 1993.

Other Books of Interest

The Reading Teacher's Survival Kit: Ready-to-Use Checklists, Activities and Materials to Help All Students Become Successful Readers
Wilma H. Miller, Ed.D.
$29.50 Paperback
ISBN: 0–13–042593–1
Grades K–8

This unique instructional resource is packed with ready-to-use time and work savers for virtually every aspect of the reading teacher's job, including over 120 reproducible activity sheets, assessment devices, and management tools to help students of all ability levels learn to read as proficiently as possible.

The strategies and materials presented give you the best of comprehension and phonics instruction for setting up an appropriate, well-paced reading program that meets the needs of individual students, small groups, or the entire class. They cover the full range of reading skills and provide a variety of games, activities, and reproducibles for teachers and tutors to effectively meet the individual reading needs and interests of the children with whom they are working. It will help ensure that every child learns to read up to his or her potential.

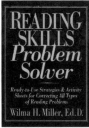

Reading Skills Problem Solver: Ready-to-Use Strategies & Activity Sheets for Correcting All Types of Reading Problems
Wilma H. Miller, Ed.D.
$32.95 Paperback
ISBN: 0–13–042206–1
Grades 3–12

Written by a nationally known authority in reading instruction, this comprehensive practical resource gives classroom teachers and reading specialists everything they need to quickly correct or remediate all types of common reading problems encountered in grades 3 and up.

Included are over 260 tested techniques and activity sheets for correcting 35 specific problems in seven major reading skill areas—from poor visual memory and mastery of consonant sounds, to difficulty identifying the main idea in a paragraph. It will help you solve student reading problems in phonics and sight word knowledge, structural and contextual analysis, literal and interpretive comprehension, and in critical thinking.

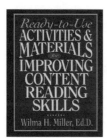

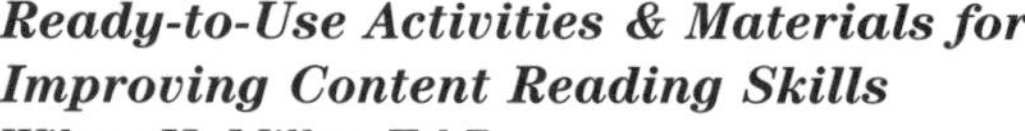

Ready-to-Use Activities & Materials for Improving Content Reading Skills
Wilma H. Miller, Ed.D.
$29.95 Paperback
ISBN: 0–13–007815–8
Grades 4–12

Evaluate and improve your students' reading, writing, study, and test-taking skills in the content areas of literature (language arts), social studies, science, and math with this exceptional resource. It first provides several ways to categorize the skills needed and offers lists of specialized vocabulary and skills required for effective reading/writing/study skill in each subject area. It then provides a multitude of ready-to-use methods and over 100 reproducible activities to help assess and improve the ability of all students to read, comprehend, write, and study.

In short, this resource gives grades 4–12 classroom teachers, content teachers, reading specialists, and special educators an unparalleled store of tested, ready-to-use information and materials for the quick, accurate evaluation and improvement of the reading, writing, and studying ability of all students.

Alternative Assessment Techniques for Reading & Writing
Wilma H. Miller, Ed.D.
$29.50 Paperback
ISBN: 0–13–042568–0
Grades 3–12

This practical resource helps elementary classroom, remedial reading, and LD teachers make the best possible informal assessment of a child's specific reading, writing, and spelling strengths and weaknesses, and attitudes toward reading.

Written in easy-to-follow non-technical language, it provides a multitude of tested informal assessment strategies and devices, such as "kid watching," retellings, journals, IRIs, writing surveys, portfolios, think-alouds, and more, including more than 200 reproducible assessment devices ready for immediate use.

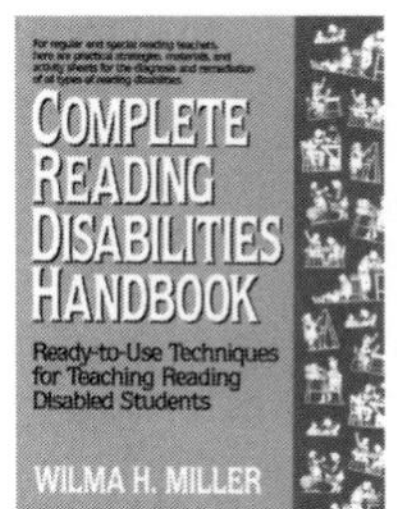

Complete Reading Disabilities Handbook: Ready-to-Use Techniques for Teaching Reading Disabled Students
Wilma H. Miller, Ed.D.
$29.50 Paperback
ISBN: 0–87628–275–3
Grades K–8

Help each child achieve his or her optimal potential in reading. This unique handbook gives reading and learning disability teachers one of the most comprehensive and practical resources available today for diagnosing and remediating all types of reading disabilities in elementary and middle school students. You'll get easy-to-follow explanations of the various courses of reading disabilities and over 100 reproducible assessment devices, corrective activity sheets, and other aids. And all of this material can be adapted for use with individual students, small groups, or an entire class.

Some of the special features in this handbook include:
* Case studies showing the causes of various reading problems
* A complete Individual Reading Inventory to determine the student's independent, instructional, and frustration reading levels
* Reproducible activity sheets for improving visual perception, letter identification, sight word recognition, structural and semantic analysis, and reading comprehension
* Specific strategies for use with children with learning disabilities

Paving the Way in Reading and Writing Strategies and Activities to Support Struggling Students in Grades 6–12
Larry Lewin
$21.95 Paperback
ISBN: 0–7879–6414-X
Grades 6–12

"Lewin's emphasis on effective instruction that integrates both reading and writing offers me just what I want most from a book: useful classroom strategies based on both research and master teacher's experience with real kids. . . . a welcome addition to my toolbox of useful books." — Jim Burke, author, *The English Teacher's Companion: A Complete Guide to Classroom, Curriculum, and the Profession* and *The Reader's Handbook: A Student Guide for Reading and Learning*

Paving the Way in Reading and Writing offers secondary teachers from across the content areas a structured approach for motivating reluctant and disengaged students to tackle difficult reading and writing assignments and thus boost their potential for academic success. Drawing on relevant theory and research and the author's extensive experience as a teacher and teacher trainer, the book presents an arsenal of practical instructional strategies along with teacher-tested tools, techniques, and activities. In a straightforward, helpful, and collegial tone, Lewin offers tips and techniques for organizing the class while helping students improve their comprehension of informational and literary text as well as strengthen their written communications. Activities combining reading and writing tasks are emphasized along with graphic exercises for engaging the more visually oriented students. The book also offers extensive listings of Web-based instructional resources and provides guidance on using the computer as a literacy tool to improve students' grammar, spelling, and research skills.

[Prices subject to change]

Other Books of Interest

Phonics First!:
Ready-to-Use Phonics Worksheets for the Primary Grades (Student Workbook)
Wilma H. Miller, Ed.D.
$3.95 Paperback
ISBN: 0-13-041462-X

Engage your students with this book of activities that provides practice in learning the letter sounds of the alphabet. These activities begin with the consonant letter and their sounds, progressing to vowel sounds, consonant blends, digraphs, diphthongs, and other aspects of phonics. It then moves on to worksheets that involve your children in creating new words and using them in context. The words are age-appropriate and the reading selections have been created using the Spache Readability Formula.

These activities can be used in any reading program with children of all ability levels. They provide the extra practice that many students need to master beginning reading skills.

Phonics First!:
Ready-to-Use Phonics Worksheets for the Intermediate Grades (Student Workbook)
Wilma H. Miller, Ed.D.
$3.95 Paperback
ISBN: 0-13-041461-1

This book of activities gives students practice in learning the various sounds of the alphabet, helping them decode new words as well as build on their knowledge of previously learned words. The activities cover a wide array of topics, including consonant blends and digraphs, vowels, rhyming words, homophones, silent letters, prefixes, suffixes, root works, plurals, syllables, and more.

Many of the worksheets engage children in thinking out new words and putting them in sentence context. Others ask students to select a correct answer from several choices. Some have students working with a partner or using a dictionary to create word lists not found on the worksheet. The words are age-appropriate and the reading selections have been created using the Space Readability Formula.

These activities can be used in any reading program with students of all ability levels. They provide the extra practice that most children need as they continue to master intermediate reading skills.

How To Reach & Teach All Students in the Inclusive Classroom: Ready-to-Use Strategies, Lessons and Activities for Teaching Students with Diverse Learning Needs

Sandra F. Rief, M.A.
Julie A. Heimburge
$29.95 Paperback
ISBN: 0-87628-399-7

For all classroom teachers, special educators, administrators, and parents, here is a remarkable new resource packed with ready-to-use strategies, lessons, and activities for helping students with diverse learning styles, ability levels, skills, and behaviors in today's inclusive classroom.

Focusing on the "whole child" and a team approach that lets you guide a varied group of students toward academic as well as social and emotional success, some strategies the book shows you are:

* How to reach all students through their multiple intelligences and learning styles
* How to manage behaviors and use positive discipline to reduce and prevent problems
* How to hook reluctant readers/writers through the use of poetry, comic strips, and other motivational materials
* How to build positive relationships, social skills and conflict resolution skills

PLUS you get more than 100 full-page reproducible management tools, such as a "Parent Volunteer Assistance Form" ... "Portfolio Item Evaluation Form" ... "Mystery Story Planning Sheet" (for thematic unit "Mystery Around Us") ... Teacher Newsletters ... Letter to parents about missing homework ... "Behavior Improvement Form" ... sample School-Home Compact ... "Cereal Box Investigation" (reading/science) ... "Survival Math Packet" ... and "Science Project Information Sheet."

In short, *How to Reach and Teach All Students in the Inclusive Classroom* gives you all the necessary information and specific techniques you need to effectively integrate heterogeneous groups of students to ensure the success of each and every child in the classroom!

Other Books of Interest

Helping Adolescents with ADHD & Learning Disabilities: Ready-to-Use Tips, Techniques, and Checklists for School Success
Judith Greenbaum, Ph.D.
Geraldine Markel, Ph.D.
$28.95 Paperback
ISBN: 0-13-016778-9

"The authors clearly explain the diagnostic process and the teacher's role in continuing to evaluate student functioning. In addition, they provide a practical and useful guide for teachers on understanding their students' range of behaviors and how they might or might not respond to them. The authors have a positive outlook and contagious belief that teachers can make a real difference in their students' lives."

-Percy Bates, Ph.D., Former Director, U.S. Office of Special Education Programs, Professor Special Education, University of Michigan

This comprehensive practical resource gives all educators of teens with ADHD and/or learning disabilities a unique store of tested strategies, tips, and tools for helping students develop the understanding and skills they need to succeed emotionally, socially, and academically.

For quick access and easy use, materials are organized into 12 chapters and printed in a big 8-1/2" x 11" format that folds flat for photocopying of any page as needed. Below is an overview of some chapter topics along with one example of the kind of help each chapter offers:

* Adolescents with ADHD and Learning Disabilities (Is It ADHD or Something Else?)

* The Learning Environment (Strategies to Develop a Supportive Emotional Environment)

* Behavioral Interventions (Teacher Checklist: Steps for Shaping Behavior)

* Preparing for the Future: Transitions to Postsecondary Settings (Parent Checklist: Helping Teenagers Prepare for College)

What's more, four appendices provide useful sources of further information, including organizations, references and websites, plus proven strategies for dealing with 20 common classroom problems encountered with ADHD and LD adolescents, from excessive movement and impulsivity to procrastination and defiant behavior.